THE ECONOMIC MODERNISATION OF IRAN, 1953–1968

Also by Ali Rahnema

Call to Arms: Iran's Marxist Revolutionaries – Formation and Evolution of the Fada'is, 1964–1976

The Rise of Modern Despotism in Iran – The Shah, the Opposition, and the US, 1953–1968

THE ECONOMIC MODERNISATION OF IRAN, 1953–1968

Architects, Agents, and Unwitting Thwarters

ALI RAHNEMA

A Oneworld Academic Book
First published by Oneworld Publications Ltd in 2025

A CIP record for this title is available from the British Library

ISBN 978-1-83643-098-8
eISBN 978-1-83643-099-5

Typeset by Geethik Technologies
Printed and bound in Great Britain by Clays Ltd, Elcograf S.p.A.

The authorised representative in the EEA is eucomply OU,
Pärnu mnt 139b–14, 11317 Tallinn, Estonia
(email: hello@eucompliancepartner.com / phone: +33757690241)

Oneworld Publications Ltd
10 Bloomsbury Street
London WC1B 3SR
England

To Ahmad Ashraf, an exemplary scholar of Iranian Studies, and a caring mentor with an ever-hearty laughter gracing his company.

Contents

Acknowledgments

In this endeavor, I am indebted to Leyla Ebtehaj who spent hours in the British National Archives searching for necessary documents that helped make this study possible. Three pairs of sharp eyes, Leyla Ebtehaj, M.H., and Kaveh Rahnema X-rayed this text with care and precision. I am most fortunate that they agreed to examine the text and helped identify and correct the knots, mistakes, and omissions in the text, and saved me from major embarrassments. The photograph of the Royal Hilton Hotel and Pahlavi Street in Tehran of 1966 on the book cover is the artistic work of late Hamid Habibi. Finally, I am grateful to Novin Doostdar, an admirably meticulous, engaging, and caring publisher, and his team, who helped realize this project.

Preface

The idea for this work originated after the completion of a previous study, *The Rise of Modern Despotism in Iran.* Having covered the political events of 1953 to 1968, I sought to give a comprehensive picture through another work focusing on the economic, cultural, and social developments of the same period. The initial project proved too ambitious. Once research began on the economic history of that period, it became clear that a thorough examination of the cultural and social aspects of the period could not be crammed into one volume. Those topics were excluded, hopefully to be revisited later.

This work attempts to depict the chronological unfolding of Iran's economic history during its formative years of modernization, starting with post-August 1953 and ending in March 1968, which marks the beginning of the Fourth Five-Year Plan. The study of this fifteen-year period demonstrates how Iran went through two of the five stages of Walt Rostow's stages of economic growth, namely pre-conditions to economic take-off, and take-off. Aspects of the two final stages, laying the foundations of economic maturity and the age of mass consumption, somewhat overlapped in Iran from 1968 onwards.

Why frame Iran's growth trajectory in terms of the descriptive and now rudimentary Rostovian model? Put simply, Rostow's outline of the stages of economic growth was broadly accepted by Iranian officials of this period as the "scientific" schema of how economic history evolved. They used it as a roadmap and compared Iran's economic performance, especially its rates of growth, to the signposts of where Iran stood along the model's unilinear economic growth path. In September 1969, the Prime Minister Amir-Abbas Hoveyda proudly reported to the Shah that "our society is moving towards what economists call the [age] of mass consumption."[1]

1 G. Nikpay (gerdavarandeh), *Surat jalesat-e showray-e 'aliye eqtesad dar pishgah Shahanshah Aryamehr, az Shahrivar 1347 ta Mordad 1348*, Surat jaleseh-e 29 Mehr 1347, Tehran: Chapkhaneh vezarat-e farhang va honar, n.d., p. 30.

The fifteen-year timeframe of this study was also chosen as it depicts a period of economic, social and political flux, fluidity and transition. During the first twelve years of this period, debates around suitable economic objectives, orientations, priorities, and policies, which regularly flared up between decision-makers, gradually came to a halt. From around 1965, one voice and one view, that of the Shah, came to dominate and dictate macroeconomic strategies and microeconomic tactics.

How economic modernization unfolded during these fifteen years is the broad topic of this research. The above is a simple research topic, but not a research question or hypothesis, as it lacks an if-then statement and an independent and dependent variable. This study, therefore, is an exploratory exercise, sifting through primary and secondary sources to find, highlight, and analyze relevant information, evidence, and details that would make sense of and shed light on the research topic. At best, it is a comprehensive report with some explanation of facts and events, driven by numerous questions pertaining to the subjects covered. The findings of this study may, hopefully, generate hypotheses for researchers interested in Iran's economic development and modernization during the second Pahlavi period.

The study of the progress and modernization of the Iranian economy during these fifteen years was driven and inspired by a series of nagging research interests and questions, constituting the intellectual motors of this work. This investigation aims at identifying the main architects and actors of Iran's economic modernization, through a study of the country's economic history. Who did what, when, how, and to what end? What happened during this period? Who in the final analysis were the key decision-makers? Who deserves credit or blame for the achievements and opportunities foregone during this specific period in Iran's economic history?

Finally, did the suppression (self or otherwise) of political ideas different from those of the Shah transform into inhibiting the presentation of economic ideas different from his? If so, did the Monarch deny the Iranian economic system its self-correcting and self-adjusting mechanisms? Did intolerance towards alternative economic ideas prevent the Shah from hearing the warning signals that would have improved and even saved the economy from heading toward a disaster?

Given Iran's oil-driven economy, this study needed to uncover and understand the role of the state, namely the Shah, Iran's public administrators such as prime ministers, ministers, state planners, and bankers, as well as members of Iran's law-making institutions, the Majles and the Senate, in this process. A consistent observation during this study was the difference between the Shah's understanding of economic concepts and that of his economists, planners, and bankers. A close read of Iran's economic history during this period may help understand why the Shah came to appreciate his economists less and less.

A thorough examination of the evolution and role of the Plan Organization in charting Iran's course of development after 1953, and its growing efficiency and power, until the fall of the spirited and competent Abolhasan Ebtehaj in 1959, helps understand how and why economic institution building in Iran was fostered and curbed. Why were the decision-making and executive powers of this pivotal and able economic institution gradually limited and replaced by the High Economic Council, presided by the Shah? What were its repercussions? What was Ebtehaj's contribution and why was he ousted? What were the economic consequences of replacing him by individuals equally competent and honest, but more deferential towards the Shah?

The development of the Iranian economy, especially after 1953 was forged and framed through a Planning mechanism. Five-Year Plans, except the First Seven-Year Plan, were supposed to indicate how the economy would allocate its resources to achieve its developmental ends. One of the biggest headaches of all post-coup governments was to draw up the Plan and then to deal with its revisions.

The process of drafting Plans and the annual task of formulating budgets, and their subsequent reviews and amendments sheds light on the workings of Iran's economic history. The extent to which Iranian planners, economists and government officials were sensitive to the directives and views of the International Bank for Reconstruction and Development (World Bank), and the International Monetary Fund in drafting plans and how this responsiveness changed over time comes under scrutiny in this study. How were the Second and Third Development Plans that were to guide the Iranian economy conceived and how did they fare? How much were the ups and downs of the Iranian economy in this period a function of planning? To what extent did economic policies, domestic and foreign, flow from the economic school of thought of the ministers or planners in charge? How and why did Import Substitution Industrialization come to prevail over free trade?

A meaningful study of Iran's economic history must understand the power dynamics between the Shah and members of his government, economic team and the legislative in determining economic goals and priorities. Did the alignment of forces change in time? To what extent was it a function of the Shah's evolving power? What role did the character and management style of each public administrator play? Why was the Shah's relationship with Abolhasan Ebtehaj or Ali Amini fulgurous, conflictual, and turbulent, but not so with Manuchehr Eqbal, Ja'far Sharif-Emami, Asadollah 'Alam, Hasan-Ali Mansur, and Amir-Abbas Hoveyda? If compliance was the key to longevity in office, why did the Shah replace Eqbal, Sharif-Emami, and 'Alam?

Iran was a developing market economy, and as such actors in the private sector, merchants, businessmen, bankers, industrialists, and mine owners were indispensable actors and key partners in its economic modernization. This study investigates Iran's business community with an eye on its evolution, transformation, contributions, and its relations with the state.

Where did their capital come from? Were Iranian entrepreneurs independent actors, or state dependent? Did their degree of autonomy depend on their trade, principles, or the financial scope and magnitude of their enterprise? To what extent did connections with the court and high government officials ensure business success? What was the role of sheer luck? How did importers of household manufactured products transform themselves into assembling the products domestically – in the process known in Iran as *montage*? Finally, what was the role of religious minorities in building the modern Iranian economy, and to what extent did religious distinctions melt away during this period?

The part played by the state, the recipient of oil revenues, in the economic history of Iran was most significant. It was the big engine that charted the course of the Iranian economy. The process by which the state began aggressively promoting heavy industrialization will be scrutinized. What role did politics, nationalism, the White Revolution, and the pursuit of re-establishing Iran's national glory play in the Shah's drive to insist on the development of the steel industry, petrochemicals, and the aluminum industry? Was it the Shah who led Iran into the era of heavy industrialization?

After the 1953 coup, the United States became Iran's biggest and most generous benefactor. This study focuses on the role that the United States played in Iran's economic and military modernization during these fifteen crucial years. What were the channels through which the US provided technical assistance and carried out military construction projects in Iran? Did various US administrations see eye to eye with the Shah on Iran's economic priorities? Was the US pushing Iran to allocate more resources to arms than to development projects?

In the process of this investigation, a series of unanticipated findings of varying significance emerged, providing greater clarity and precision in understanding the period. Among them were the fundamental financial role of the state in jump-starting industries and helping create a viable capitalist class back in 1957, the significant shift in lifestyle, taste, and consumer behavior of Iranians, from traditional to modern, resulting from economic development and modernization between 1957 and 1962, and the definitive, almost deliverer role of the Soviet Union and Soviet Bloc countries in Iran's heavy industrialization drive from 1965.

This study was not conducted in a vacuum. Simply put, the author did not start from nowhere, with a virgin mind. He has baggage, accumulated suppositions and views, which ultimately creep into how he views and analyzes the processes. But the exploratory voyage is at its most stimulating when we encounter evidence that challenges our priors. Some assumptions were attenuated, altered, scrapped, and some were confirmed. This study begins with the assumption that, despite his unsuccessful political record, the Shah's support for and promotion of economic modernization after 1953 benefited the country. At the risk of being labeled pedantic, this study hopes to present the brick-by-brick economic development and modernization process over its fifteen-year term.

Introduction

An accurate account of Iran between the 1953 coup and the 1979 revolution requires a detailed study of the political, economic, cultural, and social developments of this period. The Shah's role and agency, as the decision-maker of last resort, determined the nature and meaning of modernization as well as its outcomes. This study does not deny the role of economic and social forces, the matrix conceptualized by historical materialism, in moving and shaping the course of events. Yet it intends to investigate whether it would stand to reason to argue that in autocratic and despotic societies, making history becomes the privilege of one until he is no more.

In such societies, the handpicked legislative and judiciary act as rubberstamp institutions, and the executive holds power by the despot's grace. The press and trade organizations are under strict government control and no longer offer a space for open discussion and the clash of ideas. Functionaries, technicians, and experts may provide counsel and information, but their input is filtered through the perspective and objectives of the final decision-maker. Mohammad-Reza Shah did shape the history of Iran, as did his father, and their family's nemesis, Ruhollah Khomeyni. The modern history of Iran does give credence to the role of the individual in history and the men who left their undeniable mark on this land.

PROFILING THE SHAH TO UNDERSTAND ECONOMIC DECISIONS

A difficulty in assessing the Shah's pre-eminent role in Iran's modernization journey lies in the fact that even though the Shah did intend well for his people, often his hubristic and hasty decisions unwittingly thwarted his objectives. Worthy intentions and visions are commendable first steps, but they do not necessarily translate into desirable results. The path from good intentions to positive deeds is undetermined and sometimes perilous. The search for factors determining the success or failure of the crossing inevitably leads to analyzing the loaded and layered concept of personality. Profiling the Shah requires exploring his personality as an influential factor in his thinking and decision-making process. This slippery and speculative exercise, with all its pitfalls, may explain the extent to which he could have converted his good ideas to good deeds.

The Shah was raised in a cloistered royal bubble and attended a highly select elementary school at the court, with students of Iran's elite surrounding him. For about five years, Mohammad-Reza and his siblings were also tutored in French by Madame Arfa, a widow, whom Reza Shah had hired as a governess for the Crown Prince. During their daily tutorials, she taught the royal children the French language and gave them a taste of French life and culture.[1]

In September 1931, the almost twelve-year-old Mohammad-Reza was sent to Switzerland accompanied by his brother Ali-Reza, his childhood friend Hoseyn Fardust, and Mehrpour Teymurtash, the son of Reza Shah's Minister of Court. Le Rosey, a most exclusive boarding school, was a destination for the super-rich. Mohammad-Reza spent some five years there. He proved to be outstanding in sports and average academically. The Crown Prince was sent to Le Rosey not to obtain a *tahsilat elmi* (rigorous education) but to be educated in *mamlekatdari* (governance/administration).[2]

At Le Rosey, the Crown Prince made friends with Ernest Perron, the well-read mystical son of the gardener who was ten years his senior and worked as a janitor at the school.[3] Despite the age, cultural, and class differences between them, Perron became so dear to the Crown Prince that he accompanied Mohammad-Reza back to Iran and remained his close confident until the early 1950s.

---

1 H. Fardust, *Zohur va soqute saltanate Pahlavi*, Tehran: Entesharat-e Ettelaʿat, 1369, p. 27–28. Princess Ashraf Pahlavi, *Faces in a Mirror*, New Jersey: Prentice-Hall, 1980, pp. 16–17. Madame Arfa, whose full maiden name is unknown, should not be confused with the English Hilda Bewicke, General Hasan Arfa's wife.

2 Interview with Abdol-Madjid Alam, Foundation for Iranian Studies, p. 2.

3 Fardust, pp. 46–47; A. Milani, *The Shah*, New York: Palgrave Macmillan, 2011, pp. 48–50.

The Shah's life at Le Rosey was as sheltered as it was when he had been in Iran. Later in his memoirs, the Shah complained about the rigid and secluded social life his Iranian guardian imposed on him at Le Rosey. During his stay in Switzerland, the Crown Prince was prohibited to leave the school unchaperoned or attend school parties. Other than the pleasure of doing sports, his life was cheerless and lonely. Mohammad-Reza Shah attributes his "seriousness" and "lone behavior" to this period in his life when he was prohibited from having fun.[4] In 1936, Mohammad-Reza returned to Iran without a high-school diploma.

Contrary to his father who had been raised among the popular classes and had learnt the art of social survival in a rough and competitive environment, until the age of sixteen, the Crown Prince had neither seen much of Iran nor interacted with Iranians outside the Court. The only non-ceremonial and frank human relation that he may have had was probably with Perron, which may explain his attachment to the Swiss.

On his return, Mohammad-Reza attended the Officers Cadet College for two years, thus completing his formal schooling. It would be safe to assume that at the Officers Cadet College he received very special treatment as the Crown Prince. After finishing the Officers Cadet College in 1938, he began work with the rank of Second Lieutenant as an inspector in the army.

Within the five years between the Crown Prince's return to Iran and his ascent to the throne in September 1941, Reza Shah had not really prepared him to govern and rule for the welfare of his people. His only higher education had been a military one, and his only role model was his severe father, who had neither much time for him nor was understanding of the young man's sensitivities and mystical orientations. Reza Shah wanted a tough and decisive son made in his own image, while the Crown Prince was neither. Mohammad-Reza Shah was the first to admit that his character was different from his father.[5]

While at Le Rosey, Mohammad-Reza Shah reflected on his "future responsibilities" and how he should become "a wise monarch". These thoughts led him to focus more on "natural sciences to better understand

4 Mohammad Reza Shah Pahlavi, *Mamuriyat baray-e vatanam*, Tehran: Chap-e artesh, n.d., p. 77.

5 Mohammad Reza Shah Pahlavi, *Mamuriyat baray-e vatanam*, Tehran: Chap-e artesh, n.d., pp. 53, 66–68.

and prepare for the complex problems of industrialization ..."[6] The Shah, however, made no reference to the pursuit of any of the most common social science subjects, including economics, history, sociology, or even politics, and there is no record that he was self-taught in any of them. Yet we know that he was a keen and studious follower of military hardware and an insightful oil negotiator.

According to Khodadad Farmanfarmayan, the Shah's director general of the Plan and Budget Organization in the early 1970s, "He [the Shah] was not a well-trained individual, and he was not an intellectual", and "his analytical apparatus was extremely limited."[7] Based on the Shah's actions, interactions mainly with his cabinet members and high functionaries and sometimes with his subjects, speeches, interviews, and writings, the reports written about him in foreign sources and memoires, and oral references by Iranians, some of his attributes and characteristics, from 1953 to 1979, can be identified.

This cannot be a fully comprehensive and thorough exercise, as it is not the subject of this study but is a means to understand the economic history under consideration. At the cost of being charged with generalization, simplification, cherry-picking and amateur psychoanalyzing, an attempt, no matter how half-baked, needs to be made to discern certain personality traits of the Shah as the commander of Iran's economic development and modernization.

The Shah believed that he was chosen and protected by God for a mission and that made him feel infallible. He therefore never publicly questioned or doubted his own positions, reasoning, and actions. After 1953, the Shah also displayed certain consistent single traits, such as being authoritarian, vainglorious, unforgiving, impersonal, standoffish, hardworking, audacious, suspicious, persistent, and intolerant. Some of his traits worked as antipodes, revealing themselves during his well-known mood swings. For example, at times he could be rational and at other times irrational; other such pairs were scientific/superstitious, secular/religious, decisive/indecisive, committed/wavering, domineering/insecure, and reckless/fearful.

The Shah's behavior patterns sometimes went through phases and cycles. In his optimistic/euphoric phase, grounded in what he perceived

6 Mohammad Reza Shah Pahlavi, *Mamuriyat baray-e vatanam*, p. 77.

7 Khodadad Farmanfarmaian, Iranian Oral History Collection, Harvard University, Transcript 16, Sequence 208.

as success in his statecraft, and secure political position, the Shah would be stern, unyielding, arrogant, voluntaristic, and obsessively self-righteous. In this up-phase, his ego would eclipse his rationality, he would be unresponsive to all counsel and enter a bubble with little connection to reality. He would become a voluntarist, feeling as though he could move mountains, intervening and commandeering in all affairs of the state while frustrating and undoing the hard work of his experts in preparing plans and budgets.

When the Shah entered his pessimistic/dysphoric phase, his personality would change radically, manifesting traits in stark contrast to his optimistic/euphoric phase. His gloomy mood was usually prompted by real, perceived, or illusional dangers or setbacks. Characteristic of the Shah's down-phase was self-doubt and uncertainty about his position and security, rendering him incapable of decision-making. In his depressive moods, he would become deterministic, leaving everything to God and otherworldly protectors and leaving the affairs of the state in limbo.

In both his up and down moods, the Shah was a suspicious and distrustful person. Reversals and unfulfilled expectations made him angry; he was not fond of analyzing his shortcomings. Since he did not believe that he could be at fault, he found solace in finding culprits and scapegoats, blaming the other for a myriad of conspiracies. Shortcomings became the works of external and internal enemies, and ill-wishers. It would be incorrect to attribute his suspicious state of mind only to his weak moments. At the height of his power, the Shah had an equivalent distrust of those he felt were banding together against him.

The Shah cherished and demanded praise, adulation, and unquestionable obedience. He had little tolerance for dissent and resistance to his ideas and construed open criticism and questioning of his decisions, let alone disobeying them, as disloyalty and treason. The Shah's relation with his subjects was complicated. He often disapproved of them for not rising to his excessive expectations and fulfilling his far-fetched dreams at his speed. Towards the end of his rule, he even began to resent them for what he believed was their ingratitude for what he had done for them.

But, between 1961 and 1966, there were occasions when the Shah demonstrated empathy and compassion toward Iranians, especially the peasantry. On several occasions during this period, the Shah exhibited genuine care and warmth, proving that he could be a father figure, capable of personal attachment to and affection for his people. This warm window of proximity and attachment, however, closed after 1966.

By May 1977, the Shah seemed drained of fatherly affection and bonding, even with his own children. On one telling occasion, the Shah became delighted when Reza, his eldest son, asked to have lunch with him. Yet, as if all relations were supposed to be based on a superior mind parting wisdom and informing lesser intellects, he told his sixteen-year-old boy that, "If you want to learn something, you need to read my books and works on the history of Iran, so that you would benefit from my remarks (*sohbatha-ye man*)."[8]

CONFLICT OF INTEREST: PAHLAVI FOUNDATION, A BUSINESS EMPIRE

The Shah had double standards. His ethics and morals did not apply to all equally. He was exacting towards his people and expected them to be hard-working, productive, honest, incorruptible, and upright. He consistently spoke out against corruption and the corrupt. Yet, he was most indulgent and lenient with his courtiers, his close circle of companions, and favorite statesmen, closing his eyes to the rampant corruption around him and involving him. He did discriminate and indulge in favoritism, nepotism, and cronyism, undoing the shame and stigma of such vices. His support for his companions would not abate when cases of their corruption – be it bribery, profiteering, smuggling, or outright fraud – came to the fore.

Well before the revolution, most urban Iranians knew or had heard of the Shah's circle of companions, courtiers, and family members who stood above the law and benefited from perfect immunity. Overseas, the Shah protected his criminal friends from prosecution and went out of his way to obtain their acquittal. In Iran, they were unmolested and even rewarded.[9]

In his 1958 report on the Shah's economic activities, the British Ambassador, Roger Stevens, noted that, "The Shah's direct and personal interests alone now extend publicly into the fields of banking, publishing, wholesale, and retail trading, shipping, construction works, new industries,

8 A. 'Alam, *Yaddashtha-ye 'Alam*, ed. A.N. 'Alikhani, vol. 6, Bethesda: Ibex Publishers, 2008, p. 459.

9 A. 'Alam, *Yaddashtha-ye 'Alam*, ed. A.N. 'Alikhani, vol. 2, Bethesda: Iranbooks, 1993, pp. 194–198, 345, 360. A. 'Alam, *Yaddashtha-ye 'Alam*, ed. A.N. 'Alikhani, vol. 4, Bethesda: Ibex Publishers, n.d., pp. 126–129. See the case of Amir-Hushang Davalu.

hotels, agricultural development and even housing."[10] His business interests and participations ranged from bridge building over the Karun River ($1 million) and housing (IBEC), to the manufacture and distribution of pharmaceutical products in collaboration with a British firm.

Stevens added that the Shah promoted "the schemes in which he has a personal interest financial or otherwise". Stevens reported that the shortcut to business success was through enlisting the Shah's support, "through middle-men of dubious reputation to obtain priority treatment, cut through red tape and secure finance". He named Meybud (Mahbod), 'Ala and Behbahaniyan and the Shah's own family as his trusted "nominees or servants", through whom he operated. The British Ambassador to Iran concluded that "The crescendo of stories of direct or indirect bribery, either of His Majesty or of his confidantes and family, or both, is however impossible to ignore."[11]

THE ORIGIN AND ORGANIZATION OF ROYAL ASSETS

Immediately after the abdication of Reza Shah on 21 September 1941, the new Shah, Mohammad-Reza, donated his father's estates, which he had obtained mainly through coercion and expropriation, to the people. On 11 July 1949, he changed his mind and took back the royal estates. In 1951, the Shah established the Royal Assets and Estates Organization (*Sazeman-e amalk va mostaghelat-e saltanati*), to manage the estates of his father that he had repossessed.

On 7 May 1958, the statute of the newly established Pahlavi Foundation (*Bonyad-e Pahlavi*) was made public, and Mohammad-Ja'far Behbahaniyan was named as its director general by the Shah. Behbahaniyan had the complete trust of the Shah. The Pahlavi Foundation was a tax-exempt charitable foundation, centralizing all of the Shah's philanthropic activities. The new Pahlavi Foundation was officially registered as *Moqufat-e Khanedan-e Pahlavi* or the Endowments of the Pahlavi Family. It housed and managed all the Shah's assets.

Behbahaniyan, who had been the administrator of the Royal Assets and Estates Organization worth $133 million, was tasked with overseeing

10 FO 371/133022, EP 1102/10.
11 FO 371/133022, EP 1102/10.

the smooth transition of this organization to the newly created Pahlavi Foundation. The Pahlavi Foundation had a seven-man board of directors appointed by the Monarch. The statute of the Foundation stipulated that only the Shah could change its articles and that it was established for an unlimited amount of time.[12]

Once the Shah decided to distribute his lands by selling them to sharecroppers working on those lands, he created the *Bank-e Omran* (Construction/Development Bank). Born on 11 September 1952, the official mandate of this royal bank was to collect the installments of the land sold to the sharecroppers, provide credit to the peasants who had obtained royal lands, and to initiate farmers' cooperatives. From its inception, the Shah appointed the US-educated Hushang Rām as the director general of *Bank-e Omran*. In time, Rām became the Shah's trusted personal financial manager.

At the inauguration ceremony of *Bank-e Omran* in 1952, the Shah said that the distribution of royal lands would not have been possible without the creation of this bank and its associated cooperatives. He hoped that the extra revenues of the bank would be re-invested in rural industries, health services, and charitable organizations.[13]

After the deduction of the maintenance cost of assets, completion of unfinished buildings, expenditures of the charity organizations and investments to increase the revenue of the endowment, the proceeds of the bank were to be spent on health, cultural development, helping the needy, and religious and social affairs.[14] In 1958, *Bank-e Omran*'s receipt of installments from credit extended to sharecroppers for the purchase of their lands came to 960,000 tomans, 352,406 of which was loaned out to 63 agricultural cooperatives.[15]

In September 1960, the Shah ordered *Bank-e Omran* to be integrated within the Pahlavi Foundation and place its activities under the tutelage of Behbahaniyan, the director general of the Foundation. The bank was to be restructured and its activities transformed.[16] Subsequently, the *Bank-e*

---

12 *Ettela'at*, 18 Ordibehesht 1337; 6, 8 Mehr 1340; 4 Azar 1340.

13 Bayanate a'lahazrat homayuni shahanshah Mohammad-Reza Shah Pahlavi dar goshayesh bank omran, https://mashruteh.org/wiki/index.php?title= (retrieved 9/8/2023).

14 *Ettela'at*, 15 Mehr 1340.

15 *Tehran Economist*, 23 Mordad 1338.

16 *Ettela'at*, 22 Shahrivar 1339.

Omran began engaging in regular banking activities. It accepted individual funds as deposits, paid out interest, and lent money to borrowers at interest.

In August 1964, Asadollah and Seyfollah Rashidiyan founded the Distribution Cooperative Bank (*Bank-e ta'avoni-e tozi'*), which was to be the bank of all guilds. Two months later, the Shah visited it and put his seal of approval on it. The Shah felt indebted to Asadollah and Seyfollah Rashidiyan for their determining role in bringing down Mosaddeq on 19 August 1953 and so helped them open this bank. Nevertheless, the Distribution Cooperative Bank operated without an official permit from the banking authorities, did not comply with the reserve requirements established by the banking authorities, and lent to whomever it wanted without any government supervision.[17]

In September 1968, the Distribution Cooperative Bank became insolvent when the Central Bank failed to clear 2.2 million tomans of its cheques due to insufficient funds. In a meeting with Hoveyda, the Prime Minister, and his economic and banking advisors, Khodadad Farmanfarmayan, the deputy governor of the Central Bank, informed the Prime Minister that the situation at the Distribution Cooperative Bank "was not dire, but dangerous" and listed all the bank's legal violations and infractions.

Hoveyda agreed but responded that since the people and the *Bank-e Omran*, the National Iranian Oil Company, and the Tehran municipality had invested huge sums in this bank, it had to be saved. Hoveyda confirmed the rumors that the Shah was a shareholder in Rashidiyan's bank by acknowledging the financial participation of the *Banke-e Omran* in the Distribution Cooperative Bank. The government finally decided to bail out the bank.[18]

Gradually, the *Bank-e Omran* branched out into building hotels, upmarket housing and apartments, leisure resorts, and casinos. It also became a shareholder in other banks, industries, mines, shipping, and insurance companies and engaged in development and construction projects. *Bank-e Omran* ended up having some 100 branches in Iran, was said to have two branches in Switzerland, and owned shares in First Wisconsin Corporation in the US.

17 Be ravayat-e asnad-e savak, *Rashidiyanha*, vol. 2, Tehran: Markaz-e barrasi-e asnad-e tarikhi-e vezerat-e ettela'at, 1389, pp. 186, 229.

18 Be ravayat-e asnad-e savak, *Rashidiyanha*, vol. 2, Tehran: Markaz-e barrasi-e asnad-e tarikhi-e vezerat-e ettela'at, 1389, pp. 369, 383–386. Information in the previous two paragraphs is based on the above sources.

By October 1961, the Pahlavi Foundation owned a vast empire. It owned 100% of the shares of the following entities: *Bank-e Omran*, *Bongah-e Tarjomeh va Nashr Ketab* (The [Royal] Institute for Translation and Publication), *Sherkat Haml-o-Naql Khalij* (The Gulf Transportation Company), two hotels in Ramsar (old and new), Motel Khazar in Ramsar, Casino Ramsar, housing complexes in Ramsar, Darband Hotel and its cozy restaurant and dance floor, Kolbeh nightclub, two hotels in Babolsar (old and new), housings complexes in Babolsar, Buali Hotel in Hamedan, Sakhtsar Motel, Hotel Abali, two hotels in Chalous (old and new), two hotels in Gachsar (old and new), Vanak Hotel, Shahi Hotel, Amol Hotel, Hilton Hotel in Tehran, Shiraz Hotel, Residence Restaurant in Tehran, the land on which Khorramshahr Hotel was built, and forty-one orphanages.

The Pahlavi Foundation also owned shares in the following services and industries: *Shahr-Ara* housing project (40%), *Sherkat-e Sahami Naftkesh Iran* or Iran Oil Tanker Company (77.5%), *Bank-e E'tebarat* or Credit Bank (2%), *Bank Iran va Ingelis* or Anglo-Iranian Bank (1%), Melli Insurance Company (80%), Tehran's Mehrabad Airport Restaurant (25%), Kermanshah Sugar Company (500 shares) Hamedan Sugar Company (10%), Birjand Sugar Company (10%), Fariman Sugar Loaf Company (200 shares), Ahwaz Sugar Refinery (0.4%), Tehran Cement Company (25.5%), Iranit Tile Company (30%), B.F. Goodrich Tire Company (9.5%), Daru Pakhsh Pharmaceutical Company (50%), Shiraz or Pars Sugarloaf Company (unknown shares), and IBEC housing project in Sahebqaraniyeh, Tehran (unknown shares).[19]

Wheat and Sugar Monopoly

After the 1953 coup, *Bank-e Omran* became involved in major money-making activities unrelated to the Pahlavi Foundation. By fiat, *Bank-e Omran* obtained the exclusive right to import wheat. Wheat procurement from the US and Australia was a highly lucrative business as the annual import of wheat increased from $10,687,000 in 1960/1961–1961/1962 to

19 *Ettela'at*, 10, 15 Mehr 1340; *Tehran Economist*, 19 Tir 1338, 22 Mehr 1340. Information in the previous two paragraphs is based on the above sources. See also the report of the British Ambassador, Sir Roger Stevens; FO 371/133022, EP 1102/10.

$75,951,000 in 1971/1972.[20] The Shah's bank, unfettered by any supervision or control handled all wheat imports. It benefited from opaque financial transactions and contracts for some twenty years.

On 27 April 1974, Hoveyda appointed Fereydun Mahdavi as Minister of Commerce. Mahdavi obtained his doctorate in economics from Hamburg University. He had joined the Second National Front in his youth and had been imprisoned for some eight months for his political activities. About a month after he entered the cabinet, Mahdavi began his efforts to bring the import of wheat and sugar under government control. Soon, he faced entrenched economic powers very closely connected to the Shah.

The country's cereal, sugar, sugar loaf, and tea organizations were placed under the jurisdiction of the Ministry of Commerce. Worried about the shortage of basic foodstuffs in 1974, the Shah wanted an expert such as Mahdavi to manage the import of these goods and ensure their abundant availability on the market. So, from June 1974, the decades-long monopoly of Rām and Felix Aqayan was rescinded, and the right to import wheat and sugar was reverted to the Ministry of Commerce and placed under government control.

Behind the smooth-looking transition of 11 June 1974, a harsh tug of war was in progress at the stratosphere of Iranian political circles. Rām defended *Bank-e Omran*'s most profitable monopoly over wheat import and tried to convince the Shah to block Mahdavi's move. Felix Aqayan, an old and close friend of his Majesty and another beneficiary of the Shah's largess, who had obtained the exclusive right to import sugar from the monarch, also fought against Mahdavi's incursions into his turf.

The Shah became upset with the dispute among his appointees dragging on. Before the power transfer of wheat import to the Ministry of Commerce, the Shah instructed 'Alam, his Minster of Court, to convey the following message to Hushang Rām: "Relinquish this wheat deal. What is one, two, or even $10 million earned in this way by *Bank-e Omran*, especially since it concerns the people's daily bread."[21] The Shah's instruction to Rām intimated that he should give up this source of income which by

20 U.S Department of Agriculture, Economic Research Service, Iran: Agricultural Production and Trade, 1974, https://downloads.usda.library.cornell.edu/usdaesmis/files/jq085j963/7s75dg57b/70795b99s/ERSF-04-11-1974_Iran_Agricultural_Production_and_Trade.pdf (retrieved 29/1/2024).

21 A.'Alam, vol. 4, pp. 118–120; Fereidoun Mahdavi, Iranian Oral History Collection, Harvard University, Transcript 2, Sequences 35–36.

1974 had become comparatively insignificant; *Bank-e Omran* had bigger fish to fry.

Scandal over Shipping Companies

The National Seafaring Company under the management of a board of directors comprised of Ahmad Mahbod, Ahmad Shafiq, Princess Ashraf's ex-husband, and Mohsen Qaragozlu was created on 2 November 1956. This private company was in partnership with the Netherlands and intended to transport Iranian oil in cooperation with the National Oil Company.[22] A year later, the Shah issued an edict and bestowed the rank of Ambassador on Mahbod, the director general of the National Seafaring Company. The edict mentioned that, under orders (*hasb al-amr*) from the Shah, Mahbod had established the National Seafaring Company as well as a commercial seafaring company.[23]

In January 1959, the 35,000-ton oil tanker *Reza Shah*, the first of the Iranian fleet, began activities at Ma'shur Port in Khuzestan, with Mahbod as the Iranian member on the managing board of this tanker.[24] According to Mahbod, he had been the original owner of the two shipping companies, the National Iranian Shipping Company and the National Seafaring Company. Mahbod had gifted 15% of his two shipping companies' shares to the Shah. Later, through 'Ala, who had also been gifted 100 shares, Mahbod got news that the Shah wished to have the majority shares of the National Iranian Shipping Company and bought 50% of Mahbod's shares at 80 million rials.

Mahbod maintained that the Shah later sold the 50% shares, which he had forcefully obtained from him at a price of $1.1 million, for $12 million to the National Iranian Oil Company. As for the smaller National Seafaring Company, Mahbod claimed that he had been compelled to give it to the Shah. Mahbod, who felt betrayed by the Shah, left Iran for good in October 1960.[25]

---

22 *Ettela'at*, 11 Mehr 1335.
23 *Ettela'at*, 18 Shahrivar 1336.
24 *Tehran Economist*, 4 Bahman 1337.
25 Ahmed Maybud, Iranian Oral History Collection, Harvard University, Transcript 6, Sequences 103–104, Transcript 7, Sequences 107–108, Transcript 9, Sequence 142, Transcript 10, Sequence 151. See A. 'Alam, vol. 7, pp. 290–291 for his negative view of Mahbod.

ALL IN THE FAMILY: EHSANEH DAVALU, SULTAN OF CAVIAR

In September 1956, the Iranian press reported on a lucrative exclusive five-year contract given to a Mrs. Davalu to sell Iranian caviar abroad. Mrs. Davalu had subsequently signed an exclusive five-year contract with the Frenchman Fernand de Lalagade, giving him the exclusive right to distribute Iran's caviar in Europe.[26] In addition, there were rumors circulated in the press about 2 million in old Francs (ancient Francs) or 20,000 in new Francs being paid out as a bribe by Mrs. Davalu to obtain the monopoly.[27]

On 23 October 1956, Abdolhoseyn Nikpour delivered a scathing speech on the floor of the Iranian Senate against Amir-Hushang Davalu, a dubious and ill-reputed but very well-known member of the Shah's inner circle. Nikpour was a highly respected elected senator who had made his money as a crystal merchant and headed Tehran's Chamber of Commerce for 25 consecutive years.

Nikpour represented Iran's emerging capitalist class, which wished to free business from the corrupt influence of the state and court but was also dependent on and scared of both. In his speech, Nikpour tested how far one could go in criticizing the Shah's corrupt inner circle. He announced that Mrs. Davalu held a monopoly over 60 to 70 tons of caviar through the intermediary of Amir-Hushang Davalu.[28]

Nikpour contested that Mrs. Davalu was given this exclusive monopoly without public tender and competing bids for selling Iran's caviar overseas. He charged that a few ministers were involved in this deal but failed to name them. Even though it was evident from Nikpour's speech that Mrs. Davalu was somehow related to Amir-Hushang, the Shah's friend, since he did not refer to her first name, the public remained in the dark about her real identity.

The franchise over the sale and export of Iran's caviar industry was taken out of the control of Iran's Fisheries Company, a state enterprise, and given to a person who was the front for another person with very high connections. Based on letters received from European caviar merchants, another senator, Moayed-Sabeti, also an industrialist, referred to illegal transactions and misappropriations in the caviar deal. He called for a

26 *Tehran Economist*, 17 Shahrivar 1336.
27 *Tehran Economist*, 29 Day 1335.
28 *Ettela'at*, 1 Aban 1335.

review of the concession and recommended its cancellation, as it seemed to be against the rules.[29]

An illegal deal of such magnitude, aimed at enriching Amir-Hushang Davalu, could not have been without the consent and even direct order of the Shah. Some three months after the scandal over Davalu's caviar monopoly was publicized, an attempt was made to whitewash Davalu and the deal. On 22 December 1956, the weekly *Tehran Economist*, which had first covered the scandal, wrote a detailed article arguing that Iran's Fisheries Company could not find a better deal and that there was much ado about nothing. In this detailed retraction, no mention was made of Amir-Hushang Davalu, the Shah's friend.[30] Less than a month later, the issue of bribes and improprieties in Mrs. Davalu's contract and news of legal pursuits appeared in the press once again, still without reference to Amir-Hushang.[31]

The Shah was irritated by the recurrent talk in the Senate and the press of corruption involving his entourage. His reproach came on 28 February 1957, during the official festivities celebrating *Mab'as* (the prophetic mission of Mohammad) at Golestan Palace. The Shah said, "More than anyone else, I have curtailed the interests of those whom you call the ruling class. So, who and where is this ruling class you constantly talk about?"[32] The Shah called on all to refrain from discouraging and despairing news and talk.

Some four years and eight months after Nikpour's speech in the Senate, the public discovered that Mrs. Davalu was Ehsan/Ehsaneh Nikkhah Davalu, a cousin of Amir-Hushang Davalu's mother, Monira'zam. On 3 June 1961, in the heat of Prime Minister Ali Amini's anti-corruption crusade, Ehsan/Ehsaneh Nikkhah Davalu was arraigned for "unlawful possession" and "misappropriation/embezzlement" and subsequently arrested.[33]

After her arrest, Mrs. Davalu is said to have sent word to Princess Ashraf and Hoseyn 'Ala that if her arrest were to take a severe turn, she would spill the beans about the illegal activities of members of the royal family and their entourage. Subsequently, Mrs. Davalu was transferred to a special

29 *Tehran Economist*, 19 Aban 1335.
30 *Tehran Economist*, 1 Day 1335.
31 *Tehran Economist*, 29 Day 1335.
32 *Tehran Economist*, 11 Esfand 1335.
33 *Ettela'at*, 13 Khordad 1340.

prison. She was promised clemency and leniency.[34] Davalu and General Ruhollah Noveysi, the director general of Iran's Fisheries Company, were put on trial on 30 September 1961.

In court, certain aspects of Mrs. Davalu's lifestyle became public. It became known that Davalu's caviar company owned a one million toman cold storage facility in Tehran and a 42 million French Francs (probably old French Francs or 42 thousand new French Francs) caviar shop called Maison de Caviar on Paris' prestigious George V Avenue. In Paris, Ehsan/ Ehsaneh Davalu had taken residency close to her place of work at one of the most luxurious Parisian hotels, George V, in the eighth arrondissement.[35]

Estimating her extravagant and exorbitant cost of living long-term at George V would be difficult. However, assuming she was alone, a glimpse at the cost of her meals would be somewhat revelatory. In 1961, the price of a Tournedos Rossini, a famous main course at George V's restaurant, was 15 new French Francs. Today, the restaurant at George V does not serve a Tournedos Rossini, but at a comparably high-end establishment, Lasserre, the price of a Cœur de filet de bœuf Rossini is 105 Euros. On 20 December 1961, Mrs. Davalu was found guilty of misappropriation and embezzlement, sentenced to a year and a half of correctional imprisonment and payment of fines. It is not known whether she served her full prison term.

CONTEXTUALIZING IRAN'S MODERNIZATION EXPERIENCE

The Shah's personality traits and behavioral inclinations affected his economic decisions and leadership. They determined how his good intentions could be transformed into nationally beneficial ends. But even though he did develop and modernize the economy, the flaws in his one-man governance style and statesmanship derailed Iran's structural and long-term economic development and prosperity.

The thought of what Mohammad-Reza would have become in life and what line of work he would have chosen had he not been a king is as entertaining as it is futile. Nevertheless, it helps to speculate on his natural

34 http://www.15khordad42.ir/?page=post&id=2401 (retrieved 11/9/2023).
35 *Ettela'at*, 28 Aban 1340.

and innate capacities and interests and their relation to his pet modernization projects and their outcomes. Would Mohammad-Reza have been a good soldier and made it to the rank of a three-star general (*sepahbod*), or would he have entered the Iranian National Oil Company and ended up in an office on the 15th floor among the directors? Would he have been a first-class sportsman, coach, enthusiastic owner or manager of a sports shop or club?

In hindsight, we can rank the Shah's preferred modernization domains as military, economic, and social. As king, Mohammad-Reza did not need any intellectual, public relations, administrative, or management skills. The Shah's title assured the execution of his will, as his orders were expected to be those of God (*cheh farman-e yazdan cheh farman-e shah*). Regardless of why, the Shah chose to rely on obedience, allegiance, and fear to get things done.

From 1953, the Shah's management and leadership style was marked by lecturing, chiding, and preaching while refusing to discuss matters of substance with his people, close friends, ministers, or experts. Consultation based on informed open discussions to arrive at improved results was not practiced in the Shah's meetings with his advisers. He rejected counsel as if it was a sign of weakness for a ruling monarch. In time, he would not even listen to or read reports that departed from his thinking.

Any critical appraisal of past or present economic decisions and policies was construed as a personal attack. Perhaps the Shah found consultation and dialogue a contradiction to his belief that he was divinely selected, protected, and commissioned. The Shah's management style was that of an obstinate executive, bent on having his way, averse to hearing voices other than his own, and set in his ideas.

As the Shah's grip on the country tightened, either dissident economists and planners were relieved of their duties, left the Plan Organization, or yielded to the Shah's designs and subsequent edicts. This process was the beginning of political will imposing itself on economic imperatives, rerouting and distorting economic development.

1

Modernization and its Actors

Northwestern Europe between the sixteenth and nineteenth centuries gave birth to modernity. In short, the sixteenth-century Reformation, dovetailed by the scientific revolution of the seventeenth century and the Industrial Revolution of the eighteenth and nineteenth centuries, ushered in phenomenal economic, social, political, and cultural transformations. Irrespective of why modernization first occurred in Europe, in the twentieth century and especially after the Second World War, modernization and industrialization became the objective of "Third World" countries.

The pressing issue of economic development and a rapid escape route from underdevelopment, presented the Third World with two options: either going down the path of the socialist Soviet-type economies, and its later model of the non-capitalist road, or buying into the Western modernization package. The choice was more political than economic, and countries chose one or the other model based on the ideology of their governments and leaders. Implicit in this choice was adherence to the Western or the so-called free world camp, or the socialist camp with the non-aligned countries tilting economically and ideologically towards the socialist camp.

Both camps believed that their development models were easily grafted onto any kind of society in any continent. Many US post-war social scientists and policymakers were convinced that the type of economy and society that they had attained was the summit of a linear movement of human development and progress. They also believed that their experience and model of development could be compressed, implying historical leaps, and exported to traditional societies eager for development.

Based on this assumption, US economists, sociologists, and political scientists elaborated ready-made modernization theories to assist US-supported administrations achieve modernization in Third World countries. The Cold War compelled the US to vigorously compete with the Soviet Union in presenting its model of development and modernization as the best choice for the newly decolonized countries.

Economic growth and development were at the core of the Western modernization model. The indispensable features of modernization, such as democracy, political and individual liberties, the rule of law, and the establishment of modern government institutions, were expected to somehow miraculously dovetail, even if they were lacking at the time.

Western economic modernization required specialized bureaucracies staffed by technocrats and experts, formed and educated over time, to implement various governmental objectives and plans. Such bureaucracies had consistent rules and procedures that were uniformly applicable. The modern bureaucrat and technocrat ideally functioned according to the regulations established and were accountable for the proper application of methods. Civil servants, employed based on expertise and merit, formed the backbone of government organizations.

The Western modernity project also involved the birth and empowerment of organizations and associations that were independent from government, such as trade unions, professional and trade associations, and the free press. Such institutions were essential countervailing powers, imposing checks and balances to protect the public by scrutinizing and curbing the excesses and power of both government and business.

MODERNIZATION AGENTS: REINFORCING AND CLASHING

Economic modernization initiatives in Iran, broadly categorized by actors, conceptualizers, and designers, fall into three domestic categories, royal, governmental, and private sector, and a foreign one, the US. But what happens to history from below and the supposed role of ordinary people in economic modernization and development?

In 1953, some 70 to 75% of the population lived off the land in rural areas and were fixed in their traditional lifestyles, and only 25 to 30% of the urban population was open to change. The role of literacy as a medium of change was also limited, as about 85% of the population was illiterate. The role of the urban man on the street in modernization was therefore restricted to the extent to which he could undergo attitudinal change in tune with modernization; hence the determining role of those in society whose outlook had transcended traditional values. So, the role of the ordinary people in modernization, as they had a limited one, will be disregarded in this study. The ordinary people were not subjects of modernization, exercising agency.

The Shah's non-opposition or consent was necessary for all modernization initiatives. A more focused study of the three domestic agents demonstrates that formal boundaries between royal and governmental, private and governmental, and finally, royal and private were not always clearly discernable.

On the whole, the economic activities and decisions of the two domestic actors, the government and the private sector, constantly reinforced and wholeheartedly supported the Shah's initiatives. One exception was when the economy began to stall from the mid-1970s. Searching for scapegoats, the Shah punished the private sector and his ministers. However, the clash between the US economic modernization ethos and the Shah's practices was more pronounced and structural.

After 1953, the American modernization model, and its crucial behavioral pattern injected into the system by the Shah's embrace of all things American, trickled down to the minds of urban Iranians. Soon, those Iranians who identified themselves with the American lifestyle in its entirety found their newly acquired beliefs at odds with the Shah's leadership style, causing tensions within the system.

THE GOVERNMENT'S RESTRICTED ROLE

In an oil-based economy, where the state commands significant resource-based revenues, differentiating between the Shah's agency and his government's is complicated since the Shah appointed the prime minister and approved the ministers. Initially, the Shah supported economic or developmental ideas presented to him by individuals in the government, the Plan Organization, or other relevant institutions. These were few, but included infrastructural projects, such as building roads, dams, airports, ports, and electricity grids, and the Khuzestan Development Services in the latter part of the 1950s.

There were also economic and financial organizations and institutions that were absent in Iran. Members of the government advocated for their creation, and the Shah accepted and supported their propositions. It was Ebrahim Kashani who raised and pursued the idea of a Central Bank (*Bank-e Markazi*) with the Shah.[1]

In the 1950s, the Shah delegated authority to individual experts he trusted. Abolhasan Ebtehaj, the director general of the Plan Organization, Abdollah Entezam, the director general of the National Iranian Oil Company, and Ali Amini, Minister of Finance during Zahedi's tenure, best exemplified this breed of managers and officials, with independent decision-making leeway.

However, in the 1960s, it became difficult to clearly demarcate between the Shah's initiatives and those of the government, as governments acted on behalf of the Shah. During Ebtehaj's tenure at the Plan Organization (1954–1959), he decided on, directed, and executed the Plan, but after his ouster, this role essentially reverted to the Shah.

With Ali Amini's premiership (May 1961 to July 1962), there was a short interlude in the established Shah–government relations. Economic decision-making became almost a consensual activity between the Shah and his prime minister. Amini's economic policies and proclivities, among other factors, ultimately led to a fallout with the Shah. The two men clashed over the military budget of 1962–1963 and over Amini's anti-corruption campaign against the Shah's military brass and figures close to him.

With Amini out of the picture, and up until the 1979 revolution, apart from Shapour Bakhtiyar's short term in office, prime ministers, ministers, general directors of banks, and other government organizations, including the Plan Organization, were merely implementors of His Majesty's designs.

Government initiatives and projects were brought before the parliament as bills, were "debated", and made into laws. However, the outcome of parliamentary procedures was always predetermined. Hand-picked and well-vetted members of parliament never challenged, or God forbid, rejected bills brought before them. Members of the parliament knew that a bill would not come to the parliament unless it had the Royal blessing, and as such, it was irrefutable.

1 H-A. Mehran, *Hadafha va Siyasathay-e Bank-e Markaziy-e Iran, az 1339 ta 1357*, Tehran: Nashr-e Ney, 1394, p. 29.

Instead of going through the parliament, certain military expenditures were discussed in cabinet meetings, ratified by the ministers, and thus became legally binding decrees (*tasvibnameh*). In cases where ministers expressed doubts about such expenditures, the prime minister would prevent discussion and dissent, and for reason of state, would push through the ratification of the expenditures without a legally sanctioned due process.

Amir-Abbas Hoveyda, who was prime minister for almost thirteen years (January 1965 to August 1977), believed in "the political line established by the leader [Shah] and did his utmost [to follow that line]". Hoveyda was convinced that "one should act according to whatever seemed expedient or good to the Shah"[2] – all this to say that government initiatives from the 1960s were hardly distinguishable from royal initiatives.

THE SHAH'S BOUNDLESS AGENCY

The Shah had specific economic areas of interest in which he played a direct role. His personal purview was strategic industrial projects, such as oil, petrochemicals, steel, aluminum, copper, armaments, and nuclear power. For each of these domains, the Shah created an independent organization and structure, and in most cases, neither prime ministers nor ministers were knowledgeable about their goings-on or involved in decision-making concerning them.[3]

The Shah's personal decisions and interventions in the economic realm also belonged to this latter category, with often significant adverse social consequences. These included the Shah's decision to reduce the cost of living in June 1965, his anti-profiteering decree and anti-corruption campaigns of August 1975, and his establishment of the Royal Commission (*komisiyon-e Shahanshahi*) of October 1976, a watchdog to supervise economic activities and developments in the country.

Besides the Shah's involvement with the Iranian economy through direct engagement and through his government, he also played an active role through a financial giant initially registered as an endowment. The Shah's Pahlavi Foundation pursued economic interests in the Iranian economy. It held an array of assets, including large tracts of land. These businesses

2 Interview with A.-M. Majidi, Foundation for Iranian Studies, APT-I, pp. 5–7, 10.

3 Interview with A.-M. Majidi, Foundation for Iranian Studies, APT-I, p. 16.

ranged from import monopolies, banking, insurance, and factories to shipping, hotels, and housing projects. The Foundation founded some of these enterprises; some were transferred to it, some partnered with other businessmen, and some were holdings. While the Shah pushed his vision of economic development and modernization with national objectives through the Iranian government and his initiatives through the Pahlavi Foundation, he pursued interests that he believed had public welfare benefits.

Finally, the Shah sometimes made economic decisions that caused ambiguity as to whose interests they were maximizing. These interventions neither benefited the country nor himself directly. They seemed akin to gifting Iran's resources to others. Was he more equal than others in Iran, or did he believe he owned the country? This ambiguity further blurred the Shah's public and personal economic motives. When the Shah instructed the government to ensure the private interests of specific individuals, his assertions about prioritizing Iran's economic development and modernization became doubtful.

At the High Economic Council of 15 August 1965, the Shah enquired about the economic proposal made by the Kermit Roosevelt Group, requesting that areas in Jiroft and Minab be entrusted (*dar ekhtiyar*) to his firm for agricultural development purposes. Safi Asfia, the director general of the Plan Organization, informed his majesty that since negotiations were advancing with the French on agricultural development in the Jiroft and Minab region, the Plan Organization suggested the Hamedan region to Roosevelt.

Everyone around the table must have known why the Shah insisted on giving a project to Kim Roosevelt. Kim (Kermit) Roosevelt, the CIA operative instrumental in the 1953 coup against Mosaddeq, had since become a close friend of the Shah. The Shah was gifting him an agricultural project for his services rendered twelve years earlier. The problem, however, was that Roosevelt was an oilman working for Gulf Oil, a consultant to American Companies doing business in the Middle East, and later an arms dealer. There was no record of his prior experience in agricultural development.

Nevertheless, the Shah ordered "the Ministry of Water and Electricity and Plan Organization to study the project and report their findings to him".[4] Three months later, Mansur Rowhani, the Minister of Water and

4 G. Nikpay (gerdavarandeh), *Surat jalesat-e showray-e 'aliye eqtesad dar pishgah Shahanshah Aryamehr, az Shahrivar 1343 ta Shahrivar 1345*, Surat Jaleseh-e 24 Mordad 1344, Tehran: Chapkhaneh vezarat-e farhang va honar, n.d., pp. 126–127.

Electricity, informed the Shah that Roosevelt had been entrusted the Jiroft and Minab agricultural development project, except for dam building in the area, which had been contracted to the French. The contract with Roosevelt included a $2 million preliminary study fee and an eventual $25 to $30 million to implement the project. The Shah subsequently instructed that the contract be signed as soon as possible and added that "this project will be beneficial to the output of the region and the export of agricultural goods."[5]

How influential individuals with no relevant expertise obtained lucrative contracts in fields unrelated to their business expertise or experience is inexplicable unless it is assumed that the Shah doled out favors to whomever he wished. The baffling news in May 1958 that Bahram Shahrokh had obtained the 200 million rial contract to construct the Shahnaz Dam near Hamedan was another such case.[6]

Shahrokh, the managing director of the privately owned Hamedan Irrigation Company, was anything but an engineer or a technical expert. He was a mysterious character who worked for the German propaganda machine during the Second World War, running their Persian radio program from Berlin. After the war, the pro-Nazi Shahrokh switched sides and, in November 1950, became the director general of the Office of Propaganda and Publications while working for the publication office of the Anglo-Iranian Oil Company. At the time, it was the Shah who had demanded that Shahrokh become the director general of Iran's Office of Propaganda and Publications.[7]

THE EXPANDING PRIVATE SECTOR

The post-1953 period witnessed the growth and increasing importance of the private sector in economic modernization. Individuals' business foresight fueled the rise of a modern capitalist class. As the economy transitioned from traditional to modern, profit-seekers and entrepreneurs

5 Nikpay (gerdavarandeh), *Surat jalesat-e showray-e 'aliye eqtesad dar pishgah Shahanshah Aryamehr, az Shahrivar 1343 ta Shahrivar 1345*. Surat Jaleseh-e 24 Mordad 1344, pp. 126–127, p. 187.

6 FO 371/133049, EP 1423/1.

7 *Shahed (Haqiqat)*, 7 Day 1329.

distinguished themselves through their talent and business acumen in their respective fields of activity.

Before 1953, private initiative had produced successful merchants and entrepreneurs such as Mohammad-Taqi Barkhordar, Mohammad Namazi, Habibollah Sabet, Mohsen Azmayesh, Mahmud Khalili, Habibollah Elqaniyan, Mahmud Lajevardi, Mohammad-Jafar Kazeruni, the Arjomand brothers (Khalil, Eskandar, and Siavosh), Hoseyn Qasemiyeh, Mostafa Alinasab, Mohammad Khorram, Gholamreza (father) and Fereydun (son) Darugar, and the Kuros brothers (Kazem, Isa, and Hasan).

From 1953, the home market expanded due to increasing oil revenues, government expenditure, and the injection of US capital. The expansion in the extent of the market meant increased demand for goods and services, especially consumer goods, both durable and non-durable. More significant opportunities for successful businesses presented themselves, while low-interest government loans and the safety of deferred repayments at times of difficulty reduced investment risks. During this period, the mushrooming government projects benefited those entrepreneurs and contractors who obtained government contracts for building roads, airports, dams, and government buildings. Thus, the private sector became actively involved in Iran's economic growth.

From the late 1950s, the socio-economic environment witnessed a surge in the activities of private entrepreneurs, transforming the lifestyle of Iran's urban dwellers. The boost in private sector activity was largely aided in 1957 by the government's injection of funds. Light industries produced new and better-quality durable and non-durable consumer goods for homes and offices, bringing ease, variety, and color to urban life.

Services evolved, shaping tastes, changing eating, clothing, shopping, entertainment, and recreational habits and venues. The neutralized press did not engage in meaningful political debates, but through its growing advertisement volume for new goods and services it widened consumer horizons and propagated consumerism. The increasing number of private banks provided new financial outlets and competitive services. All those individuals who innovated, took risks, invested their private money, and threw their back into creating and managing the businesses that mushroomed in post-1953 Iran were also the mid-wives of modernization.

The Iranian economy, however, was far from a classical laissez-faire system. It was what the Shah called a "guided" capitalist system in which the state, through its monetary and foreign trade policies, directed and supported capitalists to invest in fields deemed necessary for the national economy. The mass of small shopkeepers, bazaaris, workshop owners, and manufacturers, who operated in a perfectly competitive market and did not benefit from any special government assistance or support, constituted the bulk of Iran's business community.

A numerically small but financially powerful group of participants in Iran's guided capitalism were mutants or hybrids. This important subcategory was revitalized between 1957 and 1958. This hybrid businessman was not a typical Western entrepreneur who would take a calculated risk on his novel idea and gamble his savings in the hope of a handsome profit. This type of Iranian capitalist was both innovative and state-supported. The most successful among them were commercial, industrial, and banking capitalists.

These agents of economic modernization received a significant helping hand from their connections with the court and key government personalities, such as economically influential ministers and state banks. Some new mutant capitalists may have been less successful and affluent had they not obtained state-allocated financial privileges and benefits. However, to their credit, most of these state-supported capitalists used their advantages to establish well-managed and profitable enterprises.

These 1957 to 1958 enterprises were highly capital-intensive, as they imported all the machinery from industrially advanced countries, which was not necessarily the most suitable strategy for a labor-abundant country such as Iran. Yet, they generated employment, paid out wages, created revenue, added to the demand for other enterprises, and further expanded the market. Moreover, there were those capitalists among the recipients of state financial favors who used their loans for speculation on land; some never paid back their debt and some went under. In other words, these state-supported capitalists' success was not solely down to the state's favorable terms, it also depended on their own business acumen.

It was not unusual for members of the royal family or key decision-making government officials to sit on the boards of private enterprises. This allowed them to decide on import permits, tax, or customs duty exemptions. Such connections, partnerships, or associations guaranteed particular businessmen loans and credit from government sources, which in the 1950s was very hard to come by. The factor determining why credit would go to one capitalist and not to the other was not necessarily based on the merits of a project but on a businessman's access to political power.

There were, however, also those entrepreneurs who were not politically connected and did flourish through their independent and exclusive private initiatives.

US: A DIFFERENT ACTOR

The significant involvement and activity of various American missions in Iran marked the post-1953 modernization experience. A few of these missions pre-dated 1953 tracing back to 1942–3. The diversity of US assistance programs and missions represented the breadth of US involvement, the domains targeted, and the mediums through which American-style modernization was channeled and implemented.

Listing US missions in Iran is long and somewhat tedious but essential in providing a glimpse of the map of the American presence in Iran. These missions and programs included: the Near East Foundation (rural improvement and sanitation), Point Four Program (wide-range technical assistance), Public Law 480 (food assistance), The Harvard Advisory Group (economic advisors to the Plan Organization), Ford Foundation (financing the Harvard Advisory Group and various educational and technical projects), Governmental Affairs Institute (organizational and administrative advisors to the Plan Organization), Franklin Book Programs (translating and publishing books), the American Friends of the Middle East (educational organization facilitating university and college education in the US), Iran–America Cultural Society (binational cultural and educational center), the Peace Corps (rural and community development and English teaching), United States Information Agency (promoting American politics, institutions, and values), US Armed Forces Radio and Television services (English language radio and television broadcasting), MAAG (Military Assistance Advisory Group), ARMISH (The United States Military Mission with the Imperial Iranian Army), GENMISH (The United States Military Mission with the Imperial Iranian Gendarmerie), and USACE (Army Corps of Engineers). The activity of two of these programs, Point Four and the Army Corps of Engineers, will be dealt with in more detail.

After 1953, the growing presence of the US through its generous assistance programs and missions as well as financial and military support resulted from two compelling and intertwined factors. First, since 1947, the US was engaged in a cold war with the Soviet Union and communism, which then turned into a hot war between 1950 and 1953. In a bipolar world, Iran was a resource-rich (oil) and critically located monarchy that the US preferred to keep within the "free world" led by itself. After 19 August 1953, when Mosaddeq fell, the US entered a long-term patron–client relationship with the Shah, which from 1965 gradually became a solid partnership.

Second, after the 1953 coup, the Shah abandoned Mosaddeq's foreign policy axiom of neutrality and "negative equilibrium" to keep Iran out of the Cold War and the superpowers at bay. By opting for "positive nationalism" and a close and comprehensive strategic alliance with the US, the Shah sought to fend off the threat to his power of radical nationalism and communism. Economic modernization was the US's anti-communist strategy in Iran.

ATTITUDINAL CHANGE: AGENT OF MODERNIZATION STYMIED BY BAD GOVERNANCE

The post-1953 US economic, technical, and financial missions invariably carried pronounced cultural, educational, and ideological messages. This non-material aspect of US assistance primarily affected Iranians who came into contact with the numerous American missions and programs. The introduction of American business, civil service, professional, and military standards, practices, and values resulted in a latent attitudinal transformation.

American experts, technicians, and military personnel in Iran, aided by US-educated Iranians, were active carriers of American attitudes. It was natural for the Americanized to spread the American way of thought and life through everyday practice and action. This non-traditional behavioral incursion was reinforced by equally potent foot soldiers, such as books, magazines, movies, radio, and television shows, some translated and dubbed and some in their original version.

Fostering and disseminating attitudinal modernization ranged from practicing a Western work ethic and efficiency at the workplace to discouraging corruption and not taking bribes. Encouraging initiative, thinking outside the box, respecting the division of labor, aspiring to high standards, taking pride in technical knowledge, proactivity, meritocracy, accountability, and teamwork became examples or symbols of this Americanized ethos. From March 1955, government organizations spearheading modernization, especially the Plan Organization, demonstrated an unmistakable preference for US-educated employees and provided them with higher salaries and better benefits. An intended consequence of US programs was the Americanization and modernization of Iranian work ethics.

In theory, the all-encompassing US "assistance package", including attitudinal change, was intended to help support and stabilize the Shah's regime. The full adoption of such changes, however, encountered serious difficulties. Those determinant American attitudes that would pave the way for organizational and governmental modernization but were incompatible with the prevailing ethos were ignored, resisted, and even stigmatized. It would be foolhardy to assume that exporting work ethics is as easy as exporting goods.

Conflicting Work Ethoses

In Iran, rules and laws did not delineate the boundaries of what was possible. Proximity to, alliance with, and loyalty to people in power did. Therefore, most conspicuously in government organizations, reward and punishment were the remit of hierarchical superiors. Minimizing occupational risk through obeying orders was deep-rooted in employees' psyches. A successful employee – be it a bureaucrat, banker, planner, worker, or even engineer – did not find it in his interest to question authority or take initiative. As in all traditional societies, employment and promotion were contingent upon compliance. Pushing back on an unsound idea from the top, standing by one's expert opinion, or demanding a rational explanation for unreasonable orders did not bode well in the traditional Iranian work environment.

Initiative, innovation, and enterprise gradually flourished in the private sector. Technocrats and entrepreneurs were appreciated and rewarded in Iran's mushrooming private firms and factories. In government organizations, the story was different. The technically skilled elite, even those who were US-trained and brought up to have pride in their expertise, could not form a technocratic stratum, properly speaking. The quasi-technocrats in government had the skills but not the liberty to apply their know-how and accept the consequences. They were not political activists or militants and would, therefore, compromise their professional knowledge and concede to the whims of their superiors.

For the most part, Iranian technocrats, without the protective shield of exceptional characters such as Ebtehaj and Amini, were either obliged to swallow their professional pride and function under the non-expert notions and commands of the Shah, or else leave government organizations and ministries. These young Western-educated techno-bureaucrats of the 1960s and 1970s had splendid ideas but were only able to shine if their proposals and reports concurred with and helped advance the Shah's vision and mission.

The High Economic Council (*shoraye 'aliye eqtesad*) was the highest consultative body to the Shah concerning all financial and economic matters. This high-powered Council usually met once a week; each session took about three hours. The Shah presided, sitting at the head of the table. Economically and financially related, ministers, planners, and government bankers presented reports on the agenda items. The Shah raised issues, posed questions, and lectured. Sometimes, he decided on the spot and gave definitive directives. But often, the Shah deferred, asking for a comprehensive follow-up report to be sent to his special office for his final decision.

At the 1 August 1965 meeting of the High Economic Council, Prime Minister Hoveyda, six ministers (of Finance, Economy, Water and Energy, Labor, Housing and Urban Development, and Agriculture), along with two deputy ministers, were in attendance. Asfia, the director of the Plan Organization, and Mehdi Sami'i, the governor of the Central Bank, were also present.

Mansur Rowhani, Minister of Water and Energy, reported on the technical and financial details of two dams to be constructed at Nakhjavan and Qaraviz. The technical plans, including the size and projected electricity and irrigation capacities of these dams, had been prepared in cooperation with Soviet experts and presented to the Iranian government on 6 April 1965. Four months later, Rowhani asked the Shah's permission to sign the Soviet–Iranian agreement.

The Shah responded, "If the Soviet authorities agree with the accord, sign it immediately, and increase the height of the Qaraviz Dam to produce more electricity."[8] The royal response was at best ambiguous as it implied

8 G. Nikpay (gerdavarandeh), *Surat jalesat-e showray-e 'aliye eqtesad dar pishgah Shahanshah Aryamehr, az Shahrivar 1343 ta Shahrivar 1345,* Surat jaleseh-e 10 Mordad 1344, pp. 112–113.

yes to signing the contract but with an essential technical caveat, which to him seemed minor. The Shah desired a taller dam and informed his Minister to ensure it before signing. No one at the meeting asked for clarity or questioned the technical reason for the change, let alone the financial and technical consequences of such an alteration.

The Shah's intervention, however, marked Mehdi Sami'i, the governor of the Central Bank, who was present at that meeting. Twenty years later, Sami'i recalled that in a "childish manner", the Shah wished to impose his opinion. Sami'i was baffled at how the Shah "overruled" Rowhani over a difference of a few meters in the height of a dam carefully designed by experts. Neither in the minutes of that meeting, nor in Sami'i's recollection of that day, is there a reference to Rowhani questioning or discussing the merit of the Shah's technical order.[9] Nine years earlier in April 1957, in a similar situation, the Shah had ordered a three-meter increase in the height of Golpayegan Dam.[10]

The Shah's treatment of his experts demonstrated that by 1965, attitudinal change, an important aspect of the US modernization package, was not taking root in Iran's governance structure. The modernist monarch perpetuated traditional ideas and attitudes. As a role model, the Shah demanded unquestioning compliance in all fields, failing to give wings to his experts' technical imagination and innovation despite them being far better educated and qualified than him.

How could the economy truly develop and modernize when technical facts and expert designs had to bow to superior political wills? Absolute power and unaccountability at the apex of the political power structure trickled down Iran's administrative hierarchy, preventing it from structural development and modernization.

---

9 Mohammad-Mehdi Sami'i, Iranian Oral History Collection, Harvard University, Transcript 2, Sequence 42.
10 *Ettela'at*, 10 Ordibehesht 1336.

2

US and Iran's Economic Transformation

The typical modernization project of the 1950s and 1960s for "underdeveloped" or "developing" countries included four areas: political, economic, social, and cultural. Once Mohammad-Reza Shah came to embrace the Western modernization model, he dug in his heels and chose aspects that he considered desirable. The Shah knew that if he maintained his pro-US foreign policy position and assured the flow of Iran's oil, his US benefactors would not disavow him for fear of a non-aligned alternative, regardless of his domestic politics.

As early as January 1955, the US position towards Iran was clear. Iran was considered "critically important" to the US and the "free world" for its oil resources and geostrategic and geopolitical position. Therefore, it had to be fully supported as "an anti-communist asset" in "Asia". The US was not bothered by Iran using "authoritarian means if necessary to maintain stability and carry forward desirable economic and political reform".[1] Aware of its paradoxical position of excusing "authoritarian means" to achieve political liberalization, the US naively or shrewdly hoped to encourage "the careful and gradual introduction of political and social reforms that will make the democratic forms in Iran more of a reality".[2]

After the 1953 coup, the US envisaged six objectives with their corresponding "courses of action" to help the Shah consolidate his rule and overcome his country's problems. They included new initiatives and

1 FRUS, 1955–1957, Near East Region, Iran, Iraq, vol. XII, Document 291.
2 FRUS, 1955–1957, Near East Region, Iran, Iraq, vol. XII, Document 291.

policies in the economic, technical, military, cultural, educational, and socio-political domains.[3] The US financially committed itself in order to successfully attain these objectives. Iran's post-coup modernization thus became tightly intertwined with the US government and private involvement in Iran.

The US soon realized that its post-Cold-War Third World "anti-communist" allies were eager to pursue economic and technical modernization but were opposed to its political modernization supplement. Iran was no exception to this trend. After some wrangling with the Kennedy administration during Ali Amini's premiership (May 1961 to July 1962), the Shah made it clear to the US that he would completely discard political modernization and democratization. He correctly feared that political liberalization would imply checks and balances on his rule, destabilizing his absolutist power. Only economic, technical, cultural, and social modernization, accompanied by attitudinal changes, were considered free of political consequences and warmly welcomed.

The Shah hoped that delivering economic, social, and cultural modernization would compensate for the absence of political liberalization and participation. He failed to see that those same "sanitized" but still life-changing modernizations would invariably raise political consciousness, leading to questioning of his methods and absolute power.

The Shah not only succeeded in getting the US to drop its insistence on political liberalization, but he also forced a notable change in the outlook of US policymakers and economic experts. The US development package emphasized allocating funds to infrastructural, agricultural, and industrial investments, which would jump-start the development process of underdeveloped economies. US assistance aimed at fostering economic "take-off" and paving the path to what W. W. Rostow called the society of "high mass-consumption".

In the economic textbook trade-off between guns and butter, growth and development economists of the late 1950s and early 1960s emphatically sided with less military expenditure and more developmental allocation. Walt Rostow, who became Kennedy's deputy National Security Advisor in 1961 and Johnson's National Security Advisor from 1966 to 1969, was

3 FRUS, 1955–1957, Near East Region, Iran, Iraq, vol. XII, Document 291.

a strong supporter of the Shah.[4] He was on friendly terms with the Iranian monarch and the country's political leaders and had traveled to Iran.[5]

For the Shah, modernization included a continuous rearmament program and a consistent expansion of Iran's military power. High military expenditures, a drain on economic development, were not built into the original US modernization package. However, the Shah got his way and forced the US to renege on another pivotal component of its modernization package. The Shah chose to ignore the persistent US complaint in the late 1950s that Iran did not possess the technical know-how and personnel to operate and maintain its US-acquired equipment.[6]

EVOLVING RELATIONS

From 1953 to 1964, the US became Iran's auxiliary provider, consistently aiding the country when internal resources, grain, expertise, or money fell short of demand. There were also moments like in 1962, right before the end of Amini's premiership, when the US tightened the purse to teach the Shah a lesson. Yet from 1953, following the hypothesis that modernizing and developing Iran economically and socially would guarantee the Shah's rule and ward off the communist threat, the US spent lavishly on Iran.

Relations in this initial phase (1953–1964) were primarily contributive: the US provided, and Iran received, without any financial obligations. Iran relied on US goodwill and generosity for grants and loans throughout this period, while the Shah insisted on more military hardware. Between 1950 and 1965, the US provided Iran with $820.7 million in economic grants and loans and $1,498 million in financial and military aid.[7] The lion's share of these transfers began after the coup. Between 1954 and 1957, Iran was

4 A.L. Johns, "The Johnson Administration, the Shah of Iran, and the Changing Pattern of U.S.-Iranian Relations, 1965–1967: 'Tired of Being Treated like a Schoolboy.'" *Journal of Cold War Studies*, vol. 9, no. 2, 2007, pp. 64–94.

5 A. 'Alam, *Yaddashtha-ye 'Alam*, ed. A.N. 'Alikhani, vol. 7, Bethesda: Ibex Publishers, 2014, pp. 219–220.

6 Report to the Congress of the United States. Review of the military assistance program for Iran. January 1959, https://www.gao.gov/assets/b-133134.pdf (retrieved 3/6/2023).

7 J. Amuzegar, *Technical Assistance in Theory and Practice: The Case of Iran*, New York: Praeger, 1966, p. 36.

the third largest Middle East recipient of grants, aid, and credits from the US, trailing Turkey and Israel.[8]

From 1964, US economic, technical, and military relations with Iran evolved. This second phase, characterized by Iran's reduced financial dependence, was due to an increase in oil revenues resulting from an increase in oil production and the stabilization of oil prices after the foundation of the Organization of the Petroleum Exporting Countries (OPEC) in 1960.[9] Between 1964 and 1970, Iran's oil export revenues almost tripled from $479 million to $1.14 billion.[10]

This period saw Iran move away from relying on US grants and financing its purchases through foreign loans. "Credit drawdowns mounted from a scant $28 million in FY 1964 to $952 million in FY 1970."[11] Iran did, nevertheless, remain dependent for loans on the International Bank for Reconstruction and Development (World Bank). From 1957 to 1969, Iran received fourteen loans from the World Bank worth $412 million. The World Bank extended these loans for "general development purposes", "road construction", "irrigation dams and agriculture", and "foreign exchange resources for the Industrial and Mining Development Bank of Iran".[12]

Iran's military procurements also reflected this significant transformation from grants to loans. The Shah backed his demand for more sophisticated US military hardware by insisting on paying for it. A background paper prepared by the US Department of State noted that, "Prior to 1964, all U.S. military equipment and services were provided [to] Iran on a grant basis; since that time, Iran has undertaken to pay for an increasingly large portion of its defense needs."[13]

Also, from 1964, the post-1953 wave of US experts, advisors, and personnel that came to Iran gradually diminished. The Americans involved in

---

8 *Tehran Economist*, 12 Bahman 1336.

9 CESIFO working paper no. 4118, K. Mohaddes and M. Hashem Pesaran, "One Hundred Years of Oil Income and the Iranian Economy: A Curse or a Blessing?" https://www.repository.cam.ac.uk/items/0cdba012-56a1-4edb-b1c4-382303e97720 (retrieved 12/6/2023).

10 FRUS, 1969–1976, vol. E–4, Documents on Iran and Iraq, 1969–1972, Document 165.

11 FRUS, 1969–1976, vol. E–4, Documents on Iran and Iraq, 1969–1972, Document 165.

12 J. Bharier, *Economic Development in Iran 1900-1970*, London: Oxford University Press, 1971, p. 120.

13 FRUS, 1964–1968, vol. XXII, Iran, Document 220.

numerous US government technical and construction programs handed over their activities to Iranians. During this second phase, the US presence in Iran gradually shifted from governmental to private and from export to investment. US private firms which had up to 1964, with a few exceptions, been exporters of goods and services, became interested in industrial investments.

The definitive turning of the tables, which almost resembled a role reversal, came with the quadrupling of oil prices in 1973–1974, as oil revenues jumped from $2.8 billion in 1972–1973 to $4.6 billion in 1973–1974 and rocketed to $17.8 billion in 1974–1975.[14] Iran was no longer the needy recipient of US generosity that it was in 1953 and had transitioned to a well-to-do economic force.

US EARLY PRESENCE IN IRAN: NEITHER ALTRUISM NOR IMPERIALISM

With lessons learned from two monumental US economic initiatives, namely the Tennessee Valley Authority (TVA) and the Point Four program, American politicians and economic experts concluded they had a magical formula for economic development. They came to believe that by exporting to and replicating these two initiatives in the less and underdeveloped countries of the world, they could significantly raise the standard of living of these people and put them on the track of economic development and modernization.

Tennessee Valley Authority

On 10 April 1933, about a month after Franklin Roosevelt launched the "New Deal" to pull his country out of depression and unemployment, he asked Congress to "create a Tennessee Valley Authority – a corporation clothed with the power of government but possessed of the flexibility and initiative of a private enterprise".[15] The US government was saving laissez-faire capitalism by planning and intervening in the economy.

---

14 H. Razavi and F. Vakil, *The Political Environment of Economic Planning in Iran, 1971–1983: From Monarchy to Islamic Republic*, London: Routledge, 2019, p. 63.
15 S.M. Neuse, *David E. Lilienthal: The Journey of an American Liberal.* Lexington: Plunkett Lake Press, 2018. Kindle edition. Location 3084 of 17935.

The directors of the TVA were Arthur Morgan, Harcourt Morgan, and David Lilienthal. The TVA was a multi-purpose government-mandated regional development agency. Within some sixteen years, it brought economic, social, and cultural modernization to the agrarian South, one of the US's most underdeveloped regions, through integrated planning.

The TVA carried out infrastructural projects, initiated agricultural development programs, built dams, and provided water and cheap electricity to rural areas and industrial plants. It introduced modern irrigation and farming techniques and constructed fertilizer plants. The investments attracted industries ranging from textiles to ammunition, created jobs, generated income, and brought prosperity to the area. Electricity brought radios, clothes irons, fans, water heaters, washing machines, and refrigerators to southern homes, improving living standards. The TVA exemplified modernization. It "was geared to changing the perceptions of people said to be a hundred years behind the rest of the country".[16]

The TVA's success story convinced American policymakers that it could be applied to all underdeveloped regions with similar results. Subsequently, the TVA model was touted as "the best model for global liberal development".[17] To combat the appeal of the Soviet development model, the US promoted international liberal and market development, with the TVA as its tested and proven trademark and blueprint.

From Marshall Plan to Point Four

After World War II, on 3 April 1948, the Foreign Assistance Act, better known as the Marshall Plan, named after the US Secretary of State, was enacted by President Truman. The Marshall Plan was the European Recovery Program, aimed at putting sixteen war-torn Western and Southern European economies back on their feet. The US provided these countries with $13 billion of economic aid over four years. This program was a substantial economic development plan aimed at reconstructing ruined cities, reviving industry and agriculture, and rebuilding devastated infrastructure.

16 D. Ekbladh, "Meeting the Challenge from Totalitarianism: The Tennessee Valley Authority as a Global Model for Liberal Development, 1933–1945." *The International History Review*, vol. 32, no. 1 (March 2010), pp. 47–67.

17 Ekbladh, "Meeting the Challenge from Totalitarianism," pp. 47–67.

The Marshall Plan was grounded in the liberal American establishment's long-held belief that economic prosperity and growth would prevent the spread of communism and assure political stability. The Marshall Plan helped speed up economic recovery in Europe, put industry back on its feet, provide for high gross national product growth rates, and raise income levels substantially.

In his second-term inaugural address of 20 January 1949, President Harry Truman referred to the Marshall Plan as "the greatest cooperative economic program in history" and identified "four major courses of action" to ensure "peace and freedom". Continuing the Marshall Plan for "world economic recovery" constituted his second action.

Tuman called his fourth course of action "a bold new program for making the benefits of our scientific advances and industrial progress available for the improvement and growth of underdeveloped areas". This new American initiative intended to transform underdeveloped countries by providing them with modern scientific techniques, technical knowledge, and "capital investment in areas needing development".[18]

This initiative, commonly known as the Point Four Program, was, in effect, an economic development project based on a small-scale transfer of Western technical expertise. It was to be the equivalent of a mini Marshall Plan Program to the less-developed countries of the "free world".[19] David Lilienthal, the chairman of the TVA at the time and a key player in Iran's future economic modernization, hailed the Point Four Program as "the most potent weapon ever devised, a weapon that makes the atom bomb seem a firecracker by comparison".[20]

Point Four in Iran (1951–1967)

On 27 October 1950, the Technical Cooperation Administration was established in the Department of State to implement the Point Four Program. The program relied on the expertise of academics in American universities in agriculture, medicine, and education. Point Four in Iran, as elsewhere,

18 Inaugural Address of Harry S. Truman, Thursday, January 20, 1949, The Avalon Project, https://avalon.law.yale.edu/20th_century/truman.asp (retrieved 25/5/2023).
19 Inaugural Address of Harry S. Truman, Thursday, January 20, 1949, The Avalon Project, https://avalon.law.yale.edu/20th_century/truman.asp (retrieved 25/5/2023).
20 R. Garlitz, *A Mission for Development, Utah Universities and the Point Four Program in Iran*, Colorado: University of Colorado Press, 2018, p. 18.

pursued the interrelated objectives of helping buttress national stability and security through promoting economic development and a US-style modernization.

US assistance to Iran in the 1950s intended to "strengthen the Iranian Government and people in their resistance to communist pressures, [and] bring them into closer association with the free world".[21] Even though the Point Four Program became involved with training Iran's police and providing it with surveillance material, it was primarily a development assistance program. It was divided into four periods, and although it was initially aimed at rural development, its purview expanded over time.

First Phase: 1951–1953

The first phase included the arrival of the Program staff and their adjustment to the country that was consumed by nationalist sentiments during the Mosaddeq government. Franklin Harris, the President of Utah State University and a former consultant to the Iranian government, was the first chief of mission.

After the assassination of Prime Minister Haj Ali Razmara in 1951, the US panicked that a Soviet threat with the help of the Tudeh Party might be real and imminent. On 15 March 1951, Burton Berry, the Deputy Assistant Secretary of State for Near Eastern, South Asian, and African Affairs at the State Department, argued that the best course of action in Iran would be in "support of a vigorous overt United States program to strengthen Iran, including loans, increased military aid, medical and public health programs and Point IV assistance".[22]

In early September 1951, five academics from Utah State University and their families arrived in Tehran. In October, another batch of Point Four employees from Brigham Young University and Utah University followed suit.[23] They arrived at a time when the US was focused on how to grapple with the rise of Mosaddeq, mediate between the UK and Iran over the oil nationalization dispute, and neutralize Tudeh Party agitation. The Point Four Utah employees spearheaded a project that lasted some ten years with significant long-term consequences.

21 Foreign Relations of the United States, 1952–1954, Iran, 1951–1954, Document 6.
22 Foreign Relations of the United States, 1952–1954, Iran, 1951–1954, Document 8.
23 Garlitz, *A Mission for Development*, pp. 4, 42.

On 28 November 1951, William Warne, the new director of Point Four, arrived in Tehran, replacing Franklin Harris. Warne found Mosaddeq favorable to the Program's presence and had "a very friendly, rather bantering relationship" with him.[24] During Mosaddeq's premiership, Point Four committed $23,450,000 for the fiscal year 1952. At this time, Point Four officials and experts worked with the ministries of health, education, agriculture, and the Plan Organization.[25]

Second Phase: 1953–1956

The second period in the Point Four experience began with the fall of Mosaddeq in August 1953 and ended in September 1956. With General Fazlollah Zahedi as prime minister, the Point Four Program was placed "on its firmest footing". Warne benefited from a special relationship with the Zahedis. Ardeshir Zahedi, the General's son, had been involved with the Program since its inception and had been Warne's "principal Iranian assistant". He had been at Point Four since his return to Iran from Utah State University in 1951. Immediately after the 1953 coup, the US government pledged its support for the Shah and Prime Minister Zahedi. On 8 September 1953, President Eisenhower extended $45 million to Iran in emergency economic assistance. This sum was "to be given to Iran in increments through Point Four".[26]

In this period, Point Four launched various administrative programs in addition to its strictly developmental projects. In early 1954, "Public Administration" (*umure 'umumi*) programs were begun to overhaul and improve statistical techniques, population census and national surveys, tax collection, budgeting, and commercial accounting. Point Four also established technical and communication programs in the police department. They advised the Plan Organization and municipalities on improving their administrative structure.[27] The establishment of the Institute for Administrative Affairs (*Moaseseh-e 'ulume edari*) was one of the main achievements of Point Four in this period.

24 W. Warne, *Mission for Peace: Point 4 in Iran*, Indianapolis: Bobbs-Merrill, 1956, pp. 25, 132.
25 Garlitz, *A Mission for Development*, pp. 84–85.
26 Warne, *Mission for Peace*, pp. 39, 258–259, 270. Information in this paragraph is based on this source.
27 *Ettela'at*, 21 Bahman 1335.

In 1955, Point Four became involved in establishing, modernizing, and reorganizing Iranian industries. These included the Shahr-e Ray cement plant, three sugarloaf factories in Shiraz, Kerman, and Mashhad, and the Tehran Fabric Factory (*Karkhaneh-e chitsazi-ye Tehran*). Point Four technical advisers trained railroad workers and road maintenance personnel. They set up repair shops in some nine provincial centers, where they coached some 500 workers.[28]

This period witnessed the implementation of numerous small rural development projects and technical and financial assistance to the Namazi Hospital in Shiraz and the Agricultural College of Shiraz.[29] Other new projects varied from radio production training to providing technical assistance in the construction of Karaj Dam.[30]

In March 1955, William Warne left Iran, and on 25 January 1956, Clark Gregory, the new director, outlined his developmental plans. He spoke of $8 million earmarked for technical assistance and another $5 million for the purchase and import of necessary goods. Point Four would assist Iran in agricultural development, with a focus on research, education, and technical training centered around the Karaj Agricultural College.[31]

Point Four, through Utah State University faculty members, had begun cooperation with the Karaj Agricultural College (*Daneshgadeh keshavarzi-ye Karaj*) back in 1951 with five advisers. It was from 1956 to 1961 that the expansion and development of the College became a showcase for Point Four. In this period, $1.2 million was spent on new buildings, laboratories, and student and faculty residents. Point Four introduced and promoted "American higher-educational practices", and the College adopted a credit system, enabling "students to specialize in a particular area".[32]

In late March 1956, Point Four signed a contract with the Ministry of Education to train teachers for Tehran University's Teacher Training College (*Daneshsara-ye 'ali-ye daneshgah-e Tehran*), the country's only teachers training establishment. The program, with the aid of Brigham Young University experts, was to modernize the educational program and curriculum of teacher training based on the American educational system.

---

28 *Ettela'at*, 23 Bahman 1335.

29 *Ettela'at*, 22 Farvardin, 15, 16 Khordad 1335.

30 A. Ansari, *The Shah's Iran: Rise and Fall*, London: I. B. Tauris, 2017, p. 45.

31 *Tehran Economist*, 7 Bahman 1334.

32 Garlitz, *A Mission for Development*, pp. 98–99, 103. *Ettela'at*, 9 Khordad 1336.

Point Four earmarked $108,000 for this project, while the Ministry of Education provided the buildings worth approximately $95,650.[33]

Third Phase (1956–1961)

Preparations for Point Four's third phase were under way by January 1956, but became effective around November 1956, and lasted until 1961. On 28 January 1956, while outlining Point Four's projects, Gregory announced that plans were drawn up in coordination with the respective Iranian ministries for the gradual transfer of activities from Plan Four to the Iranian government.[34]

Ten months later, on 20 November 1956, Gregory reported that Point Four had transferred the equivalent of $23 million worth of machinery, vehicles, and electric goods to eight relevant ministries and the Plan Organization. He said the transfer of assets would also include items such as wheat, sugar, medicine, motor vehicles, agricultural equipment, improved seeds, educational tools, and airport electronic devices in the future. This phase aimed at delegating the administration and execution of all technical and developmental projects to Iranians. At this point, the Point Four staff would only act as technical advisers. The Iranian press referred to this phase as "integration and merging" (*edgham va talfiq*).[35]

Integration and merging implied that ministries were prepared to take over administrative responsibility for the projects gradually and could efficiently complete the remaining projects. From the 9,000 small agricultural, technical, and developmental projects that had begun in 1953 in the rural areas under the rubric of "self-help" (*khishtan yari*), 7,000 were completed, and the remainder had to be completed and maintained by Iranian ministries. These projects all fell under the rubric of "Community Development Projects" and included building schools, public baths, mortuaries, feeder roads, bridges, clinics, water systems, and mosques in the villages.[36]

On 26 June 1957, Gregory announced Point Four's plan for allocating $12 million of aid to various programs in Iran. Six projects received a total of $5.3 million. These included the improvement of transportation on the

33 *Ettela'at*, 20 Farvardin 1335.
34 *Tehran Economist*, 7 Bahman 1334.
35 *Ettela'at*, 2 Aban 1335.
36 *Ettela'at*, 18 Bahman 1335.

Rezaiyeh Lake, the development of Iran's telephone network, the surveying of the forests in Northern Iran, the completion of installing technical instruments at Mehrabad airport, and the provision of equipment and tools for technical training. Two programs, including development aid to provinces and agricultural and irrigational development schemes in rural areas, received $2.6 million. The remaining $4.1 million was deposited at the Melli Bank and earmarked for the development of Karaj Agricultural College and the training of 1,000 students per year in various fields.[37]

Point Four announced that during 1958–1959, it would only shoulder the cost of American experts and technicians employed at the Iran office. With Gregory's departure on 24 February 1958, Harry Burn, his successor, carried out the process of gradual disengagement. Despite initial administrative and book-keeping obstacles, by 1961, Point Four programs were passed on to Iranian authorities. The critics of the integration initiative maintained that Iranians were not yet ready to take responsibility. "Both Point Four and Ford Foundation officials found that Iranian agencies failed to maintain agriculture and education projects amid the subsequent reduction of American technical aid."[38]

Fourth Phase: (1961–1967)

Point Four's last phase in Iran dates from 1961 to 1967, during which participation and activities wound down. From 1962, "the scale of the [Point Four] program was reduced", due to "the progress achieved in 1953–1962", and activities were limited to "rural development, public administration and higher education".[39] In summer 1964, "the last Utah technical assistance advisers left Iran", and "by that time, Point Four's rural improvement initiatives had faded into the background of Iranian development ..."[40] On 29 November 1967, the Point Four mission in Iran officially closed down.

37 *Ettela'at*, 5 Tir 1336.

38 Garlitz, *A Mission for Development*, p. 138.

39 J. Amuzegar, "Point Four: Performance and Prospect." *Political Science Quarterly*, vol. 73, no. 4 (December 1958), pp. 530–546.

40 Garlitz, *A Mission for Development*, p. 135.

Point Four's Legacy

The sums received by Iran from the US under the aegis of the Point Four Program were substantial. According to William Warne, from 1950 to June 1955, "the technical co-operation program in Iran operated on approximately $90,000,000" from the US.[41] Clark Gregory maintained that for the 1956 fiscal year, US assistance to Iran was $77 million of which $7 million was strictly for technical assistance and $47 million was for the purchase of necessary items such as tractors, electricity generators, construction material and textiles, $10 million was for credit and $12 million was for the purchase of wheat and sugar. This figure, he added, did not include US military assistance.[42] Jahangir Amuzegar refers to $116.2 million in technical aid grants from the US between 1950 and 1965.[43]

The discrepancy in the sums may be due to calculating only technical assistance figures as compared to all economic aid through Point Four. According to one calculation, between 1950 and 1965, Iran received some $600 million from the Agency for International Development, the successor to Point Four.[44]

During its sixteen-year activity in Iran, aside from the transfer of technical expertise, Iranian Point Four personnel were exposed to American work ethics, standards, and culture. Between 1951 and 1965, some 550 Point Four technicians and experts came to Iran and spread throughout the country.[45] By July 1957, even though the "integration and merging" phase was well underway, and numerous Iranian employees who had been lent to the Point Four team in Tehran returned to the respective ministries and organizations, the Point Four office continued to have some 1,000 employees.[46] During its activity in Iran, Point Four sent some 1,230 trainees to the US for various training programs.[47]

Point Four in Iran was also home to several US and UK-trained Iranians who became prominent politicians. These included Khalil Taleqani, Ardeshir Zahedi, Abdolreza Ansari, Hushang Rām, and Jamshid Amuzegar.

41 Warne, *Mission for Peace*, p. 272.
42 *Ettela'at*, 30 Tir 1335.
43 Amuzegar, *Technical Assistance in Theory and Practice*, pp. 29, 36.
44 M. Ali, "Iran's Relations with the US And USSR." *Pakistan Horizon*, vol. 26, no. 3 (1973) pp. 45–68.
45 Amuzegar, *Technical Assistance in Theory and Practice*, p. 247.
46 *Ettela'at*, 1 Mordad 1336.
47 Amuzegar, *Technical Assistance in Theory and Practice*, pp. 244–245.

Salaries at Point Four were much higher than any other private or government organization. The American work environment required some knowledge of English and privileged employees with expertise in Point Four related activities.

At a time when women's presence in the workforce was sparse, Point Four attracted educated women, most of whom came from prominent Iranian families. The daughters of Hoseyn 'Ala, Manuchehr Eqbal, and Nezameddin Emami all worked at Point Four.[48] Emami was the Iranian government's inspector general at Bank Melli, whose daughters Farideh and Leyla later married Hasan-Ali Mansur and Amir-Abbas Hoveyda.

Point Four personnel were, therefore, more than technical specialists, and the Program was more than a benign and innocuous small-scale development program. The Program was also an incubation agent promoting economic and cultural modernization and Americanization, and its messengers were also missionaries, "spreading American values – the American way of life".[49]

The success of Point Four in Iran was "uneven" in its various fields of practice. In his extensive study of Point Four in Iran, Jahangir Amuzegar maintains that those directly impacted by its activities, receiving "improved seed, healthier poultry or livestock, few new tools, some medical treatment or preventive inoculations, and a token of new village facilities", experienced an undoubted improvement in their lot.[50] Utah State University, a principal actor and participant in Iran's Point Four Program, assessed its agricultural program in Iran as "not so successful".[51]

THE DISCREET PRESENCE OF THE ARMY CORPS OF ENGINEERS (GULF DISTRICT)

Three years after the 1953 coup, Iran received another substantial US aid program. This one's clear objective was primarily military, but it had substantial developmental externalities. In 1956, the Army Corps of Engineers

48 Ansari, *The Shah's Iran: Rise and Fall*, pp. 12, 19, 26–27. Information in this paragraph is based on this source.
49 Garlitz, *A Mission for Development*, p. 24.
50 Amuzegar, *Technical Assistance in Theory and Practice*, pp. 9–21.
51 Utah State University, USU and Point Four in Iran, http://exhibits.usu.edu/exhibits/show/pointiv (retrieved 1/1/2024).

began an almost silent operation on a massive scale in Iran. Little was reported on its activities and contributions in the Iranian press. The government probably wanted to keep the US military presence in Iran hushed up, even though their mission was construction. Nevertheless, the Army Corps of Engineers built military quarters, barracks, cantonments, air bases, military airfields, naval bases, and civilian airports in all four corners of Iran.

When it pulled down the curtain on its construction activities in 1967, concurrent with Point Four's departure, the US Army Corps of Engineers left behind an impressive infrastructural base of civilian airports, such as the Mehrabad airport in Tehran and the Hamedan airport, army garrisons and cantonments in sensitive border areas such as Khaneh/Piranshahr, Naqadeh, Sanandaj, and Oshnaviyeh in northwestern Iran, a complete airfield in Dezful and the Shahrokhi air base in Hamedan, a complete naval base on Khark Island, along with some seventy smaller projects. During its eleven-year stay, the Army Corps of Engineers carried out over ninety projects of different types and costs throughout Iran. Point Four and the Army Corps of Engineers' contributions were free and gifted by the US.

Background to the US Corps of Engineers

In February 1947, Dean Acheson told congressional leaders that if Greece were to fall to communism, Iran, a neighbor of the Soviet Union, and all to the east would follow suit in a domino effect. When North Korea crossed the 38th parallel and invaded South Korea on 25 June 1950, the communist threat became an absolute US nightmare. From this date, aside from military aid and arms transfer or sales, the US army supported allied countries in developing and beefing up their defensive capacities. To this end, the US provided engineering and military know-how to build the physical constructions necessary for defensive and containment actions. Just as the US came to view economic development as a preventive course of action against communism from within, boosting deterrence capabilities and military preparedness of friendly countries became a prime concern to inhibit external threats.

First Phase of the Army Corps of Engineers: 1956–1962

The Bagdad Pact, a military alliance involving Iran, Iraq, Turkey, Pakistan, and the UK, with the US's strong support, was signed in February 1955.

The Army Corps of Engineers began operating in Iran in January 1956. A group of 27 technicians from the 30th Engineer Battalion's Topographic Section came to Iran to assist and train Iranian army personnel in conducting surveys. On 12 March 1956, the US Corps of Engineers officially began work, and by September 1956, contracts were signed between the US and the Iranian government.[52]

In Iran, the US Army Corps of Engineers operated under the regional name of Gulf District. The Gulf District headquarters in Tehran planned and executed military-related construction projects to modernize the Iranian armed forces. It "supervised military construction in cooperation with the US Army Mission and Military Assistance Advisory Group to Iran (ARMISH-MAAG)".[53] It also extended technical assistance to ARMISH-MAAG and provided "the appropriate design and construction directives".[54] The Gulf District was tasked with building installations for the Iranian Airforce, Navy, Army, and Gendarmerie and therefore handled projects of various size, purpose, and cost.

The construction work for projects, except those for the Gendarmerie, was carried out by a joint venture of five US firms. Once projects were completed, they were turned over to the MAAG, which subsequently handed them to Iranian authorities. Funding for the Gulf District's construction "came from the Department of Defense's Military Assistance Program and from the State Department's International Cooperation Administration".[55]

On 26 May 1957, when Morrison-Knudsen, one of five Gulf Districts' US contractors in Iran, known as M-K-O (Morrison-Kaiser-Oman), began hiring workers in Tehran to construct cantonments throughout the country, applicants poured in, bringing traffic to a halt on Shah Street. It was after the police intervened that the throng of jobseekers stood in line and order was restored. Morrison-Knudsen hired technicians, draftsmen, surveyors, skilled and semi-skilled workers, drivers, and office personnel.

52 R.P. Grathwol and D.M. Moorhus, *Bricks, Sand, and Marble: U.S. Army Corps of Engineers, Construction in the Mediterranean and Middle East, 1947–1991*, Center of Military History and Corps of Engineers, United States Army, Washington, D.C., 2009, pp. 107–110.

53 Grathwol and Moorhus, *Bricks, Sand, and Marble*, p. 171. The information in this section on the operation of Army Corps of Engineers in Iran draws heavily from this source, https://www.publications.usace.army.mil/Portals/76/Publications/EngineerPamphlets/EP_870-1-72.pdf (retrieved 4/1/2024).

54 Grathwol and Moorhus, *Bricks, Sand, and Marble*, p. 171.

55 Grathwol and Moorhus, *Bricks, Sand, and Marble*, p. 180.

It was interviewing some 100 applicants per day.[56] To carry out its local activities, M-K-O subcontracted works to four major Iranian construction firms, such as Kayqobad Zafar's Khaneh Construction Company.[57]

Grasping the scale of the Gulf Districts' projects and their effect on the Iranian economy requires a brief review of a few specific projects. The Iranian Army project at Khaneh/Piranshahr, for example, involved the construction of 290 buildings for some 5,100 troops at the cost of some $10 to $14 million.[58] Khaneh, located in Western Azarbayjan, right on the border with Iraq, was an inaccessible location. Once construction at Khaneh began in 1956, some six to seven truckloads of construction material were being transported daily from Tehran to Khaneh, whereas before this project, there was hardly any significant traffic on the dirt roads to Khaneh.[59]

In October 1958, at the peak of activities on three projects located geographically fairly close to one another, Khaneh, Naqadeh, and Oshnaviyeh, contractors employed a local workforce of some 10,000, "with about sixty Americans supervising and inspecting the work".[60] In both, Naqadeh and Oshnaviyeh, 180 buildings were constructed housing some 3,300 troops.

In Sanandaj, the capital of Kordestan province in Northwestern Iran, close to the Iraq border, the Army Corps of Engineers began work in April 1958 to supervise the construction of "a divisional cantonment of 213 buildings and support facilities including water, power, and sewage systems and ammunition storages".[61] Some 3,500 locals worked on this project between ten to twelve hours per day and seven days a week. The cost of this project, finished in January 1961, was also around $10 to $14 million.[62]

The Army Engineering Corps built numerous similar facilities for regimental combat teams (accommodating some 4,500 to 5,000 soldiers) at Hamedan, Kermanshah, Quchan, and Sarab. By March 1958, the Gulf District had built eight new gendarmerie outposts in Shahrud, Sabzevar, Torbat Jam, Malayer, Qom, Varamin, Abadeh, and Dahran.[63] These were

56 *Ettela'at*, 5, 6 Khordad 1336.
57 *Ettela'at*, 27 Khordad 1336, 20 Esfand 1336.
58 Grathwol and Moorhus, *Bricks, Sand, and Marble*, pp. 175, 178, 189.
59 *Ettela'at*, 10 Mordad 1336.
60 Grathwol and Moorhus, *Bricks, Sand, and Marble*, p. 177.
61 Grathwol and Moorhus, *Bricks, Sand, and Marble*, p. 179.
62 Grathwol and Moorhus, *Bricks, Sand, and Marble*, p. 179.
63 *Ettela'at*, 20 Esfand 1336.

part of some seventy smaller projects with costs between $4,000 to around $1 million.[64]

The Army Corps of Engineers was also involved in highly significant military projects. The Dezful airfield project for the Iranian Airforce was a significant undertaking that began in August 1957 and included "an air depot, taxiways and lighting, hangars, parking aprons, shops, living quarters for about two hundred fifty officers and one thousand two hundred enlisted personnel, and a drainage system".[65]

Subsequently, at the Iranian Army's request, the Gulf District supervised the construction of an ordnance depot with 295 buildings at the Dezful site. This major military project was completed in some three-and-a-half years. In May 1961, the base was handed to the Iranian Air Force, and US-made F-84 turbojet fighter-bomber aircrafts were landing and taking off from Dezful Airfield. The cost of this project was $23.3 million.[66]

The construction of Khark Naval Base, which began in June 1961 and was completed in March 1963, was a second example of a significant project with a price tag of just over $2 million. The facilities at Khark included "barracks with laundry, bath, and latrine installations for two hundred men; a fully equipped kitchen and mess hall; an administration building; quarters for five officers and their families; ammunition magazines; and warehouse space. The construction included electrical, water distribution, and sewage disposal systems and the roads necessary to support the installation."[67]

The Last Phase of Gulf District Projects in Iran 1962–1967

The Gulf District built its last "regimental combat team" units for the Iranian Army in Quchan, northwest of Iran and close to the Russian border. Construction began in July 1962 and ended in April 1964. From 1966, the Army Corps of Engineers supervised the construction of small projects for the Iranian army, such as twenty-seven schools located at or near army garrisons.[68] Most of the smaller projects were finished by mid-1967.

---

64 Grathwol and Moorhus, *Bricks, Sand, and Marble*, pp. 175, 178, 189.
65 Grathwol and Moorhus, *Bricks, Sand, and Marble*, p. 178.
66 Grathwol and Moorhus, *Bricks, Sand, and Marble*, p. 178.
67 Grathwol and Moorhus, *Bricks, Sand, and Marble*, pp. 183–184.
68 Grathwol and Moorhus, *Bricks, Sand, and Marble*, p. 222.

During its last five years of operation, the Army Corps of Engineers worked on two major projects, one in Hamedan and another in Khorasan. Construction of the Shahrokhi air base in Hamedan began in June 1963 and was completed in June 1965. This $4.8 million project "involved about 1,300 family-housing units, a 200-man dormitory, a squadron operations building, a theater, a post exchange, a commissary, a cold-storage plant, an officers' club, a noncommissioned officers' club, a hospital, a school, and a base headquarters building".[69] On 16 June 1965, at an official ceremony, the US Ambassador to Iran, Armin H. Meyer, handed over the Shahrokhi Air Base to the commander of the Imperial Iranian Airforce, General Mohammad-Amir Khatami. Meyer pointed out that the Shahrokhi Air Base was an essential addition to Iran's aerial defense capabilities.[70]

In 1964, the Army Corps of Engineers took on a $6 million contract to develop and expand the Mashhad air base, the last of projects funded by the US Military Assistance Program. This major project, which began in July 1964, consisted of building a 4-kilometer runway and taxiways that would allow for the use of F-5s and C-130 transport planes. It included fifteen buildings, 3,000 square meters of warehouse space, "rocket-storage facilities ... two airmen's dormitories, headquarters, and operations buildings; sewage, water, and power systems; and a road network".[71] The entire project was completed by April 1966, or in less than two years.

The Gulf District's Legacy

In July 1956, the Gulf District (Army Corps of Engineers) had a staff of fifty-five, including six American military personnel and twenty-nine American civilians, and by the end of 1957, it employed 465 civil employees, 138 of whom were Americans. At the height of its activities in March 1961, the staff at Gulf District increased to 797.[72] From 1961, the staff dwindled, and by June 1967, it had 27. Finally, after being dormant for months and having "placed approximately $170 million of construction in Iran", the Gulf District officially ended its presence in the country on 30 September 1968.[73]

69 Grathwol and Moorhus, *Bricks, Sand, and Marble*, pp. 188–189.
70 *Ettela'at*, 27 Khordad 1344.
71 Grathwol and Moorhus, *Bricks, Sand, and Marble*, pp. 195–196.
72 Grathwol and Moorhus, *Bricks, Sand, and Marble*, pp. 108–110.
73 Grathwol and Moorhus, *Bricks, Sand, and Marble*, p. 222.

The US Corps of Engineers, the American construction contractors, the Iranian engineers and student-interns they hired, along with tens of thousands of Iranian workers and masons who built the units and facilities, had cooperated in a massive construction enterprise between 1956 and 1967. Iranians and Americans had rubbed shoulders at offices and construction sites in at least ninety localities scattered throughout Iran, most of which were in the country's remotest areas.

It would be difficult to tell precisely what the Iranians learned from the Americans besides their technical know-how, work ethics, and construction skills. However, just as the American Point Four personnel became known for their professional but unassuming sleeves-up and hands-on approach, the US Corps of Engineers members must have left a similar impression. The Gulf District personnel were not messengers of modernization in the tradition of Point Four, who worked in an area over a considerable period. Members of the Corps and their American contractors were parachuted into a region, did the work, taught by example, and got out. How much the Iranians retained from this interaction, other than the buildings left behind, is difficult to guess, but they must have left some traces.

The work of the Army Corps of Engineers in Iran was exceptional for several reasons. First, the construction materials for these buildings, such as brick, tar, cement, plaster, and lime, were provided domestically. In contrast, components such as pipes, beams, wiring, and windows were imported from Europe. Gulf District contractors hired domestic and foreign transportation companies to get the necessary material to some of the remotest parts of Iran.[74]

Second, a striking feature of the US Army Corps of Engineers' performance was the speed, punctuality, and discipline with which they completed their projects. The construction of some 650 buildings in border areas of Kordestan and Azarbayjan provinces, where infrastructure was most wanting, took less than three years (July 1957 to April 1960).

Third, each completed project had significant externalities as it transformed the Iranian countryside and brought physical aspects of economic development and modernization to underdeveloped regions of the country. The US Corps of Engineers were obliged to carry out some infrastructural activities to complete their projects. In the late 1950s and throughout the 1960s and even 1970s, there were very few rural areas where brick

74 *Ettela'at*, 13 Khordad 1336.

housing, potable water, electricity, schools, and sewage systems could be found, as was the case with the Army Corps of Engineer's constructions. These construction projects provided its users with greater comfort. The Iranian military regarded the new cantonments as "modern military cities equipped with the latest living facilities".[75]

Finally, the construction of projects in underdeveloped regions of the country generated a one-time income for the local population. The construction of Hamedan Airfield was completed in February 1962. At its peak, the Gulf District in Hamedan had forty-one employees, half of whom were Iranian technicians, and its joint venture American contractors Morrison-Kaiser-Oman (M-K-O) "employed eight hundred fifty laborers daily and paid out approximately $95,000 a month in wages".[76]

75 *Ettela'at*, 15 Bahman 1336.
76 Grathwol and Moorhus, *Bricks, Sand, and Marble*, pp. 187–188.

3

Abolhasan Ebtehaj, Banker, Planner, and Developmentalist

Abolhasan Ebtehaj was fifty-four when, on 2 September 1954, he was appointed Director General of Iran's Plan Organization by the thirty-four-year-old Shah. Ebtehaj, who had spent his primary and middle school years in French, British, and American schools in Paris, Beirut, and Rasht (Iran), was fluent in French, English, and Russian. From his childhood, he was interested in numbers and financial accounts. Ebtehaj's high school education was not at a regular school. He had private tutors and was homeschooled. There is no record or mention of his high school diploma.

When the young man joined the British-owned *Bank-e Shahi* (Imperial Bank) in 1920, he was appalled to learn that the toilets were "for Europeans only". He strongly objected to this, although he was told that the rule did not apply to him.[1] Ebtehaj served at the Imperial Bank for sixteen years and was promoted to deputy general inspector, the highest rank attainable by an Iranian.

In July 1936, Ebtehaj resigned from the Imperial Bank and joined Ali-Akbar Davar at the Ministry of Finance. After Davar's suicide, Ebtehaj joined *Bank-e Melli*, Iran's National Bank, in January 1938 and left it in 1940 to direct *Bank-e Rahni Iran*, Iran's Mortgage Bank. In December 1942, he was appointed Governor of Iran's National Bank and served for nine years.

1 A. Ebtehaj, ed. A-R. Aruzi, *Khaterate Abolhasan Ebtehaj*, vol. 1, Los Angeles: Ketab Corporation, 2010, p. 27.

It is said of Ebtehaj that, "He would look at a whole bunch of figures and put his finger right on the wrong one, and call attention to it."[2] By 1950, Ebtehaj had proven himself to be a blunt, forthright, highly disciplined, exacting, efficient, honest, nationalistic, and conscientious banker and technocrat. He was also vain and self-righteous, with a foul mouth to go with his bad temper. Ebtehaj's forthrightness made him brash.

While visiting Tehran University in December 1957, Ebtehaj, as the director general of Iran's Plan Organization, proposed closing the prestigious departments of law and literature and instead expanding the engineering school. His pragmatic argument was that the country needed more technicians and engineers to turn the wheels of economic growth and development. Ebtehaj neither understood nor cared about the consequences of his statements.[3]

Ebtehaj was special because he did not reserve his straightforward and curt mannerisms for his employees and those lower than him in rank. Domestic and foreign dignitaries and men of power received his candid outbursts and incisive fury in equal portions. Ebtehaj did not like what he could not control and loathed his employees getting involved in politics or labor unions, especially the left kind. He argued that people needed to trust a bank, and a left labor union within a bank would erode their confidence.[4]

In the summer of 1946, when the National Bank of Iran (*Bank-e Melli-ye Iran*) employees founded a labor union to express their grievances, Ebtehaj broke it up forcefully. The masterminds of the labor union were the twelve outstanding students who had been selected based on an examination before the war. They were sent by the National Bank to British universities on scholarships and returned to Iran to work as economists, auditors, and chartered accountants. Ebtehaj suspected the labor union to be in collusion with the Tudeh Party of Iran.[5] Ebtehaj liked independent-minded young experts but not those whom he felt would challenge and endanger organizational discipline and the smooth running of operations. He was a model manager and technocrat but also an autocrat.

2 Khodadad Farmanfarmayan, Iranian Oral History Collection, Harvard University, Transcript 4, Sequence 41.

3 *Ettela'at*, 30 Azar, 3 Day 1336.

4 Ebtehaj, *Khaterate Abolhasan Ebtehaj*, vol. 1, p. 106.

5 Abolghassem Kheradjou, Iranian Oral History Collection, Harvard University, Transcript 2, Sequence 20.

Ebtehaj punished three of the leaders of the labor union. He fired Eprime Eshaq, the outstanding Iranian socialist economist, who later took a permanent teaching post at Oxford University. At the time, Eprime Eshaq was a member of the communist Tudeh Party of Iran, from which he resigned a year later. Ebtehaj banished Mohammad-Mehdi Sami'i, the future Governor of the National Bank of Iran and Director General of the Plan Organization, to Zahedan. Abolqasem Kheradjou was initially exiled to Abadan but managed to stay in Tehran and continued at the Bank. He later became the Governor of *Bank-e Tose'eh San'ati va Ma'dani-ye Iran*, or the Industrial and Mining Development Bank of Iran (IMDBI).

Ebtehaj met the Shah for the first time after he became Governor of Iran's National Bank in late 1942. Quickly, the two developed a strong bond of mutual appreciation, complicity, and camaraderie. Soon Ebtehaj became "one of the closest people to the Shah". In 1944, the Shah was said to have proposed the position of prime minister to Ebtehaj, and the latter had refused. According to Ebtehaj, their close friendship lasted between 1942 and 1950 while Ebtehaj was the Governor of Iran's National Bank.[6]

MULLING OVER PLANNING

In September 1945, Ebtehaj proposed drafting an economic plan to generate employment and wealth and improve the standard of living of Iranians after the end of the war. He encouraged Mahmud Bader, the Minister of Finance, and Prime Minister Mohsen Sadr to adopt a national economic plan to efficiently use Iran's gold, silver, and foreign exchange reserves. He urged the government to prevent the flight of Iran's reserves and prompted it to gather information and begin formulating a national economic plan.[7]

It was not until 6 April 1946 that the first meeting to prepare a long-term developmental "economic map" was convened at the office of Abdolhoseyn Hajir, the Minister of Finance. From 9 October 1946, Ebtehaj began arguing that a few infrastructural investment projects in Tehran were not enough to solve the plight of Iranians. He did not object to investing in

6 Ebtehaj, *Khaterate Abolhasan Ebtehaj*, vol. 1, pp. 86, 88, 238.
7 Ebtehaj, *Khaterate Abolhasan Ebtehaj*, vol. 1, pp. 307–308.

such projects but argued that they were insufficient to jolt Iran out of its underdevelopment.[8]

Ebtehaj called on the government to draw up a series of national socio-economic projects with the appropriate price tag for each in the context of a five-to-seven-year plan, which he called a map. These would include building and developing infrastructural facilities, dams, agricultural projects, factories, mines, as well as investments in education and public health. Ebtehaj believed that the government investments necessary to initiate economic development needed more capital than could be mustered at home and so foresaw borrowing overseas. He insisted that the foreign creditor "should have no political agendas or ill-intentions towards the country".[9]

Ebtehaj may or may not have read P.N. Rosenstein-Rodan's groundbreaking paper in the June-September 1943 issue of *The Economic Journal.* However, the essence of his arguments for a "Big Push" closely resembled Rosenstein-Rodan's. In "The Problems of Industrialisation of Eastern and South-Eastern Europe", Rosenstein-Rodan emphasized the initiating role of government and the subsequent partnership with the private sector. He underlined the importance of foreign capital in the development process and foresaw the necessity of less developed countries borrowing from advanced countries. For Rosenstein-Rodan, the development effort was wider than just basic industries such as public utilities, railways, roads, canals, and hydroelectric power stations. He argued that, "We have seen how complementarity makes to some extent all industries 'basic.'"[10] Rosenstein-Rodan's notion of across-the-board, large-scale investment projects in less developed countries became popularized as the "Big Push" theory and influenced many developmental economists and practitioners in the late fifties and early 1960.

KICKSTARTING THE BIG PUSH

In 1945, Ebtehaj became interested in an agricultural development scheme for the Khuzestan region and mulled over the idea of building dams over

8 Ebtehaj, *Khaterate Abolhasan Ebtehaj*, vol. 1, pp. 315–316.
9 Ebtehaj, *Khaterate Abolhasan Ebtehaj*, vol. 1, pp. 316–318.
10 P.N. Rosenstein-Rodan, "Problems of Industrialisation of Eastern and South-Eastern Europe." *The Economic Journal*, vol. 53, no. 210/211 (1943) pp. 202–11.

the Karun for irrigation and to generate electricity. He followed up his ideas by initiating negotiations with British banks to raise capital. The initiative came to a dead-end when William Fraser, the Chair of the Anglo-Iranian Company, convinced the Foreign Office against the project.[11]

On 30 October 1946, Ebtehaj followed his idea of the "Big Push" for Iran by applying for a $250 million loan from the International Bank for Reconstruction and Development. His application was turned down. Ebtehaj was aware that the country did not have accurate data, statistics, and figures on which he could base his studies, determine appropriate projects, and provide cost projections. To identify critical projects and ensure the financial soundness of the national plan, Ebtehaj heeded the advice of Max Weston Thornburg and sought the assessment of an internationally renowned civil engineering and construction firm. Thornburg, an American, was vice-president of the California Texas Oil Company and a government adviser on oil matters.

On 28 December 1946, a ten-men mission of American engineers from the American firm Morrison-Knudsen came to Iran to study the country and assess the rationality and effectiveness of the projects included in the plan. Morrison-Knudsen had long been involved in numerous substantial infrastructural projects in the US, such as the Hoover Dam. The Morrison-Knudsen experts spent three months in Iran crisscrossing the county and submitted their 320-page report in July 1947. Their preliminary survey came at a cost of "a quarter of a million dollars".[12] The report provided for "a choice among three plans of differing sizes (the largest cost $1.4 billion and contained 234 projects, the smallest cost $260,000 and contained 24 projects)".[13]

In August 1948, the Iranian parliament voted on a 25 million rial credit for the completion of developmental projects, and the government created an agency called "The Supreme Office of Planning". The brief of this agency, which later became the "Provisional Plan Organization" was to draw up a detailed seven-year plan.[14] For Ebtehaj, the seven-year plan was intended to provide a clear and comprehensive roadmap for the development of

11 Ebtehaj, *Khaterate Abolhasan Ebtehaj*, vol. 1, pp. 373–375.
12 T. Cuyler Young, "The Race between Russia and Reform in Iran." *Foreign Affairs*, vol. 28, no. 2, Jan. 1950, pp. 278–289.
13 G.B. Baldwin, *Planning and Development in Iran*, Baltimore: The Johns Hopkins Press, 1967, p. 28.
14 Ebtehaj, *Khaterate Abolhasan Ebtehaj*, vol. 1, pp. 321–326.

the whole economy, rather than ad hoc and disjointed public investment schemes. Accurate planning, he believed, was the only way Iran could close its "100-year gap with the caravan of civilization".[15]

On 20 January 1949, Mohammad Sa'ed, the prime minister, appointed Ebtehaj to head the newly formed *Sazeman-e movaqat-e barnameh*, or the "Provisional Plan Organization", mandated to draw up a seven-year developmental plan and prepare its implementation. Ebtehaj refused the position, arguing that according to the statutes of Iran's National Bank, the Governor was prohibited from accepting another job besides the one he held.[16]

The attempt at formulating and preparing a long-term developmental plan for Iran stalled. Before the Shah's first visit to the US on 16 November 1949, he seemed aloof and unsupportive of a comprehensive plan for developing the country. Truman had announced his Point Four Program ten months before and was optimistic about its impact on less developed countries. This apparently played a role in convincing the Shah of the necessity of economic development. During his four-day trip to the US, the Shah and President Truman issued a joint statement emphasizing the importance of comprehensive economic and social developmental activities.[17]

FIRST FALL FROM GRACE

For over a decade, Ebtehaj held the purse strings and stood up to the irregular and self-interested demands of princes, members of parliament, ministers, governors, and men of authority and power. In a traditional country where favoritism, preferential treatment, and quid pro quo were the norm, trickling from the top to the bottom of society, the no-nonsense Ebtehaj ruffled many feathers by refusing to play the game. However, his professionalism and expertise usually came to his aid.

On 18 July 1950, General Haj Ali Razmara became prime minister, and three weeks later, he replaced Ebtehaj with Ebrahim Zand as Governor of Iran's National Bank. This sudden reshuffling, which may or may not have been with the Shah's consent, deeply scarred Ebtehaj. He believed that the Shah was his friend and would give him some prior notice. The Shah's

15 *Ettela'at*, 21 Day 1336.
16 Ebtehaj, *Khaterate Abolhasan Ebtehaj*, vol. 1, p. 328.
17 Ebtehaj, *Khaterate Abolhasan Ebtehaj*, vol. 1, p. 330.

response to Ebtehaj's removal was ambivalent. On 7 September 1950, Ebtehaj, the banker/economist, was re-cycled as a diplomat and dispatched to France as Iran's Ambassador.

On 7 April 1952, seventeen months into his ambassadorship, Ebtehaj was replaced by Mohammad-Hoseyn Najm. Ebtehaj did not look back to Iran, which was dealing with the consequences of oil nationalization. Instead, he looked for a job in the US. His choice at the time made sense. Even though both Ebtehaj and Mosaddeq were honest, ethical, and upright nationalists, one was a dry technocrat, and the other was an emotional, charismatic, and idealist politician in search of national honor and pride. For Ebtehaj's liking, Mosaddeq's period was marred by too much excitement, indetermination, and indiscipline.

Ebtehaj accepted a position as advisor to Ivar Rooth, the Swedish managing director of the International Monetary Fund in Washington, and subsequently became director of the Fund's Middle East Department. In August 1953, after the coup against Mosaddeq, the Shah returned to power, and an agreement was reached with Britain and the International Oil Consortium. The Iranian parliament ratified the new Amini–Page oil agreement on 21 October 1954. The flow of oil resumed and "oil revenues were running at about $200 million a year".[18]

EBTEHAJ AT THE HELM OF THE PLAN ORGANIZATION

Ebtehaj returned to Iran from his IMF post in the US in August 1954. He was a self-educated economist and banker. For someone with no formal education in these fields, Ebtehaj read a lot about economics, money, banking, and finance. Throughout the 1950s and the 1960s, John Maynard Keynes' economic thoughts prevailed in universities and international organizations. If not before, then Ebtehaj must have become familiar with Keynesianism during his two years at the IMF. It would be safe to say that Ebtehaj was a Keynesian economist who firmly believed in government intervention, especially in the case of less developed countries. Given Iran's underdeveloped and weak private sector, Ebtehaj viewed the government as the principal agent of development and enabler of the private sector.

18 Hector Prud'homme, World Bank Oral Histories, https://oralhistory.worldbank.org/sites/oralhistory.worldbank.org/files/transcript/790970TRN0Prud0Box0377367B00PUBLIC0.pdf (retrieved 13/1/2023).

Ebtehaj's experience at the IMF convinced him that Iran should use its oil revenues only to generate economic growth and increase productivity and income per capita. He feared the squandering of oil revenues or their use for current expenditures. Iran, he believed, needed infrastructural and developmental projects that would provide Iranians with water to drink and cultivate, electricity, and roads.

When the Shah offered him the choice between directing the Iranian Oil Company or the Plan Organization, he chose the latter. One of Ebtehaj's most critical conditions for accepting the position was that he would have complete autonomy in exercising his responsibilities, with no one interfering in the affairs of the Plan Organization. He made this point very clear to the Shah and Prime Minister General Fazlollah Zahedi.

The Plan Organization came into existence because the existing government bureaucracies and ministries were fixed in their traditional ways and incapable of initiating and executing economic development in Iran. It was intended as a super agency, apart from and above the government, in terms of developmental decisions, project conception and execution (not implementation), and most importantly, financial power and autonomy of fund disbursement. The Plan Organization, the turbo-engine of Iran's economic development, enjoyed a privileged legal, administrative, financial, and political position.

On 2 September 1954, Ebtehaj officially took office as the Director General of the newly founded Plan Organization and built it from scratch. In less than a year, Ebtehaj had become a controversial figure, with criticism directed at him and his management style from prominent political figures. On 16 July 1955, the reputable pro-business Iranian economic weekly *Tehran Economist* came to his aid. It referred to the bickering around him in the press and set the tone for his supporters. In the article, "The defeat of Ebtehaj is the defeat of competence and honesty", probably penned by Baqer Shariat, the editor-in-chief and owner of the weekly, Ebtehaj was described as a competent European manager who valued hard work and expertise and was not interested in *partibazi* (exploiting connections) or paying and receiving bribes.[19]

19 *Tehran Economist*, 24 Tir 1334. Baqer Shariat was a member of the "Economic Center" (*Kanune Eqtesad*), whose members were French- and Swiss-educated economists. Other prominent members of the circle included Ali-Asghar Purhomayun, Gholamhosyen Jahanshahi, Ali-Naqi Farman Farmaian and Ziaeddin Shademan.

In 1957 and 1958, Iran was deprived of national income data, so assessing economic activity and growth was a matter of guesswork, and policymaking was conjectural. Based on rough estimates, Iran had a population of 19 million, 75% of whom relied on agriculture, 10% on commerce, 10% on industry and handicrafts, and the remaining 5% were engaged in government employment and the professions.

Some 70,000 of the approximately 180,000 workers in industry were in the oil industry. The government controlled "over half of the country's factory capacity", from cement, brick, and chemical factories to sugar, tea, and food processing plants. Cotton textiles, followed by sugar and cement, constituted the country's most important industrial products, outside the oil industry.

Iran's annual per capita income was between $75 and $110. Only 40% of the farmers owned land, and 1% of the landowners owned 56% of the land, while a mere 10% of the potential arable land was cultivated. Ten private firms produced roughly 3 million pairs of shoes annually for a population of 19 million. The combined budgeted expenditure of the Ministry of War, Police, and Gendarmerie for 1957–1958 was 8,352 million rials (835.2 million tomans) as compared to the 7,292 million rials of budgeted expenditure for the Ministries of Post, Telegraph and Telephone, Health, Education, Finance, and Agriculture plus road maintenance, all together.[20]

For Ebtehaj, the Plan Organization was the powerhouse that would put development in motion by using oil revenues estimated to be $1.4 billion between 1956 and 1962. Article 8 of the Second Seven-Year Plan Law, ratified by the Majles on 28 February 1956, stipulated that oil revenues, once current expenditures of the National Iranian Oil Company had been deducted, would be allocated between the National Iranian Oil Company, the Ministry of Finance, and the Plan Organization. Up to March 1958, the National Iranian Oil Company was to receive 28% of the oil revenue, the Ministry of Finance 10%, and the Plan Organization some 62%. After

20 International Bank for Reconstruction and Development, *Economic Development of Iran*, January 3, 1957, https://documents1.worldbank.org/curated/en/622341468254365503/pdf/multiopage.pdf (retrieved 21/1/2023) and International Bank for Reconstruction and Development, *Economic Situation and Prospects of Iran*, July 23, 1958, https://documents1.worldbank.org/curated/en/503761468050961050/pdf/multiopage.pdf (retrieved 22/1/2023). All statistical information in the above two paragraphs is based on the International Bank for Reconstruction and Development reports. Information in the previous three paragraphs is based on these sources.

this date and up to 1962, the Plan Organization was to receive up to 80% of the net oil revenues.[21]

Ebtehaj intended to take full advantage of the Plan Organization's lion's share of the oil income, sidetracking what he believed to be inefficient, corrupt, and incompetent ministries involved with development projects. Iran's ministries and government organizations lacked well-trained civil servants educated in public administration. Ministers and high government functionaries were chiefly political appointees, selected through favoritism or nepotism, with a myopic focus on their institutional turf.

The Plan Organization under Ebtehaj became a kind of "National School of Administration", where employees, selected based on merit and educational achievement, received hands-on training and learned by doing. It could have become a blueprint for other ministries and government organizations. Instead of extending a helpful hand to the inept ministries and connecting with them, thereby allowing the Plan Organization's ethos to permeate, Ebtehaj treated them with technical and ethical contempt. His self-righteousness and exclusiveness prevented constructive interaction and cooperation with ministries, alienated them, and created jealousies among bureaucracies outside the Plan Organization. This same haughty attitude also estranged members of parliament who were tasked with approving the bills and activities of the Plan Organization.

Subsequently, Ebtehaj's success with institutional modernization at the Plan Organization, which was based on efficiency, discipline, and ethicality, remained confined to that organization. Under Ebtehaj, the Plan Organization missed an important opportunity, and inevitably, did a disservice to national development.

Ebtehaj envisaged the Plan Organization as a government parallel to the government. When, in June 1956, the Iranian Senate requested Prime Minister 'Ala to name Ebtehaj as his deputy so that he would appear before the senators and be accountable to them for the activities of the Plan Organization, Ebtehaj refused. 'Ala was obliged to name Khosrow Hedayat, the Plan Organization and Ebtehaj's vice-director, as his deputy.[22] Ebtehaj considered himself on par with the Prime Minister and had

---

21 International Bank for Reconstruction and Development, *Economic Development of Iran*, January 3, 1957, https://documents1.worldbank.org/curated/en/622341468254365503/pdf/multiopage.pdf (retrieved 21/1/2023). *Ettela'at*, 13 Aban 1336.

22 *Ettela'at*, 31 Khordad 1335.

his deputy represent the Plan Organization at the Majles and the Senate. He did not report to the Prime Minister, the Majles or the Senate, except under exceptional circumstances.

The man was not a politician and did not realize that by estranging and antagonizing politicians, notables, and bureaucrats, he was chasing away potential allies, effectively removing his own safety net and making himself reliant on the Shah's favor alone. His maverick and cavalier behavior would be tolerated as long as the Shah supported him.

Ebtehaj formulated and discussed his plans with Plan Organization specialists, foreign bankers, and businessmen and then reported to the Shah. He would go on business trips and conferences, undertake negotiations, and tell the Shah what he had done on his return. Once His Majesty gave his green light, Ebtehaj would meet with members of the Majles or the Senate in closed and private sessions to inform them of decisions already made.[23] Whereas the Prime Minster and his ministers were formally responsible before the Majles and the Senate, Ebtehaj acted as though he was not. No wonder members of parliament did not appreciate him.

PLAN ORGANIZATION: WALKING ON TWO LEGS

Ebtehaj set out to restructure and revitalize the Plan Organization, rendering it efficient and dynamic. New, young, and Western-trained professionals, the best in their respective fields, were attracted by higher-than-average salaries and a Western-style work environment. Ebtehaj sought apolitical, honest, and patriotic experts committed to Iran's economic prosperity and unburdened by Iran's political system. Outstanding young experts, like Hoseyn Mahdavi, a Mossadeqist with progressive political views, entered the Plan Organization but exited it quickly.

The Plan Organization had the heavy responsibility of allocating funds for development projects. To break the cycle of favoritism and politically induced patronage, which wasted money and did not produce results, Ebtehaj began by establishing strict rules on doling out contracts. Professional contract appraisal by qualified Iranian and foreign experts, followed by public and, therefore, competitive tenders, minimized corruption and waste. He used the Plan Organization's technical and economic

23 *Ettela'at*, 26 Aban 1336.

competence and philosophy of fairness and frankness to countervail the arbitrariness and cronyism of the political system. He believed professionalism and efficiency could harness or overcome unscrupulous business habits and practices.

Ebtehaj envisioned the Plan Organization as a conceptual, executive, and supervisory body, all in one, in which development plans were drafted and technical projects were identified, executed, and supervised. Using the World Bank as his model, Ebtehaj created an organization with technical and economic expertise. The hybrid organization that Ebtehaj had in mind needed high-caliber and world-class know-how, which was severely lacking in Iran.

FIRST LEG: THE TECHNICAL BUREAU

In 1955, Ebtehaj began by creating the Technical Bureau. This was the technical and engineering wing of the Plan Organization responsible for drawing up and supervising the implementation of projects, such as hydroelectric and irrigation dams, railroads, ports, airports, roads, municipal utilities, and major industrial plants. To study the technical feasibility of projects, engineers, technicians, and master craftsmen needed to be recruited in a country which "did not have a single engineer specialized in building dams".[24] Through his contacts with Eugene Black, the President of the World Bank (1949–1962), Ebtehaj recruited internationally renowned engineers and technicians of different nationalities.

He arranged for Black to come to Tehran on 13 June 1956. During his three-day visit, Black met with Iranian dignitaries, businessmen, Prime Minister ʿAla, and the Shah. Before leaving Tehran, Black praised the efforts of Ebtehaj and the Plan Organization, adding that the World Bank was very interested in the activities of the Plan Organization.[25] From Black's comments on his visit to Tehran, it was evident that even though he had met the Shah and ʿAla in the past, his relation with Ebtehaj was of a more intimate, solid and professional kind.

Based on a 1955 agreement, "the [World] Bank [had] agreed to engage for the Plan Organization a group of eighty highly ranked engineers of as

---

24 Ebtehaj, *Khaterate Abolhasan Ebtehaj*, vol. 1, p. 335.
25 *Ettelaʿat*, 11, 23, 24, 26, 27 Khordad 1335.

many different nationalities as possible to form the Technical Bureau."[26] The recruitment task was given to Ebtehaj's most important catch, the Harvard-educated economist and engineer, Hector Prud'homme. Prud'homme had been a senior member of the World Bank mission to mediate between Mosaddeq's government and the UK in 1951. Black gave Prud'homme a leave of absence from the World Bank, and he arrived in Tehran on 30 August 1955.[27] He ended up staying in Iran for three years. Having hired a competent international group of engineers, Prud'homme was put in charge of the Technical Bureau in October 1955.

The prominent figures in the Technical Bureau were: Brian Colquhoun, the Scottish engineering advisor to the World Bank; Walter Binger, the MIT-educated American civil engineer; Albert de Smaele, the Cornell-educated Belgian civil engineer and ex-minister of economics; and the French Georges Leon Girard, a graduate of France's most prestigious engineering institute, the École polytechnique. Girard headed the communication and transportation section of the Technical Bureau and was involved in the construction of roads, railways, airports, and ports. His report on substantial embezzlements and major technical flaws in the Tehran–Mashhad railroad was to make significant waves in April 1957.[28]

Other figures in the Technical Bureau included the British W.T. Jackson, in charge of municipal and social projects; the British Mr. Josey, a civil engineer; the American Benjamin Brown, a health and education specialist; and the Swedish Oscar Karlstadt. The Technical Bureau made recommendations to Ebtehaj, who had the final say on projects and oversaw their implementation.

The Iranian star of the Technical Bureau was Mohammad-Ali Safi Asfia, a civil engineer specializing in mining. He was among the fourth batch of students sent to Europe by Reza Shah in 1932. He graduated from France's top engineering schools, École polytechnique and École des Mines de Paris, in 1936. In 1939, at age twenty-three, he became the youngest faculty member of Tehran University's prestigious Engineering Faculty, teaching mathematics and geology.

The Iranian alumni of French universities who were sent by Reza Shah to obtain a technical education formed a professionally close and politically

26 F. Bostock and G. Jones, *Planning and Power in Iran*, London: Frank Cass, 1989, p. 121.
27 *Tehran Economist*, 11 Shahrivar 1334.
28 *Tehran Economist*, 7 Ordibehesht 1336.

diverse circle. Their bond was one of shared competence and expertise. This circle included opposition figures such as Mehdi Bazargan (École Centrale), Yadollah Sahabi (Lille), Kazem Hasibi (École polytechnique), Ahmad Zirakzadeh (École polytechnique), and Taqi Riyahi (École polytechnique) as well as non-political figures such as Asfia and Abdolmajid A'lam (École polytechnique), a close friend of the Shah.

Asfia entered the Ministry of Mines around 1940 and began planning a piped-water network for Tehran. Soon, he became an expert on Tehran's groundwater sources. In late 1941, he collaborated with Qodratollah Tashakori, his classmate at École polytechnique, and worked as an engineering contractor. Around 1948, he worked on construction projects with Ahmad-Ali Ebtehaj (Abolhasan's brother), the future owner of Tehran Cement Company.

In 1950, Abdolmajid A'lam's engineering, contracting, and construction firm TESAD obtained the momentous project of finally constructing a water network for Tehran. For its implementation, A'lam hired Asfia as the project manager. In 1955, Abolhasan Ebtehaj approached A'lam and insisted on "borrowing" Asfia for the Technical Bureau.[29] Ebtehaj never gave him back, and Asfia ended up serving thirteen years at the Plan Organization, following in the footsteps of Ebtehaj as director general.

Asfia had most of Ebtehaj's virtues but one and none of his vices. He was a scrupulous technocrat but would not stand up to the Shah's unsound and irrational economic instructions. Asfia would not make a fuss, neither banging his fist on the table nor kicking out of his office those who had the Shah's support and illicit demands. Whereas Ebtehaj would speak his mind and push back against the Shah's excesses, Asfia would reluctantly acquiesce.

Like Ebtehaj, Asfia was meritocratic and not a sycophant. Both men were nationalists, deeply committed to Iran's economic development and highly esteemed by their employees for their professionalism and diligence. However, Asfia's temperament was such that he would compromise according to the Shah's whims rather than oppose them head-on, as Ebtehaj did.

Asfia was an outstanding and accomplished engineer with a vivid interest in and vast knowledge of all things technical. He was a humble, efficient, and most respected manager, impeccably honest, wise, and calm. He was

29 Abdol-Majid Aalam, Interview, Foundation of Iranian Studies, p. 7, https://fis-iran.org/wp-content/uploads/2021/12/Abdol-Maid-Alam-pdf.pdf (retrieved 13/1/2023).

renowned and appreciated for his fairness, tolerance, and liberal approach at work. He spoke little, but when he did, everyone listened closely.

PREPARING THE SECOND LEG: THE HARVARD ADVISORY GROUP

When Ebtehaj took over the Plan Organization, he realized the need for professional economists and approached the Ford Foundation for assistance.[30] Two years later, in 1956, the Ford Foundation sent him two economists, François Cracco and Morgan Sibbett. Ebtehaj had established good relations with Kenneth Iverson, the Near East representative of the Ford Foundation.[31] In 1958, Ebtehaj "persuaded the Ford Foundation to finance the second major bureau – the Economic Bureau".[32]

Iverson was in accord with Ebtehaj and believed Iran lacked technical expertise and needed "a sound economic development program" articulated by Western-trained Iranian economists and supported by American advisors. He, therefore, was also in favor of a more sophisticated and elaborate economic advisory group.[33] To this end, the Ford Foundation turned to Edward Mason, who was a progressive economist, a pioneer of modernization theory, George Marshall's economic advisor, and the Dean of Harvard University's Graduate School of Public Administration. The team of economic experts and advisors, who came to be known as the Harvard Advisory Group was thus vetted and assembled by Edward Mason.

On 18 April 1958, dispatching the Harvard Advisory Group to the Economic Bureau became a reality thanks to the Ford Foundation's award of an $800,000 grant to Iran over four years to study the country's socio-economic conditions. The salary of the Harvard Advisory Group, which came to $740,000, was paid from this grant.[34] A small portion ($60,000) of the Ford Foundation money went to supplement the salaries of the

30 G. Brew, "Economic Expertise and Rural Improvement in Iran, 1948-1963," Rockefeller Archive Center Research Reports, 2017, http://rockarch.issuelab.org/resources/29283/29283.pdf (retrieved 7/8/2023).

31 Brew, "Economic Expertise and Rural Improvement in Iran, 1948–1963."

32 Bostock and Jones, *Planning and Power in Iran*, p. 122.

33 Brew, "Economic Expertise and Rural Improvement in Iran, 1948–1963."

34 *Tehran Economist*, 8 Khordad 1338. According to Brew, the grant was $1.2 million; Brew, "Economic Expertise and Rural Improvement in Iran, 1948–1963."

fourteen Western-educated Iranians, nine of whom were US-educated, who were employed at the Division of Economic Affairs by 1959.[35]

Kenneth Hansen, who was to head the Harvard Advisory Group, arrived in Tehran with his team in January 1958.[36] George Baldwin, the American MIT-educated industrial economist, who stayed in Iran from 1958 to 1961 and went on to write an excellent book on planning and development in Iran, was among the first to join him. Some ten months later, on 30 October 1958, Edward Mason arrived in Tehran for a three-week stay to get a handle on the country, as well as observe the constraints and progress of his Group. Mason was struck by the lack of coordination between various economic decision-making bodies.[37]

Despite considerable turnover among members of the Harvard Advisory Group, the team remained in Iran until 1963. During its five-year stay numerous European and American economists joined the Group for varying durations. The composition and activities of Harvard Advisory Group at the Division of Economic Affairs can be divided into two distinct "generations".

The first generation of Harvard Advisory Group advisors assessed "the progress of the second development plan, its problems, and difficulties as well".[38] This was followed by the preliminary steps of producing the comprehensive Third Five-Year Plan in mid-1958. The arrival of the Harvard Advisory Group's "second generation" in 1960 and 1961 shortly overlapped with the stay of the "first generation".

The newcomers had neither been involved in critically assessing the Second Plan nor drafting the Third Five-Year Plan. They had inherited a work not of their thinking and doing, yet were made responsible for the incorporation of all previous reports into an appropriate plan, including

35 M.K. Shannon, "American–Iranian Alliances: International Education, Modernization, and Human Rights during the Pahlavi Era," *Diplomatic History*, vol. 39, no. 4, 2015, pp. 661–688. These included Dr. Gholamreza Moqhadam, Dr. Bahman Abadiyan, Dr. Hoseyn Mahdavi, Dr. Mostafa 'Elm, Dr. Farhad Qahraman, Dr. Taqi Mortazavi, Dr. Abbas Qezelbash, Dr. Shapur Rasekh, Dr. Purabbas, Mehdi Amin-Salehi, Rasul Bakhtiyar, Daryush Oskoui, Jamshid Ashrafi, and Ismail Ajami.

36 Khodadad Farmanfarmayan, Iranian Oral History Collection, Harvard University, Transcript 1, Sequence 12 and Transcript 2, Sequence 17.

37 *Tehran Economist*, 1 Azar 1337.

38 Khodadad Farmanfarmayan, Iranian Oral History Collection, Harvard University, Transcript 2, Sequence 21.

appropriate government policies, identification of specific projects, and presentation of their cost estimates.[39]

Furthermore, the Harvard Advisory Group's "second generation" arrived at the Plan Organization during a period of instability and internal disorder. Ebtehaj had gone, and the Plan Organization was in disarray. In early 1961, three different figures, each very different from the other, filled the director's post.

The "second generation" advisors included Bjorn Olsen and Paul Rasmussen, two Danish economists who worked in Iran between 1960 and 1962. Rasmussen delivered a lecture series at the newly inaugurated (1958) Institute of Social Science Studies and Research of Tehran University. Price Gittinger, the agricultural economist, was in Iran from January 1960 to June 1961. The Canadian and Harvard-trained economist Thomas McLeod was in Iran between 1961 and 1963 as the leader of the Harvard Advisory Group. He went on to write a damning report on Iran's National Planning.

SECOND LEG: THE ECONOMIC BUREAU

In 1957, or some two years after the Technical Bureau was set up, Ebtehaj formed the Economic Bureau. In contrast to the Technical Bureau, which, aside from Asfia, was initially staffed with foreign experts, the Economic Bureau was staffed with Western and US-educated Iranians. Shortly after its creation, the Harvard Advisory Group, composed of entirely Western experts, began to cooperate closely with it. The Economic Bureau was to be the country's thinktank for studying and planning economic development and working on development schemes in industry, agriculture, mining, irrigation, and energy. The difficulties due to inexistent or imprecise data and statistics persisted, rendering any meaningful economic measurement, such as elasticity, productivity, capital-output ratios, and cost-benefit tenuous, if not inconceivable.

39 T.H. McLeod, "National Planning in Iran, A report based on the experiences of the Harvard Advisory Group in Iran," 1964, file:///C:/Users/alira/Downloads/national-planning-in-iran-a-report-based-on-the-experiences-of-the-harvard-advisory-group-in-iran compress.pdf (retrieved 4/6/2023), p. xi; J. Price Gittinger, "Planning for Agricultural Development: The Iranian Experience," Center for Development Planning, Planning Experience, Series no. 2, National Planning Association, 1965, https://pdf.usaid.gov/pdf_docs/PNRAA581.pdf (retrieved 13/1/2024), p. 57.

By the time the Economic Bureau was born, the Second Plan (Seven-Year), which had started in February 1955, was three years old. The Plan Organization had four years left to prepare the Third Plan (Five-Year), which was to start in September 1962 and end in March 1968 (five and a half years). The Third Plan was to lay the basis for Iran's economic "take-off". American advisory groups, such as the Governmental Affairs Institute (GAI), George Fry Associates, and Point Four, also became involved in drafting the Third Plan.[40]

The New York-based GAI, founded in 1950 and headed by Luther Gulick, was a private non-profit organization with strong ties to the US government. It advised foreign governments and advocated planning as a tool for development. From 1957 to 1959, GAI obtained an advising contract with the Plan Organization and municipalities in Iran. Gulick traveled regularly to Tehran and met with government officials, including Ebtehaj and the Shah, to discuss the country's ongoing and future development plans.[41] GAI was tasked to "improve the organizational structure and administrative procedures of the Plan Organization".[42]

In cooperation with their Iranian colleagues, a team of eight American administrative experts from GAI spent six months drawing up a new organizational structure and began implementing it in the fall of 1957. By November 1957, the Plan Organization was divided into six sections: economic and social projects, budget, human resources and manpower, organization, publications and communications, and finally, legal. These sections were subsequently reorganized into divisions.

By September 1958, the handful of economists at the Economic Bureau were overwhelmed by the amount of work that Ebtehaj was piling on them. He constantly sought their advice. Even though they worked from 08:00 to often 22:00, they were constantly behind his assignments, instructions, and requests, "for survey evaluation, project appraisals, and studies".[43]

Within the Economic Bureau, there were two competing developmental strategies. Hansen and most Harvard Advisory Group members

40 T.M. Ricks, "U.S. Military Missions to Iran, 1943–1978: The Political Economy of Military Assistance", *Iranian Studies*, vol. 12, no. 3/4 (1979), pp. 163–193.

41 "An Adventure in Democracy," The Institute of Public Administration Collection: A Processing Blog, https://blogs.baruch.cuny.edu/ipaprocessing/2015/01/mission-to-iran-a-c-i-a-connection/ (retrieved 9/6/2023).

42 McLeod, p. 212.

43 Khodadad Farmanfarmaian, Iranian Oral History Collection, Harvard University, Transcript 2, Sequence 19.

supported small projects that would yield concrete results in a short time, visibly improving the living conditions of the majority living in rural areas. Ebtehaj and the Shah gave priority to massive multipurpose and "grandiose" development projects such as the Khuzestan Development Services, which were to yield results in the long term.[44]

However, Ebtehaj sought the advice of his experts and listened to their recommendations. He wanted to know whether the steel mill project proposed by the German Krupp company was feasible or whether the Dez Dam project made sense "on a cost-benefit basis". On the advice of the Division of Economic Affairs, which had the view that a steel mill did not make economic sense for Iran, Ebtehaj scrapped this project, although it had been very dear to the Shah.[45] On the other hand, Ebtehaj, who had initially rejected the Dez Dam project, gave it a green light, once the World Bank allocated $42 million to it.

The Plan Organization quickly became the melting pot of Iranian and Western professionals and experts. In 1958, in addition to the foreign experts working at the Technical and Economic Bureaus, some thirty consultancy firms from Europe and the US were advising the Plan Organization on the establishment and running of "a variety of industrial and infrastructure projects".[46]

Khodadad Farmanfarmayan Heads the Second Leg

Ebtehaj recruited Khodadad Farmanfarmayan, who had already started teaching at Princeton, for the Economic Bureau. Farmanfarmayan had obtained his BA and MA in economics from Stanford, where he was taught by economic luminaries such as the neo-classical giant Kenneth Arrow, the Keynesian Moses Abramovitz, and Paul Baran, the only tenured Marxist economic professor at the time. Farmanfarmayan had completed his PhD in economics from the University of Colorado in 1956. Between 1955 and

44 G. Brew, "'What they Need is Management': American NGOs, the Second Seven Year Plan and Economic Development in Iran, 1954–1963," *International History Review*, vol. 41, no. 1 (December 2017), pp. 1–22.

45 Gholam-Reza Moghadam, Iranian Oral History Collection, Harvard University, Transcript 1, Sequence 7. Mohammad Yeganeh believes that it was the Americans who firmly opposed the idea of a steel mill for Iran. See Mohammad Yeganeh, Iranian Oral History Collection, Harvard University, Transcript 2, Sequence 30 and Transcript 6, Sequence 106.

46 Bostock and Jones, *Planning and Power in Iran*, p. 123.

1957, Farmanfarmayan obtained a university fellow position at Harvard's Center for Middle Eastern Studies, where he finished writing his PhD thesis on the interrelationship between the oil industry and the Iranian economy.

At Harvard, he had fallen under the influence of Wassily Leontief and his input–output table. Farmanfarmayan became interested in constructing an inter-sectoral matrix for the Iranian economy, which would have been useful for his thesis. However, this never happened due to the unavailability of relevant data. Having been enticed and recruited by Ebtehaj during his stay at Harvard, Farmanfarmayan returned to Iran in March 1958 and joined the Plan Organization as the Acting Head of the Economic Bureau.

Before Farmanfarmayan assumed his duties, his friend from Stanford days, Gholamreza Moqadam, was hired by Ebtehaj as his deputy. Moqadam had obtained his PhD in economics from Stanford in 1956 and wished to follow an academic career at Tehran University, but the French-educated faculty of political economy limited employment to their own kind.[47] By February 1959, the Economic Bureau, renamed the Division of Economic Affairs, had some forty members, at least half of whom were Iranian.[48]

The staffing at the Economic Bureau was openly in favor of the US-educated. Admiration for a mixture of the American educational system, training in the social sciences, especially economics, the content of economics taught at American universities, and the American work style, ethics, and environment made the US-educated employees at the Plan Organization wish to reproduce themselves. It is helpful to know that "at the time the Economic Bureau was established, there were only 47 economists in Iran".[49] This number probably included European as well as US-trained economists.

Khodadad Farmanfarmayan, who was "Joe" to his friends even in Iran, had an unabashed bias for Anglo-Saxon trained economists, whom he believed were "hard economists" properly trained in micro and macroeconomics, growth and international economic theory, along with econometrics and statistics. He had a soft spot for those economists who, he claimed, knew Paul Samuelson's "sacred" text, *Economics* by heart.

47 Gholamreza Moghadam, Iranian Oral History Collection, Harvard University, Transcript 1, Sequence 4.
48 *Tehran Economist*, 2 Esfand 1337.
49 McLeod, "National Planning in Iran," p. 49.

The US-trained economists believed their education had endowed them with a distinct way of economic thinking based on maximizing returns and ends, given limited and scarce resources. It was the propagation of this economic mindset that they believed would solve Iran's economic backwardness. Farmanfarmayan did not trust the theoretical grasp of German and French-trained economists and considered them political economists, economic historians, and institutional economists.[50]

For Farmanfarmayan, the Division of Economic Affairs was instrumental in spreading Samuelsonian economics in Iran. He credited his Division with educating Iranian government officials and politicians in rudimentary economic jargon and pulling them out of the age of economic ignorance. Somewhat presumptuously, he posited that at the time, "Nobody knew, for example, what GNP meant". He maintained that economic concepts such as "GNP, investment, savings, income distribution, intersectoral relationships, rate of growth, balance of payments adjustments, monetary policy, fiscal policy, etc. – all issued forth from the Economic Bureau to leave an indelible impression on the thinking of the administrators and political authorities."[51]

The newly hired Iranian staff at the Division of Economic Affairs were experts in their fields. However, they had spent a long time away from home, had become somewhat Americanized, and had to re-familiarize themselves with the country, its people, and the way of interacting with the traditional ministries. Their detractors, either Iranian or European-trained politicians and experts, looked upon this young and entitled elite as "American Chicken" and "Massachusetts Boys". The Plan Organization itself was seen as a privileged Americanized enclave, incompatible with its Iranian surroundings, incapable of understanding Iranian administrative agencies or interacting with them.

The claim that "All transactions of the Division [of Economic Affairs] were conducted in English, written or oral" and that "discussions and committee meetings were conducted in English", and finally, "all working documents up to and including frames, were prepared in English", gives

50 Khodadad Farmanfarmayan, Iranian Oral History Collection, Harvard University, Transcript 2, Sequence 18.

51 Khodadad Farmanfarmayan, Iranian Oral History Collection, Harvard University, Transcript 2, Sequence 26.

context to the hefty US cultural and academic weight within the Division of Economic Affairs.[52]

The Western-educated Iranian superstars at the Division of Economic Affairs were also criticized by their American Harvard Advisory Group colleagues, who were in Iran between 1961 and 1963. The "second generation" of Harvard Advisory Group employees accused their Western-educated colleagues of being culturally displaced, confused, self-righteous, not properly able to speak their mother tongue, and contemptuous of their compatriots. They were chided for their unfamiliarity with Iranian bureaucracies, government practices, and the mode of operation of ministries that were supposed to implement the developmental projects.[53]

The work environment and decision-making process at the Division of Economic Affairs set it dramatically apart from the rest of Iranian administrative and governmental establishments. Farmanfarmayan believed that the participatory, consultative, non-hierarchical, and knowledge-based process of discussions and deliberation would establish a model of "democratic due process" at the workplace, eventually permeating throughout the Plan Organization.

Nevertheless, Farmanfarmayan was a realistic expert who "insisted that we [the Division of Economic Affairs] were advisors" to the Plan Organization's director general, the prime minister, or His Majesty. He recommended that his staff should not be disappointed if their well-thought-out proposals were turned down or ignored. The radius of the democratic and transparent administrative practices of his office was limited to the Plan Organization and no further.[54]

52 McLeod, pp. 93, 109.

53 McLeod, pp. 54, 59, 61, 63, 70.

54 Khodadad Farman Farmayan, Iranian Oral History Collection, Harvard University, Transcript 2, Sequence 24. The quote in this paragraph and the one before are from this document.

4

Ebtehaj's Development Initiatives

On 14 March 1956, Ebtehaj held a press conference to give a comprehensive report of the Plan Organization's development prospects. He announced that two contracts had been signed in December 1955 with a German and a British firm to build two cement plants at Dorud and Manjil. Another contract had been signed with three French firms on 29 February 1956 to build the Sefidrud Dam.

To meet the country's excess demand for textiles, Ebtehaj signaled the creation of two new textile plants, the completion of Tehran's *chit* (printed cotton) factory, and the extension of financial assistance to private firms. The Plan Organization also intended to meet the country's excess demand for sugar through the output of a new plant in Fasa and two factories which were to come into operation in Kerman and Khorasan within a year. The sugar factory in Marvdasht would expand from 650 tons to 1,000 tons within a year.

Ebtehaj reported on the formation of a new state bank, *Bank-e E'tebarat-e San'ati* (Industrial Credit Bank), which was to support and encourage private investment. The Industrial Credit Bank extended loans to jump-start industries, particularly those whose home production lagged behind domestic demand. This bank began operations on 30 July 1956.

Ebtehaj told the press that even though he fully supported home industries, he did not favor prohibiting imports and called for a well-studied policy of applying tariffs and import duties where they were needed. In the field of transportation, Ebtehaj announced that substantial repairs had begun on the ports of Khorramshahr and Bandar-e Shahpur. At the end of his press conference, he was asked about the high salaries of foreign experts at the Plan Organization. Ebtehaj lost his temper and said, "all countries in the world need foreign experts" and "we are not overpaying anyone".[1]

DAVID LILIENTHAL AND THE KHUZESTAN DEVELOPMENT SERVICES

Between 12 and 16 September 1955, Istanbul hosted the annual meeting of the World Bank and the International Monetary Fund. Ebtehaj attended this gathering in Turkey and met with David Lilienthal for the first time at the Hilton hotel. Ebtehaj spoke about the developmental possibilities in Iran and asked for Lilienthal's input, and the latter responded enthusiastically. On his return to Tehran, Ebtehaj reported on his meeting and informed the Shah that he wished to invite Lilienthal to Iran. The Shah, who knew of Lilienthal's achievements, eagerly welcomed the idea.[2]

Ebtehaj was aware of Lilienthal's impressive work as one of the directors of the Tennessee Valley Authority and knew how he had successfully initiated economic progress in one of the most depressed and backward areas in the US. Ebtehaj was convinced Lilienthal could do the same for Iran's Khuzestan Province. Khuzestan was Iran's most prosperous oil-producing region but one of the most underdeveloped and poor agricultural areas due to its scorching heat, salty soil, and lack of irrigation water.

In June 1955, a few months before Lilienthal and Ebtehaj met in Istanbul, Lilienthal and his business partner Gordon Clapp founded their own Development and Resources Corporation (D&R). The mission of D&R was to "provide development services to underdeveloped countries."[3] Lilienthal and Clapp arrived in Tehran on 21 February 1956 and left for Khuzestan two days later. After their week-long inspection of the region, Lilienthal met with Ebtehaj on 1 March 1956 and submitted a lengthy report on his observations.[4]

On 7 March, Lilienthal and Clapp gave an interview to the Iranian press, in which they emphasized "the incredible developmental potentials

1 *Tehran Economist*, 26 Esfand 1334.

2 Ebtehaj, *Khaterate Abolhasan Ebtehaj*, vol. 1, pp. 382–385.

3 S.M. Neuse, *David E. Lilienthal: The Journey of an American Liberal*, Plunkett Lake Press. Kindle Edition. Location 11615 of 17935.

4 *Ettela'at*, 11 Farvardin 1334.

of Khuzestan".[5] A week later, Ebtehaj announced that Lilienthal and Clapp were to conduct a two-year study of the Khuzestan region for developmental purposes. In his transparent style of informing the people, Ebtehaj reported that the study would cost some $350,000 and that no one could predict the full cost of the complete agricultural and industrial development project.[6]

Lilienthal was impressed with Khuzestan's natural resource availability. To revive the region, he argued, it needed water, electricity, fertilizer, industry, and the re-introduction of sugar cane, which had once been cultivated but had been abandoned since the thirteenth and fourteenth centuries due to negligence in upkeeping irrigation canals.[7]

On 29 March 1956, Lilienthal's D&R corporation signed a contract with Iran's Plan Organization to reproduce the Tennessee Valley Authority experience in Khuzestan. This comprehensive, integrated regional development plan included: project studies for the development of Khuzestan; construction of the Dez Dam and its associated electricity plants and high-tension electric transmission lines; rebuilding the electric distribution system in Ahvaz and irrigation programs; establishment of an agro-industrial sugar cane production and processing project at Haft Tappeh; construction of the Aqajari-Ahvaz natural gas pipeline; and the building of a plastic and fertilizer plant in Ahvaz.[8] Lilienthal believed that Khuzestan would become the "powerhouse" of a modern Iran, export electricity to other regions, and substantially increase agricultural production.[9]

The contract stipulated that the Plan Organization had to review and approve all projects before D&R could embark on them. D&R, acting as Iran's agent, signed contracts with the firms involved in the various projects, supervised them, and paid them directly out of funds made available by the Plan Organization. An independent accounting firm reporting to the Plan Organization was to audit the accounts every six months. Both parties were entitled to terminate the contract "upon short notice".[10]

5 *Tehran Economist*, 19 Esfand 1334.
6 *Tehran Economist*, 26 Esfand 1334.
7 A. Seyf, "Production of Sugar in Iran in the Nineteenth Century," *Iran*, vol. 32 (1994), pp. 139–143. *Ettela'at*, 11 Farvardin 1334.
8 FO 371/127096, EP 1106/14.
9 D.E. Lilienthal, "Enterprise in Iran: An Experiment in Economic Development," *Foreign Affairs*, vol. 38, no. 1 (1959) pp. 132–139.
10 Lilienthal, "Enterprise in Iran," pp. 132–39.

In consultation with D&R, Ebtehaj, who had the last word, assigned each part of the multi-purpose scheme around the Dez Dam to the most established and reliable contractors. Rather than relying on one country to execute the development tasks, thereby obtaining an asymmetrical hold on Iran's development process, the Khuzestan development project was given to an international group of highly competent firms based on their expertise. Tenders were put out for each project, and firms with the lowest cost won the bid.

A British firm carried out the "aerial mapping of Khuzestan." The building of the hydraulic dam, coveted by the US Morrison-Knudsen engineering and construction firm, was contracted to the Italian engineering and dam construction firm Salini Impregilo, experts in high-arch dams. The Japanese Hitachi Mitsubishi Hydro supplied the turbines for the hydropower project, and West Germany's Siemens received the contract for furnishing the electric generators. A joint-bid involving the Los Angeles engineering firm and C. Brewer & Co, a Hawaiian sugar cane company, obtained the sugar cane plantation project. The sugar mill and refinery were manufactured by a Dutch company, and the "petrochemical design and market development for plastic" was "assigned to a leading Italian chemical company".[11]

Until 1956, Iran was bereft of rudimentary statistics and primary geographical and demographic surveys. Only in December 1956 was the first national census of modern Iran conducted, determining that Iran had a population of 18,944,821, with Tehran accounting for 10% of the population. The census also determined that some 80% of all Iranians lived off the land, and half of Iran's 3,500 doctors lived in Tehran.[12]

Given the data scarcity, Lilienthal earmarked three years to prepare and gather information on the projects. Identifying the location of the Dez Dam and constructing the irrigation canals, conducting a thorough soil analysis of the entire region, and deciding on what to cultivate where and which grain of sugar cane would best suit Khuzestan were all time-consuming processes, and all were necessary.

By the summer of 1957, D&R had an executive vice-president, a chief representative, and a vice-president for engineering in Iran, along with

---

11 D.E. Lilienthal, "Enterprise in Iran," pp. 132–139. Ebtehaj, *Khaterate Abolhasan Ebtehaj*, vol. 2, pp. 826–817. All information in this paragraph is based on the above sources.

12 FO 371/127142, EP 1822/1.

"thirty employees and ninety local hires". A year later, "the payroll had grown to include 64 employees and 437 local hires".[13] An essential aspect of the contract with D&R involved the training of Iranians in all aspects of the work and the final relinquishing of responsibilities to Iranians. Between 1955 and 1960, Lilienthal visited Iran nine times.

WORLD BANK LOAN AND ITS CONSEQUENCES

In January 1957, ten months after signing the integrated development scheme with Lilienthal's D&R, the World Bank gave Iran its first loan of $75 million. In preparation for obtaining this loan, Eugene Black, President of the World Bank, visited Tehran on 13 June 1956.[14] Subsequently the World Bank sent several economic and technical missions to Iran to review the projects in the Second Plan and assess the Khuzestan project. The World Bank loan was probably motivated by Eugene Black's trust in the professionalism and expertise of both Abolhasan Ebtehaj and David Lilienthal and confidence in Iran's ability to repay its debt out of its oil revenues.

Worried about the sordid history of incurring foreign debts and the subsequent lamentable intervention of foreign powers in Iranian politics, a few Majles deputies rallied against the World Bank credit. On 27 November 1956, Seyyed Ahmad Tabatabai-Qomi, the MP from Qom, addressed the loan as "a grave act against the interests and status of this country".[15] Seyyed Ja'far Behbahani, the influential MP from Tehran, opposed the loan and raised concern about Iran's inability to pay back this loan and warned against the adverse effects of the hegemonic control of a foreign entity over Iran. Abolhasan 'Amid-Nuri, the influential MP from Babol, spoke against the loan and believed that it was not in Iran's interest. To settle the issue, the deputies met with the Shah, and subsequently, on 27 December 1956, the Majles ratified the loan by a vote of eighty-eight in favor, four against, and eight abstentions.[16]

---

13 Neuse, *David E. Lilienthal,* Kindle location 11637 of 17935.

14 *Tehran Economist,* 26 Khordad 1335.

15 *Ruznameh-e Rasmi-ye Keshvar Shahanshahi-ye Iran,* 12 Azar 1335, *Mozakerat-e Majles-e Showray-e Melli,* 6 Azar 1335, Neshast-e 36.

16 *Tehran Economist,* 8 Day 1335. *Ruznameh-e Rasmi-ye Keshvar Shahanshahi-ye Iran,* 11 Day 1335, *Mozakerat-e Majles-e Showray-e Melli,* 6 Day 1335, Neshast-e 47.

Having been forced to approve the World Bank loan, the Majles chose to get back at Ebtehaj and the Plan Organization. On 12 October 1955, despite strong opposition, Ebtehaj had succeeded in convincing the Majles to pass a bill on the development of provinces.[17] The Plan Organization had offered to help the municipalities of 276 cities (excluding Tehran) with 50% of the expenses of their development projects, while the remaining half was to be shouldered by the local municipalities.[18] These projects included the provision of basic amenities from electricity and potable water to feeder roads, public baths, and slaughterhouses.

Suddenly, on 8 January 1957, the Majles passed a bill obliging the Plan Organization to provide long-term loans to municipalities in case they were unable to cover their 50% share of expenses.[19] In effect, the Majles was forcing the Plan Organization to foot the whole bill of municipal projects, while the Plan Organization had budgeted for only half such expenditures. The finances earmarked for municipal development during the Second Seven-Year Plan were set at slightly below £60 million.[20]

The Plan Organization identified some 1,000 projects, mostly electricity supplies, water schemes, and inner-city roads, and some 200 projects were put out to tender. By December 1957, some 180 municipal contracts were in progress, and 4,000 individuals were working on these projects. Local contractors had completed the asphalting of some forty to fifty town roads. The Plan Organization had divided and outsourced the consultancy aspect of its provincial development schemes to the French in the North, Germans in Central Iran, and Americans in Southern Iran.[21]

THE INDUSTRIAL AND MINING DEVELOPMENT BANK OF IRAN

Ebtehaj attended the International Industrial Conference held in San Francisco between 14 and 18 October 1957. This was the hub for some 600 business leaders from sixty countries to meet and discuss "how to raise standards of living for the peoples of the world through increased

17 *Tehran Economist*, 22 Mehr 1334.
18 *Ettela'at*, 12 Day 1335.
19 *Ettela'at*, 18 Day 1335.
20 FO 371/127096, EP 1106/1.
21 FO 371/127096, EP 1106/15; *Tehran Economist*, 23 Mehr 1334.

capital investment and economic growth".[22] Those attending the conference believed in the Western "free-world" economic philosophy, private enterprise, and entrepreneurship. *Time* magazine mentioned five key attendees, among them A.H. Ebtehaj of Iran.

Eugene Robert Black, a partner in the Wall Street investment firm Lazard Frères & Company, accompanied his father, Eugene Black, President of the World Bank, at this conference. The younger Black informed Ebtehaj that André Meyer, the powerful senior partner at Lazard Frères & Company urgently wished to see him in New York. After the end of the conference, Ebtehaj flew to New York and met with Meyer, who suggested the creation of a private industrial development bank in Iran to promote domestic and foreign investments in the budding private sector.

On his return to Tehran, Ebtehaj obtained the Shah's approval.[23] "Shortly thereafter, Chase International Investment Corporation joined Lazard in sponsoring the bank."[24] The two giant New York investment banking firms became the initiators of and contributors to one of Iran's most successful financial institutions, the Industrial and Mining Development Bank of Iran (IMDBI). Prime Minister Eqbal, who never got along with Ebtehaj, tried to obstruct the establishment of the IMDBI. On 1 March 1959, only two weeks after Ebtehaj was removed from the Plan Organization, a Memorandum of Agreement was signed with the Iranian government. The Majles subsequently ratified the memorandum, which the Shah finally confirmed in May 1959.

Conceptually, the IMDBI was the brainchild of two New York investment banking firms, Ebtehaj, and the World Bank. The purpose of the IMDBI was to help create, expand, and modernize Iran's private industrial, mining, and transportation enterprises by providing long- and medium-term loans and developing a capital market. This private bank was to assist the private sector, support established entrepreneurs, and jump-start new ones. The IMDBI was to act as the powerful engine of capitalist development in a predominantly traditional society. Aside from financial

22 *Time*, October 14, 1957.

23 Ebtehaj, *Khaterate Abolhasan Ebtehaj*, vol. 1, pp. 425–427.

24 International Bank for Reconstruction and Development, *Report and recommendations of the President to the executive directors on a proposed loan to Industrial and Mining Development Bank of Iran*, August 4, 1959, https://documents1.worldbank.org/curated/en/940751468253789340/pdf/multiopage.pdf (retrieved 7/2/2023).

assistance, the IMDBI aimed to "assist Iranian industry on technical, financial, managerial and administrative matters".[25]

The IMDBI had shareholders from six European countries, as well as from the US. Its largest shareholders were the two financial institutions of Lazard Frères and Chase International Investment Corporation.[26] Sixty percent of the IMDBI's equity capital ($3.1 million) belonged to Iranian shareholders and 40% ($2.1 million) to foreign concerns. In terms of loans, the IMDBI received $8 million from the Iranian government, $5.2 million from the World Bank, $5.2 million from the US government Development Loan Fund which was earmarked to finance the foreign exchange cost of imported material, equipment, and services. From the $37.1 million of loans that constituted the source of IMDBI's capital, $18.7 million came from the Plan Organization's Industrial Credit Bank (*Bank-e E'Tebarat-e San'ati*) and the Special Revaluation Fund.[27]

On 24 August 1959, the IMDBI began selling its shares to the public in all branches of the Melli Bank. A total of 1,900 Iranians bought shares in IMDBI. Among them, Habibollah Sabet was one of the major shareholders.[28] On 5 October 1959, the first General Assembly of IMDBI's shareholders was convened. The elected members of the Iranian managing board of the bank were Habibollah Sabet, Aqa Khan Bakhtiyar, Kaveh Farmanfarmayan, Habibollah Elqaniyan, Isa Kuros, Mehdi Sami'i, and Mohammad Bonakdar.[29] Almost all were reputable and well-established businessmen and industrialists. Nine days later and some eight months after Ebtehaj's resignation, his brainchild, the IMDBI, began official operations from a rented building on Boulevard Karaj.[30] By the end of October 1959, the World Bank had extended a loan of $5,200,000 to the IMDBI.[31]

---

25 International Bank for Reconstruction and Development, *Report and recommendations of the President to the executive directors on a proposed loan to Industrial and Mining Development Bank of Iran*, August 4; 1959.

26 International Bank for Reconstruction and Development, *Press Release No. 597. $5.2 million, Loan to Iran,* (August 13, 1959), https://documents1.worldbank.org/curated/en/278661590742790624/pdf/Announcement-of-Five-Million-Two-Hundred-Thousand-Dollars-Loan-in-Iran-on-August-13-1959.pdf (retrieved 23/1/2023).

27 Baldwin, pp. 117–118.

28 *Tehran Economist*, 3, 10 Mehr 1338.

29 *Ettela'at*, 13 Mehr 1338; *Tehran Economist*, 17 Mehr 1338.

30 *Rahavard*, Shokrollah Baravariyan, Bank-e tose'h san'ati va ma'dani-ye Iran, (Paiz 1395), No. 116, pp. 152–168.

31 *Tehran Economist*, 6 Azar 1338.

The IMDBI's management was entrusted to non-Iranian shareholders for the first five years, while Isa Kuros was appointed as chairman of the board of directors. Willem A. Van Ravesteijn, a Dutch banker, became the managing director, and Mehdi Sami'i, the former Vice-Governor of Bank Melli Iran, became the associate managing director. Like the Plan Organization, the IMDBI attracted talented, young Iranians. One of the first recruits of the IMDBI recalled that most of the secretaries and assistants were "educated overseas, had a firm grasp of English and Persian, and were professionally trained, well-dressed, smart-looking, congenial, and excellent at their jobs".[32]

In April 1961, an internal publication of the IMDBI, intended for its shareholders, made pertinent points about viable industrial investments. Reacting to the mismanagement and misappropriation of funds borrowed by influential capitalists, the IMDBI publication warned about enterprises with the lion's share of capital coming from loans and credits. It insisted that at least 60% of the capital had to come from privately accumulated funds. It emphasized the necessity of a proficient managerial, technical, financial, and accounting nucleus for the success of an enterprise. The IMDBI promised to consider all these considerations before approving a loan. The financial position of the enterprise applying for a loan and the importance of their product in the overall development scheme of the country were also essential factors for the IMDBI's green light.[33]

The first General Assembly of the IMDBI was convened on 13 July 1961. The small shareholders of the bank complained about their non-representation on the managing board and the executive committees, their inability to sell their shares and the low 4% rate of return on their shares. However, Mohammad-Rahim Motaqi-Iravani, a significant shareholder of the bank and the owner of *Kafsh-e Melli* (National Shoe), representing the large shareholders, praised the one-year activity of the bank.[34]

The first annual report of the IMDBI acknowledged that by 20 March 1961, the bank had received 593 loan applications. Based on the bank's strict criteria, 375 applications were refused for incomplete files, another 183 were turned down as they did not meet the bank's requirements, and only 35 loans were awarded, from which 31 led to

32 *Rahavard*, Shokrollah Baravariyan, Bank-e tose'h san'ati va ma'dani-ye Iran, (Paiz 1395), No. 116, pp. 152–168.
33 *Ettela'at*, 9 Ordibehesht 1340.
34 *Tehran Economist*, 31 Tir 1340.

a signature of contracts worth 101 million tomans. The firms receiving loans and technical, managerial, and accounting assistance produced cartons, bricks, cement, dairy, plastic, biscuits, matches, canned food, and textiles.[35] By March 1962, the IMDBI had given out forty loans worth 117 million tomans.[36]

At the 20 June 1962 General Assembly of the IMDBI, Khalil Taleqani, chairman of the board of management, reported on the annual activities of the bank from March 1961 to March 1962. He announced that during an economic crisis in the country, the IMDBI had a good year and increased its rate of return on shares from 4 to 6%. The bank planned to allocate some 100 million tomans among industries between March 1962 and March 1963. The board's composition – those who had been in office since October 1959 – remained almost intact. Habibollah Elqaniyan and Mohammad Bonakdar left the board, and Saeed Hedayat joined it.[37]

After five years, the IMDBI's management was handed over to Iranians, and Abolqasem Kheradjou became Governor-General in the summer of 1963. Kheradjou was of impeccable honesty, a manager in the style of Ebtehaj, a London School of Economics graduate, and a chartered accountant. Before his appointment at IMDBI, he had worked at the World Bank for six years. He was the World Bank's deputy director of the Far East Department and subsequently deputy director of the Development Finance Companies Department at the International Finance Corporation. By 31 August 1969, the World Bank had extended $105 million in loans to the IMDBI.[38]

CAPITALISTS, CONTRACTORS, COURTIERS, POLITICIANS, AND MERCHANTS BECOME BANKERS

Between Ebtehaj's return from the International Industrial Conference held in San Francisco in October 1957 and his removal from office in February 1959, a number of new banks, including joint foreign–Iranian

35 *Ettela'at*, 28 Tir 1340.

36 *Tehran Economist*, 22 Ordibehesht 1341.

37 *Tehran Economist*, 9 Tir 1341.

38 The World Bank Group Archives, Travel Briefings: Iran-Travel Briefs 01 (01/11/1969–01/12/1969). Folder ID: 1772516. Industry-IMDBI/IFC folder, p. 1, https://pubdocs.worldbank.org/en/71141387399257556/World-Bank-Group-Archives-Folder-1772516.pdf?redirect=no (retrieved 9/2/2023).

private banks, sprouted up. Even though a few of these banks officially commenced activities within eight months of Ebtehaj's removal from office, their application process had all begun during his time as the head of the Plan Organization.

The Iranian press referred to 1957 as the year of the scramble of foreign interests for deals in Iran and the year of banking activities.[39] From late 1957, businessmen and bankers in Iran were actively looking for interested foreign partners, and the press reported that Ebtehaj was seeking out foreign capital in Iran.[40] Ebtehaj's detractors maintained that the Plan Organization was created to recycle Iran's oil revenues back into the pockets of Western governments and capitalists.[41] However, the proliferation of private banks in this period had nothing to do with Ebtehaj.

The principal reason for the mushrooming of foreign and domestic private banks between 1957 and 1960 was the absence of a proper Iranian central bank controlling credit and the money supply. Without clear regulations and requirements for opening and operating banks, including lending conditions, reserve requirement specifications, and a watchdog institution supervising and controlling financial transactions and loaning mechanisms, banks could become the personal coffers of their major shareholders and friends.

At this time, American, European, and Japanese banks suddenly found the Iranian market attractive for commercial and financial activities. Even though the legality of joint banks was questioned, foreign banks entered partnerships with Iranian banks, based on the ownership of 49% of the capital, while the remainder went to private Iranian citizens.[42]

A Franco-Iranian bank, *Bank-e E'tebarat-e Iran*, (Credit Bank of Iran), with the participation of three French banks, *Crédit Lyonnais*, *Banque Nationale pour le Commerce et l'Industrie* and the *Banque d'Indochine*, was the first to move into the Iranian banking system. It officially opened for business on 1 July 1958 in the presence of Hoseyn 'Ala, the Minister of Court. The Iranian shareholders of the Credit Bank of Iran were prominent industrialists, courtiers, and politicians.

39 *Khandaniha*, 12 Farvardin 1337, 16 Farvardin 1337.

40 *Khandaniha*, 21 Aban 1336, 29 Bahman 1336.

41 *Khandaniha*, 12 Azar 1336.

42 *Ettela'at*, 16 Khordad 1338. Mostafa Tajaddod announced that based on his knowledge of banking laws in Iran, joint partnerships with foreign banks were illegal.

The President of this bank was Ahmad Shafiq, Princess Ashraf Pahlavi's second husband.[43] Ahmad Shafiq was a partner in numerous financial activities, such as one with Reza Afshar, providing hospitality services for the new Mehrabad Airport.[44] Other prominent shareholders of the bank were Abunasr Azod, the owner of Ahvaz Sugar Refinery, Ali Vakili, the chairman of Tehran's Chamber of Commerce, Hasan Kuros, the owner of Chitsazi-ye Ray textile company and shareholder of Esfahan Sugar Company, Abdol Hossein Behnia, and Mohammad Shahkar, members of parliament.[45]

On 12 June 1958, the Dutch *Banque des Pays Bas* and two other smaller foreign banks formed a partnership with *Bank-e Tehran* (Bank of Tehran) founded in 1953 and owned by Mehdi Laleh, a well-known merchant. Bank of Tehran owned 60% of the stock, and the three other banks owned the remainder. The Iranian managing board was composed of Mostafa Fateh, Mehdi and Abolhasan Laleh, and Mohammad and Abbas Naraqi.[46] By the end of August 1958, Mehdi Sami'i, the governor of the Melli Bank, informed interested British bankers that Iran's "Banking Control Board would soon have to begin turning down applicants, as the numbers were getting too many for the business of Tehran".[47]

Six years after leaving Iran during the Mosaddeq period, British banks made a return. The formation of a £1 million *Bank-e Iran o Ingelis* (The Bank of Iran and Britain) with the participation of the Chartered Bank and Eastern Bank LTD was announced on 2 October 1958.[48] The Bank was officially opened on 10 March 1959 during an elaborate ceremony attended by some 2,000 of Tehran's businessmen, bankers, and politicians.[49] The chairman of the bank's directors was Abbasqoli Neysari, Minister of Commerce in Eqbal's cabinet and the owner of twenty shares, each worth 1,000 tomans in the bank.[50] The mixed Iranian and British managing board of the bank included prominent Iranian businessmen such as Habibollah

43 FO 371/133024, EP 1111/13; *Ettela'at*, 11 Tir 1337.
44 Their corporation was called "*Sherkat-e Sahami-ye Service Forudgah-e Mehrabad (mehmankhaneh)*" and registered as a corporation in July 1958.
45 *Ettela'at*, 28 Khordad 1337.
46 *Tehran Economist*, 21 Tir 1337.
47 FO 371/133024, EP 1111/24.
48 FO 371/133024, EP 1111/22 (A).
49 *Ettela'at*, 23 Esfand 1337.
50 *Tehran Economist*, 25 Bahman 1337.

Sabet, Mohammad-Mehdi Lari, Qasem Harati, and Jafar Taqiniya. Esmail Dehlavi was the deputy director of the bank.[51]

In December 1958, the British Bank of the Middle East received approval to establish the joint *Bank-e Iran o Khavar-e Miyaneh* (Bank of Iran and the Middle East). It opened its doors with 120 employees on Ferdowsi Street on 6 May 1959.[52] The British Bank of the Middle East owned 49% of the shares, and fifty-nine Iranian investors held 51%.

Titans of Iran's industrial and commercial class, such as Habibollah Sabet, Hoseyn Hamedaniyan, the owner of Shahnaz Weaving and Textile Company, Gholamreza Naser, and Mehdi Namazi were the major shareholders of the Bank of Iran and the Middle East.[53] Mehdi Namazi and his cousin Mohammad, along with Abdolhoseyn Nikpour were also founding partners of Bank Pars, which had begun operation in July 1953.[54] The four board directors of Bank of Iran and the Middle East were Senator Qolamhoseyn Khoshbin, the chairman, Habibollah Sabet, Hoseyn Namazi and Hoseyn Khajehnuri, ex-manager of the Agricultural Bank and a wealthy landowner.[55]

The Dutch entered Iran's financial market for a second time when, on 13 April 1959, *Bank-e Iran o Holland* (the Mercantile Bank of Iran and Holland) began its activities. The Netherlands Trading Society owned 25% of the bank's shares, and Iranians held 75%. The principal Iranian shareholders of the bank were Soleyman and Ahmad Vahabzadeh, franchise owners for the German car DKW firm and US-made Caterpillar tractors, respectively. The bank operated from a building owned by the Vahabzadehs.[56]

In June 1959, the Swiss joined the bandwagon of partially foreign-owned banks. The major Swiss shareholder of *Bank-e Iran o Swiss* (Bank of Iran and Switzerland) was the Union Bank of Switzerland, which held 49% of the shares. Iranian shareholders, one of the most influential of which was Abbas Eskandari, held 51% of the capital. The Iranian manager of the

51 *Ettela'at*, 26 Aban 1337, 3 Day 1337.
52 FO 371/133024, EP 1111/10.
53 *Tehran Economist*, 11 Ordibehesht 1338.
54 *Tehran Economist*, 30 Shahrivar 1336. In June 1958, Nikpour obtained the shares of Mehdi and his son Shafi in Bank Pars and in return gave them his shares in Davud Rajabi's Iran Machine Company (*Tehran Economist*, 31 Khordad 1337).
55 FO 371/133024, EP 1111/30.
56 *Tehran Economist*, 21 Farvardin 1338. Soleyman Vahabzadeh became a senator (6th Majles Sena) in September 1971.

bank was Musa Abtin. This bank intended to give small loans to numerous merchants instead of one big loan to one or two businessmen.[57]

The Bank of Tokyo was the last of the foreign banks to establish a foothold in Iran and established *Bank-e Beynolmellali-ye Iran o Japon* (International Bank of Iran and Japan). This bank was registered on 15 September 1959 and officially inaugurated on 1 October 1959. Mostafa Mesbahzadeh, the owner of *Keyhan* newspaper, was the chairman of its board of directors.[58] The Bank of Tokyo owned 30% of the shares. Mahmud Lajevardi, representing Ariyan Company, held 33% of the shares.[59] The bank's capital was 20 million tomans, and it claimed about 100 prominent shareholders, many of whom were merchants trading with Japan. Among its major shareholders and members of the board of directors were Abolqasem Lajevardi, Mohammad Namazi, Qasem and Abbas Tahbaz, Ali Tavakoliyan, and Mohammad-Mehdi Talebi.[60]

Between 1958 and 1960, thirteen private banks were established in Iran, nine of which were joint ventures with foreign banks, leading the government to cease authorization of new commercial banks in 1960. The four new Iranian private banks included *Bank-e Asnaf-e Iran* (Iran's Guild Bank), *Bank-e Kar* (Labor Bank), *Bank-e Eqtesadi-ye Iran* (Iran's Economic Bank), and *Bank-e Iranian* (Iranians' Bank). The only fully foreign bank that remained was *Bank-e Iran o Russ* (Bank of Iran and Russia), which was formed in 1923.[61]

Bank-e Asnaf (Iran's Guild Bank) opened its doors in April 1958. Its founder and principal shareholder, General Ali-Akbar Zargham, had entered Eqbal's government on 4 April 1957 as Minister of Customs and Monopolies. The private *Bank-e Kar* (Labor Bank) began operation on 10 June 1958. After two years of operation, it had three branches in Tehran and had invested in a sixteen-storey building on Hafez Street. The main shareholders of the bank were Abdolmajid A'lam, a most influential

57 *Ettela'at*, 25 Esfand 1337; *Tehran Economist*, 22 Khordad 1338.

58 FO 371/140824, EP 1111/16.

59 *Tehran Economist*, 27 Day 1337; *Ettela'at*, 10 Mehr 1338. A-A Sa'idi, and F. Shirinkam, *Moqeiyat tojar va saheban-e sanaye' dar Iran-e asr Pahlavi, Khanedan Lajevardi va Lajevardiyan*, Tehran: Game No. 1398, p. 207. Mahmud Lajevardi, his brother Akbar Lajevardiyan and Mahmud's three sons Ahmad, Qasem, and Habib Lajevardi went on to create Iran's first holding company, the Behshahr Industrial Development Corporation.

60 *Ettela'at*, 25 Shahrivar 1338, 10 Mehr 1338.

61 R.E. Benedick, "The Money Market in Iran," *The Pakistan Development Review*, vol. 2, no. 3, 1962, pp. 406–421. *Tehran Economist*, 26 Esfand 1340.

contractor and a close friend of the Shah, Siyamak Farzad, Javad Mahin, Azizollah Khabirpur, and Saeed Hedayat.[62] *Banke Eqtesadi-ye Iran* (Iran's Economic Bank) was inaugurated in September 1959. On 31 January 1960, Abolhasan Ebtehaj's *Bank-e Iranian* (Iranian's Bank) was the last private bank that appeared during this period.

The Central Bank

Creating the Central Bank (*Bank-e Markazi*) as distinct from the commercial National Bank (*Bank-e Melli*) was long in the making. The original idea of the Central Bank came from Ebrahim Kashani and Mehdi Sami'i, who subsequently solicited the help of François Cracco. The Belgian Cracco, had been sent to the Plan Organization in 1956 on a Ford Foundation grant, then transferred to the *Bank-e Melli*, where he began working on a proposal for a "mother of all banks".[63]

Both houses ratified the bill establishing a Central Bank on 28 May 1960, and on 16 August 1960, the new governors of the National Bank and the Central Bank were appointed. Ahmad Majidiyan, the deputy of the Melli/National Bank, was promoted to its governor, and Ebrahim Kashani, the head of the Melli/National Bank, became the first governor of the Central Bank. The two banks were to collaborate and cooperate for a one-year trial period before the official separation of functions.[64]

The Central Bank was to take over the printing of money, national economic surveys and studies, supervision of and control of foreign exchange and banks, and maintaining an equilibrium in the balance of payments. As the government's bank, the Central Bank was also responsible for the book-keeping of government accounts and municipalities and the issuance of government bonds and treasury bills.[65]

---

62 *Tehran Economist*, 22 Mordad 1339.

63 H-A. Mehran, *Hadafha va Siyasathay-e Bank-e Markaziy-e Iran, az 1339 ta 1357*, Tehran: Nashr-e Ney, 1394, pp. 20–22. According to Mehran, Cracco's first name was Francis. But according to Gregory Brew ("Economic Expertise and Rural Improvement in Iran, 1948–1963") who refers to Cracco's correspondences with the Ford Foundation based on his archival research at the Rockefeller Archive Center, Cracco's first name was François. I privilege Brew's finding. Francis, however, is the English equivalent of François.

64 *Ettela'at*, 25 Mordad 1339. *Tehran Economist*, 29 Mordad 1339.

65 *Ettela'at*, 30 Mordad 1339.

The formulation and implementation of monetary policy and the coordination of financial and monetary policies with the High Economic Council fell under the jurisdiction of the Central Bank. To this end, a Money and Credit Council (*showray-e poul va e'tebar*) was created within the Central Bank. The Money and Credit Council has been dubbed the "legislative body of the country's banking system". A prime task of the Central Bank was the formulation and execution of the economic stabilization program and liaising with the International Monetary Fund through regular reports.[66]

66 Mehran, *Hadafha va Siyasathay-e Bank-e Markaziy-e Iran*, pp. 26, 31.

5

Ebtehaj Cornered

Ebtehaj's refusal to dole out appointments and contracts as personal favors, even when requests came from the Shah and the Court, made him powerful enemies. It also placed him on a collision course with those who believed that *partibazi* or cronyism was standard cultural practice. The modernist Ebtehaj believed differently. Pressure on him by the Court and government members was a regular strain. The Shah, the Court, or influential government members would have a favorite contractor or candidate for major and lucrative national projects. They would pressure the Plan Organization to select and accommodate their nominees. When Ebtehaj, having done his research, questioned and rejected their candidate for incompetence or irregularity in the contracting procedure, the reigning powers in Iran would feel snubbed. But for the Plan Organization, contracts costing the country huge sums were not private favors to be dispensed.

RAHIM-ALI KHORRAM AND THE MAZANDARAN ROAD (HARAZ) PROJECT

Ebtehaj had barely started his term as director general of the Plan Organization in September 1954 when he received a letter from the Shah's Special Royal Bureau (*Daftar-e makhsus-e shahanshahi*) with specific instructions. The Special Royal Bureau was the executive arm of the Court. One of its functions was to officially inform various government organizations of the Shah's decisions, appointments, and orders. Formal correspondence on the Bureau's unique stationery conveyed such orders.

The Shah's Special Royal Bureau instructed Ebtehaj to give the project of building a road to Mazandaran to Rahim-Ali Khorram, the owner of *Asphalt-e Rāh* construction company. Ebtehaj recalled that in his discussions with the Shah, when he was considering the post of director general at the Plan Organization, one of his principal conditions for accepting the job was that he would not accept illicit exhortations.

The Plan Organization therefore informed the Special Royal Bureau that strict procedures required the road project to be put in for tender and that it could not simply hand over the project to Khorram. Soon, a second letter from the Special Royal Bureau followed, insisting that the project had to be given to Khorram. The Plan Organization, under Ebtehaj's direct instructions, informed the Special Royal Bureau that "there was no difference or distinction between Khorram and other contractors and that he too can participate in the bidding for the project."[1] Luven Palanchiyan, a young Armenian engineer and graduate of Tehran's School of Engineering who owned a well-established roadbuilding firm, won the tender and began work on the Haraz Road to Mazandaran in September 1955.

Khorram's rise to great fortune was typical of how some went from rags to riches through some initiative but mainly through making use of connections, outright fraud, and strong-arm tactics. Khorram, a heavily built man, was allegedly illiterate and had begun his career as a simple construction worker (*amaleh*). He subsequently bought a roller and began his road-building career by obtaining a contract from the mayor of Tehran, Mahmud Davalu, in 1945 to tarmac Ganjei Street in the Amiriyeh district of Tehran. By September 1960, his company, *Asphalt-e Rāh* employed some 4,000 workers.[2] Khorram had close ties to the Court, especially to Hamid-Reza and Mahmud-Reza Pahlavi. He was known for fawning over the Court and the Shah by spending millions on festivities marking the birthday of the royal family.[3]

In 1962, a major scandal surrounding Rahim-Ali Khorram made the headlines. Khorram's construction company, *Asphalt-e Rāh,* had obtained a contract, after Ebtehaj had left the Plan Organization, to build 40% of Abadan Airport. According to a SAVAK (*Sazeman-e Ettela'at va Amniyat-e Keshvar*; the Bureau for Intelligence and Security of the State) report dated 30 June 1959, Prince Hamid-Reza, the Shah's brother, had been

1 Ebtehaj, *Khaterate Abolhasan Ebtehaj*, vol. 1, p. 347.
2 *Tehran Economist*, 21 Aban 1339; *Ettela'at*, 23 Esfand 1339.
3 *Khandaniha*, 13 Shahrivar 1341.

instrumental in getting Khorram his contract.[4] SAVAK was Iran's dreaded secret police.

Despite reports in December 1960 that the Abadan airport was rapidly progressing, by January 1962, it still remained unfinished. At the same time, it also became known that Khorram's work had not been carried out according to the Plan Organization's specifications and that he had fled the country leaving 170 bounced cheques behind him. Khorram was subsequently accused of embezzling funds from the tarmacking contracts of Tehran's streets that he had obtained from Tehran's municipality over a period of ten years, as well as misappropriation of state resources, and tax evasion.[5]

Khorram was arrested on 29 August 1962 and charged with illegal land occupation in *Shahr Ara* and *Tarasht* and numerous bounced cheques, in addition to previous accusations. In 1962, Khorram's wealth was estimated at 400 million tomans and the Tehran municipality was said to have owed him 36 million tomans. Khorram was alleged to have paid substantial bribes to high officials in return for lucrative contracts.[6] Yet he was summarily released and went on to become one of Iran's richest "businessmen".

ROBERT GREIF, AHMAD MAHBOD, AND THE DAMS OF LATYAN AND LAR

In 1957, the Plan Organization carefully studied two crucial dam-building projects, Latyan and Lar. The main objective of these two dams was to provide potable water for Tehran. While the Plan Organization was conducting its preliminary research, the Shah decided on Mr. Greif as his chosen candidate for constructing the $86 million Latyan and Lar dams.[7]

Ebtehaj, however, regarded Greif as immoral and incompetent. Robert Greif was a Swiss contractor, consultant, and middleman. He had had shifty dealings in Latin America while setting up a telephone network and was

4 The Center of Historical Documents Survey. *Moruri bar zendeghi va fesadha-ye Rahim-Ali Khorram*, https://historydocuments.ir/?page=post&id=3328 (retrieved 11/11/2023).
5 *Ettela'at*, 7 Day 1339; 4 Day 1340; *Tehran Economist*, 7 Bahman 1340.
6 *Tehran Economist*, 23 Day 1340. *Ettela'at*, 7, 8 Shahrivar 1341.
7 The value of the contract ($86 million) is based on FO 371/133049. ECD/ 14210/58; *Ettela'at*, 29 Mordad 1337.

wanted by the law.[8] The British Embassy in Caracas, Venezuela, described Greif as "undoubtedly a clever and successful, but unscrupulous, operator who needs watching."[9] The said Embassy did, however, mention that in Greif's 1953 to 1955 dealings "nothing" had "gone seriously wrong" from a "financial point of view".[10] In Venezuela, Greif represented the Swiss company Emeg AC of Zurich.

Greif's powerful contact in Iran was Ahmad Mahbod (Meybud), a person very close to the Shah, and his "representative for a number of projects".[11] Mahbod, a senior counselor at the Court, was also a close confidant of Hoseyn 'Ala, the Minister of Court. Mahbod played an instrumental role in brokering Iran's path-breaking oil contract with the Italian firm ENI (Italian National Oil Organization) in March 1957, which gave Iran 75% and ENI 25% of the royalties.[12] Among US firms dealing with Iran, Mahbod had the tainted reputation of "openly asking for bribes to be passed on to higher levels".[13]

In May 1957, Greif and his team traveled to Tehran to discuss the dam projects and met with the Shah, Prime Minister Eqbal, and members of his cabinet. Eqbal's cabinet and his economic team briefed Greif on the technical and legal aspects of the Lar project. Greif's proposals were subsequently discussed at the High Economic Council, and the Shah gave his approval for the contract.[14] Greif left Tehran on 24 May 1957, without having obtained a final confirmation, and the construction of the dam remained in limbo.[15]

On 19 June 1957, almost a month after Greif left Tehran, the Shah, who had been on a lengthy European tour, suddenly ordered a progress report on the Greif contract which he had approved before his departure. Worried about the Shah's urgent demand from Paris, Gholamali Meykadeh, the director of the Tehran Water Organization, told the press that everyone supported the project, but they were still conducting further studies. On

8 Ebtehaj, *Khaterate Abolhasan Ebtehaj*, vol. 1, p. 433.

9 FO 371/133048, EP 1421/16.

10 FO 371/133048, EP 1421/16.

11 FO 371/133048, EP 1421/17.

12 In September 1957, ENI and the National Iranian Oil Company established the *Societé Irano-Italienne des Pétroles* (SIRIP).

13 FRUS, 1955–1957, Near East Region; Iran; Iraq, vol. XII, Doc. 377.

14 *Ettela'at*, 30, 31 Ordibehesht 1336, 1 Khordad 1336.

15 *Ettela'at*, 4 Khordad 1336.

30 June 1957, Meykadeh went to Europe, met with the Shah in Geneva, and informed him of the interest of a British firm in the project.

The Shah instructed him to go to England and pursue the matter with the British firm. Meykadeh returned to Iran after a one-month fact-finding trip to Europe and reported to the Shah at the High Economic Council that the Lar Dam project would go ahead. On 10 December 1957, Greif and Meykadeh met again with the Shah, while the High Economic Council was still hesitating between the British Taylor Woodrow civil engineering firm, which specialized in power plants, and the Greif proposal.

Finally on 19 April 1958, Meykadeh announced that an agreement had been reached with Greif over the construction of Lar Dam. Between the winter of 1957 and the spring of 1958, Greif had substantially reduced his initial cost price for the project due to the competitive prices of Taylor Woodrow.[16] On 14 June 1958, the press announced that both the Lar and Latyan dams were contracted to Greif's company.[17]

Behind the scenes, the tug of war between Ebtehaj and the government was reaching its apex over major economic and developmental decisions. On 12 October, Eqbal was able to take legal control of the fate of the two dams. The government was permitted to contract the dams "independently".[18] The Plan Organization was relieved of any role in the matter. The government subsequently decided to defer the construction of the Lar Dam and proceed with the Latyan Dam, to which $35 million was allocated.[19] In September and October 1958, a few months before Ebtehaj left the Plan Organization, rumors circulated in the press about his decision to resign over disagreements with Eqbal and his team over the contactors of the Latyan and Lar dams.[20]

Construction of the Latyan Dam, renamed Farahnaz, did not begin until 1963 and was completed in May 1967. It was eventually contracted to the French construction firm Sacer, not to Greif's company. By 1961, Greif's chief contact in Iran, Ahmad Mahbod, had had a serious falling out with the Shah over money matters and had left Iran. The construction of

16 *Ettela'at*, 17 Esfand 1336, 30 Farvardin 1337.
17 *Ettela'at*, 24 Khordad 1338, 23 Mordad 1338.
18 *Ettela'at*, 21 Mehr 1337.
19 *Tehran Economist*, 1 Mehr 1337, *Ettela'at*, 10, 21 Mehr 1337.
20 *Tehran Economist*, 29 Shahrivar 1337.

the Lar Dam was eventually carried out by the Italian firm Impregilo. It did not begin until 1974 and was finished in 1982.

YUNES AQA VAHABZADEH AND THE ELECTRIFICATION OF TEHRAN

Within the Second Seven-Year Plan context, special priority was given to providing electricity to Tehran as well as large and smaller cities. The Plan Organization invited the American Sanderson & Porter engineering company, which specialized in building electrical power plants, to Iran. After six months of study, in the Spring of 1957, they presented their detailed study for Iran's electrification project to the Plan Organization.[21]

Albert de Smaele, the Belgian civil engineer and ex-minister at the Plan Organization's Technical Bureau, was charged with studying the electrification projects. He had been pivotal in planning and implementing the Belgian electricity network. Having done his research, conducted his studies, and traveled to Europe to meet with and investigate prospective contractors, de Smaele recommended that the electrification of the whole country, including some 220 provincial towns, be given to a consortium of French, British, German, and Belgian firms.

The Plan Organization had done all the groundwork for creating a national and single electricity organization called *Sherkat-e Vahed-e Barq Iran* (Iran's Single Electricity Company), with its regional networks. The consortium of foreign firms would act as managerial, technical, and administrative contractors of the Iran Electricity Company for ten years. They would provide the credit for necessary investments at low interest rates and train Iranian technicians and experts to operate the networks.[22]

Under the umbrella of a unified national project, foreign firms would make up for their losses of electrification in small towns with the profitable project of Tehran. Ebtehaj supported de Smaele's recommendation. Even though he had heard rumors that Tehran's electrification project was to be separated from the national project and given to an Iranian merchant,

21 *Ettela'at*, 3 Tir 1336.

22 *Ettela'at*, 22, 31 Tir 1336.

he nonetheless stressed to the Shah the compelling case for de Smaele's recommendation, hoping to get his approval.[23]

The Shah's choice for Tehran's electrification project was Yunes Vahabzadeh. The Tehran electrification project was the most lucrative part of a comprehensive nationwide scheme worth $60 million. The Tehran project was initially estimated to be some $19.8 million. Later, it was estimated at around $23 to $30 million. The press reported that Vahabzadeh was to receive a 3% commission, but Vahabzadeh told the Shah that he would receive a 5% commission.[24]

Ebtehaj knew that Vahabzadeh did not have the faintest notion of electrification and power plants. He was an influential merchant, financier, and middleman with connections to the Shah. On 2 December 1957, the press reported that the Cabinet and the High Economic Council, presided over by the Shah, had approved giving Tehran's electrification contract to Vahabzadeh and the contract had been signed.[25] The fact that Vahabzadeh's proposal did not even include the name of potential suppliers of machinery, let alone well-founded cost estimates for the project, demonstrated that the criteria of the decision-makers for giving him the contract were neither expertise nor cost-efficiency.

The contract with Vahabzadeh for Tehran's electrification made the Plan Organization's idea of a single national electrification company redundant, and it undermined the involvement of the consortium of French, British, German, and Belgian firms. Having obtained the lucrative contract, Vahabzadeh went abroad looking for firms to build a 50,000-kilowatt power station and an 80,000-kilowatt plant generated by the Karaj Dam. The contract for building Tehran's electrical plant was sub-contracted to the US Westinghouse Company.[26]

On 7 August 1958, Roger Stevens, the British Ambassador to Tehran, commented on the Greif and Vahabzadeh affairs. He reported that even though he had no evidence, it was generally assumed in Tehran that "large-scale payments were made over the Latyan Dam project or the recent

23 Ebtehaj, *Khaterate Abolhasan Ebtehaj*, vol. 1, pp. 412–413.

24 *Ettela'at*, 16 Tir 1335, *Tehran Economist*, 4 Bahman 1337. Ebtehaj, *Khaterate Abolhasan Ebtehaj*, vol. 1, p. 413.

25 *Ettela'at*, 11 Azar 1336; FO 371/133051, EP 1534/2.

26 *Tehran Economist*, 17 Aban 1337.

Tehran power plant scheme". Such payments were said to have been "by dubious financiers with strong royal support".[27]

THE TOUCHY JOHN MOWLEM CONTRACT: EBTEHAJ OR THE SHAH?

The John Mowlem fiasco caused Ebtehaj a lot of headaches. The road-building contract with John Mowlem was signed on 10 May 1955.[28] The Plan Organization gave John Mowlem, an English road construction consultancy firm, a contract to build 6,000 kilometers of roads in eight years. John Mowlem thus became the managing agent "for the whole of the Plan's road programme".[29] According to British sources, it was the Shah who had "personally chosen John Mowlem".[30] John Mowlem's firm also benefited from the friendship, association, support, and patronage of Asadollah Rashidiyan, a most anglophile person close to the Shah and a key organizer of the 19 August 1953 coup against Mosaddeq.[31]

Mowlem, in turn, contracted the massive road-building project to three Iranian contractors. The first stretch of road built under Mowlem's supervision between Qazvin and Takestan was completed in November 1956. On 2 March 1957, this newly built stretch broke up under use.[32] Five days later, on 7 March, Abolhasan 'Amidi-Nuri, a vocal member of the parliament, began questioning and criticizing the road-building activities of John Mowlem and the monies received by this company. He insisted that John Mowlem had not even constructed one kilometer of road.

The inefficiency, lethargy, and incompetence of John Mowlem were an embarrassment to Ebtehaj, who had been averse to giving a contract to this firm in the first place, and the Shah, who believed Mowlem had wasted Iran's time and money.[33] Even the British Embassy in Iran believed that the John Mowlem affair had been "a disastrous story and whomever was

27 FO 371/133022, EP 1102/10.
28 *Khandaniha*, 4 Aban 1336.
29 FO 371/127117, EP 1372/9/A.
30 FO 371/127117, EP 1372/26.
31 FO 371/127117, EP 1372/22; FO 371/127117. EP 1372/23; FO 371/127117. EP 1372/3(A).
32 FO 371/127117, EP 1372/1.
33 FO 371/127117, EP 1372/18.

responsible for selling Mowlem to the Iranians did H.M.G [Her Majesty's Government] a very bad turn indeed".[34]

On 18 December 1957, after five months of haggling and Mowlem's ardent stand that it should continue with the road-building contract, Ebtehaj followed the Technical Bureau's recommendations and ended the Mowlem contract. The Plan Organization announced that since John Mowlem had not fulfilled his obligation, the contract was terminated.[35]

Subsequently, Ebtehaj distributed the road-building job among different road consulting engineers from different countries, with each getting a contract of not more than 700 kilometers.[36] According to British Embassy sources in Tehran, both the Shah and Prime Minister Eqbal were against the termination of John Mowlem's contract.[37]

THE MACHINATIONS BEHIND A FERTILIZER PLANT

In 1956, the Plan Organization outsourced a study to the reputable Belgian chemical firm UCB (Union Chimique Belge) on the appropriate site for a much-needed fertilizer plant. The study concluded that a fertilizer plant must be close to gas fields, water sources, and port facilities. Ahvaz was the natural site for a fertilizer plant due to its proximity to Iran's gas fields, access to the Karun River, and the existing port and transportation facilities. Ebtehaj, therefore, supported the findings of the professionals and followed up on the construction of Iran's fertilizer plant at Ahvaz.[38]

On 18 September 1957, Ebtehaj announced that plans for the fertilizer plant in Ahvaz had been finalized, and it would probably be built on the banks of the Karun River. The plant was estimated to cost $19 million and would produce around 170 tons of fertilizers daily. The construction of the plant was subsequently put to a public international tender.[39]

34 FO 371/127117, EP 1372/24.

35 FO 371/127118. EP 1372/42 (A). Iranian sources mention 23 December 1957 as the termination date, see *Ettela'at*, 2 Day 1336.

36 FO 371/133044, EP 1372/8; *Ettela'at*, 5 Day 1336. The foreign companies replacing John Mowlem included Kampsax (Danish), SAUTI (Italian), Amon & Whitney (American), ETCO (Franco-Iranian) and OFER (French).

37 FO 371/127117. EP 1372/26.

38 Ebtehaj, *Khaterate Abolhasan Ebtehaj*, vol. 1, pp. 439, 441.

39 *Ettela'at*, 27, 31 Shahrivar 1336, 3 Mehr 1336.

However, the Shah, Eqbal, and Ja'far Sharif-Emami, the Minister of Industry and Mines, had different plans for Iran's fertilizer plant. They favored building the plant in Shiraz, and their preference was not based on any solid cost-efficient or technical study. At the time, there existed "a very stiff competition and rivalry" between Sharif-Emam and Ebtehaj, and the two would become entangled in heated disagreements and feuds.[40] Eqbal welcomed this cleavage and supported Sharif-Emami to undermine Ebtehaj's power. According to Sharif-Emami, it was the Shah who had suggested the fertilizer plant in Shiraz.[41]

On 30 November 1958, Sharif-Emami announced the signature of a contract with the French Schneider group to build the fertilizer plant in Shiraz, and the British firm John Brown to build the gas pipeline from Gachsaran to Shiraz.[42] In his interview with the press, Sharif-Emami insisted twice that this project was the Shah's initiative and had his full support. He thanked Eqbal's cabinet, the High Economic Council, and the National Iranian Oil Company for their cooperation but did not mention the Plan Organization. Instead, Sharif-Emami made a veiled reference to the behind-the-scenes disagreements over this project by thanking the Shah for overruling and overcoming all opposition.

This critical deal was signed without a public tender for the projects. The total cost of the fertilizer plant, including building, machinery, and a gas pipeline from Gachsaran to Marvdasht in Shiraz, was put at $36 million.[43] Half of the cost for the project was to be paid by the National Iranian Oil Company and the other half was to be paid from the Special Revaluation Fund.[44]

Ebtehaj contended that contrary to Ahvaz, Shiraz did not possess any of the prerequisites for a fertilizer plant. Its distance from necessary

40 Jafar Sharif-Emami, Iranian Oral History Collection, Harvard University, Transcript 6, Sequence 137; Transcript 7, Sequence 147–150.

41 Jafar Sharif-Emami, Iranian Oral History Collection, Harvard University, Transcript 7, Sequence 151.

42 *Tehran Economist*, 1, 15 Azar 1337; *Ettela'at*, 10 Azar 1337.

43 Cyrus Ebrahimzadeh, Economics of Petro-Chemical industries in Iran; Tahqiqat é Eqtesadi, https://ensani.ir/file/download/article/20101122150154-mte011pdf34.pdf (retrieved 2/2/2024). The annual report of the Ministry of Industry for 1960–1961 (1339) puts the cost figure at $32 million. NIPNA, https://www.nipna.ir/fa/newsagency/10170/ (retrieved 2/2/2024). A third cost figure is quoted at £10.5 million. See *Tehran Economist*, 1 Azar 1337.

44 *Ettela'at*, 10 Azar 1337.

gas resources made it twice as costly.[45] Once he became aware of the *fait accompli*, Ebtehaj reacted harshly, referring to the Shiraz deal, which had been concluded behind his back, as "criminal" and treasonous. On 18 January 1959, the disagreement between the Eqbal and Sharif-Emami team and Ebtehaj became public. On the Majles floor, Eqbal asked, "I do not know what treason has been committed. They wish to disturb public opinion because we are doing positive work."[46]

In Ebtehaj's estimation, the Sharif-Emami contract was drawn up in the most inefficient and unprofessional manner, primarily since it was awarded without international competitive bidding.[47] According to Cyrus Ghani, "one of the Shah's mistresses had apparently been involved in negotiating the contract."[48] According to Ebtehaj, after the Shiraz fertilizer affair, the Shah was indignant and resented him over his opposition to the contract, and Ebtehaj, too, had decided to resign.[49]

In November 1958, Sharif-Emami had promised that a fertilizer plant with a productive capacity of 90,000 tons of ammonium nitrate per year would be ready in twenty-one months.[50] By November 1961, or three years after the contract for the construction of the Shiraz fertilizer plant was signed, the completion of the project stalled. The government announced that it was some 24 million tomans short to complete the plant and begin production.[51] The delays in completion were a major embarrassment to its staunch proponents.

Finally, on 18 January 1962, Prime Minister Ali Amini, Abdollah Entezam, the director general of the National Iranian Oil Company (NIOC), and Mohammad-Taqi Sarlak, the Minister of Industry and Mines, met to discuss the modality of transferring the unfinished Shiraz fertilizer plant to the NIOC, Iran's financial "fire-fighter" of last resort.

At this meeting on the top floor of the new NIOC building on Takht-e Jamshid Street, the NIOC agreed to shoulder the remaining 30 million

45 For various accounts of the Shiraz Fertilizer Plant debate, see: *Tehran Economist*, 15 Azar, 20 Day, 27 Day 1337, 7 Bahman 1340; *Khandaniha*, 2 Esfand 1337; *Ettela'at*, 3, 8 Aban 1341; Ebtehaj, *Khaterate Abolhasan Ebtehaj*, vol. 1, pp. 439–441.

46 *Tehran Economist*, 4 Bahman 1337.

47 Ebtehaj, *Khaterate Abolhasan Ebtehaj*, vol. 1, p. 438.

48 Bostock and Jones, *Planning and Power in Iran*, pp. 155–156, 218.

49 Ebtehaj, *Khaterate Abolhasan Ebtehaj*, vol. 1, pp. 440, 443.

50 *Ettela'at*, 10 Azar 1337.

51 *Ettela'at*, 23 Aban, 29 Azar 1340.

tomans necessary to finish this project. The Shiraz Fertilizer Company was subsequently placed under the tutelage of NIOC, and Reza Razmara, a graduate of Tehran University's School of Engineering and the University of London, became its director general. After five years, the Shah and General de Gaulle inaugurated this fertilizer plant on 18 October 1963.[52]

52 *Ettela'at*, 28 Day 1340, 16 Esfand 1340; *Tehran Economist*, 2 Azar 1342.

6

Uphill Struggle, Negotiating Economic Development

Ebtehajism symbolized a modern Iranian meritocratic economic philosophy that firmly believed in free and competitive markets, dispassionate technical objectivity, the superiority of Western technical expertise and social sciences, and the drive to acquire them through international organizations and the sanctity of honest and fair contracts. He and his young and nationalist followers believed in technocracy, economic growth and development, and, most importantly, the incorruptibility of civil servants as the means of overcoming Iran's economic underdevelopment.

Ebtehaj and his team, stuck firmly to their professional and ethical guns, and often came off as spoilt brats to the Iranian political establishment. Their dry, businesslike style of operation and interaction seemed haughty and discourteous in a political environment where exaggerated niceties were essential elements of any social, political, or business rapport. The Plan Organization's boss and his boys were unfamiliar with the popular Persian saying, "slitting a throat with cotton", the prevalent mode of operation in high government circles. They were an anomaly in Iran's institutional scene of the time, and so they naturally faced backlash. At first, their rise to power and survival was by the Shah's grace.

In the early days of Ebtehaj's office, the Shah was his staunch supporter, giving him protection and considerable leeway. On numerous occasions, the Shah supported Ebtehaj in confronting powerful government officials. He even ignored the US administration's grumblings about Ebtehaj. Upon arrival, Ebtehaj clashed with the powerful Prime Minister General Zahedi over negotiations underway with the British construction firms, John Mowlem and Group One.

Zahedi was anxious to conclude both agreements. Ebtehaj rejected the Group One contract because the company was merely an intermediary with no construction experience. He agreed to the John Mowlem contract, but he insisted and obtained a 30% discount from John Mowlem. Ebtehaj also inserted a clause allowing Iran to terminate the contract if, after two years, the stipulated progress had not been made on the roads under construction.

On 6 April 1955, Hoseyn 'Ala replaced Zahedi as prime minister. The American Ambassador to Iran, Loy Henderson, believed that one of the reasons for Zahedi's removal from power was his opposition to Ebtehaj.[1] The Iranian press speculated that disagreements and clashes between Zahedi and Ebtehaj over the allocation of development projects among contractors had reached a boiling point before Zahedi's removal. Zahedi is said to have demanded Ebtehaj's dismissal, which the Shah had refused.[2]

Though Ebtehaj and 'Ala got along fine, the press began criticizing Ebtehaj and the Plan Organization in April 1956. The first volley came in a lengthy article published in the progressive weekly *Ferdowsi* on 24 April 1956. The author, who was probably Mahmud 'Enayat (*Mim 'Ayan*), criticized the slow progress of building the Karaj Dam. He chided the Plan Organization for its extravagant expenditures, wasteful contracts with foreigners, and sluggishness in completing essential projects. 'Enayat posited that the Plan Organization was not spending money on people's basic needs but on non-essentials and accused it of misplaced priorities and expenditures without forthcoming revenues.[3]

Less than a month after the *Ferdowsi* article, the US administration began complaining about the Plan Organization's performance and the person of Ebtehaj. On 17 May 1956, partly echoing 'Enayat, the US administration voiced its frustration over the Plan Organization's pace of implementing projects. Jeffrey Kitchen, the deputy director of the Office of Greek, Turkish, and Iranian Affairs, wrote, "after two years the people are beginning to doubt the effectiveness of the Organization which seems only to compound long-range plans while sitting on millions of dollars.

1 FRUS, 1955–1957, Near East Region, vol. XII, Document 304.
2 *Khandaniha*, 26, 29 Farvardin 1334.
3 *Ferdowsi*, 4 Ordibehesht 1335.

The Shah has staked his future on Ebtehaj who is widely hated and must be counted a political liability."[4]

The highly placed Iranian contacts of the American Embassy in Tehran must have conveyed a very negative image of Ebtehaj to the Americans, who subsequently reported it to Washington and Kitchen. The image of Ebtehaj as a disliked and resented figure in Iran was not limited to the American administration, but also circulated among the British. By January 1957, the British Embassy had commended Ebtehaj for having done "a remarkable job at the Plan Organization". It referred to "his only shortcoming being his unwillingness to make concessions to political expediency". However, on 18 January 1957, Roger Stevens, the British Ambassador in Iran, referred to Ebtehaj as "unhappily detested by nearly everyone".[5]

In February 1957, towards the end of 'Ala's Premiership, deputies in the Majles and the Senate and the mainstream press intensified their criticism. This time, it was the influential daily *Ettela'at* that repeated Kitchen's concerns and wrote about the "lingering doubts" of the people about the activities of the Plan Organization two years after the start of the Second Plan. It reminded Ebtehaj of the urgency of showing tangible results and urged him to prioritize the most pressing projects.[6]

Ebtehaj, however, was unwilling to forego detailed and thorough studies and surveys before launching into operation. Careful consultation and preparation to identify the first-best options internationally were integral to his management style. In a speech on 26 February 1957 at Tehran University, he defended his track record and hammered home the importance of balanced growth and development based on careful technical and financial studies. He reminded Iranians that "implementing economic projects without careful preliminary studies was much more dangerous than not implementing them at all." Ebtehaj referred to the financial failure of several major projects launched without sufficient prior studies. He acknowledged that it was difficult to implement projects in a short period and identified the paucity of technical and professional manpower as a significant problem of the country, explaining the need for hiring foreign experts.[7]

4 FRUS, 1955–1957, Near East Region; Iran; Iraq, vol. XII, Doc. 356.
5 FO 371/127072, EP 1012/1. FO 371/127073.
6 *Ettela'at*, 8 Esfand 1335.
7 *Ettela'at*, 8 Esfand 1335.

Ebtehaj's explanations did not fall on receptive ears, and soon a few Majles deputies joined the anti-Plan Organization campaign. On 12 March 1957, Tabatabai-Qomi, the MP who had criticized the Plan Organization for receiving loans from the World Bank, lamented that it was difficult to criticize the Plan Organization "as if it was a government unto itself".[8] The notion that the Plan Organization was a government unto itself was later repeated by 'Amidi-Nuri, another MP. The Plan Organization and Ebtehaj were also chided in the Senate by Senator Abbas Mas'udi, the owner of the daily *Ettela'at*, for the absence of coordination between it and the ministries, especially the Ministry of Roads, responsible for executing infrastructural projects.[9]

In the anti-Plan Organization chorus that was becoming ever more vocal in March 1957, Jamshid A'lam, the one-time special physician of the Shah and an MP, played a peculiar role. Jamshid A'lam led a political crusade against the Iran Party, an important member of Mosaddeq's old National Front. Pandering to the Shah's dislike for Mosaddeq and the National Front, A'lam presented a bill to the Majles demanding the banning of the Iran Party as illegal. Once the Majles outlawed the Iran Party, A'lam began a witch hunt for Iran Party members in the Plan Organization, all of whom were honest, well-educated, and capable engineers. He accused them of favoritism towards their own old party members and went as far as reading their names in the Majles and demanding that they be fired.

For Jamshid A'lam, like his Royal mentor, Iran Party members were traitors. By extension, he accused the Plan Organization and Ebtehaj of acting against state security.[10] The curious political attack on the Plan Organization by a member of the Shah's intimate circle of friends could not have been without the Shah's consent. The A'lam episode was a clear indirect warning from the Shah to Ebtehaj.

Attacks of various kinds, economic and political, on Ebtehaj and the Plan Organization were compounded by the continuous negative opinion of the US administration. On 28 March 1957, President Eisenhower's special assistant, James Richards, wrote that the "Plan Organization appears to have no coherent program. Apparently Plan director Ebtehaj, personal appointee of Shah, [is] responsible in considerable part for [the]

8 *Ettela'at*, 21 Esfand 1335.
9 *Ettela'at*, 26 Esfand 1335.
10 *Ettela'at*, 23 Esfand 1335.

ineffectiveness [of] the development effort because of vanity and failure [to] delegate authority."[11]

Once Manuchehr Eqbal became prime minister on 3 April 1957, he and his government turned the verbal campaign against Ebtehaj and the Plan Organization into an operational assault. Less than a month after Eqbal became prime minister, the Iranian press unveiled the new prime minister's plans to transfer all factories under the Plan Organization's control to the government. Concomitantly, they speculated about Ebtehaj's decision to resign if Eqbal was to have his way.[12] Rumors even circulated that Eqbal had complained to the Shah about Ebtehaj and had asked his Majesty to issue orders to "discipline" him.[13]

Another tide of opposition to Ebtehaj and the Plan Organization arose three months after Eqbal became prime minister. From the end of June 1957, the pro-Eqbal press repeated the old criticisms levied against the Plan Organization: procrastination and wasting time while urgent projects needed to be undertaken; paying large sums of money to foreign companies as consultancy fees and project assessments; payment of phenomenal salaries to its Iranian and foreign personnel; absence of tangible results; squandering public funds and outsourcing services and projects that Iranians could have easily carried out at a much lower price.

The press even opined that launching development schemes was "not a difficult task" and that Ebtehaj was wasting the people's money. But behind the non-professional technical and financial reproaches lay the real political bone of contention: Ebtehaj's Plan Organization wielded more economic and financial power than Eqbal's government. It was more established and recognized by the financial international community than Eqbal and even the Shah, and it had become a veritable "government more powerful than the government".[14]

A major source of jealousy among Iranian high officials was Ebtehaj's privileged financial status. It was rumored that Ebtehaj and Abdollah Entezam, the director general of the National Iranian Oil Company received

11 FRUS, 1955–1957, Near East Region; Iran; Iraq, vol. XII, Doc. 399.
12 *Khandaniha*, 14 Ordibehesht, 1336.
13 *Khandaniha*, 21 Ordibehesht 1336.
14 *Khandaniha*, 4, 15, 29 Tir 1336. Information in the two previous paragraphs is based on these sources.

the highest salary of any government employee. Each were said to receive the staggering salary of 15,000 tomans ($2,000) per month in 1957.[15]

HARD ECONOMIC DECISIONS

In July 1957, Eqbal faced a 600 million toman budget deficit.[16] Even though he benefited from an increase in oil revenues and tax receipts, the deficit proved daunting in the absence of forthcoming US aid. To overcome the deficit, Eqbal tried to increase his government's share of revenues at the Plan Organization's expense. Eqbal also tried to nibble away at profitable factories, such as sugar, under the control of the Plan Organization by placing them under a ministry.

The estrangement and rift between Eqbal and Ebtehaj became public knowledge in July 1957. The press wrote about Eqbal's decision to resign if Ebtehaj was not removed. A group of parliamentarians was said to have met with the Shah, demanding Ebtehaj's dismissal.[17] Even when Ebtehaj's three-year term as the director general of Plan Organization came to an end in September 1957, and a window of opportunity opened for Eqbal to remove him from power, the Shah continued to support Ebtehaj.

The Plan Organization argued that oil money was Iran's capital and should be invested rather than spent in the non-developmental current budget. Instead of reducing developmental funds to finance the budget deficit, the Plan Organization suggested savings in the government's current budget, a rise in taxes, and their efficient collection to raise government revenue. When Gholamreza Moqadam, one of the stars at the Division of Economic Affairs, presented the detailed figures of how proper taxation of contractors and industrialists could help solve the government's deficit, Eqbal's response was acerbic: either you become Minister of Finance and do it yourself or "keep quiet".[18]

Neither the Prime Minister nor his Minister of Finance were interested in changing their traditional and bureaucratic method of going about business by maintaining the status quo, using up oil money for current

15 *Sepid o Siyah*, 4 Bahman 1336.
16 *Khandaniha*, 15 Tir 1336.
17 *Khandaniha*, 25, 29 Tir 1336.
18 Gholamreza Moghadam, Iranian Oral History Collection, Harvard University, Transcript 1, Sequence 10, 11.

expenditures, and avoiding hard decisions. Ebtehaj's professional team at the Plan Organization represented the opposite. This young blood had returned home from the West and had entered the civil service to change and modernize decision-making based on established economic criteria.

Eqbal considered the Plan Organization as a bothersome rival, the young members of which, under the protective shield of Ebtehaj, argued back with facts and figures, operated only by the book, and did not unquestioningly defer to the economic opinions of their elders. Eqbal's most crucial problem with the Plan Organization was that it maintained a firm grip over drawing up, executing, and supervising national development projects. He was, therefore, determined to curtail the operational power of the Plan Organization by forcing it to relegate all its executive responsibilities and functions, as well as the profit-making factories and organizations under its purview, to appropriate government ministries.

Despite the pressure and criticism against the Plan Organization and its hiring of foreign experts, Ebtehaj got his way with the Iranian legislature. On 14 January 1958, the joint Majles-Senate Commission approved the Plan Organization's request for a budget of $775,000 for the fiscal year 1958–1959, beginning on 21 March 1958, to hire foreign experts recruited from United Nations Organizations and the World Bank.[19] The order to approve Ebtehaj's controversial request must have come from the Shah. Having been reassured of the Shah's continuing support, Ebtehaj strongly objected to Eqbal's plan to gut the enterprises under the Plan Organization's control and threatened to resign in late February 1958.[20]

VICIOUS CYCLE OF BALANCING BUDGETS 1958–1959 AND 1959–1960

The problems with the 1957–1958 budget deficit dragged on to the March 1958–1959 budget and intensified as the government intended to raise government salaries. To relieve pressure on the Iranian government's economic and budgetary problems in the fiscal year of 1958, Iran's Foreign and Finance Ministers traveled to Washington. They met with prominent American officials on 26 September 1957.

19 *Ettela'at*, 25 Day 1336.
20 *Khandaniha*, 10 Esfand 1336.

Aliqoli Ardalan, Iran's foreign minister, informed the Americans that the average salary of government workers in Iran was 4,000 rials (400 tomans), equivalent to some $52 per month, and that anything below that bordered on poverty. He added that "70% of Iranian family income was below this figure". Ardalan warned the American administration of the "serious social and political problems" facing Iran. The price tag for the increase in salaries planned was some 6 billion rials (600 million tomans).

Ardalan added that Iran's 1957–1958 budget was 21 billion rials (2.1 billion tomans), and the military budget constituted 45% of this sum. To enable the Iranian government to finance the 6 billion rials, Ardalan asked the US to help with Iran's military budget so that funds could be released to increase government salaries. The response of the Secretary of State, John Foster Dulles, was not favorable. He told the Iranian mission that Iran should do more in collecting taxes and that the problem was Iran's "excessive defense burden".[21]

The Iranian budget problem of 1958–1959 was closely tied to the inflexible and high military expenditures for that year, the need to increase salaries of government employees, and the Shah's emphasis that the US, as Iran's military ally, should help bill some of the military expenditures. So, in November 1957, the Shah requested the US government for a $50 million loan for budgetary support and threatened that if the US did not provide it, he would have to accept Soviet assistance.[22] Throughout 1957, the Shah insisted on more military aid.[23]

The US responded negatively to the Shah's insistence on increased military aid. On 10 December 1957, Dulles wrote to Selden Chapin, the US Ambassador in Iran, and enumerated the reasons why further assistance was not forthcoming.[24] According to Chapin's report of 29 May 1958 to the US Department of State, the "Shah's military ambitions, and his preoccupation with large modern military establishment pose a major problem for not only economic but also political health of [the] country".

21 Foreign Relations of the United States, 1955–1957, Near East Region; Iran; Iraq, Volume XII, Document 408.

22 Foreign Relations of the United States, 1955–1957, Near East Region; Iran; Iraq, Volume XII, Document 412.

23 Foreign Relations of the United States, 1955–1957, Near East Region; Iran; Iraq, Volume XII, Document 409.

24 Foreign Relations of the United States, 1955–1957, Near East Region; Iran; Iraq, Volume XII, Document 413.

Chapin warned that the Shah should not be led to believe that the US would "underwrite an increasing part of the Plan Organization's program", allowing him to use Iran's foreign exchange "for other purposes". He finally emphasized the necessity of clearly informing the Shah that the US would neither assist him in significantly enlarging his army nor provide him with economic assistance above its prior commitments.[25]

In late January 1958, the Iranian press reported that for the financial year March 1958 to March 1959, Iran faced a budget deficit of some 1,100 to 1,300 million tomans.[26] The lion's share of the deficit was attributed to a 300 million toman increase in the army's budget, a 100 million toman increase in Iran's gendarmerie budget aimed at increasing salaries, and another roughly 250 million tomans to increase government salaries. The Iranian press speculated that American military aid would enable funds earmarked for increased military expenditures to relieve the deficit somewhat.[27]

Fixing the ledger was not simple. Increasing revenues from direct taxation, especially from the rich, was doomed. The large landowners, merchants, capitalists, and contractors who were benefiting from the construction and development boom in the country were all so well connected that their taxes hardly came to more than that of grocers, carpenters, and petty shopkeepers. It was common knowledge that members of the parliament, ministers, and courtiers owned some of the biggest contracting companies, and were shareholders in major companies and banks, and therefore benefited from an iron-clad political protective shield.[28]

As Ebtehaj, Abdollah Entezam, the director general of the Iranian National Oil Company, Eqbal, and Ali-Asghar Naser, the Minister of Finance, were haggling over the budget deficit, the Shah summoned the senators. The subject of this rather unexpected meeting, on 11 February 1958, was directly related to the budget deficit and its leading cause, the military budget.

The Shah's address focused on the importance of Iran's military might in the region. He argued that membership in the Baghdad Pact did not imply that "our friends" would pay for our military expenditures. The Shah

25 Foreign Relations of the United States, 1958–1960, Near East Region; Iraq; Iran; Arabian Peninsula, Volume XII, Document 235.

26 *Ettela'at*, 3,7 Bahman 1336, 1 Esfand 1336. *Khandaniha*, 19 Bahman 1336.

27 *Khandaniha*, 8 Bahman 1336, *Ettela'at*, 16 Day 1336, 7 Bahman 1336.

28 *Khandaniha*, 22 Bahman 1336.

relayed US apprehensions about financing Iran's budget deficit, and said that, "our friends" ask whether Iranian taxpayers have fully complied with their obligation before we consider further assistance.

The Shah minimized Iran's military expenditures and claimed that only "17 percent of the country's income was spent on defense". He effectively argued that the military budget was not negotiable, and he called for more strict means of collecting taxes. The Shah threatened those finding loopholes and shirking their responsibility to pay taxes with grave punishments such as imprisonment.[29]

Faced with the Shah's insistence on increasing the military budget, there was no magical way to balance the budget. All that could be done was to reallocate investment money to current expenditures. The bulk of the gap was painfully filled by transferring funds from oil revenues, initially earmarked for the Plan Organization and developmental expenditures.

On 20 February 1958, it was announced that the Plan Organization's share of oil revenues, targeted initially at 80% for 1958–1959, was slashed to 60%. The National Iranian Oil Company allocated some of its own funds intended for investment and infrastructural development of the oil industry to fill the deficit. In a last-ditch attempt to reduce the budget deficit, $23 million of the $150 million loan from the Export–Import Bank earmarked for the Agricultural Bank was rechanneled to the government's current budget.[30]

Amid the budget debate, Eqbal hoped to chip away at the Plan Organization and change the balance of power between the government and the Plan Organization. Even though he tried to transfer the profit-making sugar factories of the Plan Organization at Marvdasht, Shazand, Rezaiyeh, and Shahabad to the Ministry of Monopolies and Customs, which would have added some extra 60 million tomans to the government's budget, he failed to do so.[31] The sugar factories remained under the control of the Plan Organization, which had to pay 60 million tomans to the government. After much juggling and jostling, on 25 February 1958, Eqbal presented the budget with an official 140 million toman deficit to the Majles.[32]

---

29 *Ettela'at*, 22 Bahman 1336.
30 *Ettela'at*, 16, 24 Bahman 1336, 1 Esfand 1336.
31 *Ettela'at*, 3 Esfand 1336.
32 *Ettela'at*, 6 Esfand 1336.

The US did come to Iran's help. For the US fiscal year 1958, the American government had initially earmarked a total of $84,120,000 for Iran under the rubric of the Total Mutual Security Program. This included military and economic assistance. However, by June 1958, the US had increased its assistance for 1958 to $105,108,000. For the fiscal year 1959, the US planned to reduce its Total Mutual Security Program to $85,965,000, and Iran was forced into a most challenging economic situation.[33]

FALLOUT OF THE 1958–1959 BUDGET

Once the Majles had ratified the 1958–1959 budget, Ebtehaj reacted to the 20% reduction of the Plan Organization's share of oil revenues. On 3 March 1958, he announced that, "It would be difficult for the Plan Organization to carry out its developmental and construction responsibilities according to the law."[34] The Iranian press warned of the dramatic consequences of the government's policies. Mehdi Bahrehmand, the economics editor of *Ettela'at*, wrote, "If the present monetary policy continues, within a few years, developmental programs will vanish, and the budget's deep purse will swallow all oil revenues." Channeling investment funds into current expenditure, Bahrehmand argued, was inflationary and would set in motion a vicious circle of higher prices and future budget deficits, disrupting the economy.[35]

On 19 March 1958, the debate on the budget deficit reached a new height in the Senate. In a fiery speech, Jamal Emami, a prominent senior senator known for his bluntness, criticized the size of the 1.2 billion toman military budget and announced that it was "unsuitable for the military budget to constitute 50 percent of the total budget". Eqbal's reaction was predictable. In a somewhat unconvincing defense, he corrected Jamal Emami by pointing out that the 50% figure referred to the budget of the army, police, and gendarmerie and not the army alone.

Eqbal then formulated a counterattack, which became a standard argument to silence all questioning of the size of the military budget. He insinuated that Emami was unpatriotic, if not treasonous, and spoke

33 Foreign Relations of the United States, 1958–1960, Near East Region; Iraq; Iran; Arabian Peninsula, Volume XII, document 237.

34 *Ettela'at*, 12 Esfand 1336.

35 *Ettela'at*, 5 Esfand 1336. Bahrehmand signed his articles as M.B.

about "those treacherous elements that first attacked and weakened the army and then tried to destabilize the country". Eqbal indulged his King, apologized for the military budget being less than what it should be, and added emotionally and incoherently that, "without the army, there would be no living people (*hich mellat-e zendehi*) in the world."[36] Debate in the legislature over the military budget was quickly becoming a taboo.

Discerning the insensitivity of the Eqbal government to the importance of developmental expenditures and the Shah's prioritizing of military expenditures, Ebtehaj went on the offensive to put economic development back on the national agenda. On 18 July 1958, Ebtehaj delivered a ninety-minute speech in English at the Iran–America Cultural Society. Speaking to Iran's economic and political elite, Ebtehaj laid out the tangible problems of getting development underway. He emphasized the importance of detailed studies to determine developmental priorities and identify the most productive projects, given the country's paucity of financial and human resources.

As if responding to 'Enayat's critical article on the Karaj Dam, Ebtehaj detailed the grave infrastructural problems in the country when it came to building a dam. Roads and electrical power plants had to be constructed, and cement and various inputs had to be made available, transported, and safely stored. The staff working on the dam had to be provided with housing, medical, educational, and hygienic facilities. He defended using foreign consultants because of their expertise and know-how, as well as the pioneering role of government in launching mother industries, which was too costly for the private sector.

To highlight the importance of Plan Organization activities for the country, Ebtehaj provided a detailed report of its activities and concluded that "contrary to the erroneous arguments that are heard once in a while", with a 9% rate of growth of the gross domestic product in 1957 as compared to 1956, "Iran was moving towards a sound and speedy economic progress."[37] At this time however, Ebtehaj's detractors were hard at work. On 23 August 1958, the Iranian press reported on anti-Ebtehaj leaflets distributed in the Majles and the Senate.[38]

By late 1958, Ebtehaj faced another challenge to the finances of the Plan Organization. The substantial budget deficit for March 1959 to March 1960,

36 *Ettela'at*, 28 Esfand 1336.

37 *Tehran Economist*, 11 Mordad 1337.

38 *Tehran Economist*, 1 Shahrivar 1337.

rooted, once again, in the increased military budget, worried and embittered him. Disappointed with the orientation of national priorities, in December 1958, Ebtehaj confided in Eugene Black, President of the World Bank. He told Black that the Shah was again trying to divert oil revenues to the general budget and "that Iran's financial difficulties were a result of the United States military's pressing upon the Shah armed forces in excess of Iran's needs".[39]

Ebtehaj, however, knew that it was the Shah who was constantly pushing for higher military expenditures. For Ebtehaj and his team at the Plan Organization, money spent on military projects was funding misspent and wasted.[40] At this point, by blaming the US military, Ebtehaj was using Black to convey to the US administration and military establishment his disapproval of oil money being taken out of developmental expenditures and put into military expenditures. Ebtehaj was naively hoping that, somehow, the US would convince the Shah to reconsider his priorities.

The prospect of transferring development funds to current and military expenditures frustrated Ebtehaj. It must have been around December 1958 that Khodadad Farmanfarmayan went to see Ebtehaj. He pointed out that while expenditures by the Plan Organization during the Second Plan were limited to 8.7 billion tomans, Ebtehaj had committed to 10.3 billion tomans. An edgy Ebtehaj thumped his fist on the table and retorted, "When are you going to understand that if I don't commit those funds, the government will take away those funds and misspend it on military projects."[41]

EBTEHAJ'S SHIFT IN FORTUNES: THE 1959–1960 BUDGET

From early February 1959, the political tides turned against Ebtehaj. Shifts in the fortunes of influential political figures in Iran were always prompted by the Shah. A united front composed of a few ministers, such as Ja'far Sharif-Emami, the Minister of Industry and Mines, a few MPs, and a

39 FRUS, 1958–1960, Near East Region, Iraq; Iran; Arabian Peninsula, vol. XII, Document 259.

40 Khodadad Farmanfarmayan, Iranian Oral History Collection, Harvard University, Transcript 3, Sequence 30.

41 Khodadad Farmanfarmaian, Iranian Oral History Collection, Harvard University, Transcript 3, Sequence 30.

handful of newspapers, began once again attacking Ebtehaj, his management of the Plan Organization, and the substantial budget deficit for the year beginning in March 1959 and ending in March 1960.[42]

According to British and American diplomatic sources, the budget deficit for 1959–1960 was $107 million, $65 million (60%) of which was due to the Ministry of Defense's expenditures over and above the original estimates.[43] From January 1959 the press reported on the possibility of a $20 million reduction in the Plan Organization's budget for the fiscal year March 1959 to March 1960. This reduction was to go towards the government's budget deficit.

A representative of the International Bank for Reconstruction and Development (World Bank) flew to Iran to warn against decreasing development funds in favor of current expenditures. On 15 January 1959, four days before a decision was to be made on reducing Plan Organization funds at the High Economic Council, Ebtehaj tried to force the Shah's hand by announcing that "the Shah's commitment to the progress of developmental projects in the country is such that he would not permit the reduction of such funds."[44]

Talk of further reducing the Plan Organization's funds was getting Ebtehaj hot under the collar. At the High Economic Council meeting presided over by Shah on 19 January 1959, no official decision was reached on the fate of the Plan Organization's budget for the fiscal year 1959–1960. The Shah's waning support for the role of the Plan Organization in Iran's development and the ambiguity over the Organization's future financial stature was becoming ever more manifest. In the eyes of the Shah, the stars and fortunes of Eqbal and Sharif-Emami were rising, while Ebtehaj was losing his luster.

The Ominous Outburst

On 7 February 1959, George McGhee, President Eisenhower's special envoy, and Admiral Arthur Radford, the Joint Chiefs of Staff ex-chairman, arrived in Tehran. Radford was a seasoned, highly decorated and tough naval commander known for his hawkish military views. President Eisenhower sent this team on a fact-finding mission to study Iran's economic

42 *Khandaniha*, 14 Bahman 1337.
43 FO 371/140825. EP 1112/2.
44 *Ettela'at*, 25 Day 1337.

development and military requirements and assess US assistance in these fields. The mission met with the Shah, Eqbal, and Ebtehaj.

Concurrent with the arrival of Eisenhower's envoys, Eqbal met with the Shah on 7 February 1959 to discuss the government's 300 million toman budget deficit after all economies were made. After this meeting, it was reported that, "more oil revenues would be allocated to reduce the budget deficit." The press did not get into the details, but it was apparent that the Plan Organization's 1959–1960 budget would again be reduced to finance the budget deficit, again due to the augmented military budget.[45]

On 9 February 1959, amid speculation about further cuts in the Plan Organization's budget, Ebtehaj, Farmanfarmayan, Hansen, and Moqadam met with Admiral Radford, George McGhee, and Kenneth Iverson. Having heard Radford's comments on Iran's military needs, Ebtehaj lost his temper, banged his fist on the table, and said, "Admiral Radford, Iran needs economic development, not military power." He angrily stressed that a strong economy with rising living standards would be the real defender of the country and not military might. Admiral Radford's face turned red as Ebtehaj lectured him on Iran's national priorities.[46]

One day before leaving Iran on 11 February, Eisenhower's envoys met with the Shah for two hours. An important topic in their discussions revolved around the military budget. It can be surmised that the issue of increasing Iran's standing army of 160,000 to 200,000 and improving military hardware and its impact on Iran's developmental projects were discussed. The night before their departure, Admiral Radford and George McGhee met with Ebtehaj at the American Officers Club for some five hours.[47]

OUSTING EBTEHAJ TO SERENELY FUNNEL OIL REVENUES

On 12 February 1959, the Prime Minister personally attended the Nineteenth Majles and introduced an urgent bill called "Granting

45 *Ettela'at*, 20 Bahman 1337.

46 Khodadad Farmanfarmayan, Iranian Oral History Collection, Harvard University, Transcript 4, Sequence 44. The correct date of this meeting is 20 Bahman 1337 or 9 February 1959. See *Ettela'at*, 21 Bahman 1337. For a somewhat similar version of this meeting see: Interview with Manuchehr Gudarzi, Foundation for Iranian Studies, p. 36.

47 *Ettela'at*, 22 Bahman 1337.

responsibility of executing the Second Seven-Year Plan to the Prime Minister". Eqbal posited that to avoid overlaps in executing development projects and to centralize affairs, the Plan Organization should become a technical consulting bureau (*daftar-e fani*), and all its responsibilities should be transferred to the prime minister. He argued that to dispense with its responsibilities properly, the government needed to bring the Plan Organization under its direct authority. Eqbal emphasized that it was his prerogative to determine the director general of the Plan Organization and insisted that the Majles vote on the matter immediately.

Faced with a lightning assault by Eqbal, most of his ministers and members of the parliament were taken off guard. The loyal opposition in parliament argued that the bill aimed to replace Ebtehaj with the Prime Minister. Members of Asadollah 'Alam's *Hezb-e Mardom* (Peoples Party) in the Majles left the floor in protest before a vote was taken on the immediate urgency of putting the bill to the vote. Eventually, on 13 February, after a few speeches for and against, a highly agitated Majles voted in favor of Eqbal's bill by standing up.[48]

Two days after the Plan Organization was placed under the tutelage of Eqbal (14 February 1959), it was officially announced that its 1959–1960 budget would be cut by $22 million. Instead of $152 million from oil revenues, the Plan Organization was promised some $130 million, with the difference going to the budget deficit.[49] The Shah–Eqbal coup against Ebtehaj had cost the country $22 million in development projects, which were rerouted to the current and military budget. Also, the budget of the National Iranian Oil Company was halved, putting its expansion and infrastructural programs on hold.

The consequences of cutting back the Plan Organization budget were manifold. In the cultural domain, numerous construction projects were put on hold. Among frozen construction projects were: three hospitals attached to the universities of Esfahan, Shiraz, and Mashhad; thirty technical workshops in schools; three vocational schools in Sanandaj, Rasht, and Zahedan; three technical schools at Yazd, Ahvaz, and Qazvin; four agricultural technical schools; six practical agricultural schools; and the technical school and hydraulic workshops at Ahvaz University. Finally,

48 *Ruznameh-e Rasmi-ye Keshvar Shahanshahi-ye Iran*, 30 Bahman 1337, Mozakerat-e Majles-e Showray-e Melli, 23 Bahman 1337, neshast-e 271; *Ettela'at*, 23, 25 Bahman 1337.

49 *Ettela'at*, 13, 26 Bahman 1337.

there was the suspension of construction and purchase of equipment for rural schools.[50]

As for provincial development, 144 projects were frozen, including asphalting provincial roads. These cutbacks were due to slashing the Plan Organization's social expenditure budget by 300 million tomans.[51] During the fall and winter of 1960, the press was regularly reporting on the budgetary shortcomings of the Plan Organization and its inability to complete the developmental projects of the Second Seven-Year Plan.[52]

The Shah–Eqbal move was aimed at pushing Ebtehaj out of power, breaking the technocratic power and pride of the Plan Organization, ending its independence of thought, initiative, action, and policies, and placing it under a compliant leadership, thus converting the Plan Organization into a timid government bureaucracy. However, most importantly, with Ebtehaj out of the way, the Shah could allocate the sums he believed necessary to the military budget without any debate or resistance.

The Shah intended to replace the obstinate Ebtehaj with techno-bureaucrats who would serve him without questions asked. Rumors circulated that most of the Plan Organization's responsibilities would be transferred to Sharif-Emami's Ministry of Industry and Mines.[53] Around noon of Thursday 12 February, once Ebtehaj was informed of Eqbal's machinations in the Majles, he resigned immediately, and the news of his resignation made headlines on Saturday 14 February 1959.

After four years and a few months, Ebtehaj, the "bête noire", was pushed out of the Plan Organization. He knew that without the Shah's consent no power in the land could have handed over the Plan Organization to another. Ja'far Sharif-Emami recalled Eqbal informing him that the Shah had instructed him to "take away his [Ebtehaj's] responsibilities and duties".[54] The Plan Organization was thus deprived of an honest and veritable technocrat.

In his editorial of 14 February 1959, Abbas Mas'udi, the owner of *Ettela'at*, who had been critical of Ebtehaj in the past, came to his defense. At the time, this was a courageous act since it was evident that the Shah

50 *Ettela'at*, 21 Farvardin 1338.
51 *Ettela'at*, 21 Esfand 1338.
52 *Ettela'at*, 1, 2 Aban 1339.
53 *Ettela'at*, 25 Bahman 1337
54 J. Sharif-Emami, Iranian Oral History Collection, Harvard University, Transcript 7, Sequence 157).

wanted Ebtehaj out. Mas'udi opined that Ebtehaj was paying for his honesty, no-nonsense attitude, aggressiveness, and stubbornness. These characteristics, Mas'udi argued, had made him many enemies, whose illicit interests and arbitrary transactions had been forcefully curtailed by Ebtehaj. Mas'udi suggested that Eqbal should let Ebtehaj do the great job that he had been doing and hoped that the country would have many more like him.[55]

On 2 March 1959, Ebtehaj's deputy, Khosrow Hedayat, replaced him as Minister Without Portfolio and deputy prime minister in charge of the Plan Organization. Safi Asfia became Hedayat's deputy. Hedayat was a well-respected figure with different skill sets from Ebtehaj. He was a diplomat, adept in the art of public relations, and endowed with the political skill necessary to navigate the rough Iranian political scene safely.

Hedayat was loyal to Ebtehaj's line of economic thought and the Plan Organization's independence. With Ebtehaj's departure, however, members of the Plan Organization knew that a critical page had been turned in their history and that they had lost their special status, autonomy, privileges, and protective shield. They had effectively been orphaned, and many thought of resigning. The Hedayat period became one of "quiet", and "healing of wounds".[56]

On 28 May 1959, the World Bank announced the extension of a $72 million loan to Iran. Three months after his departure, the loan that Ebtehaj had long negotiated was at hand. This was the largest loan extended by the World Bank to any country for the purpose of extensive road construction and reconstruction. Of Iran's 25,000 kilometers of roads, only a small portion were paved and fit for motor vehicles. This loan was to be spent on constructing 2,000 kilometers of asphalted roads.[57]

Yet the Plan Organization had been enfeebled. On 21 February 1960, a year after Ebtehaj's forced resignation, it was announced that the share of Plan Organization funding from oil revenues in the Second Seven-Year Plan, which ended in 1961, was to be cut by $280 million. This shortfall in the Plan Organization's budget deferred some projects, put some on

55 *Ettela'at,* 25 Bahman 1337

56 Khodadad Farmanfarmayan, Iranian Oral History Collection, Harvard University, Transcript 4, Sequence 46.

57 International Bank for Reconstruction and Development, Press Release No. 588, $72 Million Loan to Iran, May 29, 1959, https://documents1.worldbank.org/curated/en/484061590042881375/pdf/Announcement-of-Seventy-Two-Million-Dollars-Loan-to-Iran-on-May-29-1959.pdf (retrieved 13/2/2023); *Ettela'at,* 8, 10 Khordad 1338.

hold, and forced the Plan Organization to borrow money internationally to finish the more pressing projects.[58]

The post-1953 Iranian political system sometimes tolerated personalities such as Ebtehaj, whose economic objectives and priorities differed from the Shah's. As time passed and the Shah's position hardened, accommodating incongruent political and economic players became difficult. After Amini's departure in 1962, squares could no longer fit into the Shah's circular political system, inhibiting dissenting views, numerous voices, negotiation, compromise, and adaptation. The economic priorities and policies defined by the Shah thus lost their ability to be analyzed, revised, and improved. Gradually, the economic realm became ossified and inflexible, just like the political realm.

A partial cause of Ebtehaj's demise was his inflexible, undiplomatic, and brisk demeanor. But the main reason was his independent-mindedness, and his unwillingness to sacrifice what he believed was in the national interest for political expediency. His technocratic professionalism became an obstacle in the Shah's quest to impose absolute authority and legitimacy in the economic realm.

58 *Ettela'at*, 1 Esfand 1338.

7

The Special Revaluation Fund: Forging Economic Take-Off (1957–1962)

W.W. Rostow's famous economic take-off stage, which supposedly propelled underdeveloped countries into the orbit of "sustained" development, necessitated a stimulus of some form. This economic stimulus in Iran came from the government channeling domestic and foreign loanable funds to a wide range of manufacturing enterprises.

The economic and financial events of 1957 and 1958 triggered an unprecedented industrial transformation in the country with far-reaching consequences. The government intervened in the economy and distributed the equivalent of some $94 million in loans to specific industrialists at low interest rates. This was an attempt to industrialize and modernize the economy, to generate employment and income. Jump-starting industrialization by the private sector came in tandem with attracting foreign investment, banking, expertise, and economic participation.

On 12 May 1957, the Majles approved a bill called Stabilizing the Exchange Rates (*Tasbit-e nerkh-e arz*).[1] Six days later, under pressure from Eqbal who threatened that he had discussed the issue with the Shah and that he would resign unless the senators voted in favor of the immediate consideration of the bill, the Senate, Iran's upper house, ratified the bill to re-value the price of Iran's gold reserves.[2] The preamble to the bill stated

1 *Ettela'at*, 22 Ordibehesht 1336.

2 *Ettela'at*, 25, 28 Ordibehesht 1336.

that, since Iran had become a member of the IMF and the organization recommended a single rather than multiple exchange rates, Iran was going to readjust its currency.

The government, therefore, increased the value of a dollar from its previous (27 December 1947) official rate of 32.2 rials (3.22 tomans) to its market rate of 75.5 rials (7.55 toman), thus revaluing the dollar and devaluing the rial.[3] The Eqbal government argued that this devaluation of the rial would release blocked-up funds and eventually help Iranian exports.

Within this bill, there was a clause revaluing the price of each gram of gold from 36.2 rials to 85.2 rials, thereby more than doubling the rial equivalent of gold reserves. The extra rials generated from this bookkeeping alteration were to be placed in a special account at the Melli Bank.[4] Based on a law passed on 24 July 1954, the reserve of the money in circulation in Iran was composed of gold (60%) and foreign exchange or the dollar (40%).[5]

The concurrent revaluation of both gold and the dollar reserves generated an excess of 7.6 billion rials (760 million tomans) or $94 million.[6] This considerable sum, accrued from the difference in the revised valuation, was put into the Special Revaluation Fund. This device made it possible to increase the money supply significantly.[7] The monies from the Special Revaluation Fund were earmarked to boost the private sector and foster robust Iranian capitalists. Three and a half years after the initial law, on 15 January 1958 the High Economic Council, in the presence of the Shah, sent a bill to the parliament earmarking 350 million tomans of the total Fund to agricultural projects.[8] In effect, however, the lion's share of this sum was spent on industrial loans.

Loans were allotted for projects other than those specified in the Second Seven-Year Plan and were therefore placed outside the reach of the Plan Organization. Loans to individual applicants could not exceed

3 This pegged exchange rate of 7.5 tomans to one US dollar remained constant from 1957 until 1973.
4 *Ettela'at*, 23 Ordibehesht 1336.
5 *Ferdowsi*, 31 Ordibehesht 1336.
6 *Ettela'at*, 29 Ordibehesht 1336.
7 International Bank for Reconstruction and Development, *Economic Situation and Prospects of Iran*, July 23, 1958, https://documents1.worldbank.org/curated/en/503761468050961050/pdf/multiopage.pdf (retrieved 22/1/2023); FO 371/140824, EP 1111/11.
8 *Ettela'at*, 24 Day 1336.

half the total cost of the project, and applicants were required to have 30% of the total cost at hand when applying. Once the project was approved, Bank Melli provided the loan to the recipients. Loans were at an interest rate of 4 to 6%, and foreign investors with Iranian partners could benefit from these credits.

The bylaws of the Special Revaluation Fund stipulated that the High Economic Council would be tasked with producing a five-year program for the country's developmental, industrial, and agricultural priorities and needs. This program was to be drawn up with the cooperation and coordination of the ministries of Industry and Mines, Commerce, and Agriculture, as well as the Melli Bank and the Plan Organization.

Based on this overall program, credit was to be gradually disbursed among applicants. Requests for credit had to be submitted to appropriate ministries with an initial project assessment outlay and the projected time for the completion of the project. All projects eligible for credit had to be then ratified by the High Economic Council, and it was the responsibility of this body to annually evaluate the activities of the recipients to determine whether the projects were on track or needed revisions.[9]

The High Economic Council, with the Shah at its head, was suddenly catapulted to the center stage of economic decisions, overshadowing the Plan Organization. Its composition and brief, which had long been under consideration, were finalized on 14 December 1955. It was mandated to centralize and coordinate economic policies. It comprised five ministers – finance, trade, agriculture, finance, and industry and mines, plus the director generals of the Melli/National Bank and the Plan Organization. The High Economic Council had a secretary general, proposed by members and approved and appointed by the Shah for five years. The government was tasked with obtaining the advice of this body on all matters pertaining to economic, agricultural, industrial, financial, fiscal, and monetary policies before making any decisions. The Council was presided over by the prime minister in the Shah's absence.[10]

The five-year program, within which credit was to be allocated to priority industries, never saw the light of day. This led to suspicion that the allocation of loans from the Special Revaluation Fund would be marred by influential economic and political players controlling the purse and

9 *Ettelaʿat*, 18, 19 Shahrivar 1336; *Tehran Economist*, 23 Shahrivar 1336.

10 *Tehran Economist*, 25 Azar 1334, 30 Azar 1336.

channeling funds to their own partners, allies, and friends. The absence of well-defined criteria and guidelines facilitated the peddling of influence instead of allocation based on merit, efficiency, and professionalism.

Only a month after the by-laws of the Special Revaluation Funds had been announced, the High Economic Council ratified the first loans.[11] Within the first fifteen months, Sharif-Emami announced that the value of loans requested and the loans extended exceeded the Special Revaluation Fund, and asked applicants to desist from applying.[12] The unusual speed at which loans were disbursed undermined the original idea that credit would be gradually allocated based upon established national priorities and careful consideration of well-prepared proposals by the appropriate ministries and subsequently the High Economic Council.

Ebtehaj believed that the Special Revaluation Fund had to be efficiently and fairly allocated based on merit and had to be removed from the hands of Iranian politicians, lest it vanish into a black hole of nepotism. He insisted on the importance of rigorous economic standards and equally severe technical and specialized guidance and supervision.[13]

By placing the Special Revaluation Fund outside the control of the Plan Organization, Ebtehaj worried that favoritism would lead to mismanagement and wasting this one-time opportunity. Ebtehaj believed that the Special Revaluation Fund should have been placed under the control and management of the professional, non-governmental, and partially foreign-owned Industrial and Mining Development Bank of Iran (IMDBI). Later, Sharif-Emami recalled that he and Eqbal colluded to ensure that the Special Revaluation Fund monies would go to ministries and not the Plan Organization.[14]

By March 1958, a commission composed of representatives of the Ministry of Industry and Mines, Ministry of Finance, Bank Melli, and the High Economic Council reviewed and approved the loans. Once the contracts were finalized, Bank Melli was given the authority to pay the loans. Later, the final say on the allocation of loans was passed on to the Ministry of Industries and Mines, headed by Sharif-Emami.

11 *Ettela'at*, 16 Mehr 1336.

12 *Ettela'at*, 8 Day 1337.

13 *Ettela'at*, 21 Day 1336. Ebtehaj, *Khaterate Abolhasan Ebtehaj*, vol.1, p. 427.

14 Jafar Shrif-Emami, Iranian Oral History Collection, Harvard University, Transcript 6, Sequence 137–138.

By 7 July 1959, 869 businesses had applied for loans, and the Ministry of Industries and Mines had ratified 234 loans worth 433 million tomans. Some twenty-six months after the Special Revaluation Fund was founded, only 27% of the applicants had received loans. Only 20.1 million tomans of the loans extended or 4.6% of the total sums disbursed were repaid.[15] By 20 March 1960, the Bank Melli had received 1,068 applicants for loans and approved 316, totaling 585 million tomans. Within some three years of the approval of the Special Revaluation Fund, the government had allotted 77% of all the monies in it.[16]

FORTUNATE BENEFICIARIES OF THE FUND

Most loans went to textiles, including cotton cloth and yarn, woolen yarn, knitwear, and jute. Twenty-two new textile mills benefited from the Special Revaluation Fund. It was hoped that such investments would render Iran self-sufficient in cloth. Other industries benefitting from the Special Revaluation Fund included building materials, such as cement, bricks, tiles, pipes, iron and steel castings, nails, plastic, tires, leather, paint, nuts, and bolts, and a variety of consumer goods, such as matches, vegetable oil, enamelware, aluminum utensils, heaters, batteries, laundry detergent powder, and refined sugar.[17]

Among those industrialists who benefited from this scheme were the owners of Azar yarn-weaving factory in Esfahan, Farahbakhsh textile factory in Tehran, the Lajevardis' Behshahr Vegetable Oil Company in Tehran and Behshahr, Esfahan Cement Corporation, Nakhkar yarn-weaving company in Tehran, Iran Paint Corporation in Tehran, Taqi Rasuliyan and Mohammad Taheri's Yazdbaf textile company in Yazd, Hasan Kuros' Chitsazi-ye Ray textile company in Tehran, the Arjomand brothers' Arj metal works and heater producing company in Tehran, Mohsen Azmayesh's Azmayesh factory producing metal works and home furniture in Tehran, Kahkeshan chinaware and tile company, Baran sugar refining

15 *Ettela'at*, 21 Tir 1338.
16 *Tehran Economist*, 24 Ordibehesht 1339.
17 International Bank for Reconstruction and Development, *Economic Situation and Prospects of Iran*, July 23, 1958, https://documents1.worldbank.org/curated/en/503761468050961050/pdf/multiopage.pdf (retrieved 22/1/2023); FO 371/140824, EP 1111/11; *Ettela'at*, 30 Day 1336.

company, Forugh textile company, Parbas window and door company, Taklis zinc company, Abbas Akhavan's Iran Nail Company, a pasteurized Milk Company in Khuzestan, Mission Corporation producing leather goods in Tehran, an ice-producing factory in Bandar Abbas, Lubel Corporation producing macaroni in Tehran, Shrimp Corporation in Khorramshahr, Senator Moayed Sabeti's Mashhad Sugar Company, Gholamreza Afghani's metal works company in Tehran, Mozafar Industrial company specializing in the production of rails, Abbas Aynehchian's Tehran Copper Smelting and Rolling company, Khorasan Commercial and Industrial Company specializing in cotton ginning, Sharq Cardboard Company, Hasan Khosrowshahi's Tolid Daru pharmaceutical corporation in Tehran, Gholamhoseyn Mas'ud's copper mining company in Esfahan, Behbahani brothers' metal works and home appliances General Mekanik Company in Tehran, Asadollah Fatahiyan's Galosh Company, Ali-Akbar Eqbal's ice-producing company in Fars, Vahdat's ice-producing factory in Esfahan, Heydarqoli Biglari's Central Heating Company, Jourabchi Brothers' Weaving company, Abounasr Azod's Ahvaz Sugar Refinery, Abdollah Moqadam and Habibollah Elqaniyan's Momtaz Weaving Company in Tehran, Habibollah Elqaniyan's aluminum company, Pars and America in Tehran, Morad Eriyeh's Tehran Manufacturing Factories comprised of Iran Tile and Chinaware Company, Tehran Plastic Company, and Tehran Industrial Wool weaving company, Davud Rajabi's Iran Machine Manufacturing Company, Mehdi Mirashrafi's Esfahan Wool Weaving Company, Abdolali Farmanfarmayan's petrochemical company, Naft-e Pars, Mohammad-Taqi Saravi's brick producing company in Amol.[18]

Ebtehaj believed that under the government's auspices, a substantial amount of the Special Revaluation Fund was loaned out to "people lacking the competence and qualification to undertake industrial projects". He accused the commission responsible for allocating credit under the presidency of the Minister of Industry and Mines, Ja'far Sharif-Emami, of illicit collusion. Ebtehaj argued that at the time, those who wanted to get a loan "knew which middlemen and fixers to approach, and what percentage to pay to whom to obtain their objective".[19]

18 This list is compiled on the bases of the following sources: *Ettela'at*, 2, 14, 16, 20 Aban 1336, 1 Esfand 1336, 15, 19 Bahman 1337, 6 Ordibehesht, 19 Tir 1340; *Khandaniha*, 25 Aban 1336; *Tehran Economist*, 17 Aban, 22 Azar 1337, 17 Day 1339.
19 Ebtehaj, *Khaterate Abolhasan Ebtehaj*, vol. 1, p. 428.

Sharif-Emami did play a significant role in distributing the Special Revaluation Fund.[20] The approximately 350–400 industrialists who were fortunate enough to eventually benefit from the bulk of this unique financial situation must have been well connected. Many Iranian industrialists who benefited from these loans thanked Sharif-Emami for his good office and help when their factories were finally inaugurated, mainly between 1960 and 1962.

The industrialists who received loans from the Special Revaluation Fund lauded its spectacular impact on the Iranian economy. Abunasr Azod, a Qajar Prince, a sugar tycoon, and the principal shareholder and managing director of the Ahvaz Sugar Refinery, was the recipient of a 13 million toman loan from the Special Revaluation Fund. His enterprise also benefited from the financial participation of the Pahlavi Foundation.[21] Azod, a founding member of the newly revived Iran Chamber of Industry and Mines, argued that the vital credit scheme initiated by the government redirected private capital from unproductive land speculation into fruitful investments, ushering in a modern industrialization spree in the country.[22]

The monies loaned out through the Special Revaluation Fund in 1957 created a symbiosis between the state, the Crown, and a privileged capitalist class. Selected industrialists not only received substantial loans but were also rewarded by obtaining an exemption from tariff and import duties over the import of the industrial machinery used in their factories. In February 1959, the Eqbal government exempted ninety-six factories, including some of those who had received loans from the Special Revaluation Fund, from paying taxes for five years.[23] Certain industrialists were clearly pampered and enriched, while others, without political connections, were sidelined.

Among the beneficiaries of exemptions from custom and import duties for the import of machinery and inputs were owners of Siman Iran, Siman Esfahan (Ali and Hoseyn Hamedaniyan), Siman Tehran (Ahmad Ebtehaj), Siman Shomal (Yazdi brothers and Qasem Barati and later Ahmad Ebtehaj), Khomein Mines, Nakhkar, Behshahr (Lajevardis), Pars Qou Industries (Hoseyn Ghassemiyeh and Amir-Hoseyn Amir Saleh), Yazdbaf

20 Jafar Sharif-Emami, Iranian Oral History Collection, Harvard University, Transcript 6, Sequence 137–138.

21 *Tehran Economist*, 6 Esfand 1339.

22 *Ettela'at*, 13 Esfand 1341.

23 *Ettela'at*, 21 Bahman 1337.

(Mohammad-Taqi Rasuliyan and Mohammad Taheri), Pelasco (Habib Elqaniyan), Don Baxter Laboratories in Iran, and Tehran Pharmaceutical Company.[24]

As the critics of the loan distribution and allocation process contested, "most of the credit and privileges went to influential businessmen in Tehran, and provincial businessmen were less able to benefit from this scheme."[25] As early as 9 August 1960, Ahmad Majidiyan, the deputy director of the Melli Bank lamented that certain industrialists were unwilling to repay their loan installments, and they might have spent the money for other purposes.[26]

Four years after the disbursement of the Special Revaluation Fund, in September 1962, Taher Ziai, the Minister of Industry and Mines, complimented the debtors of small and medium-sized industries for having repaid their debts on time and criticized the big industrialists for delays in their repayment due to their unsound business plans.[27] On 25 December 1965, or eight years after the disbursement of the Special Revaluation Funds, Sharif-Emami confided in his audience at the Central Bank of Iran that, "In 1957 some 360 million tomans were allocated to industry, yet unfortunately, they spent the money on other things ... but now the time of extending political loans and exerting pressure on the banks is over."[28]

Many years later, Hasan-Ali Mehran, the Governor of the Central Bank (1975–1977), contended that most of the Special Revaluation Fund projects were quickly ratified without attention to their economic feasibility and viability. Mehran believed that a considerable amount of the extended credits went into speculative transactions such as real estate.[29] It is not known how many of the recipients of the Special Revaluation Fund failed to repay their debts to the Melli Bank.

However, the positive consequences of disbursing the Special Revaluation Fund on domestic production of manufactured goods were undeniable. The sincere wish of the Shah to promote infant industries, especially in "certain consumer goods industries", and his support for home capitalists, played an essential role in the manufacturing revolution of the

24 *Ettela'at*, 7 Day 1336, 17 Bahman 1336.
25 *Ettela'at*, 18 Esfand 1341.
26 *Ettela'at*, 18 Mordad 1339.
27 *Ettela'at*, 20 Shahrivar 1341.
28 *Ettela'at*, 5 Day 1344.
29 Mehran, *Hadafha va Siyasathay-e Bank-e Markaziy-e Iran*, p. 33.

late 1950s and early 1960s. In May 1959, the Shah informed the British Prime Minister that although numerous firms were selling television sets in Iran, he would "give preference to any company which manufactured its sets inside Iran". He added that "such a company would have no import duties to pay and would be free of taxes for five years."[30]

CONSEQUENCES OF PRIVATE AND PUBLIC SECTOR INVESTMENTS

The state's hefty injection of capital into the private sector, and the Plan Organization's widespread infrastructural projects, added to the boom in joint and domestic banks, creating an unprecedented environment of business optimism and confidence. The Iranian economy experienced a short-lived period of boom and prosperity as the credits obtained were expended, factories were built, labor was hired, and national output, income, and demand increased.

Between March 1957 and March 1958, some 603 private companies were registered at Iran's Companies Registration Office, thirty-six of which were foreign.[31] The number of private companies registered between March 1958 and March 1959 jumped to 681.[32] The number of permits for the construction of factories and workshops issued by the government between March 1957 and March 1958 stood at 116, and this number jumped to 487 between March 1959 and 1960.[33] With the morose economic environment of March 1961 and March 1962, the trend reversed. The number of newly registered private companies plummeted to 405, and the number of bankrupt firms exceeded that of the three previous years.[34]

Within five years, "between 1955 and 1960, the number of manufacturing establishments rose from around 2,700 to 7,800, while the labor force employed increased from 124,600 to 158,800." Yet 80% of these establishments employed less than eleven employees, while only thirty-three employed more than 500.[35] By November 1960, 110 new factories,

30 FO 371/ 140853, EP 1432/1.

31 *Tehran Economist*, 4 Ordibehesht 1338.

32 *Tehran Economist*, 7 Khordad 1339.

33 *Tehran Economist*, 14 Khordad 1339.

34 *Ettela'at, 29 Esfand 1340*; *Tehran Economist*, 22 Ordibehesht 1341

35 FO 371/157626, EP 1102/45.

beneficiaries of loans from the Special Revaluation Fund, began operation, employing some 18,996 workers and 134 engineers.[36]

This surge in private business, producing intermediate and final consumer goods, both durable and non-durable, construction materials, and services, ranging from retail to banking, was unprecedented in Iran's economic history. Yet this economic upsurge must be understood, contextualized, and relativized in terms of the country's broader picture. According to British sources, by February 1960, of Iran's 20 million population, three-quarters or 15 million lived in "forty-thousand scattered villages" with inadequate communication and transportation and "enormous distances" to travel. Some 75% of the population was illiterate, and the estimated income per capita was $75.[37]

According to Iranian sources, however, in August 1960, Iran's income per capita was approximately $125. The rural population, constituting 67%, was estimated to have an income per capita of $51. The distribution of income among the urban population was highly stratified. The lower income categories, constituting some 60% of the urban population, earned between $356 and $712 per annum, with the majority in this category tending towards the lower bracket. The middle income bracket, making up 25% of the urban population, had an income per capita of $713 to $1,428, and the top 15% earned $1,429 and above.[38]

Boom Goes Bust Via Stabilization Program

The 1957–1960 boom, fueled by the distribution of the Special Revaluation Fund, overheated the economy. "An overexpansion of domestic credits to the private sector led to a demand-pull boom, rising inflation and the exhaustion of foreign exchange reserves to perilously low levels."[39] To control the adverse consequences of the boom, a stabilization program was introduced which in turn pushed the economy into a recession. In the

---

36 *Tehran Economist*, 5 Azar 1339.
37 FO 371/149818, EP 1731/2.
38 *Ettela'at*, 25 Mordad 1339. United Nation puts Iran's population in 1959 at 21 million. See Statistical Office of the United Nations, Department of Economic and Social Affairs. Demographic Year Book 1968, Twentieth Issue, United Nations, New York, 1969, https://unstats.un.org/unsd/demographic-social/products/dyb/dybsets/1968%20DYB.pdf (retrieved 27/4/2024).
39 J. Amuzegar, *The Dynamics of the Iranian Revolution: The Pahlavis' Triumph and Tragedy*, Albany: State University of New York Press, 1991, p. 174.

middle of the recession, new factories opened, much-needed infrastructure became available, and output expanded.

In August and September 1959, high-ranking members of the International Bank for Reconstruction and Development (World Bank) gathered in Tehran to help the Iranian government develop a stabilization program to balance its budget and avoid using development funds for current expenditures.[40] The World Bank gently warned the Eqbal government that loans were contingent upon a balanced budget and controlled inflation rates.

It was not until 26 October 1959 that the contours of the stabilization program became public. Hasan-Ali Mansur, the Prime Minister's economic deputy and chair of the High Economic Council, announced major contractionary fiscal and monetary policies. The government vowed to decrease purchasing power (*qoveh kharid*) by reducing aggregate demand (*taqazay-e koli*) and implementing contractionary monetary policies. It proposed balancing the budget by cutting government expenditures, increasing revenues by more rigorous taxing, curtailing credit expansion, imposing controls on loans by newly created private banks, increasing interest rates, and selling government bonds.

Mansur referred to a two-year inflationary pressure building up in the country due to expansionary fiscal and monetary policies and the need to bring it under control. He acknowledged that the consumer price index stood at 109 in 1956, increased to 114 in 1957, and again jumped to 141 in 1958, indicating an inflation rate of 32% since 1956. Mansur was in no position to mention that the economic imbalances and problems of mid-1959 were caused by the Eqbal government's mismanagement and the High Economic Council's decisions that he headed and the Shah presided over.[41]

On the bright side, by the time Ali Amini became prime minister in May 1961, the much-criticized investments undertaken by Ebtehaj and the Plan Organization at the time were coming to fruition, one by one. On 25 October 1961, one day before his birthday, the Shah, accompanied by the Queen, Amini, Safi Asfia, the director general of the Plan Organization, and a large contingency of political, military, and diplomatic dignitaries inaugurated the Karaj Dam. Karaj was the first of three Plan Organization dams to reach the finishing line.

---

40 *Ettela'at*, 28 Mordad 1338.

41 *Ettela'at*, 3, 4 Aban 1338.

The contract for constructing the Karaj Dam had been signed with the US firm Morrison-Knudsen Company on 21 October 1957. Its design had been contracted to the US Harza Engineering Company, a world leader in dam, power plant, and irrigation systems engineering. Both the foreign designers and constructors were placed under the supervision and authority of the Karaj Water and Electricity Organization.

The Karaj curved and concrete dam was 180 meters high from the base. It was located 23 kilometers from Karaj on the way to Chalus. The 792,000 cubic meters of concrete used in the dam came from Ahmad-Ali Ebtehaj's Tehran Cement Company. The dam's turbines were British, and its electric generators were Japanese. Some 100 foreign experts supervised its construction, and approximately 3,000 Iranian workers, engineers, technical experts, and staff worked daily on the site. The Plan Organization bore the brunt of the project's total cost of some 450 million tomans. The dam's primary purpose was to provide electricity and potable water for Tehran.[42]

A STROLL THROUGH NEWLY BORN PRIVATE INDUSTRIES

Accompanied by his prime ministers, the Shah customarily broke ground of new and important firms, inaugurated new factories, and cut ribbons. From 1961, however, he was traveling far and wide in Iran, inaugurating the nascent industries of the Special Revaluation Fund. The Shah's visits to the new factories, systematically reported in the press, bestowed status and prestige on the owners. They also amounted to considerable political and economic collateral for the lucky industrialist's future dealings with ministries, government organizations, and banks.

As factories began producing intermediary and final consumer goods, the Shah took pride in the country's gradual industrialization process. In 1961, the Shah inaugurated one plant after another. He demonstrated his interest and satisfaction by carefully inspecting the new plants, observing their production process, examining their output, posing questions, and talking with their owners, engineers, and workers. The visited factories produced a range of goods from blankets, biscuits, metal furniture, plastic

42 *Ettela'at*, 3 Aban 1340. The information in the last two paragraphs is based on this source.

pipes for agricultural irrigation, plastic tablecloths, and heaters to pharmaceutical goods. They were all beneficiaries of the Special Revaluation Fund.

The Shah's Agenda of Factory Visits

On 3 January 1961, the Shah, accompanied by Ja'far Sharif-Emami, prime minister since August 1960, and members of his cabinet, inaugurated *Sherkat Bafandeghi-ye Momtaz* (Momtaz Weaving Company), one of Iran's three biggest weaving and textile factories. The Momtaz plant was located on Shahr-e Ray Road and cost about 120 million tomans, of which the cost of machinery and installation was 83 million tomans. It operated with 40,000 spinning machines and 1,029 weaving machines. The factory employed 2,158 workers, of whom 112 were women, and had a technical and office staff of 85. The employees were said to have been insured and benefited from the free services of a doctor and an aide who were present at the factory dispensary.

Abdollah Moqadam, who gave a long report and praised the Shah for "wise guidance", was one of the company's main shareholders. He was a prominent merchant from Qazvin, who had turned industrialist. Among Moqadam's principal partners at Momtaz were the two Elqaniyans, Habibollah and Davud. Abdollah Moqadam and the Elqaniyan brothers were also founders and partners in Iran's first vegetable shortening (solid vegetable oil), called Gol.[43] Momtaz was one of the beneficiaries of credit from the Special Revaluation Fund and had also obtained loans from the Melli Bank and the IMDBI.[44]

A week later, on 10 January 1961, the Shah, accompanied by Sharif-Emami and a few ministers, inaugurated the newly established Aladdin Industrial Company. This was a joint company, with 30% of the shares belonging to the US and British Aladdin company and 70% to Iranians. The factory was located 15 kilometers from Tehran on the road to Karaj. The Aladdin factory employed 170 workers, office staff, and three British technical experts. Aladdin's outputs, of comparable quality to the British mother company, were kerosine heaters and samovars. The factory could

43 S. Elghanayan, *Titan of Tehran: From Jewish Ghetto to Corporate Colossus to Firing Squad – My Grandfather's Life*, NY: The Associated Press, 2021, p. 50.

44 *Tehran Economist*, 10, 17 Day 1339, 12 Farvardin 1340, 27 Aban 1340; *Ettela'at*, 13, 14, 17 Day 1339.

produce 100,000 heaters, heater cookers, and stoves per year.[45] The principal Iranian shareholder of Aladdin was Ali Khosrowshahi, who later founded the Minoo Group.

On this occasion, Taher Ziai, Minister of Industries and Mines, reported on the positive impact of some 70 million tomans of credits extended through the Special Revaluation Fund to the producers of metal household products. His report of Iran's three-year progress in just one industrial output was staggering. From 1956 to 1959, he posited, the production of kerosene heaters had jumped from 10,000 to 37,000, the number of boilers had increased from 300 units to 13,000, the output of Primus or portable cooking stoves had gone from 57,000 to 230,000, the production of kerosine samovars had grown from 38,000 to 190,000 thousand, and finally the output of paraffin lamps had grown from 500 to 238,000.[46]

On the same day, after having visited the Aladdin factory, the Shah paid a visit to the industrial complex of *Karkhanejat tolidiy-e Tehran va Sazeman-san'ati-ye Pashmbaf Tehran, va Chinisaziy-e Iran* (Tehran Factories, Tehran Wool Weaving Industrial Organization, and Iran Chinaware Production). All three factories were owned by Morad Eriyeh and managed by his son Rafi. Morad Eriyeh had begun his career as a successful textile merchant in Kashan, was dear to the Shah, and was a four-time representative of the Jewish community in the Majles.

The Tehran Factories specialized in various plastic and plastic-related goods, such as sponge mattresses, hardened plastic chairs, plastic pipes for agricultural irrigation, plastic tablecloths, nylon wraps, linoleum, and safety helmets. The Tehran Wool Weaving Industrial Organization produced high-quality woolen blankets. It operated with twenty-six blanket weaving machines and could produce 50,000 woolen blankets annually. Eriyeh's *Parniyan* brand of blankets became very popular in Iran. The Iran Chinaware Production factory produced some 5 million ceramic and porcelain tiles. It became one of Iran's biggest tile factories, well-known for its *Irana* brand. All three factories operated with imported, up-to-date, and capital-intensive machinery.[47]

Right after inaugurating the Twentieth Majles at 10 a.m. on 21 February 1961, the Shah visited the Azmayesh factory at 3:30 p.m. The election to the Twentieth Majles had been politically controversial.

45 *Ettela'at*, 21, 22, 26 Day 1339.
46 *Ettela'at*, 22 Day 1339.
47 *Ettela'at*, 21, 22 Day 1339.

The first election having been annulled, all eyes were on the "cleaner" parliamentarians of the second round. At this time, the monarch found more joy in visiting the new firms rolling off the mill than dealing with the political quagmire he had created by wishing for a predetermined and fixed "free" electoral system.

Having changed from his official military uniform in which he attended the Majles inauguration, the Shah sat behind the wheel of his own car and drove to the factory. Prime Minister Sharif-Emami, a few ministers, bank directors, and high military officials were awaiting him. Before 1954, Mohsen Azmayesh had owned a small productive unit with a capital of 200,000 tomans, employing thirty workers and producing bus seats. As his enterprise gradually grew, Azmayesh subsequently spent 5 million tomans to expand and modernize his factory. Of this sum, the government provided 1.54 million tomans in credit from the Special Revaluation Fund.

By 1961, the Azmayesh factory employed 200 workers. It produced oil heaters, water heaters, refrigerator frames, metallic beds, chairs and tables, and seating for buses. Azmayesh produced about a third of oil heaters and half of water heaters manufactured in Iran and succeeded in selling heaters to the army, which had previously imported them from the US. At the end of his hour-long visit, the Shah was impressed with the achievements of the Azmayesh factory and warmly encouraged Mohsen Azmayesh, the self-made entrepreneur and owner and managing director of the plant.[48]

On 25 April 1961, the Shah inaugurated the B.F. Goodrich tire factory at Tapeh Sefid. The B.F. Goodrich Corporation of Iran was a joint Iranian–American company registered in Iran on 14 June 1958 and the first substantial non-oil private US investment in Iran. Its brief was to produce car and truck tires under license from B.F. Goodrich. The mother corporation, directed by David Rockefeller, held 55% of the shares, while the Iranian partners, or some 175 shareholders, owned 45%. The corporation's major Iranian shareholders were Khalil Taleqani and the Pahlavi Foundation. Khalil Taleqani had held ministerial positions and became chairman of the board of management of IMDBI.

The B.F. Goodrich Corporation of Iran received 12 million tomans of credit from the Special Revaluation Fund to be repaid over ten years at a 4.5% interest rate. It also obtained a 7.5 million toman loan from the IMDBI

48 *Ettela'at*, 3 Esfand 1339. Mohsen had changed his name from Eshtehardiyan to Azmayesh.

and a $1 million loan from American sources. B.F. Goodrich was flagged as one of the most successful cases of attracting foreign capital. The factory was built by a Swedish contractor. It employed some 300 workers and eighteen specialists, eight of whom were US-trained Iranians, and the rest were Americans. In April and May 1962, the factory faced some financial problems due to relaxed import restrictions and the significant headway made by Japanese-made Bridgestone tires, imported by the Lajevardians, and American Goodyear tires. However, it turned out to be one of Iran's major tire companies.[49]

Amini's Agenda of Factory Tours

Once Amini became prime minister on 5 May 1961, he became actively involved in visiting factories without the Shah. As a matter of principle, Amini believed in leaving the economy to the private sector, but he was far from a bookish laissez-faire economist. As an economic realist in an underdeveloped country lacking an independent capitalist class with sufficient capital accumulation and a government with significant foreign earnings from its oil, Amini believed in a mixed economic system. He was a Keynesian, not through theoretical economic studies, but by intuition, sheer practical experience, and necessity.

Amini did not believe that government-appointed bureaucrats could run efficient and profitable factories, and he looked favorably upon privatizing those public-sector industries that were losing money. At the same time, he believed in indicative planning, in which the government would decide, guide, and supervise the macro economy and invest in mother industries for which the private sector could not muster the necessary capital. Amini possessed a strategic view of how the national economy should function.

Amini, who had inherited an economy in recession with a prevalent sense of gloom among the business community, embarked on a campaign of giving hope and confidence to Iran's industrialists and assuring them that the economic crisis was not as bad as they thought. He would go around saying, "There was no reason to panic", as "there were medications for this known disease", and that "the economy would soon regain health."[50]

49 *Ettela'at*, 7 Ordibehesht 1340; *Tehran Economist*, 5 Esfand 1340; 5, 19 Khordad 1341.
50 *Ettela'at*, 21 Aban 1340.

Amini's visits were far less ceremonial than those of the Shah. He toured factories, met with their owners, managers, engineers, and workers, and lauded their efforts and products. His sociable, humorous, and talkative character made his visits rather special. During his factory-hopping across the country, Amini tried to raise the spirits of Iran's industrialists, engineers, and workers.

On 28 June 1961, Amini inaugurated Habibollah Elqaniyan's refrigerator manufacturing plant. Elqaniyan, one of Iran's most successful entrepreneurial figures, obtained the license for his refrigerator plant from the General Steel Company of Canada, which also provided the machinery for the plant and a Canadian technician to supervise the production process. The new factory, *Karkhanejat-e yakhchal sazi va ojaq sazi-ye Iran* (Iran's Refrigerator and Oven Factories) was but one of Elqaniyan's factories that operated under his mother company, *Karkhanejat-e sherkat-e sahami-ye sanaye' Pars va Amrika* (Pars and America Corporation's Factories).

This new factory was built next to an aluminum and a plastic goods plant, also owned by Elqaniyan. The building of the plant began in 1959. Elqaniyan had benefited from the support of the Ministry of Industry and Mines and its Minister at the time, Sharif-Emami, as well as loans from the Melli Bank. In his report to the Prime Minister, Elqaniyan declared that 75% of all plastic goods found in all Iranian markets were the products of his factory and that the quality of his refrigerators was on par with imported refrigerators.[51]

On 10 November 1961, Amini visited the Momtaz Weaving factory owned by Abdollah Moqadam and the Elqaniyan brothers, which the Shah had visited back in January 1961. Amini's inspection tour of Momtaz was primarily a public relations stunt demonstrating the company's financial viability during the economic crisis. In September 1961, news came that Momtaz had been unable to pay its workers since the end of June, the workers were planning to go on strike, and the factory was partially closed. Amini's visit ended all speculations, and the press reported that the factory was open, working at full capacity, and financially viable.[52]

To further boost the standing of Abdollah Moqadam and show confidence in his business standing and that of his partners, on 13 November 1961, or three days after Amini visited one of his factories, the Shah and the Queen

51 *Ettela'at*, 8 Tir 1340; FO 371/157626, EP 1102/35.

52 *Ettela'at*, 12, 13, 14 Shahrivar, 20 Aban 1340; *Tehran Economist*, 27 Aban 1340.

inaugurated another of Moqadam's factories. They were accompanied by Amini and two of his ministers and a large entourage of bankers, industrialists, merchants, courtiers, and the military brass. This second textile plant, called *Karkhanejat-e risandegi va bafandegi-ye pashmi-ye Moqadam* (Moqadam's Spinning and Weaving Factories of Woolen Goods), was entirely owned by Moqadam and his family.

According to the press, this modern plant, located in Nazarabad, some 75 kilometers from Tehran, possessed its own electricity-generating plant and operated with 2,000 spinning and forty-four weaving machines imported from Italy. The factory employed 672 workers and five Italian experts, supervising production and training Iranian technicians and specialists. When the Shah inquired why so few workers were involved in the spinning process, he was told that the imported highly advanced and capital-intensive machines did not require many workers. The plant imported its wool from Australia and had the capacity to produce 50,000 meters of woolen fabrics and 5,000,000 meters of silk garments per year.

The construction of the modern spinning and weaving factory in a small village had the initial developmental consequences expected of industrialization. Moqadam reported to the Shah that newly constructed brick housings with running water and electricity were gradually replacing mud huts. The new industrial town had two schools, one for girls and the other for boys, a public bath, and a sports ground. The factory's doctor, dispensary, and pharmacy were said to be free for employees and their dependents and were also open to the public.

According to Moqadam, the workers benefited from a hot meal at the factory dining hall and were charged minimum rates based on their income. The factory had constructed twelve housing units for its experts and engineers and ninety-eight for its workers. The Shah was told that the activities of the factory had quadrupled the average annual income of a household in the area from 3,000 tomans to 12,000.[53]

On 8 November 1961, flanked by a few of his ministers, Amini went to Kashan and, in the early afternoon, visited the Kashan Spinning and Weaving Factories. Hasan Tafazoli, Mahmud Keyhan, Hasan Mohammadiyan, and Ali Farshchi owned and managed this plant. It was equipped with 14,000 spinning wheels and 508 weaving looms imported from England and

53 *Ettela'at*, 25 Aban 1340. Information in the previous five paragraphs is based on this source.

installed with the help of British technicians. It produced various kinds of cotton, wool, silk yarn, and thread, as well as a variety of textiles.[54]

On the same day, Amini also visited the Kashan Velvet Company, owned by Akbar Lajevardiyan and Hasan Tafazoli. This factory was composed of two distinct units. The first produced thick velvet for upholstery, curtains, trench coats, and blankets. It started operations on 11 March 1959 and succeeded in replacing Japanese imports. The second line of production that Amini inaugurated, produced highly refined chiffon velvet, a French specialty, used primarily for women's clothing. The import of 50 European machines, the presence of a French technical expert, and the skilled labor of local workers allowed for high-quality products.[55]

The Shah and Amini Factory Rounds

On 20 November 1961, accompanied by Amini, the Shah flew to Esfahan and visited the sugar and sugar loaf factory of *Sherkat sahami-ye qand-e Esfahan* (the Esfahan Sugar Corporation). This company had been registered under the names of Kayqobad Zafar, Soltanmorad Bakhtiyar, Abbasqoli Bakhtiyar, Yahya 'Adl, and Kazem Jafrudi back in August 1958, and was to construct sugar factories, refineries, and other industries. The five founders of the company were prominent and well-to-do professionals, members of parliament, contractors, and, most notably, known to be close to the Court and the Shah. The other shareholders of the company included well-known Iranian businessmen and political figures such as General Teymur Bakhtiyar and Aqa-Khan Bakhtiyar, the Kuros brothers, and Hoseyn Hamedaniyan.

Teymur Bakhtiyar, the director general of SAVAK, and his cousin Aqa-Khan Bakhtiyar, a member of the National Iranian Oil Company's board of directors, were also in attendance. Soltanmorad Bakhtiyar, the factory's director general, welcomed the Shah by addressing himself as the Shah's slave (*gholam*). This manner of speech was gradually becoming the custom.

The Esfahan Sugar Company began construction in May 1959 with the help of a French company that provided its modern machinery and began production in October 1960. The factory used sugar beet to produce white

54 *Ettela'at*, 21 Aban 1340.
55 *Ettela'at*, 20 Aban 1340.

sugar powder and sugar loaf. The demand for sugar beet encouraged farmers to double their output to 40,000 tons within two years.[56]

The Shah followed up his tour of factories and flew to Shiraz on 21 November 1961, where he inaugurated the Shiraz/Pars Sugar Loaf Factory. This factory's construction began in June 1959 under the supervision of the British firm John Brown. The machinery installed was modern and imported, enabling the factory to produce 1,000 tons of sugar daily. It was reported that the factory had its own dispensary, pharmacy, and medical staff and fifty housing units with piped water for workers. The factory also possessed a new mosque.

The factory benefited from significant technical and financial help from the Ministry of Industry and Mines and the Melli Bank. The shareholders of Pars Sugar Loaf Corporation were renowned merchants and industrialists, including Mohammad-Reza Fatemi-Shirazi, Mostafa Qolizadeh, Jalil Montakhab, and Hoseyn Namazi. One of the "relatively significant" shareholders of the Shiraz/Pars Sugar Loaf Factory was the Pahlavi Foundation.[57]

On 25 November 1961, Prime Minister Amini, accompanied by his wife, Batul Vosuq, with her hair partially covered under a head scarf and wearing dark glasses, visited *Karkhaneh-e nasaji-ye Fakhr-e Iran* (Iran's Pride Textile Factory) at Hashtgerd near Karaj. This was a special occasion, and probably why the Prime Minister's wife accompanied him. The factory's founder and general manager was a female entrepreneur, Fakhre Iran Namazi, hence the name of her factory. Fakhre Iran's maiden name was Dahesh, her brother Hoseynqoli was the factory's general manager, and her husband was the Iranian tycoon and philanthropist, Mohammad Namazi.

Construction of this factory had begun in September 1959, and its machinery was entirely Japanese at the cost of some 80 million tomans. The 25,600 spinning and 850 weaving machines had been installed and supervised by Japanese technicians and engineers, and a group of them continued to work at the plant. The factory could produce 80,000 meters of textile daily and would employ 1,800 workers once it reached full capacity. The unit had its own electricity-generating diesel engines. Five

56 *Ettela'at*, 29 Aban 1340, 2, 5 Azar 1340; *Tehran Economist*, 4 Azar 1340. The information in the previous three paragraphs is based on these sources.

57 *Ettela'at*, 5 Azar 1340.

hundred housing units had already been built for the workers, engineer staff, and their families.[58]

On 2 December 1961, the Shah, accompanied by the Queen, flew first to Asadabad and then drove to the Birjand Sugar Company, otherwise known as the Qahestan Sugar Corporation. Birjand was the fiefdom of Asadollah 'Alam, the Shah's loyal Minister of Court, and it was located some 130 kilometers west of the border with Afghanistan.

In December 1959, at the behest of Asadollah 'Alam and his cousin Amirhoseyn Khozeymeh-'Alam, the Shah had ordered a group of experts to identify the ideal location for a sugar factory in the region. The construction of the factory had begun on 1 November 1960, and it was contracted with the John Brown firm, which had built the Shiraz/Pars Sugar Loaf Factory. The factory's entire machinery was imported from Belgium and installed by Belgian technicians and engineers. It employed 150 workers and used sugar beet to produce some 500 tons of sugar per day.

This important investment in a most backward region of the country received financial assistance from the Pahlavi Foundation and credit from the Special Revaluation Fund. Asadollah 'Alam and Amirhoseyn Khozeymeh-'Alam, along with other private investors, were shareholders in the factory. After their factory tour, the royal couple had lunch at 'Alam's estate before returning.[59]

After a two-month lull in factory visits, on 26 January 1962 the Shah inaugurated Mohammad Khorram's new safe deposit box and house furniture plant. The Prime Minister was absent, grappling with numerous political and economic headaches. The ministers of Industry, Mines, and Labor, along with other high officials, accompanied the Shah during his one-and-a-half-hour visit.

Mohammad Khorram (not to be confused with Rahim-Ali Khorram) was a pioneer in the field of safe deposits, and his first small workshop dated back to 1926. The Khorram brand of safe boxes, with its traditional logo of a fist over an anvil, was a well-known mark of excellence to consumers. At his new 7 million toman factory on the Tehran-No Road, Khorram employed seventy-four workers, two Iranian engineers, and twelve administrative staff. The factory had huge hydraulic presses, six production halls, two

58 *Ettela'at*, 5 Azar 1340. The information in the previous two paragraphs is based on this source.

59 *Ettela'at*, 11, 12, 14, 16 Azar 1340. The three previous paragraphs are based on these sources.

storage hangars, a restaurant and dining room for the employees, and a mosque. Unlike most industrialists, who benefited from different kinds of government loans, Khorram's factory was solely financed by his savings.[60]

From 21 January 1962, Amini was fighting on five major fronts. He was confronted with the disastrous political consequences of a bloody attack on Tehran University, the bid by his right-wing flank of Asadollah Rashidiyan and Teymur Bakhtiyar to oust him from office, the stern opposition of Iran's feudal class to Arsanjani's unstoppable push for land reform, the significant push-back and political harassment of those discredited military and political figures such as Zargham, and finally the urgency to finalize and balance the March 1962 to March 1963 budget. He, therefore, did not have much time for his usual factory visits. Yet, on 11 February 1962, before his European tour, Amini made time to visit the Willys Jeep plant.

In June 1958, Ja'far Akhavan, who had the franchise for importing Willys Jeeps, had begun building an assembly line for producing this popular vehicle in Iran. Sixteen months later, on 7 October 1959, the Shah, accompanied by Ja'far Sharif-Emami, inaugurated his assembly plant 14 kilometers away from Tehran on the road to Karaj.[61] At its inauguration, Akhavan's plant employed some 110 workers, assembled five to six cars daily from various imported pieces, and hoped to manufacture the vehicle's doors, seats, roofs, radiators, shock absorbers, and hoods in the next three years.[62]

Some three years later, Akhavan informed Amini that the number of workers at the plant had increased to 256 and that ten cars were produced per day. However, the plant had not made much progress in manufacturing the expected components at home and was only capable of producing the Jeep's top, seats, and doors. At the same time, everything else was imported and assembled. Akhavan again promised that with the help of American engineers in the next three years, the plant could manufacture everything except electric components, tires, windshields, and batteries in Iran. This, however, was not to happen.

Amini praised Akhavan's initiative and efforts. He spoke of the importance of producing general necessities at home and emphasized that at least 75% of the Jeep's components had to be produced in Iran if it was to be considered as a "serious/vital activity". The Prime Minister added

60 *Ettela'at*, 7 Bahman 1340.
61 *Ettela'at*, 15 Mehr 1338.
62 *Tehran Economist*, 24 Mehr 1338.

that home production of components was crucial as it translated into jobs for Iran's youth.[63]

On 6 May 1962, two days before his trip to Jeddah, flanked by his ministers of commerce, industry, and mines, Amini visited Shahpasand cooking oil and Golnar soap factories. These two major factories belonged to the Behshahr Industrial Group, owned by the Lajevardis. The Shahpasand solid cooking oil enterprise had factories in Behshahr, Gonbad Kavus, Gorgan, and Khorramshahr. The construction of the main plant on the road to Karaj had begun in 1957. The Shahpasand factory was equipped with automated and capital-intensive machinery. Aside from its cooking oil production unit, Shahpasand was vertically integrated with its own can-producing, painting, and printing units.

The Behshahr Industrial Group also owned the Golnar soap factory at the same location. This fully automated plant with imported machines produced soap on a mass scale, distinct from many other manufacturing units, still using small-scale, essentially cottage industry methods. This soap factory was said to be the biggest automated unit in the Middle East. In May 1962, it produced clothes-washing soap bars and planned to produce body and hand soaps in the future, which it did.[64]

In April/May 1962, Iranian production of soap was about 20,000 tons per year. It lagged behind neighboring countries producing some 90,000 tons a year with a comparable population of 20 million.[65] Some two months after Amini's tour of Shahpasand, he was replaced with ʿAlam, whose style of interacting with the business community and industrialists would differ from Amini's.

63 *Ettelaʿat*, 23 Bahman 1340; *Tehran Economist*, 28 Bahman 1340.
64 *Tehran Economist*, 15, 22 Ordibehesht 1341.
65 *Tehran Economist*, 8 Ordibehesht 1341.

8

Iranian Economy between 1957 and 1961: A Seesaw of Credit Expansion, Inflation, Stabilization, and Recession

In 1956, the Iranian economy experienced a major credit crunch, with real interest rates charged in the bazaar hiking to 30%. Numerous merchants in Tehran and major cities, such as Esfahan, Mashhad, Ahvaz, Abadan, and Tabriz, went bankrupt. Companies were dissolved due to insolvency, business transactions in the bazaar plummeted, uncertainty prevailed, and textile factories, especially in Esfahan, shut down.[1]

The moderate economic prosperity that began in early 1957, due to the steady expansion of Iran's oil revenues, the Plan Organizations' investments in various projects, and the $75 million loan extended to Iran by IBRD, was boosted by the government's approximately $47 million extension of credit to the private sector. Between 1957 and 1959, the banking sector had more than tripled its provision of credit to the public.[2]

The consequence of such a significant injection of capital and credit expansion for the private sector overheated the economy. Banks in competition with one another were eager to lend money. Merchants and businesses, expecting the boom to continue, threw caution to the wind and went on a borrowing spree. Loans were extended with minimal and sometimes no collateral. Banks were allowed to engage in foreign exchange operations with no centralized supervision.

1 *Ettela'at*, 17, 25 Tir 1335, 2 Mordad 1335, 25 Shahrivar 1335, 8 Azar 1335.
2 *Ettela'at*, 21 Khordad 1340.

Imports increased, and foreign exchange reserves nose-dived as importers were easily provided with unrestricted foreign exchange. Iran's foreign exchange reserves of $143 million in 1958 dwindled to $10 million in September 1960.[3] Iran was suddenly unable to meet the foreign financial commitments of its merchants and businessmen, losing its international credibility. The country faced a real predicament: to sell its gold reserves or borrow overseas. It chose to do the latter.

In tandem with the foreign exchange crisis, "domestic prices, which had been fairly stable up to October 1958, rose by nearly 20% in the succeeding twelve months."[4] The high rate of inflation from March 1959 to March 1960 was partly the consequence of the unregulated extension of loans by the new banks. Between March 1959 and March 1960, the government printed 150 million tomans. The Melli Bank, which also acted as the Central Bank at the time, loaned out 51 million tomans to the private banks, which was 26 million tomans more than the previous year.

In the second half of 1959, the Melli Bank was forced to adopt contractionary monetary policies and curtailed the credit expansion of the new private banks. Consequently, there was a rise in interest rates, with free-market interest rates reaching between 18 and 24%.[5] By August 1960, the free-market interest rates reached between 28 and 30%.[6]

REVOLVING DOOR OF THE MINISTRY OF COMMERCE: INCONSISTENT ECONOMIC POLICIES

On 31 March 1957, Manuchehr Eqbal became prime minister, and he presented Mostafa Tajaddod as his Minister of Commerce. Tajaddod was the successful founder of Iran's oldest private bank, *Bank-e Bazargani* (Commercial Bank) as well as a member of Parliament from Sari. In his first interview with the press, the forty-nine-year-old French- and German-educated Tajaddod opined that the most important factor for the prosperity

3 *Ettela'at*, 21 Khordad 1340.
4 International Monetary Fund, Annual Report 1960, 26 September, 1960, https://www.imf.org/external/pubs/ft/ar/archive/pdf/ar1960.pdf (retrieved 12/2/2023).
5 *Tehran Economist*, 28 Esfand 1338; *Ettela'at*, 5, 10 Khordad 1339.
6 *Tehran Economist*, 5 Shahrivar 1339.

of the country was to "leave people's business to themselves and assure the freedom of enterprise."[7]

Tajaddod was left to his own devices since the Eqbal government had no clear economic philosophy or coordinated national policy. Tajaddod believed in the "absolute freedom of trade". He was against quotas, which he argued caused smuggling and increased prices.[8] For him, unfettered imports increased competitiveness, rendered home products more efficient, and eventually reduced prices domestically, benefiting consumers. Tajaddod did not believe in pampering inefficient home industrialists producing higher priced products than their foreign competitors.

One of Tajaddod's first moves was to free the import of almost all previously banned goods, even milk, cheese, crabs, and edible snails. The few banned imports included alcoholic beverages, pork fat, toys, pornographic pictures, and paintings. Even the import of second-hand goods, including clothing and shoes, was permitted.[9] Minimal import duties and commercial taxes were imposed on selected goods.

In line with his free market approach, on 12 August 1957, the government monopoly over the ownership of sugar factories was rescinded, allowing the private sector to enter the home sugar manufacturing market.[10] It was after this decision that loans from the Special Revaluation Fund were directed towards private sugar and sugar loaf companies.

Industrialists and Tehran's Chamber of Commerce were the first to oppose Tajaddod's unbridled and "absolute free trade" policies.[11] His detractors believed that Iranian infant industries needed protection and his policies would wipe out home industries and reduce incentives to invest in industries.[12] The press complained that allowing import of luxury items such French steak and Dutch cheese was unnecessary, causing a drain on foreign exchange and worsening Iran's balance of payment deficit.[13]

Tajaddod's free trade policy coincided with the creation of the Special Revaluation Fund, which had generated $94 million as credit to industrialists. The money loaned out went looking for limited domestic resources, leading to inflation. The loan recipients who also imported machinery for

7 *Ettela'at*, 11 Farvardin 1336.
8 *Ettela'at*, 18 Farvardin 1336.
9 *Ettela'at*, 8, 9 Ordibehesht 1336.
10 *Ettela'at*, 22 Mordad 1336; *Tehran Economist*, 26 Mordad 1336.
11 *Ettela'at*, 16 Ordibehesht 1336.
12 *Khandanihha*, 21 Ordibehesht 1336.
13 *Khandanihha*, 3 Day 1336.

their new plants, placed further pressure on foreign exchange reserves. Tajaddod's argument that unfettered imports were the best antidote to inflation worsened the trade balance.

On 21 November 1957, the Iranian press reported on Mostafa Tajaddod's sudden resignation. Although it was announced that he had resigned because of ill health, Ebtehaj recalled that the Shah had been offended by Tajaddod's disparaging comments about the Plan Organization at the High Economic Council and had relieved him immediately of his position.[14]

On 7 December 1957, Abbasqoli Neysari succeeded Tajaddod at the Ministry of Commerce. Tajaddod's open-door policy had, by this time, led to a flood of imports. Faced with insufficient demand, it had created a glut, leading to a stagnation of business in the bazaar. The unsold imported goods threatened the bazaar with increased bankruptcies. The draw on foreign exchange reserves to finance the imports went hand in hand with a balance of trade deficit. Despite growing opposition from the business community and the precarious position of the Iranian economy, Neysari did not wish to make waves and continued with his predecessor's free trade policy.

During Neysari's tenure, Iran faced serious economic problems that the Eqbal government had been brushing under the carpet. It was experiencing a growing trade deficit, a reduction in oil revenues, an increase in government expenditures, and dwindling foreign reserves. Iran's oil revenue during 1958–1959 was $241 million. The High Economic Council knew that due to the decrease in oil prices during 1959–1960, revenues would decrease by some $26 million. Furthermore, Iran's balance of payment deficit (*kasri-ye ta'adol pardakht*) during 1958–1959 stood at $49.2 million.[15]

Iran's economic problems were exacerbated by the obligation to repay its international debt, which stood at about $40 million during 1958–1959 but increased to $62 million in 1959–1960. Furthermore, while during 1958–1959, the US had given Iran some $45 million in military aid, it was not clear whether it would continue with the same level of assistance in 1959–1960.[16] Added to the bleak international economic picture was the downturn in the domestic economy.

After 18 months, Neysari was removed from office on 11 June 1959. Abdolhoseyn E'tebar replaced him as Minister of Commerce on

14 *Ettela'at*, 30 Aban 1336. Ebtehaj, *Khaterate Abolhasan Ebtehaj*, vol. 1, p. 438.
15 *Ettela'at*, 29 Day 1339.
16 *Ettela'at*, 5, 27, 29 Khordad 1338, 5 Ordibehesht 1339.

13 June 1959. Twenty-four hours after E'tebar's nomination, inauspicious news came that two well-known merchants in Abadan had gone bankrupt, causing panic among the business community.[17]

E'tebar differed dramatically from his predecessors as he had a holistic approach to the Iranian economy. He was a staunch supporter of balancing foreign trade, protecting domestic industries, promoting exports through subsidies, banning the import of luxury goods, limiting imports of non-essential goods through increasing import duties, and calling to order countries such as Japan, which were flooding the Iranian market with their exports, but not honoring their contracts of importing Iranian goods.

Based on his economic convictions, E'tebar moved to reverse the four-year free-trade policy initiated by Tajaddod. He proposed a complete ban on imported cars and tires to encourage domestic production until January 1962. He hoped that within two and a half years, foreign car producers would set up factories in Iran, and domestic producers could assemble cars.

E'tebar believed in "a nationally guided economy". In such a system, "private property, initiative, and competition would be respected, but all matters relating to production and distribution would be placed under the protection and direction of governments". He was a proponent of "indicative planning", very much in vogue in post-war Europe, and believed it would guarantee the country's prosperity. E'tebar publicly announced that oil revenues had to be set aside and spent only on developmental and infrastructural projects.[18] The fact that E'tebar was opining on what should be done with oil revenues did not sit well with the Shah.

Eqbal and his government were not pursuing a systematic economic vision and were not ready for a policy change. On 6 August 1959, the Ministry of Commerce announced that commercial policies would not alter until March 1960. Even though the Shah seemed to support E'tebar's initiatives, Eqbal and his economic team wavered in implementing E'tebar's policies, and they were put on indefinite hold. The inertia of Eqbal to find a solution to Iran's dwindling foreign reserves, and his commitment to free trade, resulted in Iran's foreign exchange reserves shrinking by $62 million from March 1959 to March 1960.[19]

---

17 *Ettela'at*, 23 Khordad 1338.
18 *Ettela'at*, 6 Mordad 1338.
19 *Ettela'at*, 7 Khordad 1339.

One of the main bones of contention between E'tebar and Eqbal's team was the trade situation between Iran and Japan. E'tebar wished to rectify Japan's trade policy, which exported freely to Iran yet imposed restrictions on imports from Iran, such as rice. He believed in retaliating through the imposition of similar import restrictions on Japan. Those influential merchants who were in the export-import business with Japan, and who were later to found the export-import Tehran-Tokyo Corporation, namely Abolqasem Lajevardi, Akbar Lajevardiyan, and Abolqasem Purkamal, must have objected to import restrictions from Japan. Abolqasem Lajevardi and Mohammad Namazi were also major shareholders in the Iran and Japan Bank. Furthermore, Abolqasem Lajevardi was also politically close to Eqbal. During the disastrous late July 1960 parliamentary elections (Twentieth Majles), Abolqasem Lajevardi had been a candidate of Eqbal's Melliyun Party from Kashan.[20]

Even though E'tebar had some success limiting Japanese imports, it was not until July 1961 that Jahangir Amuzegar, Amini's Minister of Commerce, acknowledged that the trade agreement with Japan was unfair and that Japan had not honored its promises. Subsequently, in October 1961, Amuzegar rescinded the old commercial agreement between the two countries.[21]

Another significant difference of opinion over economic policy existed between E'tebar and the Secretary-General of the High Economic Council, Hasan-Ali Mansur, Eqbal's new Minister of Labor. Mansur believed that the foreign exchange crunch faced by the government should be resolved by banning luxuries and placing import duties on semi-necessities. The High Economic Council, however, failed to identify which goods were luxury and which were semi-necessities, ultimately leaving room for the selective import of luxury goods, as semi-necessities.

E'tebar, who believed in the government's guiding role in trade policy, maintained that the government should spend its limited foreign exchange only on clearly defined necessities, and finance the import of all other goods through exports alone. E'tebar's position on how to save on foreign exchange distorted free trade and was anathema to the position of the International Monetary Fund.[22]

20 *Ettela'at*, 3 Mordad 1339.
21 *Ettela'at*, 21 Tir 1340; 23 Mehr 1340.
22 *Ettela'at*, 3 Bahman 1338.

On 31 January 1960, E'tebar was ousted and replaced by Hasan-Ali Mansur, thus strengthening the position of the "free trade" lobby and reassuring the IMF. In his first interview, Mansur promised perfect coordination and cooperation between various economic ministries and agencies to ensure balance in payments and price stability. He began his press conference by referring to the social and economic transformations that had taken place "under the leadership and guidance of the Shahanshah (king of kings)" and concluded by pledging to be "evermore successful in fulfilling the progressive wishes (*manviyat*) of the Shahanshah".[23] This kind of pledge of allegiance and fawning by supposed technocrats towards the Shah's economic leadership and expertise was an unhealthy novelty.

Less than two months after his appointment, Mansur began singing the praises of the government's guiding role in trade policy and the necessity of allocating foreign exchange only to necessities.[24] On 17 April 1960, Mansur announced his new measures concerning imports and exports for the year March 1960–March 1961.[25] But to the surprise of economic observers and businessmen, the new trade policies remained primarily on course with the country's free trade position, as strongly advocated for by the IMF since 1955.

Mansur increased import duties on certain items such as refrigerators, plastic goods, and cars. He prohibited the import of certain other goods, such as plastic shoes and heavy trucks, but not kerosine stoves, heaters, and enamelware, which were being produced in Iran. Mansur's new import policies raised suspicions that the government was pleasing particular economic interests, such as the Mahshid Shoe Industry, which belonged to Mohammad-Sadeq Mahshid, one of the forefathers of Iran's shoe industry.[26] By 20 June 1960, despite Iran's critical and worsening foreign exchange position, Mansur kept repeating that Iran's "foreign exchange situation was completely satisfactory".[27]

After the widespread rigging of the elections to the Twentieth Majles on 29 August 1960, the Shah abruptly removed Eqbal and forced the resignation of those who had been elected to the Majles until then. The

23 *Ettela'at*, 12 Bahman 1338.

24 *Ettela'at*, 19 Esfand 1338.

25 *Ettela'at*, 27 Farvardin 1339.

26 *Tehran Economist*, 10 Ordibehesht 1339. Ali Asghar Sa'idi, Fereydun Shirinkam, *Mohammad-Rahim Mottaqi-Iravani*, Tehran: Gam-e No, 1398, p. 108.

27 *Ettela'at*, 30 Khordad 1339.

Shah immediately appointed Sharif-Emami as prime minister. In the new cabinet, the post of Minister of Commerce remained vacant until 3 October 1960, when Sharif-Emami appointed Ali-Asghar Purhomayun to this position.

By the time Sharif-Emami was appointed prime minister, the country's foreign exchange crisis had become ever more alarming. Suddenly news came of an immediate hike in the rate of import duties on a large variety of final goods. Reacting to Iran's worsening balance of trade and dwindling foreign exchange, the Sharif-Emami government increased import duties on luxury, semi-luxury, and semi-necessity goods.

This sudden policy change resulted from the IMF's new recommendations. Worried about Iran's inability to repay its international debt, the IMF wished to stop the drain on Iran's foreign exchange by further restricting its imports. After five years of promoting free trade and unrestricted imports, the IMF was reversing its recommendations.[28]

The doubling or more of import duties applied to a range of items including perfumes, cosmetics, luggage, silk and woolens, neckties, vacuum cleaners, refrigerators, television sets, tape recorders, chandeliers, crystalware, chinaware, hard liquor, cars, bicycles, metallic toys, tiles, kerosine-burning heaters, metallic and aluminum chairs, and tables.[29] Raising import duties, in turn, fanned the ongoing soaring domestic prices. No sooner were the new rates announced than, under pressure from the chinaware merchants, the government withdrew the increase in import duties on this article.[30]

During 1959 and 1960, the fall of oil prices and the rapid increase in imports pushed Iran's balance of payments into a deficit. In 1959, the decrease in oil prices, initiated by Shell and followed by other oil-producing companies, led to a $25 million drop in Iran's earnings. On 10 August 1960, the consortium of oil companies marketing Iran's oil announced that the price of Iranian oil would decrease by 7% due to competition from increased Soviet oil exports at discounted prices on the world market.[31]

The government's mixed signals, vacillating between various degrees of free trade, protectionist, and self-sufficiency economic policies reflected the struggle between commercial and industrial interest and the absence

28 *Ettela'at*, 23 Shahrivar 1339.

29 *Ettela'at*, 12, 15, 16 Shahrivar 1339; *Tehran Economist*, 19, 26 Shahrivar 1339.

30 *Tehran Economist*, 26 Shahrivar 1339.

31 *Ettela'at*, 19, 20, 22, 25 Mordad 1339.

of a clearly defined developmental, commercial, and industrial policy. Even Asadollah ʿAlam, leader of the soft opposition (*hezb-e mardom*) People's Party, criticized the government for its incoherent and confusing fiscal, monetary, and commercial policies, holding it responsible for Iran's threatening inflation rates.[32] Meanwhile, during the year 1959 to 1960, "domestic prices rose by an estimated 15 to 20%."[33]

In May 1960, an interesting article appeared in the Iranian press. It was written by a young economist, Jahangir Amuzegar, who was then teaching in the US. Amuzegar's prescription for dealing with Iran's inflation was in tune with the free marketeers and the IMF: either supply had to increase or demand decrease. He ruled against price-fixing as economically inefficient and socially inequitable and insisted on reducing demand by keeping government expenditure in check, applying contractionary monetary policies, and taking money out of the hands of the rich, either by increasing taxes on them or encouraging them to save rather than consume.[34] A year later, on 20 June 1961, Prime Minister Amini introduced Jahangir Amuzegar as his Minister of Commerce.[35]

Once the Eqbal government had curtailed the Plan Organization's development projects due to funneling oil revenues to current expenditures, it sought the help of the IMF. Iran hoped to benefit from the IMF's emergency financing by using Special Drawing Rights. It also tried to obtain loans from the US government's Development Loan Fund.

On 21 and 22 June 1960, a high-powered eight-man economic team headed by Mansur, Minister of Commerce, and Khosrow Hedayat, director general of the Plan Organization, went to Washington looking for a loan of about $150–200 million.[36] The Iranian economic team returned almost empty-handed, having only obtained $17.5 million from the IMF.[37] Economic prospects became more bleak when, after three consecutive bumper crops, the 1960 harvest proved to be poor, necessitating the

32 *Tehran Economist*, 24 Ordibehesht 1339.

33 International Monetary Fund, Annual Report 1960, September 26, 1960, https://www.imf.org/external/pubs/ft/ar/archive/pdf/ar1960.pdf (retrieved 12/2/2023); *Ettelaʿat*, 17 Shahrivar 1341; FO 416. 177, Iran: Annual Review for 1959.

34 *Tehran Economist*, 17 Ordibehesht 1339.

35 *Ettelaʿat*, 30 Khordad 1340.

36 *Ettelaʿat*, 29, 30, 31 Khordad 1339; *The Iran Economist*, 4, 18 Tir 1339.

37 *Tehran Economist*, 25 Tir 1339.

"provision of 250,000 tons of wheat by the United States".[38] The poor crop, in turn, aggravated inflation.

IMF, ECONOMIC STABILIZATION AND ITS CONSEQUENCES

By July 1960, the US National Security Council acknowledged that private credit had expanded sharply in Iran during the last two years, the external debt had increased, and the country faced "relatively heavy debt payments in the next few years". It reported that "the Iranians have yet to develop a comprehensive stabilization program to deal successfully with their present difficulties."[39] The IMF also believed that "in order to bring demand into line with available resources", the authorities had to "cut back planned development expenditure", and the Bank Melli Iran was obliged to impose "limitations on its credit operations in the private sector".[40]

In October 1960, the Sharif-Emami government, which had recently come to power, adopted a new stabilization program to "reverse the considerable decline since 1958 in foreign exchange reserves", and restore equilibrium in its balance of payments.[41] Austerity measures were imposed, "state salaries were frozen, and additional development projects scrapped."[42] This also implied "drastic reductions in the rate of expansion of internal borrowing".[43] During the three years following the stabilization program, "the annual growth rate fell to 2 or 3%", while the population growth rate was estimated to be 2.6%, leaving the annual national income per capita stagnant at $180.[44] According to Sharif-Emami, the IMF's stabilization program was a precondition for future credit.[45]

38 FO 416. 177, Iran: Annual Review for 1960.
39 Foreign Relations of the United States, 1958–1960, Near East Region; Iraq; Iran; Arabian Peninsula, Volume XII, Document 293.
40 International Monetary Fund, Annual Report 1960, September 26, 1960, https://www.imf.org/external/pubs/ft/ar/archive/pdf/ar1960.pdf (retrieved 12/2/2023).
41 International Monetary Fund, Annual Report 1961, September 18, 1961, https://www.imf.org/external/pubs/ft/ar/archive/pdf/ar1960.pdf (retrieved 12/2/2023).
42 Brew, "Economic Expertise and Rural Improvement in Iran, 1948–1963."
43 H. Mahdayy, "The Coming Crisis in Iran," *Foreign Affairs*, vol. 44, no. 1 (1965), pp. 134–146.
44 Mahdayy, "The Coming Crisis in Iran," pp. 134–146.
45 J. Sharif-Emami, Iranian Oral History Collection, Harvard University, Transcript 8, Sequence 172; *Tehran Economist*, 23 Ordibehesht 1340.

A positive externality or side benefit of the stabilization program was that it necessitated financial discipline, accountability, and transparency in the ministries involved with economic activities. Such ministries resented abiding by regulations imposed on them from the outside as a violation of their bureaucratic and political turf. The mitigated outcome of the program proved that traditional economic ministries were less successful in acting in an economically responsible way than institutions such as the young Plan Organization or the even younger Central Bank.[46]

An unfavorable outcome of the stabilization program was the significant rise of insolvencies, dissolutions, and bankruptcies among merchants and industrialists. Bouncing checks and stagnating transactions caused panic, alarm, and uncertainty in Iranian markets during the second half of 1960. The press regularly reported on such incidences in Tehran and other main cities. Between 6 and 13 August, six significant bankruptcy cases were registered in Tehran.[47]

By September 1960, there were rumors that the government had bailed out a few prominent merchants whose bankruptcies would have had major adverse domino effects on the economy.[48] By January 1961, the Iranian press reported on the rising number of businessmen in Tehran and the provinces who ended up in jail for bouncing checks – among them prominent business figures.[49]

At the late December 1960 meeting of the High Economic Council, with the Shah present, Khosrow Hedayat, the Head of the Plan Organization, informed members that Iran's stabilization policies had assured the US.[50] Irrespective of the financial hardships at home, establishing confidence among Iran's major creditors, especially the US, was of prime importance to the Iranian government.

On 15 January 1961, the Shah reiterated that Iran was following a stabilization program, and even though it had created problems, it was necessary for the stability and health of the economy. The next day, in a joint session of Sharif-Emami's cabinet and the High Economic Council, presided over by the Shah, the importance of total commitment to economic

46 Gholam-Reza Moghadam, Iranian Oral History Collection, Harvard University, Transcript 2, Sequence 32.

47 *Tehran Economist*, 18, 25 Tir, 1, 15, 22 Mordad 1339.

48 *Tehran Economist*, 19 Shahrivar 1339.

49 *Tehran Economist*, 17 Day 1339.

50 *Tehran Economist*, 10 Day 1339.

stabilization was reiterated as the only way to curtail inflation and balance the domestic budget and the international payments. The Shah asserted that the 1961 budget had to be drawn strictly according to the guidelines of stabilization policies in place.[51] Balancing the domestic budget became a major and almost unsurmountable challenge to the Sharif-Emami government and its successor.

Faced with growing pressure from the private sector for credit, the IMDBI issued a report in late January 1961, emphasizing the importance of holding firm to the government's stabilization program and praising the Central Bank's policy of limiting credit supply. It acknowledged the hardships caused by the program but asserted that they were temporary. The report concluded that, obtaining the twin objectives of "price stabilization" at home and "balancing the balance of payments", necessitated the rigorous application of credit restrictions.[52]

In 1961, all eyes were on the stabilization program. On 28 February 1961, the US National Intelligence Estimate on Iran's economic prospects was glum and sullen. Yet it acknowledged that "the new stabilization program holds some promise for putting Iran's finances in order and for developing responsible and competent economic management."[53]

On 14 March 1961, Ebtehaj told the press that the stabilization policies were "a bitter and unpleasant medicine most necessary for our sick economy". He gave four reasons for the country's dismal economic condition. First, "inflationary credit expansion", second, "absolute freedom of converting rials to foreign exchange", third, the absence of centralized planning and coordination of developmental projects and the expenditure of funds. And finally, fourth, the excessive extension of credit by foreign firms to their franchise owners to sell their products in the Iranian market.[54]

From around March 1961, the Plan Organization was unable to pay its contractors for the developmental projects that they had carried out.[55] Some 35% of the Plan Organization's budget went to Iranian contractors for their various construction services.[56] Once the Plan Organization had to cut back its expenditures drastically, Iranian contractors in turn were

51 *Ettela'at*, 27, 29 Day 1339, *Tehran Economist*, 8 Bahman 1339.
52 *Ettela'at*, 11 Bahman 1339.
53 Foreign Relations of the United States, 1961–1963, Volume XVII, Near East, 1961–1962, Document 16.
54 *Ettela'at*, 23 Esfand 1339.
55 *Ettela'at*, 11 Khordad 1340.
56 *Tehran Economist*, 2 Day 1340.

unable to pay back their debts and the worker's wages. The government's decision to put a hold on government spending made the Plan Organization incapable of meeting its financial obligation, aggravating financial crises throughout society.

By January 1962, the government's stabilization policies began to yield results. The point-to-point inflation between January 1961 and 1962 indicated that the cost of living had decreased by 0.3%. Both the outflow of foreign exchange and Iran's foreign debt had been reduced. A crucial factor contributing to Iran's management of its foreign exchange crisis was that the Amini government had banned 210 import items, a decision that the IMF viewed as a necessary but temporary evil.

Nevertheless, the IMF monitored the Iranian economy and dispatched a team of ten experts to Tehran for a month of study. The first two of the high-powered economic groups arrived on 30 January 1962. Their official brief was to meet with the Plan Organization's leadership team, review and assess the Third Plan, examine the possibility of securing foreign credit, and give economic and financial advice to the Iranian government.[57]

FINDING A NEW CAPTAIN FOR THE PLAN ORGANIZATION: FALLAH AND ARAMESH

The damage done to the Plan Organization after Ebtehaj's departure in February 1959 was partially controlled by appointing a highly respected insider, Khosrow Hedayat, his second in command. Eqbal wanted Ebtehaj out of the picture and was content with leaving Hedayat in nominal control, with himself as the ultimate decision-maker.

Once Sharif-Emami became prime minister in August 1960, he wavered on what to do with the Plan Organization. At first, he wanted a strong but reliable head willing to gradually cleanse Ebtehaj's influence from the Plan Organization without alienating the proud but disgruntled leadership team and the key members of the two bureaus, the pillars of the Organization. Hedayat was a vestige of the Ebtehaj era, so he had to go, and he wanted to go. Sharif-Emami thought that kicking Khosrow Hedayat upstairs by sending him to Brussels as Iran's Ambassador to Belgium and replacing

57 *Ettela'at*, 11 Bahman 1340.

him would be easy. But instead, Hedayat's departure further weakened the political position of the Plan Organization.[58]

On 9 January 1961, Sharif-Emami made a clumsy move, and appointed Reza Fallah, a Birmingham University-educated oilman and an outsider to the Plan Organization, as its head. Fallah was an outstanding oil specialist, trusted by the Shah, but without any actual knowledge of national planning or the activities and organizational structure of the Plan Organization. To Sharif-Emami's surprise, Fallah's tenure proved very short, as he returned to the National Iranian Oil Company on 17 January 1961. The Plan Organization's leadership team had seemingly vigorously opposed this appointment, with the press reporting that Safi Asfia had even threatened to resign.[59]

With Fallah's ill-fated appointment, Sharif-Emami realized that the Plan Organization family was too tightly knit. Sharif-Emami witnessed how key members heading different departments, even the gentle and reserved Asfia, would kick and shout if they felt the person in authority had no familiarity with the Organization and the expertise to lead.

To the surprise of Iranian pundits and experts, on 18 February 1961, or a month after the Fallah fiasco, Ahmad Aramesh was appointed director general of the Plan Organization.[60] Aramesh had been Minister of Labor and Propaganda in Ahmad Qavam's cabinet (December 1946). He had been a journalist for a time, and one of his last positions from 1954 to 1957 had been membership in the Plan Organization's Supervisory Board, a group of advisors constituted by the Majles and Senate to oversee the Organization's activities.

Aramesh was a political activist whose true colors were difficult to discern and who was said to have aspired to become prime minister. He was neither a nationally known figure nor known for his economic expertise. Yet his three years on the Plan Organization's Supervisory Board had familiarized him with its activities. The fact that Aramesh was the Prime Minister's brother-in-law and was trusted by him must have played an important role in his appointment.

By assigning Aramesh, Sharif-Emami signaled his intention to cleanse the Plan Organization of Ebtehaj's influence, economic philosophy, and

58 Khodadad Farmanfarmayan, Iranian Oral History Collection, Harvard University, Transcript 4, Sequence 48.

59 *Ettela'at*, 19, 27 Day 1339; *Tehran Economist*, 1 Bahman 1339.

60 *Ettela'at*, 30 Bahman 1339.

ethos. As far back as July 1955, Aramesh had presented the Majles with what he believed was incriminating evidence against Ebtehaj. The press at the time spoke of the clash between the two and Aramesh's efforts to remove Ebtehaj from the head of the Plan Organization.[61]

Aramesh was in office for about two and a half months. While Sharif-Emami was experimenting with the Plan Organization's leadership, effective work, other than preparing the Third Plan, stalled because of administrative and political uncertainty. Khodadad Farmanfarmayan, the Head of the Division of Economic Affairs at the time, recalled that while Aramesh headed the Plan Organization, he would go to Asfia's office every morning, sit and chat, and then go back to his room without doing "any work at all".[62]

The young but heavyweight director-technocrats at the Plan Organization, Khodadad Farmanfarmayan, Cyrus Babak Sami'i, and Manuchehr Gudarzi, opposed Aramesh's appointment and refused to go to work.[63] According to the Iranian press, the dissidents were brooding over the absence of coordination among government agencies to implement the economic stabilization program. However, the real reason behind their defiance was that they expected Asfia to become director general and opposed the political appointment of Aramesh.

After refusing to go to work for some ten days, Farmanfarmayan met with the Shah, and having obtained certain promises, he and his two colleagues returned to work.[64] Farmanfarmayan had told the Shah that Aramesh "was not interested in any development work" and was at the Plan Organization "just politicking". The Shah had replied, "all right, you go and report to Asfia."[65]

The Shah was acknowledging that Asfia was the Plan Organization's de facto director, while Aramesh was its political face. His Majesty did have a bias for parallel, and even opposing, leadership to avoid the concentration and centralization of power at the head of sensitive organizations. He was trying it out at the Plan Organization.

Aramesh's appointment disappointed all those young and educated enthusiasts who had come to the Plan Organization with the vision of

61 *Ferdowsi*, 27 Tir 1334.
62 Khodadad Farmanfarmayan, Iranian Oral History Collection, Harvard University, Transcript 4, Sequence 49.
63 Interview with Manuchehr Gudarzi, Foundation for Iranian Studies, pp. 41–42.
64 *Tehran Economist*, 13, 20 Esfand 1339; FO 371/157624, EP 1102/10.
65 Khodadad Farmanfarmayan, Iranian Oral History Collection, Harvard University, Transcript 4, Sequence 49.

putting the wheels of development and economic growth in motion. In the absence of Ebtehaj, they were exposed to too much politicking, which they were neither interested in nor cut out for. Foreigners like Kenneth Hansen, who headed the Harvard Advisory Group, could simply pack their bags and leave. The Iranians were either stuck or invested and most persisted. According to Kenneth Hansen, Aramesh "was a man who had been for sale to the Americans, British and others for years and had no conception of his task".[66]

SHARIF-EMAMI'S PERSISTENT ECONOMIC PROBLEMS

On 21 November 1960, some three months after Sharif-Emami became prime minister, John Bowling, the Officer in Charge of Iranian Affairs at the State Department, presented a bleak picture of the Iranian economy, especially in view of the Shah's military ambitions. He projected an annual per capita GNP increase of less than 3% for Iran's next five years, while "real military expenditures" were to "almost double" over those years. Bowling concluded, "All of this means that Iranian economic development will be slowed to a walk with the enormous growth of local military expenditures."[67]

In January 1961, the Iranian press reported that a forthcoming $22 million grant from the US, accompanied by a $15 million credit from the Export–Import Bank and a $26.2 million loan from the Development Loan Fund (DLF) signaled US satisfaction with Iran's economic stabilization policies.[68] In April 1961, news came that the DLF loan which was to be spent on the construction of a deep-water harbor near the port of Bandar Abbas had been "put on hold".[69] With hopes of obtaining promised foreign credit weakening, the Iranian government had to tighten its belt further.

The main problem of Sharif-Emami's government remained the old curse of balancing the March 1961 to March 1962 budget, with economic stabilization looming above and foreign exchange reserves sufficient for about two weeks of the country's needs. Faced with a 475 million toman

66 FO 371/157624, EP 1102/10.

67 Foreign Relations of the United States, 1958–1960, Near East Region; Iraq; Iran; Arabian Peninsula, Volume XII, Document 303.

68 *Tehran Economist*, 17 Day 1339; Foreign Relations of the United States, 1958–1960, Near East Region; Iraq; Iran; Arabian Peninsula, Volume XII, Document 305.

69 FO 371/157624, EP 1102/13.

budget deficit, the government was compelled to further reduce the already lean budgets of various ministries, such as education, health, agriculture, and industries. Furthermore, such nominal reductions hardly made a dent in the deficit. The army, police, and gendarmerie were the only areas where meaningful cuts could be made but these were off bounds because of the Shah's economic preferences.[70]

The Iranian government had promised the IMF to reduce government expenditures by 7%. By 9 March 1961, they had failed to do so.[71] Yet on 18 March 1961, right before the beginning of the Iranian New Year, and the long thirteen-day national holiday, the government rushed a so-called finalized budget to the Majles. As the contents of the budget became public, it became evident that the budget presented by the Sharif-Emami government contained major flaws and outright disinformation.

In the hasty budget presented to the Majles, the government claimed that between March 1960 and March 1961, it had reduced its debt to the National Bank (Bank Melli) from 1.068 billion tomans to 890 million tomans. In fact, the government had not paid a penny towards its 1.068 billion toman debt and had instead added an additional 36 million tomans to its debt.

The government's claim to have extended 150 million tomans to the Plan Organization during the fiscal year 1960–1961 also proved incorrect. It came to light that the Ministry of Finance gave the Plan Organization only 60 million tomans. The government was intentionally dissimulating its unfavorable financial position and budget deficit for the fiscal year March 1961 to March 1962. Yet, while the government was burying its head in the sand, the Iranian press, the parliament, and those who followed the news were in the know.[72]

The first elections to the Twentieth Majles were annulled for widespread ballot rigging, and Eqbal, the prime minister, was sacrificed and fired. The new elections during Sharif-Emami's government produced a more combative Majles, inaugurated on 21 February 1961. In the debates over the new budget, which was finally ratified on 25 April, several members voiced criticism of the government, the elections to the Majles, and both the Plan Organization, especially under the leadership of Ebtehaj, and the

70 *Tehran Economist*, 20 Esfand 1339; *Ettela'at*, 21 Khordad 1340.
71 FO 371/157628, EP 1111/5.
72 *Ettela'at*, 28 Farvardin 1340. The information in the previous two paragraphs is based on this source.

National Iranian Oil Company, and its director general, Abdollah Entezam. Both organizations were presented as symbols of wastefulness, exuberant salaries, and largess towards foreigners.

A DIGRESSION: DUEL BETWEEN ARAMESH AND EBTEHAJ

In the heated and highly charged Majles debates over the budget on 9 April 1961, Ahmad Aramesh, the new head of the Plan Organization, pursued his own agenda. He defended the material achievements of the Plan Organization, such as building roads, railroads, ports, airports, dams, electricity plants, water pipe installations, schools, hospitals, and training centers, in addition to establishing cement, textile, and sugar factories, while also criticizing and attacking the conduct, managerial style, and decisions of his predecessor, Ebtehaj.

Aramesh accused the Ebtehaj administration of profligacy and squandering money, especially on foreign advisers. He stated that past contracts concluded with foreign contractors had seldom been beneficial for the country and failed to secure national interests. Aramesh announced that "people have all rights to be discontented with the Plan Organization." He washed his hands of past activities and pointed an accusing finger at the person responsible at the time (Ebtehaj), claiming that he should be held accountable for his actions. Aramesh assured members of parliament that "as long as he headed the Plan Organization, unlawful activities and acts against the national interest would not be committed." Aramesh and Sharif-Emami were preparing a legal case against Ebtehaj on the grounds of compromising national interests in favor of foreigners.[73]

Aramesh's attacks on Ebtehaj were not left unanswered. Ebtehaj, the pugnacious and self-righteous technocrat, was not willing to let insinuations and insults slide by, and he reacted swiftly. Intending to unmask Aramesh's populism, Ebtehaj provided facts and figures refuting Aramesh's claims. He referred to the legal contract with Lilienthal and Clapp, which he claimed was the target of Aramesh's attacks. He explained how professional Iranian and international accountants had closely monitored all transactions. Ebtehaj asked why, twenty-six months after his departure,

73 *Ettela'at*, 31 Farvardin 1340.

the authorities had still not terminated the Lilienthal and Clapp contracts, which they deemed against national interests. He reminded Aramesh that the Plan Organization had the legal prerogative to terminate the Lilienthal and Clapp contracts after a two-month notice.

Ebtehaj observed that not only was their contract not terminated, but the Sharif-Emami government had chosen to renew it some two years after his departure. Ebtehaj quipped that the so-called "harrowing" and "heart-aching" contracts with Lilienthal and Clapp were signed again by Aramesh in February 1961. Furthermore, Ebtehaj revealed that the responsibilities of Lilienthal and Clapp were extended in the contract signed by Aramesh, and their annual fee had been increased by $75,000.[74]

Six days after Ebtehaj's response was published in the major dailies, Aramesh retaliated. Sharif-Emami was out of office at this time, and Aramesh had been laid off by Amini. In his open letter of 7 May 1961, Aramesh presented himself as the nationalist David at war with the unpatriotic Goliath. He repeated his allegations and argued that Ebtehaj believed foreigners cared more for Iranians than their own countrymen.[75] Two days after Aramesh's letter, on 9 May 1961 Ebtehaj accused Aramesh of demagogy in a blistering riposte.[76]

On 21 May, the Plan Organization provided a comprehensive response to Aramesh's claims. The lengthy report was published in the major dailies and pointed out Aramesh's repeated errors without ever naming him. This was a thorough acquittal of Ebtehaj and his management decisions at the Plan Organization, especially in relation to Lilienthal's Development and Resources Corporation.[77] The report also indicated that after a short lapse, with Asfia in charge, power in the Plan Organization was once again in the hands of Ebtehaj's old inner circle.

74 *Ettela'at*, 11 Ordibehesht 1340.
75 *Ettela'at*, 17 Ordibehesht 1340.
76 *Ettela'at*, 17 Ordibehesht 1340.
77 *Ettela'at*, 31 Ordibehesht 1340

9

Amini Inherits an Economy Coming Apart at the Seams

Sharif-Emami's economic quandaries were not very different from those of his predecessor, whose inconsistent economic policies had created an unprecedented economic crisis from October 1960. Whereas the Nineteenth Majles, which Eqbal had to deal with, had been docile, the Twentieth Majles was more outspoken. During the Twentieth Majles' very short life of some ten weeks, Sharif-Emami, his bills, and his administration came under considerable fire.

The deliberations, blunt questions, and speeches of the new parliamentarians and their twice-censuring of the government signaled the birth of a legislative body that was taking its responsibilities seriously and attempting to establish itself as independent from the executive. The fact that the "unruly" Majles could not be harnessed by the Prime Minister and that major anti-government demonstrations, reminiscent of Mosaddeq's premiership, had broken out perturbed the Shah.

On Friday, 5 May 1961, the Shah replaced Sharif-Emami with Ali Amini, who had the strong support of the Kennedy administration.[1] The Iranian press reported that Amini had long been enamored with becoming prime minister and characterized him as "reformist and radical". Amini presented himself as an honest savior of the country, promising to combat corruption and cronyism and putting the country in order.[2]

1 A. Rahnema, *The Rise of Modern Despotism in Iran*, London: Oneworld Academic, 2021, pp. 180–181.

2 *Ettela'at*, 16 Ordibehesht 1340.

Amini was a trained economist and a man of accounts and budgets. He possessed a strong sense of economic realities and had conducted numerous major international economic negotiations on behalf of his country. Blunt and a firm believer in financial and economic transparency, Amini was also a seasoned politician adept at public relations. He had been Minister of Economy in Mosaddeq's government and Minister of Finance in Zahedi's. Now in 1961, he was being appointed prime minister to resolve Iran's economic problems, implement land reform, and push for political liberalization.

On the evening of 7 May 1961, Amini delivered the first of his many speeches, and it was an ominous one. He referred to the "nearly empty coffers of the state", "wasted capital of the country", "an unbalanced budget", "rising prices", "poverty", and "disrespect for financial rules". He described Iran as being caught in "a terrifying economic and financial whirlpool". He insisted that unnecessary expenditures had to end, the credit crunch had to be tolerated, and serious savings had to be made in both the private and public sectors. To obtain a bright economic future, Amini called on Iranians to tighten their belts.[3]

Amini understood the economic crisis that the country was in and was aware of its causes. However, most importantly, he could see that the economy was on the brink of a disaster if policies of monetary and fiscal rigor were not immediately implemented. Iran's balance of payment deficit problem was becoming critical. It had grown from $61.8 million between March 1959 and March 1960 to around $80 million between March 1960 and January 1961.[4] Amini, the disciplined economist, was fully in favor of the IMF's bitter pill of a stabilization program to place the Iranian economy on a firm footing. Amini also possessed the political stamina to weather the storm of discontent that such stringent policies produced.

The recession was taking its toll. For the first time, the price of real estate in Tehran had plunged by 25% in Takht-e Jamshid and Iran-Shahr neighborhoods and 60% in Abbas-Abad and Shemiran. The construction industry had come to an almost standstill; numerous merchants had become insolvent, and a few had committed suicide. Some ten weaving and textile factories had gone bankrupt, and industries were laying off workers

3 *Ettela'at*, 18 Ordibehesht 1340.
4 *Ettela'at*, 29 Day 1339.

and downsizing. Some 80% of the country's engineers were unemployed while purchasing power had shrunk.

The credit crunch, worse than that in 1957, paralyzed business in the bazaar. Merchants were owed debts they could not collect and debts they could not pay, causing some to go bankrupt. Unpaid promissory notes on their maturity between March 1960 and March 1961 amounted to 685 million tomans and had almost doubled from March 1959 to March 1960. Business and the bazaar scrambled to remain solvent. Uncertainty prevented even the better-off bazaar merchants from transacting. The consumption of bread decreased in Tehran, and Iran's per person consumption of textiles over a year dropped below minimum basic need standards.[5]

On 9 May 1961, Amini introduced his cabinet. His economic and financial team consisted of Ali-Asghar Purhomayun, Minister of Commerce, who had held this position in the Sharif-Emami government; Abdolhoseyn Behnia, Minister of Finance; Gholamali Farivar, Minister of Industry and Mines, and Safi Asfia, at the helm of the Plan Organization. On the same day, the Shah issued a royal edict dissolving both houses of the parliament indefinitely, giving Amini a free hand to run the country by fiat.

In the absence of the Majles, Amini's government immediately began reassessing the 1961–1962 budget, even though the Majles had ratified Sharif-Emami's 1961–1962 budget on 25 April 1961. Behnia announced that the finalization and implementation of the budget was subject to the approval of the government.[6] In the absence of a finalized budget, the government operated on a month-by-month budget in order to pay its civil servants.[7]

BANNING IMPORTS AND TIGHTENING CREDIT

Iran's customs officials reported that between March 1960 and December 1960, some 10,212 television sets, 37,214 refrigerators, 10,481 cars, 117,916 radios, 3,920 record players, 5,200 tape recorders, and 21,953 neckties worth a total of 1.85 billion rials ($26.4 million) had been

5 Information in the three previous paragraphs is based on *Ettela'at*, 4, 5, 6, 26, 27 Tir, 29 Esfand 1340; 20, 29 Shahrivar 1341.
6 *Ettela'at*, 20 Ordibehesht 1340.
7 *Ettela'at*, 22 Khordad 1340.

imported.[8] Iran's foreign exchange hemorrhaging imposed a serious review of Iran's import policies.

Amini moved radically to ameliorate Iran's balance of payments problem and the country's loss of financial credibility abroad. Sharif-Emami's government had toyed with curbing imports by raising import duties on many items. Amini, however, outright banned the import of numerous items considered luxury and semi-luxury, and prohibited banks from opening a line of credit for such imports. He argued that luxury items were not necessary for average Iranians.

The list of 210 banned import items included cars, elevators, refrigerators, television sets, radios, water heaters, heaters, ovens, washing machines, dishwashers, furniture, chinaware, cosmetics, alcoholic beverages, cooking oils and shortenings, soap, textiles, nylons, ties, and bras. Advertisements for many of these items, especially house appliances, filled the pages of Iranian dailies. The government hoped to save some $50 million per annum from its restrictions on imports.[9]

Out of necessity to minimize the outflow of foreign exchange, the economic measures taken by the Amini government translated into solid steps protecting home industries and domestic industrialists against imports. However, the economic downturn and limitations on credit extension by banks curtailed their ability to take full advantage of the new trade policies.

The Amini government announced that since the credit extended from the Special Revaluation Fund to industrialists had sometimes been mismanaged and even misappropriated, lending conditions would be tightened. According to the new regulations, until there was full repayment of loans by firms that had received money from the Special Revaluation Fund, their financial management would be placed under the control and aegis of a government-appointed supervising team.

The establishment daily, *Ettela'at*, quoted an unnamed high-ranking bank official saying that extension of credit had been "primarily based on the person of the borrower, and was thus a personal affair" and that bankers had been "less concerned with how the credit would be used".[10]

However, the ban on imports created financial problems for big international merchants. Abolhasan Diba best expressed the predicament of importers after the government's ban on 210 items. Diba was a prominent

8 *Ettela'at*, 16, 17 Khordad 1340.
9 *Ettela'at*, 15, 18 Khordad 1340.
10 *Ettela'at*, 12 Azar 1340.

businessman, a powerful road, railroad, bridge, and building contractor, a hotel owner, as well as the founder of *Sherkat nesbi Abolhasan Diba va sharik* (the Proportional Liability Company of Abolhasan Diba and Partner) which held the franchise for Swiss Schindler elevators in Iran.

Diba complained that because of the ban on imports, Schindler had ended their line of credit; their cargo of elevators was stranded at ports of entry; in some cases, parts of the elevators had been installed, and the entry of the parts that were on their way had been blocked; past orders placed with Schindler could no longer be paid, while customers were demanding delivery and installment of their ordered goods. Finally, since financial disputes were to be settled in Swiss courts, Diba predicted that his company would lose and be condemned to pay indemnity to Schindler. Diba argued that the government's sudden ban on goods and its retroactive application was the best recipe for bankrupting reputable merchants.[11]

From March 1961 to March 1962, the stabilization program required the government to repay 250 million tomans of its debt to the Central Bank. Amini's government announced that even with all the anticipated savings, the government would only be able to repay 60–100 million tomans of this debt. The government's inability to repay its full debt obliged the Central Bank to further reduce its credit extension by the gap. The prospects for easing the credit crunch in 1961–1962 seemed slim.

AMINI'S SEARCH FOR FOREIGN FINANCING

Given Iran's critical foreign exchange situation and essential import needs, the Amini government was desperate to obtain grants or loans from the US to alleviate the country's financial problems. During the summer of 1961, the urgency of the foreign exchange shortage was temporarily averted. On 7 July 1961, the US announced the dispatch of 8,200 tons of wheat to Iran as a grant within the Food for Peace Program (PL 480). The value of the grant, including transportation costs, was $850,000.

A couple of days later (9 July), authorities at the Plan Organization acknowledged that a $15 million loan by the US Export–Import Bank, which had been ratified before Amini took office, was finally deposited at the Central Bank. This loan was earmarked for road-building projects

11 *Ettela'at*, 7 Tir 1340.

by the Plan Organization. At this time, Iran also received a $33.3 million loan from the US Development Loan Fund. On 24 July 1961, the US Export–Import Bank awarded $7 million of tied loans to Iran. Iran was to spend the credit on purchasing sixteen locomotive engines from General Motors and road-building machinery.[12]

The US aid provision and loans covered Iran's foreign exchange requirements until September. The nineteen-day trip (13 June–2 July) to Iran by five IMF representatives headed by John Guanter, the IMF's deputy director of the Near East, brought relief to the Iranian government. From October 1961, the IMF allowed Iran to take advantage of its stand-by agreement of $20 million.[13] Guanter's trip also resulted in a revision of the stabilization program and "some relaxation of credit restrictions in the private sector".[14]

Guanter's prior trips to Tehran had usually been anxiety-ridden for the Iranian authorities, as in private the IMF's representative chided them for not strictly adhering to the stabilization program. Back in August 1960, during his visit to Tehran, Guanter had criticized the government's credit expansion of 1958–1959, which he believed was responsible for inflation, an increase in imports, and Iran's foreign exchange crisis.[15] Needless to say that at the time, it was the IMF which had recommended unrestricted imports.

Surprisingly, during his short six-day visit in late November 1961, Guanter was full of praise for Amini's economic team and highly optimistic about Iran's future economic situation. He was delighted to see that Iran had repaid $20 million of its debt to the IMF, and on 25 November 1961, the country's foreign exchange reserves stood at a healthy figure of $112 million.[16]

AMINI'S GORDIAN KNOT: THE MARCH 1962–MARCH 1963 BUDGET

The March 1961 to March 1962 (Iranian year 1340) budget was eventually finalized on 16 August 1961. The American Ambassador to Iran, Julius

12 *Ettela'at*, 17, 18 Tir, 3 Mordad 1340.
13 FO 371/157629, EP 1111/27.
14 FO 371/157629, EP 1111/24.
15 *Ettela'at*, 27 Mordad 1339.
16 *Tehran Economist*, 11 Azar 1340.

Holmes, wrote, "No single problem has occupied as much of Amini's time as the formulation of the 1340 [1961–1962] Budget." Amini's government spent more than three months trimming expenditures. It eventually ratified a budget with a 255 million toman (approximately $36 million) deficit.[17] One of the reasons for the deficit was pay raises for teachers following their strikes and demonstrations that had played an important role in bringing down the Sharif-Emami government.

Amini took serious steps to reduce government expenditures and increase revenues. Aside from imposing austerity measures on the use of official cars or expenses on entertainment by ministries, Amini introduced cutbacks in senior staff positions in government organizations. He recalled numerous cultural counselors, and denied educational subsidies to the children of the rich studying overseas. Amini prohibited exemptions from paying import duties and tariffs, which were awarded to numerous industrialists and were also a source of bias and favoritism.[18]

The Amini government's economic credo was severe government cost-cutting, and the Plan Organization was not exempt from this practice. Having laid off numerous "consultants" who were said to have been paid handsome incomes for not doing much, in mid-June 1961, the Plan Organization announced 7.6 million tomans of savings compared to the budget that Aramesh had presented.[19]

On 4 January 1962, Amini attended an important meeting, with all his economic men at the Ministry of Finance, to review the March 1962 to March 1963 budget, which he desperately hoped to balance. Amini's revenue sources were clear. He hoped that oil revenues would increase, but he was not sure they would. He did not expect revenues from customs or import duties to increase, and he knew that, given the economic recession, tax receipts would decrease.[20]

While increasing the revenue side did not seem encouraging, he needed to adjust the expenditure side, especially its military component, over which he had no control. For Amini, the idea of an across-the-board 10%

---

17 Foreign Relations of the United States, 1961–1963, Volume XVII, Near East, 1961–1962, Document 102; *Ettela'at*, 26 Mordad 1340. Holmes cites the figure of 216 million tomans as a deficit.

18 *Ettela'at*, 15, 16 Khordad 1340; FO 371/157629, EP 1111/22.

19 *Ettela'at*, 24, 25 Khordad 1340.

20 *Ettela'at*, 14 Day 1340.

reduction on current ministerial expenditures seemed reasonable, even though it implied cutting jobs.

But the real problem was elsewhere. Amini had already begun to allude to the reason for the endemic budget deficit to the extent that he was politically able to. He could not publicly talk about the Shah's fixation or obsession with increasing military expenditures at the cost of developmental projects. In the meeting at the Plan Organization on 3 January 1962, a day before Amini was scheduled to meet his economic team at the Ministry of Finance, the Shah reiterated that the military budget had to increase.

The antagonistic contradiction over resource allocation, which eventually led to Ebtehaj's removal, was again in the making. Amini limited his criticism to the fact that the budget was skewed because the public sector wage bill was too high and government expenditure on developmental projects was too low. He voiced his skepticism about balancing the budget, and added that "many expenditures could not be omitted ... while health and education projects had to be expanded."[21]

From the end of December 1961 and throughout January 1962, Amini had regular private meetings with the Shah at the Marble Palace. These twice-a-week meetings lasted one-and-a-half to two hours. There are no records of their contents, but it is most probable that their discussions revolved primarily around economic issues, especially how to balance the budget, except a few meetings after 21 January 1962, the focus of which must have been the bloody clashes at Tehran University and their political consequences.[22]

From around 15 January 1962, Amini took personal charge of the budget. He gathered the heads of the accounting offices of all ministries and government organizations at the Ministry of Finance. He lectured them on the economies they had to make during the two remaining months of the budgetary year 1961–1962 and spoke about preparing the 1962–1963 budget and cutting administrative costs. He scheduled two to three meetings per week at the Ministry of Finance to meet with officials of different ministries over budgetary issues.[23]

At the end of January 1962, Amini ordered the dispatch of two budgetary and accounting experts from the Ministry of Finance to every ministry and government organization. Their job was to carefully study all budget

21 *Ettela'at*, 13 Day 1340.
22 *Ettela'at*, 2, 4, 6, 11, 16, 30 Day 1340; 4, 18, 23, 28 Bahman 1340.
23 *Ettela'at*, 28, 30 Day 130.

items, reduce current spending by 10%, supervise cuts in superfluous expenditures, and help draw up more slender budgets.[24] In cooperation with government ministries, the Plan Organization dispatched some fifty well-trained specialists to help draw up the developmental (*'omrani*) budget of ministries.

Through Amini's efforts, economies were made. In the Office of Sugar and Sugar Loafs, administrative costs were halved, while the Transportation Office reported a 25% reduction of administrative costs or some 4 million toman. Other government organizations, such as the Office of Tea, claimed similar savings.[25] These small savings were important but insufficient. By the end of February 1962, Amini pressed all ministries and governmental organizations to reduce their budgets and hoped to have the budget finalized by 6 March 1962. By the time the new Iranian year of 1341 came around on 21 March 1962, the budget had still not been finalized.

Jahangir Amuzegar's Commercial Policies and its Consequences

While the problem of balancing the 1962–1963 budget persisted and the prospect of increased government revenue from oil and taxes dimmed, the government attempted to raise revenue through changes in its commercial policy. Unable to increase tax revenues for the year 1962–1963, to help balance the budget, the government hoped to increase its revenue by relaxing its previous import prohibitions and instead imposing custom duties (*gomrok*) and commercial taxes or import duties (*sud-e bazargani*) on imports. While import and customs duties had different consequences on importers, home producers of the imported goods, and consumers, they generated revenue for the government.

From late February 1962, industrialists, merchants, and the bazaar eagerly awaited the government's new customs regulations and commercial policies for the year 21 March 1962 to 21 March 1963. Industrialists hoped for high import duties on final goods produced at home and low or no duties on the import of the intermediary goods used in the production of those goods, therefore minimizing the rise in their import costs and higher protection from cheaper imports.

24 *Ettela'at*, 5 Bahman 1340.
25 *Ettela'at*, 7 Bahman 1340.

On 18 March 1962, right before the New Year (*Nowruz*), in anticipation of the government's new trade policies, the powerful Iran's Union of Industries published an open letter to Amini in the press. Morteza Besharat, the Union's director general, expressed his concerns about the government allowing the free import of woolen textiles. He asked the Prime Minister to pay attention to the plight of woolen textile producers in Iran. He quoted government statistics to prove that the current supply of such goods in the country exceeded its annual demand. He warned that the free import of woolen textiles (at lower than home-made prices) would undoubtedly lead to the bankruptcy of the textile industry. Besharat pleaded for restricting imports and imposing import duties on imported woolen textiles, even those already in customs warehouses, which were to be cleared after 21 March 1962.[26]

On 20 March 1962, one day before the New Year holidays, Jahangir Amuzegar, Minister of Commerce, who had replaced Purhomayun in July 1961, announced that the government's new regulations were based on the country's "foreign exchange capabilities as well as ethical and social considerations". Wishing to foreclose future accusations of cavalier decision-making, the Minister of Commerce announced that his ministry "had received 250 suggestions, from which 60 were accepted, 40 rejected and 150 almost rejected". By telling the business community on New Year's Eve that 84% of their recommendations were ditched, Amuzegar was probably preparing them for commercial policies not to their liking.[27] This type of transparency and accountability by ministries, however, would disappear after the fall of the Amini government.

Amuzegar announced that the government's previous commercial policy of banning a wide range of imports had produced serious foreign exchange savings and enabled it to repay $110 million of its foreign debt and accumulate $100 million of foreign exchange reserves. Having managed the foreign exchange crisis of 1960–1962, Amuzegar, a free trader, tried to revert Iran's commercial policy to a quasi-free trade system. The International Monetary Fund, which had temporarily tolerated protectionist policies to assure Iran's ability to repay its debts, was now prodding the country to transition to free trade.

26 *Ettela'at*, 27 Esfand 1340.
27 *Ettela'at*, 29 Esfand 1340.

The government's economic priorities had shifted from economizing on foreign exchange to raising revenue. Lifting the ban on imports and imposing customs and commercial taxes or import duties on them instead enabled Amuzegar to obtain his government's key objective, namely increasing revenues to help balance the domestic budget. For 1962–1963, the government hoped to earn 800 million tomans from its new foreign trade and commercial regulations.

According to the new commercial policy, two-thirds of the previously banned import items, or 180 goods, were now allowed to be imported. However, customs duties and commercial taxes or import duties of some 1,400 items, from industrial inputs to final products, were raised by various percentages. The government kept its ban on the import of cars, textiles, heaters, cooking stoves, refrigerators, and water-cooled air conditioners. Importing television sets, radios, record players, and tape recorders was also prohibited. However, the import of their detached parts was allowed only if they were assembled at home, and 25% of the final goods were produced in Iran.

The government also allowed the import of previously banned items such as perfumes, all types of cosmetics, champagne, bananas and citrus fruits, and hoped to raise revenues from the upper classes by putting import duties on such items. As for cattle and rice, both their import and export, with different government duties, was permitted.

The government's protection of home industries, even that of assembling manufactured goods, with an eye to their eventual total production at home, made sense. Yet the new regulations seemed less consistent when it came to lifting the ban on importing electric pumps, radiators, boilers, and water heaters, which had been prohibited before. Just like heaters, cooking stoves, refrigerators, and water-cooled air conditioners, the import of which was still prohibited, high-quality boilers and water heaters were being produced at home by companies such as Arj, Azmayesh and ten other manufacturers, while General Mekanik was producing first-rate radiators.

The main reason for the government's decision to lift the ban on such items was probably twofold. First, the government needed the revenues from the import duties on such items, and banning more items would have reduced their expected revenues. Second, home production of such items was insufficient to satisfy home demand, placing unwarranted pressure on their price.

To assure industrialists and importers of some degree of stability and predictability, crucial to business, Amuzegar insisted that the import-export policies and regulations announced would not be subject to change. Yet only a few days later, faced with widespread criticism against commercial taxes or import duties on drugs and pharmaceutical goods and the subsequent rise in their prices, he announced their annulment.[28]

The issue of import duties on primary and intermediary goods, industrial machinery, and spare parts of machinery used for the production of domestic goods posed major problems for home producers. It neutralized some of the benefits gained from placing customs duties on final goods and increased the cost of home production. Import duties on the inputs of Iranian firms producing final goods naturally irked Iran's nascent industrial class. From the Iranian industrialists' point of view, they were financing the increase in government revenues by incurring higher production costs.

Iranian industrialists subsequently reacted almost in unison. Some, such as Siavush Arjomand and Davud Rajabi, criticized the rise in import duties and commercial taxes or import duties on inputs, and openly demanded in the press that they be rescinded. Other industrialists, representing the pharmaceutical, textile, and cooking oil industries, remained more discreet and spoke against the new regulations without revealing their identities.

Iran's Syndicate of Metal Industries called for a meeting and voiced its criticism. Esfahan's Syndicate of Factories and Industries met with the Minister of Industry and Mines and lodged its own complaint. The Iranian press became an important conduit for publicizing views opposed to various aspects of Amuzegar's new regulations.

In support of lifting the ban on 180 import items, Amuzegar argued that relaxing import bans benefited consumers, making domestic producers more efficient while promoting healthy competition among them. His opponents, economists and industrialists, argued that open door policies of past governments were responsible for the foreign exchange crisis and the present recession, and there was no reason to experiment with a policy that had proven disastrous and that would run the blossoming Iranian industries into the ground.[29]

Amuzegar was targeted as the mastermind behind relaxing the protectionist policies and came under considerable attack. His haughty comments

28 *Ettela'at*, 14, 18, 19 Farvardin 1341.

29 Information in the last five paragraphs is based on *Ettela'at*, Farvardin 7 1340; *Tehran Economist*, 11, 18, 25 Farvardin 1341, 1, 8, 15, Ordibehesht 1341.

that "the import-export regulations were not formulated to attract the public's acclaim", and that the business community's criticism was rooted in "old and outmoded economic theories, unrelated to twentieth-century economic realities", made him even less popular.[30]

Under pressure, Amuzegar announced that he had set up a special committee to analyze and assess the complaints against the new regulations. He even hinted at changing them if mistakes had been made. Yet he kept repeating that the new commercial regulations were the product of "sufficient studies".[31] The press reported that the bazaar and commercial activities in general were in recession, awaiting the recommendations of Amuzegar's special committee and hoping for alterations in the new commercial regulations.

On 6 May 1962, there was news that the Ministry of Commerce had revoked all new commercial taxes or import duties (*sud-e bazargani*) on the import of primary and intermediary goods, industrial machinery, and spare parts of factories. The Ministry of Commerce also refunded those who had imported goods and paid the new and higher rate of import duties, under the condition that their goods were already in the warehouses or that a letter of credit had been opened for their import prior to March 1962.[32]

Faced with a sustained barrage of criticism from industrialists, Amuzegar backed off and accused the business community of unwillingness to sacrifice their interests for the good of the country. He asked, "So what are we going to do to eliminate the budget deficit ... how long can we balance our budget by borrowing overseas?"[33] The government failed to obtain all the revenues it hoped from indirect taxes on imports.

This was a victory for Iranian industrialists, but it could not have been possible without the green light from Amini, who had his ears to the ground, believed in negotiation, and was sensitive and responsive to the needs of the private sector. Once the new regulations were changed, Amini said that the altered position reflected his government's concern for "rationality and fairness".[34]

The free expression of open and candid opposition to government policies by industrialists, business syndicates, employers' organizations, and

30 *Ettela'at*, 21 Farvardin 1341.
31 *Ettela'at*, 29, 30 Farvardin 1341.
32 *Ettela'at*, 16 Ordibehesht 1341; *Tehran Economist*, 22 Ordibehesht 1341.
33 *Ettela'at*, 16 Ordibehesht 1341.
34 *Ettela'at*, 17 Ordibehesht 1341.

the press, and most importantly, the tolerance shown by the government, constituted signs of socio-economic vitality during the Amini period, which would cease after his ouster. The Amini government felt accountable to the business community but not necessarily to the political community, which continued to demand the re-opening of the parliament.

In later administrations, governments did make concessions to widespread opposition to economic measures, such as Mansur's increase in the price of kerosene and petroleum in November 1964. However, they did not allow for open debates on such issues in the press. As the Shah's absolutist power grew and his prime ministers became more office secretaries than decision-makers, there was no room left for discussion and negotiation between the Monarch's decisions and the experts at the ministries and Plan Organization, let alone the private sector. It would be fair to say that during Amini's administration, the Iranian private sector felt to be at its most involved and consulted in national decision-making, a process that would not be continued later.

INDUSTRIALISTS MOVING TOWARDS MONOPOLISTIC COMPETITION

While Iranian industrialists were trying to fend off international competition by calling for barriers to imports of their final goods, competition among themselves became tight as each vied to obtain a larger share of the market. Those manufacturers using modern production methods with the latest European machinery raised the flag of quality control in the name of consumers. They tried to run out the market producers of lower quality and with poor production standards. They called on the government to establish a standardization process. This impetus first came from the food industry.

Already in December 1959, an intensive advertising brawl over the vegetable oil market had broken out between Shahpasand and Qou shortening brands. Shahpasand was an already well-established and reputable brand owned by the Lajevardis (Behshahr Industrial Group). Qou, which was entering the market, was owned by Hoseyn Amir-Saleh and Hoseyn Qasemiyeh (Pars Factories). Before putting its product on the market, Qou had advertised it as hygienically produced in sealed tin cans with a production date printed on them. Qou's machinery was imported, and production was carried out by Swedish engineers and supervised by Fred Heina, a long-time American expert in the industry.[35]

After weeks of intense advertising in the press, Qou was finally marketed on 13 January 1960, coinciding with the birth of Imam Ali. Between January and February 1960, the two brands conducted a disparaging and aggressive campaign against one another through their advertising firms, with Fakupa representing Shahpasand and Kanun Tuti representing Qou. Each accused the other of producing shoddy products and using poor-quality inputs. This type of product denigration to control the vegetable oil market was unprecedented. Soon, the war between Qou and Shahpasand calmed down in the press. Their owners must have realized that their escalating advertising war was costly and counterproductive.[36]

By 1962, Iran had at least nine cooking oil or vegetable shortening (solid vegetable oil) brands competing with one another: Shokufeh, Jahan, Khorus Neshan, Narges Shirazi, Gol, Naz, Varamin, Qou, and Shahpasand. Some of these factories, such as Shokufeh and Gol, had been around for a long time, and some, such as Qou and Shahpasand, were new capital-intensive factories with brand-new machines and up-to-date standards. In July 1960, Qou, for example, boasted that its product was of such high quality that it was being exported to Germany.

In an open letter to Amini in April 1962, Shahpasand, owned by Mahmud Lajevardi and his sons, claimed to be the biggest producer of solid vegetable oil in Iran. Shahpasand called for the active participation and supervision of the Ministry of Health to ensure the production of high-quality domestic products in the industry. It suggested the formation of a professional committee of food experts to draw up a set of production standards that all firms would follow in the industry. Shahpasand proposed that a team of experts from the Ministry of Health should be present at plants producing cooking oil to supervise and inspect the refining process, implement standardized hygienic codes, and package and store the final commodities. Finally, it recommended that the quality of products be tested and controlled in well-equipped laboratories and that quality control certificates should be issued to producers so that consumers would be informed of those brands that failed to be certified.[37]

35 *Ettela'at*, 29 Azar 1338.

36 *Ettela'at*, 14, 15, 20, 21 Day 1338.

37 *Tehran Economist*, 8 Ordibehesht 1341.

Shahpasand called for quality control and standardization to help consumers make sound choices and drive out poor-quality competition. Factory owners using high-cost modern equipment promoted consumer welfare and safety through the pursuit of their own private interests and profits. Amini's removal of the ban on importing 180 items, including cooking oil, threatened the coexistence of new and old manufacturers, producing goods of different quality, packaging, ingredients, and hygiene and sanitation standards. The concentration of capital and the spirit of oligarchic capitalism was spreading through Iranian industry.

10

Amini's Dealings with Business, Labor, and Ebtehaj

In his 1960 book *Mission for My Country*, the Shah's views are difficult to discern when it comes to employers' organizations or business syndicates. The Shah wrote that one of the basic principles of his "philosophy of economic progress" was to create an "economy so organized that the individual rights of workers, farmers, managers, scientists, and engineers, and everybody else productively engaged, are protected and enhanced".[1]

Even though he did not directly refer to industrialists, businessmen, entrepreneurs, and employers, one can surmise that he favored their rights and interests. Nevertheless, it is difficult to conclude that the sudden spate of employers' organizations formed by industrialists, manufacturers, and merchants, which began in early 1961 during Sharif-Emami's premiership, was at the Shah's behest, even though they could not have existed without his tacit support. Ali-Naqi Alikhani, maintained that as long as the members of such organizations did not create political problems, the Shah was not particularly concerned with them.[2]

During Amini's premiership, the Shah became interested in and supportive of the state-dependent capitalists, with whom he could identify ideologically and culturally and who would be the builders of industrial Iran. The Shah initially viewed their organizations as inoffensive and even in line with his vision of modernization. The honeymoon lasted as long

1 M.-R., Pahlavi, *Mission for my Country*, London: Hutchinson, 1961, p. 180.
2 Ali-Naghi Alikhani, Iranian Oral History Collection, Harvard University, Transcript 11, Sequence 205.

as the Shah did not suspect the employers' organizations as being pushy or meddling.

Engaging with the working class and inviting their genuine participation was a different story. This was not a smooth and easy process during the Pahlavis' reign. In *Mission for My Country*, the Shah insisted on the importance of independent syndicates as proof of Iran's pursuit of economic democracy. The Shah lauded "free trade unions" and affirmed his firm belief in them as "instruments of democracy". Yet he was unequivocal about the kind of unions he aspired to for Iran. He wrote, "Trade unions should be wisely separate from political parties. Trade unions should concern themselves primarily with improving the economic situation of their members, while parties have a much broader role to play."[3]

The Shah did not indulge politicized workers' unions because of their leftist history. Workers' unions reminded him of crises when his power and authority were constantly challenged in the factories and on the streets. The Shah expressed anxiety over past experiences when "in some cases ... the unions were sponsored or infiltrated by the Tudeh party."[4] The Shah was interested in the abstract idea of "free trade unions". But trade unions, at the time, naturally became politicized and swayed towards leftist and pro-labor ideologies. As such, even the most well-managed, supervised, and controlled labor unions eventually became dissentious.

According to Habib Ladjevardi, "After the coup of 1953, the security measures employed by the government to eliminate what it regarded as Communist influence had succeeded, at least temporarily, in destroying all remnants of the labor movement and subjugating the workers, or – as it is said in Persian – 'putting them in their place.'"[5] Promoting depoliticized labor unions and organizations, and expecting them to act with the same energy and engagement levels as the traditional Western labor unions, proved difficult in Iran.

In 1961, the American Embassy officials in Tehran reported, "The government of Iran can be said to have double standards. Their public attitude is, 'we should have free democratic unions'. Privately through

3 Pahlavi, *Mission for my Country*, pp. 183–184.
4 Pahlavi, *Mission for my Country*, p. 183.
5 H. Ladjevardi, *Labor Unions and Autocracy in Iran*, Syracuse: Syracuse University Press, 1985, p. 198.

SAVAK they coerce and intimidate workers and their leaders to prohibit formation of effective trade unions."[6]

Amini, the liberal prime minister, was probably more democratically oriented than his post-coup predecessors and successors. Yet, he was governing in the absence of parliament. The fact that the Majles, the symbol of Iran's constitutional and democratic monarchy, was dissolved under his watch, must have weighed on him. One way to soothe his guilty conscience was to hammer at his favorite theme that "the principle of democracy and freedom is based on direct contact between the people and the government."[7]

Amini hoped that in the absence of meaningful trade unions, he could create an environment in which white and blue-collar workers could raise their concerns and problems with government officials in something resembling town hall meetings. In this way, he tried to build trust between the people and the government, and involve the people in what his government intended to do and was doing. By promoting freedom of expression at meetings, Amini encouraged workers, merchants, and employers to vent their grievances and express their demands. The Prime Minister met with potters, bakers, tailors, municipal workers, teachers, students, bankers, merchants, and industrialists to hear them out and get them involved and invested in the country's development.

Abbas Mas'udi, the owner of *Ettela'at*, played an instrumental role in supporting and organizing such meetings. Tailors, bakers, lorry and bus drivers, hairdressers, waiters, hotel employees, workers in the sugar, tobacco, and oil industry, insurance companies, pharmacists, and even bird sellers met at *Ettela'at's* main lecture hall or the newly built *Ettela'at* Club and engaged in lengthy discussions. Sometimes, as many as 2,000 people gathered at these almost town-hall meetings, with officials and ministers in attendance.

What was important was that a day or two later, the troubles, complaints, and suggestions of those present, and who represented the working classes, were reflected in the pages of *Ettela'at*. The voiceless and neglected were given a forum and a voice, and they were made to feel that they counted and were active participants in shaping society. While workers of all sorts practiced the art of discussion and argumentation, officials

6 Ladjevardi, p. 225.
7 *Ettela'at*, 26 Bahman 1340.

at least heard the problems of those who actually turned the economic wheels. Mas'udi's remarkable initiative dove-tailed with Amini's efforts to engage economic agents in society and promote economic participation at a time when labor unions were shunned and forums for meaningful political engagement were wanting.

Contrary to the labor unions, Iran's old commercial and new industrial capitalist class, empowered in 1957, could pursue their interests more openly. The economic recession of 1960–1962 deeply worried the business community and compelled them to huddle together. Soon, members came to realize that in their unity, there was power.

The incidence and variety of guild gatherings and assemblies reached an unprecedented level during Amini's premiership. The new captains of industry, who subsequently formed various employers' organizations, wielded an impressive array of industrial and financial power. Most of them were beneficiaries of the Special Revaluation Fund. They were industrialists, producing intermediary and final goods using Western machinery and technology.

Many were also major importers and franchise holders of final goods. To top off their commanding financial position, most either had shares and/or sat on the boards of directors of private banks. Some were also shareowners and sat on the board of directors of the IMDBI. Amini's economic opening, without political liberalization, and his commitment to actively engage and empower the private sector gave wings to guilds and industries to organize.

EMPLOYERS' ORGANIZATIONS/SYNDICATES TAKING OFF

Once Amini came to power in May 1961, he engaged personally with the business community. Less than three months after his appointment, Amini met with some 3,000 to 4,000 businessmen, traditional bazaar-type and modern-type merchants, and industrialists of small, medium, and large firms. On 1 August 1961, Amini was accompanied by eight of his ministers in the jam-packed main hall of Tehran's Chamber of Commerce. Even though small businessmen, merchants, bazaaris, and industrialists constituted the majority of the Chamber of Commerce, its leadership was in the hands of a few influential and well-established businessmen.

The spokesperson for the industrialists was Ali Khosrowshahi, and for the merchants/bazaaris was Bozorg Abuhoseyn. They were highly respected, trusted, and influential figures in Iran's business community. Both emphasized the financial hardships their community was experiencing. Abuhoseyn's presentation was candid, concise, and telling. He enumerated six major causes for "this miserable [economic] condition". He argued that the proliferation of private banks meant competition between them, leading to a spur of uncontrolled credit at favorable rates. Some of those who obtained loans at 6 to 7% interest from the new banks, he claimed, were neither merchants nor industrialists but middlemen who then lent the monies borrowed at the market (bazaar) rate of 18 to 20%.

Abuhoseyn lamented that just as one day the government watched passively over the uncontrolled expansion of credit, the next day it suddenly blocked all credit facilities and imposed draconian taxes, charges, and fees on economic activities, including construction, plunging the business community into crisis and the economy into recession and unemployment. The inability of government ministries and municipalities to pay some 200 million tomans to contractors for works completed, he argued, only exasperated the situation. Abuhoseyn was telling it as it was, honestly and courageously.

The highlight of Ali Khosrowshahi's speech was his call for a "national salvation movement", with the active and assertive participation of the business community. Kazem Kuros, the chairman of Tehran's Chamber of Commerce, posited that merchants, industrialists, and the business community were henceforth adamant about playing an active role in all economic and social activities that affected their livelihood. He called on the business community to take a leadership role in the economic policies of governments and collectively act to create a healthy economic environment.

The Iranian business community was signaling to the Amini government that economic salvation necessitated their involvement in economic policies. This was an assertive posture. The business community must have received the green light from Amini to enter such a space without fearing reprisals. At this meeting, Amini proposed forming a commission composed of governmental economic and financial authorities, and representatives of merchants, industrialists, and businessmen, with himself present at the first meeting, to discuss issues and map out solutions.[8]

8 *Ettela'at*, 11 Mordad 1340.

A week after the industrialists and merchants voiced their complaints about the government's squeeze on credit provision, Amini changed the governors of the Central Bank and Bank Melli. On 8 August 1961, Purhomayun replaced Ebrahim Kashani at the Central Bank, and Yusef Khoshkish replaced Ahmad Majidiyan at Bank Melli. These changes were construed as measures to placate and appease the merchants, industrialists, and the bazaar. Amini indicated that the new governors would usher in some relaxation of credit restrictions and provide more financial facilities.[9]

However, expanding credit to the private sector jeopardized Iran's position with the IMF and its agreement over a ceiling on Iran's private credit expansion. The agreement with the IMF held Iran's private credit expansion to 3 billion rials (300 million tomans) by 21 September. However, by 21 August, this figure had been surpassed. Credit expansion stood at 3.5 billion rials (350 million tomans).[10] This was a risk Amini was willing to take as a goodwill gesture towards the business community.

On 17 September 1961, a group of prominent industrialists, led by Khalil Taleqani, Abolqasem Lajevardi, Hasan Kuros, Ja'far Akhavan, and Abdolali Farmanfarmayan, visited Amini. They presented him with a project for establishing the Iran Chamber of Industry and Mines (*Otaq-e sanaye' va ma'aden-e Iran*) to promote greater cooperation between industries and prevent unnecessary competition. The emerging Iranian industrialists wanted their own platform, exerting their distinct guild identity. This was not a new idea. Back in 1957, Sharif-Emami had "submitted to the Majles a draft proposal for a chamber of industries and mines, but approval had been blocked by Senator Nikpour and his allies, who wanted to prevent the weakening of the Tehran Chamber" of Commerce.[11] Amini welcomed the idea, promised to study the project, send it to appropriate ministries, and subsequently act on it.[12]

The Iran Chamber of Industry and Mines identified three objectives for itself, rendering it a somewhat amphibious entity. First, it was to support, develop, and reform Iranian industries and mines. Second, it aimed to centralize and crystallize the position and ideas of industrialists and mine-owners. Finally, the Chamber was supposed to "cooperate" with

9 FO 371/157629, EP 1111/36.

10 FO 371/157629, EP 1111/38; FO 371/157629, EP 1111/45.

11 Ahmad Ashraf, "Chamber of Commerce, Industries, and Mines of Persia," *Encyclopædia Iranica*, vol. V, Fasc. 4, pp. 354–358.

12 *Ettela'at*, 26 Shahrivar 1340.

the government to "implement its objectives" concerning improving the country's industrial and mining conditions. Its mandate was also to counsel the government on taxation, tariffs, and import duty policies, facilitate the issuance of industrial and mining licenses, and assist in creating a stock market for the shares of industries and mines.[13]

The Iran Chamber of Industry and Mines was not an independent organization of private business asserting its interests vis-à-vis the government but rather a business–government hybrid resembling Italian-style baby corporatism. The presence of Sharif-Emami and Entezam on its Board assured the umbilical cord between state and business, compromising the sovereignty of purely business interests.

On 15 October 1961, while a group of industrialists was meeting the High Economic Council to discuss the by-laws of the Iran Chamber of Industry and Mines, industrialists from Tehran and the provinces gathered to inaugurate *Sandikay-e sanaye' Iran* (Iran's Syndicate of Industries). Regardless of their specialized line of activity, entrepreneurs and industrial owners could become members of this syndicate.

Amini's presence, along with his economic and financial ministers at this assembly, was testimony to his support for the growing voice and presence of such guild associations. Amini hoped to institutionalize the economic power of the business community and perhaps establish a political constituency for himself. During his Premiership, Amini had failed to ally himself with the National Front, the major political force opposed to the Shah's absolutist rule. He was now considering the power of organized business as a possible counter-power to the Shah's growing autocratic tendencies.

The main speaker at the 15 October 1961 gathering was Hasan Kuros. He spoke about the "pitiful state of national industries" and told the Prime Minister that private manufacturers were drowning in debt, had exhausted their reserves, and were facing major daily difficulties paying their workers and purchasing raw materials to maintain production.

Kuros attributed the industrialists' grave situation to the government's previous "open-door policies" and the "unfortunate competition" between public and private firms. He hammered at the importance of supporting home industries, prohibiting imports, and building a protective wall around Iranian manufacturers with tariffs and import duties to industrialize the country, create jobs, increase income, and boost demand.

13 *Ettela'at*, 3 Aban 1340.

Amini's response was sympathetic and candid. He confirmed his government's intention to support domestic industries by continuing protectionist policies. He gave the news that the National Iranian Oil Company and all ministries, including the Ministry of War, had been instructed to purchase their needs from home producers. Amini then reminded the discontented industrialists that they, too, were responsible for the present conditions.

He posited that instead of rushing and pushing to borrow money lent out lavishly by previous governments, businesses should have been more cautious. Amini reminded the business community of its greediness and added, "maybe they were not thinking of repaying their debts to the government, as they are failing to repay them today." He told his business audience that, "our situation today is not good, but it is not worse than before." Amini called on the industrialists to officially register their syndicate as soon as possible so that they could "negotiate with the government and intervene in affairs of the state".[14]

The organizers of Iran's Syndicate of Industries (*Sandikaye sanaye' Iran*) soon changed their name to *Ettehadiyeh sanaye' Iran* or Iran's Industries Union.[15] On 6 November 1961, twenty members of Iran's Union of Industries, ten from Tehran and ten from the provinces, had a special audience with the Shah. This was a highly significant event. The Shah had visited the factories of many of these industrialists in the past, but giving them a group audience was recognition of their collectivity as an influential guild.

A group picture of some of Iran's "most-favored" industrialists after their audience appeared in the daily *Ettela'at*. Their names are important, as some continued their successful careers and some fell by the wayside, giving their privileged position to newcomers. The industrialists who were given audience by the Shah included Morteza Besharat, the founder of Iran's Industries Union, Abdollah Moqadam of Moqadam Wool Weaving factories, Ahmad Farhangi of Jahan Wool-Weaving and Blanket factory, Ahmad Purqadiri of Atlas Weaving Company, Habibollah Elqaniyan of Aluminum and Plasco Companies, Ahmad Lajevardi of Shahpasand Cooking Oil, Hoseyn Qasemiyeh of Qou Cooking Oil, Mohammad Qoreyshi of Margarine Factories, Mohammad-Sadeq Mahshid of Mahshid Shoes, Ja'far Akhavan of Jeep Willys, Mahmud Dehdashti of Cotton

14 *Ettela'at*, 24 Mehr 1340. The information in the previous three paragraphs is based on this source.

15 *Ettela'at*, 30 Mehr 1340.

Swabbing Production, Ali-Naqi Kashani of Semnan Weaving Company, Akbar Lajevardiyan of Kashan Velvet Weaving Company, Ahmad Akhavan-Alizadeh of Quchan Sugar Loaf Factory, Mohsen Jurabchi, importer of industrial machinery, printing machines, and medical implements, Kermanshahchi of Narges Shirazi Cooking-Oil, Hasan Sadaqiyani of Ray Leather Producing Factory, Hoseyn Kazeruni of Vatan Textile Company, and Mohammad Taheri of Yazdbaf Textile Company.[16]

In his lengthy presentation to the Shah, Morteza Besharat pledged the allegiance of Iran's Industries Union members to the Shah and requested guidance and support to domestic industries against imports. The Shah promised his support and assured the industrialists that the army had been ordered to procure all its necessities from domestic producers.[17]

One day after Iran's Industries Union members met with Shah, Iran's Syndicate of Metal Industries (*Sandikaye sanaye' feleziy-e Iran*) announced its birth. On 7 November 1961, Morteza Sarmad, the honorary president, announced the composition of the board of directors, which included the cream of the cream of Iran's metal industrialists. The predominantly Western-educated members included Davud Rajabi of Iran's Machine Manufacturing Company, Alidad and Kaveh Framanfarmayan of Nir Pars Industries, Siyavush and Cyrus Arjomand of Arj Industries, Shapur, Iraj, Enayat and Hedayat Behbahani of General Mekanik Company, Mohsen Azmayesh of Azmayesh industries, and Khosrow Eqbal of Rialco Industries.

Of the five members of the Behbahani family running the General Mekanik Factory, all four children of Abolqasem were engineers educated at the University of Michigan. The General Mekanik Company was founded on 17 April 1954 by Abolqasem Behbahani with a capital of 1.5 million tomans. It was the first producer of kerosene heaters in Iran and, in 1957, built its first fully automatic water heater and boiler.[18]

Nir Pars Industries of Alidad and Kaveh Farmanfarmayan specialized in manufacturing profile doors and windows, large water and oil tankers, and floodgates for dams. Alidad was educated at the Universities of Wisconsin and California, while Kaveh was educated in Germany. Their factory, located in Yaftabad, southwest of Tehran, began operation in 1957 and employed 140 workers by April 1962.[19]

16 *Ettela'at*, 16 Aban 1340.
17 *Ettela'at*, 16 Aban 1340.
18 *Ettela'at*, 29 Ordibehesht 1341.
19 *Ettela'at*, 20 Ordibehesht 1341.

The prime objective of Iran's Syndicate of Metal Industries was to lobby for the protection of home industries, improve productivity and quality, prevent harmful competition, and prepare and present useful long-term economic plans to the government.[20] On 4 December 1961, Sarmad announced that the syndicate had been officially registered and had started its activities.[21]

The year 1962 did not bode well for Amini. Two days after student unrest and the army's bloody assault on Tehran University shook the country and destabilized Amini's government, some eighty members of Iran's Industry Union met with the Prime Minister. While Amini was politically under pressure and weakened, the industrialists demonstrated their political support for him.

At a one-hour meeting on 23 January 1962, Hasan Kuros pledged his Union's support for Amini and expressed hope that he would overcome the country's problems. Then, one by one, Kuros, Akbar Lajevardiyan, Ali-Naqi Kashani, and others recounted their financial difficulties. These ranged from excess production in the textile industry and duties imposed by municipalities to inhibiting duties for exporters and the price cutting of nationalized textile and sugar companies.[22]

On 21 June 1962, less than a month before Amini was laid off, Iran's sugar producers announced the creation of Iran's Syndicate of Sugar-producing Factories (*Sandikay-e karkhanehha-ye qand Iran*). Three days later, Abunasr Azod invited the owners and managers of the sugar and sugar loaf industry to a two-day seminar at the exclusive Tehran Club.

Azod's modern Ahvaz Sugar Refinery had begun operation in April 1959, employed 850 workers, and produced some 150 tons of sugar products daily. The Shah had visited it on 9 March 1960. Azod was a beneficiary of the Special Revaluation Fund and one of the leading forces behind breaking the government's monopoly over sugar production, paving the way for private sector involvement. One of Azod's main innovations was launching the cultivation of sugar beet in Khuzestan and its use as input for his sugar factory.[23]

At the end of their gathering, the participants issued a four-clause resolution on 25 June 1962. The fourth clause insisted on creating a sugar

20 *Ettela'at*, 18 Aban 1340.
21 *Ettela'at*, 13 Azar 1340.
22 *Ettela'at*, 4 Bahman 1340.
23 *Ettela'at*, 18 Esfand 1338, 31 Khordad 1341; *Tehran Economist*, 16 Tir 1341.

syndicate composed of private and public sector factories to share, discuss, and address their common problems, from producing the industry's raw material to producing and selling the final product. It stated that the object of this syndicate was to increase productivity in the sector and respond to the ever-growing domestic demand.[24]

On 24 June, a three-day seminar on advertisement was organized by the weekly *Tehran Economist*. Most owners of advertising agencies, with a few exceptions, and representatives of dailies, weeklies, and radio and television, gathered at the newly constructed Marmar Hotel. At the end of their second meeting, aside from their disagreements on a few issues, the participants lamented the delay in creating a syndicate and called for its formation within ten days.[25]

The formation of employers' organizations, both in the manufacturing and service sectors, was spiraling. These new bodies hoped to foster dialogue, solidarity, and cooperation among industry members and influence government policy.

THE CONSTRUCTION SYNDICATE UNDER SUSPICION

Not all syndicates were looked upon by Amini and the public in the same way. With the credit crunch and economic crisis affecting all sectors of the economy, even Iran's well-off and profitable construction and building contractors represented by *Sandikay-e sherkathay-e sakhtemani* (Syndicate of Construction Firms) began complaining. The Syndicate of Construction Firms was one of Iran's oldest official guild organizations, tracing its date of birth to 2 March 1948. As the government began allocating funds to infrastructural projects, especially after 1953, Iranian construction firms flourished, and some made great fortunes. Even when the supervision of big projects was given to foreign contractors, their implementation was left to Iranian builders.

Between 1957 and 1962, some well-known and politically well-connected Iranian construction firms became embroiled in scandals involving nepotism, bribery, tax evasion, misappropriation, and embezzlement of funds. In 1957, the well-established Mosalas construction company,

24 *Tehran Economist*, 16 Tir 1341.
25 *Tehran Economist*, 9, 16 Tir 1341.

owned and run by notable engineer-architect-politicians such as Mohsen Forughi, Kayqobad Zafar, and Kazem Jafrudi, was said to have received a 6% supervision fee over the construction of the new Senate building. Their fees were said to have come to 3.6 million tomans.[26]

The new Senate building was inaugurated on 7 October 1959 but remained incomplete. It was first estimated to cost 30 million tomans. By the time it was almost finished, it had cost some 80 million tomans.[27] Financial misappropriation in the construction of the Senate building came to the fore with the arrest of the managing directors of Sivand Company, the building contractors, and Mosalas Company, its supervising company.

On 9 April 1962, Heydar Ghiyai, Sivand's architect, along with Mohtashami and Safaie, members of Sivand's managing board, were arrested and imprisoned.[28] Heydar Ghiyai, the Beaux-Arts educated and avant-garde architect of the Senate building was also the architect of Moulin Rouge and Radio City, two of Tehran's most prestigious movie theaters at the time. Hoseynqoli Kiyani, the ex-managing director of Sivand, was arrested later. It was rumored that some 40 million tomans had been embezzled in the construction of the Senate building.[29]

In July 1962, the Ministry of Justice ordered the expropriation of 22,500,000 tomans of properties belonging to Mohsen Forughi, Ghiyai, Mohtashami, Safaie and Kiyani. Forughi's name had been kept out of the press even though he had been in prison, along with Ghiyai, Mohtashami, Safaie and Kiyani, all in connection with alleged embezzlements in constructing the Senate building.[30] Mohsen Forughi was Mohammad-Ali Forughi's son, who played a key role in Mohammad-Reza Shah's ascension to the throne. Mohammad-Ali Forughi who had been Reza Shah's prime minister thrice, became Mohammad-Reza Shah's first prime minister. Forughi and Ghiyai were released on bail in August 1962. The bail of 20 million tomans was said to have been put up by Arjomand, Tajaddod, Eriyeh, and Batmanqelich.[31]

26 *Ferdowsi*, 28 Khordad 1336.
27 *Ettela'at*, 20 Farvardin 1341.
28 *Ettela'at*, 21 Farvardin 1341.
29 *Ettela'at*, 20, 21 Farvardin 1341; *Tehran Economist*, 25 Farvardin 1341.
30 *Ettela'at*, 17 Tir 1341.
31 *Sepid o Siyah*, 2 Shahrivar 1341.

In January 1962, scandals around Rahim-Ali Khorram, the self-made, go-getting hustler who owned *Asphalt-e Rāh,* became public. Khorram, who had obtained numerous lucrative government contracts from building roads to airports, was accused of embezzlement, tax evasion, and graft. He fled the country, leaving behind a string of creditors. The stories of misappropriation by road and building contractors had added to the public's suspicion of their ill-gotten gains and their unscrupulous deals with government organizations which gave them their juicy contracts.

So when the Syndicate of Construction Firms, with their dubious reputation, met with Amini on 20 December 1961 to bemoan their dire financial condition, their cause and grievances sounded somewhat contrived and shifty. The chair of the syndicate's board of directors, Abdolmajid A'lam, expressed hope that all the misunderstandings and misgivings around the activities of construction firms among the people and government officials would be cleared. Abdolmajid A'lam was close to the Shah. He was the founder of the reputable TESAD construction company, a shareholder of *Bank-e Kar* (Labor Bank), and a co-founder of *Sherkat Palm* (Palm Company) with Ahmad Bahrami.

The main speaker at this meeting was Kazem Jafrudi, the director general of the Syndicate of Construction Firms. Jafrudi was also one of the three key members of Mosalas Construction Company, still being investigated for embezzlement. Jafrudi's very long speech revolved around four main axes. First, he presented Iranian construction and building firms as selfless developers and pioneers of Iran's infrastructural modernization, almost like heroes who would venture where no one else would go in the country. Second, he argued that Iranian construction firms were as good as, if not better, than foreign firms and that contracts should be given to them also as an act of nationalism and anti-colonialism.

Third, Jafrudi claimed that there were 400 construction companies in Iran, and the syndicate represented only 125 to 130. Among the construction firms, he admitted that some were incompetent, corrupt, and shady. However, he emphasized that most building companies were efficient, professional, and honest and deplored the constant maligning of construction firms.

Fourth, Jafrudi posited that due to significant cutbacks in government projects, most building companies were on the brink of bankruptcy and forfeiture. Jafrudi divulged that only ten companies out of the 130 top contractors had amassed great fortunes, and the rest were only making ends meet. He recommended that the Central Bank relax its contractionary policy and provide much-needed bank guarantees.

Amini's reaction was far from empathetic. He first reminded the audience that Mosalas Construction Company, where Jafrudi was a shareholder, was one of those top ten building companies. Amini remarked that the bulk of construction works in Iran was in the hands of a "cartel" and that the smaller companies run by educated young engineers could not find contracts. He invited the beneficiaries of this cartel, who had accumulated wealth and influence, not to flaunt their wealth by riding "their Cadillacs" to the less fortunate southern districts of Tehran. Amini was setting aside the Iranian political *t'arof* or pleasantries, customary at these occasions. He tried to explain why the ordinary people looked suspiciously and unaffectionately upon the wealthy construction contractors.

Amini defended the Central Bank's policy of drastically reducing credit expansion and told his audience that they needed to "accept the bitter medicine" for the country's good. He also chided those private banks that had, in the past, extended bank guarantees to unsound projects. His main comforting words for the building contractors were that the government had recommended that, under equal conditions and circumstances, and even if the Iranian prices were slightly higher, preference should be given to Iranian contractors. Amini's protectionist policy now included building contractors, but his interaction with them demonstrated that there was no love lost between him and their privileged cartel.[32]

EBTEHAJ CROSSING RED LINES AND IMPRISONED

Out of public office, Ebtehaj returned to one of the professions that he knew best. On 31 January 1960, the first branches of Ebtehaj's newfound private bank, Bank Iranian, opened their doors. Ebtehaj held 30% of Bank Iranian's equity, and the bank's activities picked up very quickly because of his reputation. True to his proud and cavalier self, Ebtehaj continued to freely opine on the state of the Iranian economy at home and abroad, irking Iranian political decision-makers, and especially the Shah.

32 *Ettela'at*, 30 Azar 1340. Information in the previous seven paragraphs is mainly based on this source.

In June 1961, Ebtehaj gave a long technical speech about Iran's economic situation to the shareholders of Bank Iranian. The daily *Ettela'at* began printing sections of his speech on 11 June 1961.[33] In his address, Ebtehaj criticized Iranian political decision-makers for not having listened in 1959 to the sound advice of the World Bank and Iranian economists at home, and blamed Iran's economic crises on those deaf ears.[34]

He strongly admonished government-to-government economic aid and loans and argued for an international approach. He identified economic dealings with international institutions, such as the World Bank, as the only viable means of achieving rapid economic progress. Ebtehaj insinuated that bilateral dealings could lead to corruption and stressed that the aid and credit monies should not be put at the disposal of politicians, who would "for political, and personal interests as well as favoritism, spend the money for projects not necessarily in the people's interest". Ebtehaj insisted that the criteria for extending developmental loans "should not at all be based on political and military considerations" but purely on the viability of economic projects.[35] Ebtehaj then criticized the management structure of the new joint banks in Iran, arguing that having foreign managing directors of banks in Iran was unprecedented and against national interests.[36]

Three months after accusing political decision-makers of the abysmal state of the Iranian economy, Ebtehaj delivered a speech before the International Industrial Conference held in San Francisco between 11 and 15 September 1961. At this conference, he repeated his criticism of bilateral economic loans and aid and urged developing countries to seek credit and help from international organizations such as the World Bank. He argued that receiving loans from "an international agency frees development aid from the lingering suspicion of imperialistic interference." For Ebtehaj, international agencies could neither be easily influenced by private business interests in recipient countries nor were they swayed to provide loans for military and political considerations.[37]

33 *Ettela'at*, 21 Khordad 1340.

34 *Ettela'at*, 22 Khordad 1340.

35 *Ettela'at*, 29 Khordad 1340.

36 *Ettela'at*, 30 Khordad 1340.

37 R.L. Baker, *Business Leadership in a Changing World: A Report on the International Conference at San Francisco, September 11-15, 1961*, New York: McGraw Hill, 1962, p. 240.

Ebtehaj argued that governments in underdeveloped countries receiving credits and loans must be subjected to an international audit to prevent corruption and graft while helping honest businessmen.[38] He raised his primary concern and said, "Where the recipient government is corrupt, the donor government understandably appears, in the judgement of the public, to support corruption."[39]

Even though it was obvious that Ebtehaj's comments and concerns were based on his first-hand experience in Iran, he did not specifically refer to Iran, except in one highly controversial statement. He said, "I can think of no better summary of all the disadvantages and weaknesses of the bilateral system than the modern history of my own country. Not so very many years ago in Iran, the United States was loved and respected as no other country, and without having given a penny of aid. Now, after more than a $1 billion of loans and grants, America is neither loved nor respected; she is distrusted by most people and hated by many."[40]

Ebtehaj was not mincing his words. He implicitly informed the international community that the Iranian government was corrupt and that international supervision was required to ensure the spending of economic credit for designated developmental and welfare purposes. Ebtehaj's assault on government-to-government aid for promoting corruption in the recipient country implicated Amini and the Shah. Amini must have taken Ebtehaj's comments badly and personally, especially as he led an anti-corruption campaign by indicting and prosecuting dishonest and unscrupulous government and military officials. Furthermore, Ebtehaj's comments could have adversely affected the efforts of Shah and Amini to obtain desperately needed funds from the US to relieve the budget problem and finance the Third Five-Year Plan.

On 30 October 1961, less than a week after Ebtehaj's speech in the US, when the Shah visited the Dez Dam and ordered cement to be poured into its base, thus inaugurating the last phase of its construction, many were asking why Ebtehaj was absent. Dez Dam had been one of Ebtehaj's pet projects. An official told the inquisitive and the busybodies that Ebtehaj had been invited but had refused to attend. The daily *Ettela'at* paid tribute

38 Baker, pp. 235–236.
39 Baker, p. 239.
40 Baker, pp. 239–240.

to the missing architect of the project and wrote, "Ebtehaj was missed, and many asked after him."[41]

On 11 November 1961, Ebtehaj, the anti-corruption advocate, was arrested for misappropriating government property. This was less than a month after his speech in San Francisco and less than a fortnight after his absence at the opening of the Dez Dam ceremonies. The case against him was allegedly based on "unallowed (*qeyr mojaz*) expenditure of 700 million toman from public funds". No indication was given as to what the money had been spent on to verify if it was "unallowed".

After a five-hour interrogation, Ebtehaj was sent to the Police Prison (*zendan-e shahrebani*), where he lingered for some seven months. Before being dispatched to prison, Ebtehaj told reporters that he was proud of what he had done and that he would do everything all over again. Ebtehaj added that "thieves were freely roaming the streets, and I am being conducted to where they should be."[42]

The day after his arrest, key government officials engaged in the Iranian game of *ki bud ki bud man nabudam*, or who arrested Ebtehaj, since I did not order it! Amini sheepishly announced that he had no knowledge of Ebtehaj's detention and that it was the Ministry of Justice's doing. Nureddin Alamuti, the Minister of Justice, responded, "This affair has nothing to do with me since the judiciary does its own work."[43] Three days after Ebtehaj's arrest, the Prime Minister added more confusion to the affair by saying, "Ebtehaj is an honest man, but he has been arrested for illegal possessions (*tasarofat qeyr qanuni*)."[44] Amini's reactions to Ebtehaj's arrest reflected his internal qualms and contradictions over the whole affair.

Nobody in the country was willing to take responsibility. Such an important decision, however, could not have been made without the prior knowledge and consent of both the Shah and Amini. This seemed like a typically arbitrary and politically motivated case of arresting the gadfly first and then concocting a legal case. Ebtehaj's arrest had a pronounced effect on the comportment of Iran's future politicians.

Abdolmajid Majidi, a prominent and respectable minister in Hoveyda's many cabinets for ten years and later director general of the Plan and

41 *Ettela'at*, 14 Aban 1340.
42 *Ettela'at*, 21 Aban 1340.
43 *Ettela'at*, 21, 22 Aban 1340.
44 *Ettela'at*, 24 Aban 1340.

Budget Organization for four years, recalled the image of Ebtehaj in prison when he visited him. The encounter scared him. Majidi recalled that the fear of ending up in prison like Ebtehaj, who he believed was imprisoned for opposing excessive military expenditures, prevented him from "swimming against the current", going against Shah's designs, and even resigning from office.[45]

The Shah did not like Ebtehaj's independence of thought, action, and refusal to cater to his wishes. The Shah was probably jealous that after forcing Ebtehaj out of the Plan Organization, he continued to be respected by his peers and successful. Ebtehaj, however, was allowed to become a thriving banker in a country where success usually necessitated public allegiance to his majesty and a dose of groveling.

Amini and Ebtehaj shared similar notions of the importance of meritocracy, aversion to corruption, and were both sticklers for honesty. Amini was primarily a politician, and Ebtehaj was a technocrat. Amini liked politics and enjoyed being in the limelight. One could envisage him sacrificing old and like-minded friends to remain in power. Ebtehaj, however, prided himself on being an expert and a technocrat par excellence. He was too arrogant and proud to sacrifice and compromise his hard-earned technical reputation for political office.

Amini failed to understand that, having worked for the Shah and having come to know him well, Ebtehaj was no longer interested in the public sector and was, therefore, not his political rival, even though rumors circulated that he wanted to become prime minister. Amini allowed his hubris to get the better of him and belittled the economic wizard of unquestionable integrity.

And then, there was an old skeleton in the career closets of Amini and Ebtehaj. Back in 1955, when Amini was Minister of Finance, he clashed with Ebtehaj when the latter objected to the Ministry of Finance's supervisory role over oil revenues. When 'Ala became prime minister and Amini was moved from the Ministry of Finance to Justice, rumors were that the switch was made to appease Ebtehaj.[46]

Imprisoning Ebtehaj made waves. Voices in the domestic and foreign press expressed surprise and disdain at his arrest, characterizing him as

45 Interview with Abdol-Majid Majidi, Foundation for Iranian Studies, APT-I, pp. 14–15.

46 *Khandaniha*, 6 Khordad 1344.

an honest man whose services to the country were undeniable.[47] To placate the growing pro-Ebtehaj chorus, the Amini government organized a press a conference.

Alamuti, the Minister of Justice, claimed that Ebtehaj's arrest was not politically motivated but based on hard evidence. Alamuti claimed that Ebtehaj had misappropriated public funds and was guilty of "criminal activities". He repeated the old allegations against Ebtehaj and claimed that monies spent by the Plan Organization "were not with regards to the country's needs" and "had not resulted in considerable benefits for the country".[48]

Gordon Clapp, Lilienthal's business partner in the Khuzestan development project, arrived in Tehran on 10 December 1961 to participate in the inauguration of the Khuzestan Sugar Plant by the Shah. The sugar plant at Haft Tappeh used sugar cane and was an integral part of Ebtehaj's baby, the comprehensive Khuzestan development scheme. The yield per hectare at Haft Tappeh was reported to be higher than that in Cuba. On his return from Haft Tappeh, Clapp visited Ebtehaj in prison.[49] Ironically, Ebtehaj's schemes were coming to fruition while he lingered in prison, and the Shah took full credit for them.

When Ebtehaj was finally granted his freedom on the outrageous bail of some 1,000 million tomans or approximately $143 million, which was collected and presented to the authorities by Ebtehaj's friends, he refused to leave prison.[50] He strongly objected to putting up bail, even though he had the means, and stayed for twelve more days in Tehran's Police Hospital. In the war of wills between Ebtehaj and the Shah, the former won. On 14 June 1962, Ebtehaj was eventually freed without bail and only on the condition that he would not leave Tehran.[51] Despite Alamuti's claim about hard evidence against Ebtehaj, he was never put on trial, supporting the theory that his arrest was arbitrary and purely political.

Ebtehaj's incarceration sent a clear message to the honest, educated, and meritocratic Iranian professionals that they could remain faithful to their own personal ethics and criteria, but that they should not expect or try to impose their high standards on the system, especially when their

47 *Tehran Economist*, 9 Day 1340.
48 *Ettela'at*, 1 Bahman 1340.
49 *Tehran Economist*, 25 Azar 1340. *Ettela'at*, 18 Farvardin 1344.
50 *Ettela'at*, 14 Khordad 1341; *Tehran Economist*, 19 Khordad 1341.
51 *Ettela'at*, 26 Khordad 1341.

principles clashed with those of the Shah. After Ebtehaj, honest and incorruptible technocrats remained in the system, but they realized they had to live and work like the three wise monkeys: see no evil, hear no evil, and speak of no evil within the system. Candid, professional, and economically sound advice and recommendations that clashed with the Shah's were thus deemed redundant and hazardous.

11

The Second and Third Development Plans (September 1955 to September 1962)

In late 1954, the First Seven-Year Plan was discontinued, and the Parliament ratified the Second Seven-Year Development Plan Law on 28 February 1956. This plan was to last until September 1962. The new plan, drafted and completed in less than nine months, was to "be more in line with the country's increased oil revenues".[1] In March 1956, a year and a half into Ebtehaj's directorship and hardly a month after the Second Plan became law, the Plan Organization informed the World Bank that its revenues were insufficient to meet its planned expenditures and requested a short-term credit.

On 22 January 1957, the World Bank responded favorably and extended a $75 million loan for "general development" in Iran.[2] This was the Bank's largest loan to any country in 1957. It provided short-term financing for Iran's Second Seven-Year Development Plan, and it was the first time that the Bank was giving a non-specific loan rather than its usual credit for clearly designated projects. To supervise and monitor the substantial

1 F. Daftary, "Development Planning in Iran: A Historical Survey", *Iranian Studies*, vol. 6, no. 4 (1973) pp. 176–228.

2 *Iran – Second Seven Year Development Plan Project (English)*. Washington, DC: World Bank Group, http://documents.worldbank.org/curated/en/419731468044354002/Iran-Second-Seven-Year-Development-Plan-Project. Retrieved 17/1/2023.

loan, on Ebtehaj's request, the World Bank sent a permanent representative to Tehran.[3]

The Second Plan was initially allocated a budget of $933 million. In 1957, costs were adjusted upwards, and projected investments were raised to $1.1 billion for seven years.[4] The Second Plan was broadly defined and imprecise regarding specific objectives. It aimed at "increasing production, developing exports, preparing public necessities within the country, developing agriculture and industries, discovering and exporting minerals and subterranean resources, improving and completing means of communication, improving public health, fulfilling any operations designed for the development of the country, raising the educational and living standard of the people and improving living conditions".[5]

HOW DID THE SECOND PLAN FARE?

The Plan Organization was tasked with implementing the Plan out of government revenues from the sale of oil. Government ministries, such as finance, industry, and mines, competed with the Plan Organization for the revenues from the sale of oil. The Second Plan (1956–1962) had two distinct phases. The first phase began on 28 February 1956, with the ratification of the Plan by the Majles, and ended on 12 February 1959, with the ouster of Ebtehaj. The second phase was marked by the messy attempt to incorporate the Plan Organization into the government bureaucracy, detach the industries under its control and transfer them to the Ministry of Industry and Mines, and finally end its independence and authority as the country's chief planning and executive body of development projects.

First Phase: Ebtehaj Period

In its first phase, the Plan Organization was involved in eight distinct types of developmental operations. First, it engaged in comprehensive regional

3 International Bank for Reconstruction and Development, *(World Bank) Twelfth Annual Report (1956–1957), 24 September 1956*, https://documents1.worldbank.org/curated/en/885171467986357159/pdf/multi-page.pdf (retrieved 21/1/2023).
4 F. Daftary, "Development Planning in Iran: A Historical Survey," *Iranian Studies*, vol. 6, no. 4 (1973) pp. 176–228.
5 Daftary, "Development Planning in Iran: A Historical Survey," pp. 176–228.

development projects, such as the Khuzestan Development Services, in cooperation with foreign consulting firms, such as Lilienthal's Development and Resources Corporation.

Second, the Plan Organization hired foreign expert consultants to plan, supervise, and manage specific construction projects such as roads, dams, airports, railways, and ports. The contracts given to John Mowlem (British) for roadbuilding, Morrison-Knudsen (American) and Harza Engineering Company (American) for constructing dams, and SAUTI (Italian) and Kampsax (Danish) for roadbuilding were of this type.

Third, the Plan Organization cooperated in joint ventures with the Point Four organization in Iran to establish specific industries. By late December 1957, the newly established Tehran Bottle Company produced bottles for the blossoming soft drink and pasteurized milk market. Point Four and the Plan Organization provided the capital of this company. The former provided $200,000 for equipment purchase, and the Plan Organization put up 1 million tomans (around $133,000) for the construction of the bottle plant and other expenses. The technical aspects of the factory were under the supervision of an American specialist.[6]

Fourth, the Plan Organization cooperated with Iranian industrialists to establish partnerships. In March 1955, the Plan Organization joined forces with Abdolhoseyn Nikpour to revive his glass company and founded the Iran Glass Company, responding to the growing demand for glass windows. In September 1957, the Plan Organization expanded its joint venture with Senator Nikpour. It established the Iran Bottle and Glass Company to provide bottles for Iran's first pasteurized milk factory, *Shir-e pastorizeh Tehran* (Tehran Pasteurized Milk Company). The joint capital of Iran Bottle and Glass Company was 10 million tomans, its director general was Abbas Mo'tamedi, and it produced 13,000 bottles per day and employed 315 workers.[7]

Fifth, the Plan Organization entered into joint programs with foreign firms. In February 1958, an agreement was reached between the Plan Organization and an American paper and pulp firm (Allan) to build a 50-ton/day factory. The Plan Organization was a 51% owner of the firm and put up 40 million tomans.[8]

---

6 *Ettela'at*, 5 Day 1336.

7 *Ettela'at*, 19 Day 1336; *Tehran Economist*, 12 Bahman 1336.

8 *Ettela'at*, 13 Bahman 1336.

Sixth, the Plan Organization forged triangular partnerships with a ministry and an international organization. It supervised construction and managed the factory upon completion. The state-run Tehran Pasteurized Milk Company, which began operations in November 1957 and was inaugurated by the Shah on 9 January 1958, fell under this rubric. The factory's equipment was gifted by UNICEF ($430,000), the land on which the plant was built was donated by the Ministry of Health, and the Plan Organization paid for construction and installation costs (8 million tomans). The factory employed 80 workers and was run under the technical supervision of a Danish specialist. Ebtehaj's deputy in charge of agricultural affairs at the Plan Organization, Dr Kazemi, was its Chief Executive Officer.[9]

This dairy product factory began producing 10,000 half-liter bottles daily at 9 rials per bottle. It also produced pasteurized butter, yogurt, ice cream, and dried milk.[10] In the triangular negotiations between the Plan Organization, UNICEF, and the Ministry of Health, it was determined that 15% of the milk produced would be distributed gratuitously among children in primary schools, orphanages, and foster care homes.[11] By November 1960, the output of the company had increased almost tenfold to 48,000 liters per day from its initial output of 5,000 liters per day in November 1957.[12]

Seventh, the Plan Organization independently invested in infrastructural projects, the development of which was deemed necessary for the economy's overall growth. The Plan Organization outsourced the construction of such projects to foreign firms. In response to the growing demand for housing and dam construction, the Plan Organization invested heavily in cement production. The Ray, Fars, Lowshan, and Dorud plants helped triple cement production between 1955 and 1959. In December 1955, the construction of the Dorud cement plant was contracted out to the British firm Edgar Allen, a pioneer in the industry since the turn of the century.[13] The Plan Organization also invested heavily in sugar refineries.

Finally, the Plan Organization launched small projects, such as distributing fertilizer and pesticides among farmers, which "was very successful

9 *Ettela'at*, 18,22,27 Aban 1336; 19 Day 1336.
10 *Tehran Economist*, 14 Day 1336.
11 *Ettela'at*, 22 Aban 1336.
12 *Ettela'at*, 23 Aban 1339.
13 *Tehran Economist*, 18 Azar 1334; *Ettela'at*, 26 Bahman 1336.

and a major factor in raising agricultural productivity".[14] Experts from the Food and Agricultural Organization cooperated with Iranians to carry out this program. By February 1958, the Plan Organization had purchased ten agricultural aircrafts and seventy fertilizer trucks.[15]

Second Plan: Post-Ebtehaj Period

In the post-Ebtehaj period, uncertainty about the structure, function, leadership, and role of the Plan Organization, compounding the limitations placed on its resources, impacted the Second Plan. After Ebtehaj, control over the Plan Organization became the prime minister's purview. Between Ebtehaj's exit in February 1959 and the end of the Second Plan on 22 September 1962, Iran had four prime ministers. The fourth prime minister, 'Alam, appointed on 19 July 1962, did not have much of a role in the Second Plan. Until the arrival of Amini in May 1961, the Plan Organization was in a practical leadership turmoil. Its activities were almost on hold, as it was trying hard to complete the projects it had taken on within the context of the Second Plan.

The problems that the Plan Organization, and therefore the implementation of the Second Plan, faced during the post-Ebtehaj period were political, organizational, and financial. Having lost its political clout, Eqbal transferred the executive functions of the Plan Organization to relevant government ministries. Based on a cabinet decree, on 24 September 1959, Eqbal detached government-owned factories from the Plan Organization. Such factories were handed over to the Ministry of Industry and Mines for eventual sale to the private sector. This included textile, sugar loaf, chemical, and silk industries.[16]

In the post-Ebtehaj period, the Plan Organization's internal operational procedures, work practices, and established management style were disrupted by political ambitions, appointments, and experimentations, and this adversely impacted the realization of the Second Plan objectives. The internal organizational structure of the Plan Organization was constantly under scrutiny and being restructured, while unpredictability and insecurity crippled it. The Plan Organization lost its zeal and self-confidence.

14 Khodadad Farmanfarmayan, Iranian Oral History Collection, Harvard University, Transcript 2, Sequence 22.
15 *Ettela'at*, 14 Bahman 1336.
16 *Tehran Economist*, 22 Ordibehesht 1341.

From 1959, the investment expenditure of the Second Plan was significantly reduced due to cost overruns and a substantial reduction of the Plan Organization's share of oil revenues. The Plan Organization's share of oil revenues, which was supposed to constitute 80%, dropped to 48% in 1959 and 55% in 1960.[17]

Due to the combination of post-Ebtehaj political, organizational, and financial factors, there was a glaring divergence between the original intentions and outcomes of the Second Plan. The Plan intended to "construct or improve 10,700 kilometers of road". It only completed 5,503 kilometers at an 80% higher cost.[18] The lion's share of investments went to big projects such as the Dez, Sefid Rud, and Karaj dams and the Khuzestan Development Services.

THE SECOND PLAN UNDER SCRUTINY

A detailed report on the activities of the Plan Organization during the Second Plan was published in June and July 1962. It indicated that the provision of piped water had been completed in twenty-three cities and was underway in seventy-eight cities, while the tender for construction was issued in another seventy-two cities. In urban street construction, the asphalting of roads in ninety cities had been completed, while in twenty-three cities, it was underway, and in eleven cities, it was about to begin. Delays in certain cities were due to the necessity of first carrying out works for constructing pipe water networks and subsequently asphalting the city streets.[19]

Safi Asfia and Khodadad Farmanfarmayan believed the Second Seven-Year Plan to be positive. Their list of the Plan's accomplishments included the building of roads, railways, airports, and ports, mechanization of farms and distribution and maintenance of tractors, provision of some 170 cities with electricity, sewage systems, and water supplies, as well as advances in health, education, and professional training. The Second Plan was said to have established cement, textiles, and sugar industries and constructed three major dams. Farmanfarmayan argued that, most importantly, the public sector expenditures triggered off activities in the private sector,

17 FO 371/157626, EP 1102/54.
18 Daftary, "Development Planning in Iran: A Historical Survey," pp. 176–228.
19 *Tehran Economist*, 9, 22 Tir 1341.

giving rise to "the emergence of a whole new group of entrepreneurs in the private sector".[20]

The Second Plan was also credited for laying "the infrastructural and organizational base" of more comprehensive future development plans. During the first phase of the Second Plan, Ebtehaj was multi-functioning. He was effectively building the Plan Organization, securing funds from international organizations, signing a major contract with Lilienthal's Development and Resources Corporation, assessing old contracts, and executing new ones. Political considerations did not intervene in the functioning of the Plan Organization and subsequently the implementation of the Second Plan during the Ebtehaj period. This changed during the second phase.

Based on preliminary estimates, the Plan Organization suggested that Iran's growth rate between 1955 and 1959 had been 4 to 5%.[21] Bostock and Jones, however, argued that during the first five years of the Second Plan, Iran achieved an impressive annual growth rate of 7 to 8% from 1955 to 1960.[22]

The criticism and shortcomings laid at the door of the Second Plan fell into three main categories. First, problems with planning, its technique, and scope. Second, institutional and financial factors, and finally, problems with implementing the projects. Farhad Daftary, Francis Bostock, and Geoffrey Jones criticized the Second Plan for its planning and institutional deficiencies.

Daftary's list of at least seven flaws covers those of Bostock and Jones. According to Daftary, first of all, the Second Plan lacked "a clearly defined development policy". Second, it failed to be comprehensive and was unconcerned with "the overall rate and pattern of development in the economy". Third, it remained mute on how investments of the Plan Organization were to be coordinated with those of the government, causing tension between the two. Fourth, "the absence of all types of statistical information" necessary for comprehensive planning posed a serious impediment. Fifth, it was merely "a list of investment programs and projects, the selection of which did not follow from the application of any specific investment criteria".

20 Khodadad Farmanfarmayan, Iranian Oral History Collection, Harvard University, Transcript 4, Sequence 47. For a comprehensive report of the achievements of the Second Plan up to October 1961, see: Plan Organization Activities, General Department of Publications & Broadcasting in FO 371/157626 EP 1102/54. *Ettela'at*, 29 Ordibehesht 1341.

21 *Tehran Economist*, 10 Day 1339, 27 Esfand 1339.

22 F. Bostock and G. Jones, *Planning and Power in Iran*, p. 127.

Sixth, the Second Plan reflected unfamiliarity with "planning methodology and techniques". Seventh, the investments by the Plan were mainly "in a few big capital-intensive projects".[23]

Jahangir Amuzegar, Francis Bostock, and Geoffrey Jones criticized the Second Plan for institutional, financial, and implementational flaws. Bostock and Jones believed that "limited funds, and lack of data, trained planners, and interdepartmental coordination" prevented the second Plan from being "an attempt at 'comprehensive' planning".[24] Amuzegar argued that the big projects "showed substantial cost overruns", causing public revenues to fall short of the "unexpectedly high public outlays". For Amuzegar, the foreign credit crunch exasperated the match between the planned investment projects and their realization.[25]

An internal Plan Organization review of the Second Plan also identified three shortcomings: "the complications of planning", "inadequately trained manpower", and "institutional factors". The lack of a "coordinated and comprehensive national plan" was flagged as the "main obstacle to a faster rate of economic and social development".[26]

DRAFTING THE THIRD FIVE-YEAR PLAN

In mid-1959, under Eqbal's premiership, the Division of Economic Affairs was tasked with preparing the Third Five-Year Plan which was to go into effect on 23 September 1962. At this time, Khosrow Hedayat had replaced Ebtehaj, and the Division of Economic Affairs had decided that a five-year plan would be more suitable for Iran than a seven-year plan.

The Third Plan began with an assessment of the Second Plan compiled in a report called, "Measuring the progress and undertakings of the Second Seven-Year Plan." The task continued with producing "a series of documents" called "plan frames". Each "plan frame", such as the "Third Plan Frame for Agriculture", was the product of one specialized branch of the Division of Economic Affairs.

23 F. Daftary, "Development Planning in Iran: A Historical Survey", *Iranian Studies*, vol. 6, no. 4 (1973) pp. 176–228.
24 F. Bostock and G. Jones, *Planning and Power in Iran*, pp. 126–127.
25 Amuzegar, *The Dynamics of the Iranian Revolution*, p. 174.
26 McLeod, "National Planning in Iran," p. 4.

The Division of Economic Affairs "consisted of a General Economics Group, which also coordinated the planning effort, and five sections concerned with particular sectors of the economy".[27] Each section focused on developmental fields such as agriculture, industry, transportation, electricity, education, and health.

Each "plan frame" presented the complete developmental plan of a particular field of economic activity, including policy recommendations, approximative allocation of development funds, and the broad outlines of its programs.[28] Developing "plan frames" took about sixteen months (March 1960–July 1961). According to US sources, during the Aramesh period (February–May 1961), work on "plan frames" virtually ceased.[29]

The preparation of each "plan frame" involved the participation of hundreds of government technicians and foreign advisors.[30] Once each "plan frame" and their associated developmental requirements were identified, and integrated, a whole picture or an aggregate development plan emerged. The final phase of preparing the Third Plan required identifying specific projects, their associated costs, and the establishment of "an order of priority between and within sectors".[31]

This last and crucial phase had to be carried out with an eye to evaluating the funds available. The planners had to forecast government revenues and foreign capital injections, including investments and loans. The task was made more difficult by the changing trade and fiscal policies of successive governments as witnessed by the three governments of Eqbal (1957–1960), Sharif-Emami (1960–1961), and Amini (1961–1962).

---

27 J. Price Gittinger, "Planning for Agricultural Development: The Iranian Experience," Center for Development Planning, Planning Experience, Series no. 2, National Planning Association, 1965, p. 55, https://pdf.usaid.gov/pdf_docs/PNRAA581.pdf (retrieved 13/1/2024).

28 Gittinger, "Planning for Agricultural Development: The Iranian Experience," pp. IX–X, 59.

29 Foreign Relations of the United States, 1961–1963, Volume XVII, Near East, 1961–1962, Document 46.

30 Gittinger, "Planning for Agricultural Development: The Iranian Experience," pp. 59–60.

31 McLeod, "National Planning in Iran," p. 8; Gittinger, "Planning for Agricultural Development: The Iranian Experience," pp. 59, 62.

PROMOTING THE PLAN ORGANIZATION AND THE THIRD FIVE-YEAR PLAN

With the departure of Ebtehaj, the Plan Organization was pushed to become more integrated with other government ministries and organizations. As early as April 1960, key players in the Division of Economic Affairs emerged from their isolation and embarked on a public relations campaign. They hoped to reach out to the broader public, mend fences, shed the Ebtehaj era image of aloofness and haughtiness, inform the public of their assessment of the Second Seven-Year Plan, and speak about their plans for the Third Five-Year Plan.

In May 1960, at the invitation of Ehsan Naraqi, director of the Institute of Social Studies and Research, Iran's first and prestigious think tank for social studies, Khodadad Farmanfarmayan, the director of the Division of Economic Affairs, Abdolmajid Majidi, the French-educated head of the budget office, and Hoseyn Kazemzadeh, the US-educated head of the office of projects, held a conference followed by a question-and-answer session.

Kazemzadeh spoke about the Plan Organization's recent experiences, its achievements as well as its shortcomings. He enumerated three main problems facing the Plan Organization: carelessness in planning, change of projects during implementation, and unexpected reductions in finances. Kazemzadeh concluded that despite such shortcomings, the Plan Organization's overall performance exonerated it from unfounded criticisms.

Majidi outlined, in detail, how the Plan Organization was denied the finances it was promised and how the significant shortfall of promised revenues adversely impacted its performance. Farmanfarmayan deplored the fact that those who were in positions of leadership (*dar ras-e omor*) at the Plan Organization "did not know where they were going and what they were doing".[32] Farmanfarmayan's harsh words were directed at Eqbal who had become the official head of the Plan Organization.

In the context of their outreach effort, the Plan Organization team, headed by Farmanfarmayan, paid daily visits to various ministries, government organizations, and the Tehran Chamber of Commerce to engage their members in a dialogue on the Third Plan, inform them of it, and

32 *Tehran Economist*, 24 Ordibehesht 1339.

solicit their input.[33] From the summer of 1960, regular monthly and semi-monthly meetings were held between key decision-makers in the Plan Organization, all relevant ministries, and government agencies such as the Melli/National Bank and the Central Bank to discuss and work on the Third Plan.[34]

THE THIRD PLAN, AMINI, AND THE US

From May 1961, with Amini in power and the dismissal of Aramesh, the Plan Organization regained its spirit and composure under the leadership of Asfia. The Plan Organization's Division of Economic Affairs had Amini's ear. Contrary to his predecessors, the new Prime Minister trusted the specialists and valued their expertise. Economics mattered to Amini, and Iran's economic crisis was one of his biggest headaches. Amini felt close to the US-trained economists, listened to their advice, and spent hours in the High Economic Council discussing solutions to internal and external imbalances, inflation, and the money crunch. During Amini's premiership, the High Economic Council no longer met in the presence of the Shah. After each session, the Prime Minister would present the Shah with a report on the technical discussion and the policies resulting from them.[35]

Under Amini's Premiership, winds of change blew from all directions. The political crisis, which had begun with the shooting of Abolhasan Khanali, the Tehran teacher, by the police during the peaceful Tehran Teachers' demonstrations and had led to the fall of the Sharif-Emami government, rattled the Kennedy administration. Worried about a "potentially dangerous situation in Iran", at the US National Security Council meeting of 5 May 1961, President Kennedy recommended establishing the Iran Task Force, a "crisis-type task force" mandated to closely monitor Iran's political, social, and economic developments. The Iran Task Force held its first official meeting on 8 May, the day Amini replaced Sharif-Emami. At this meeting, Phillips Talbot, who served as chairman, reported that "the new government in Iran is expected to be a stabilizing force and that

33 *Tehran Economist*, 24 Ordibehesht 1339.

34 *Tehran Economist*, 2 Mehr 1339.

35 Khodadad Farmanfarmayan, Iranian Oral History Collection, Harvard University, Transcript 8, Sequence 94.

the Task Force will concentrate on medium-range objectives rather than immediate crises."[36]

One of the Task Force's main concerns was ensuring the smooth functioning of the Iranian economy. Even before embarking on the Third Plan, the US was realistically concerned whether Iran could successfully complete the Second Plan's objectives. On 8 May 1961, the Task Force asked the US Embassy in Iran, "How much aid [is] required by [the] Plan Organization [to] complete [the] Second Plan assuming [that] $10 million [is] transferred from 1340 general revenues?" Edward Wailes, the US Ambassador, responded, "[We] believe [the] $40 million estimate for hard-core Plan Org aid requirement [is] still valid."[37]

On May 18, the Iran Task Force informed President Kennedy that Iran was "pretty far down the road to chaos", and that the US "had better do everything feasible to give the Amini 'experiment' a fighting chance". To this end, the Task Force developed "a pretty good action program". The Task Force informed the President that its "action plan" was "oriented more toward economic needs and social reform than toward paying the Shah military *baksheesh* again".[38]

To alleviate Iran's immediate "cash crisis", the Task Force observed that the Plan Organization "can't pay its current bills" under the Second Plan. As for "longer-range economic aid", the Task Force recommended that the US "reorient" its efforts to support Iran's "Seven Year Plans".[39] For the immediate future, it recommended that the Iranian government should be immediately informed that the US intended "to make a cash grant of $15 million payable as soon as required by the Iranians". The Task Force also recommended that the US government "Be prepared to make an additional $5 million grant of FY [fiscal year] 1962 funds to the Government of Iran for general budgetary purposes if, at a later date, the situation in

36 Foreign Relations of the United States, 1961–1963, Volume XVII, Near East Region, 1961–1962, Document 41.

37 Foreign Relations of the United States, 1961–1963, Volume XVII, Near East Region, 1961–1962, Document 46.

38 Foreign Relations of the United States, 1961–1963, Volume XVII, Near East, 1961–1962, Documents 50.

39 Foreign Relations of the United States, 1961–1963, Volume XVII, Near East, 1961–1962, Documents 50.

Iran requires such action."[40] The US government was firmly committed to supporting Amini both economically and politically.

On 27 May 1961, eighteen days after introducing his cabinet to the Shah, Amini visited the Plan Organization. His core comments revolved around three major axes with bearing on the drafting of the Third Plan. First, he acknowledged that the Plan organization had rendered considerable services, insisted that it step up its efforts, and praised Asfia for his "know-how and abilities". Second, he asserted that the Plan Organization should diminish its operational and executive responsibilities of carrying out projects. Third, he insisted that the Plan Organization rely on short-term investment projects, which would provide quick results.[41]

The idea of transforming the Plan Organization into just a planning rather than a planning and executing body was supported by members of the Division of Economic Affairs, the Iranian government and economic experts at the British Embassy.[42] In July 1961, the Committee on Reorganization for the Third Plan, under the chairmanship of Cyrus Babak Sami'i, recommended that the Plan Organization "divest itself of its responsibilities of the execution and operation of projects" and recommended a "greater degree of integration with the regular machinery of the government".[43]

Following this advice, Amini veered away from Ebtehaj's vision. Ebtehaj had been emphatic on the plan plus execution role of the Plan Organization and the importance of long-term infrastructural projects. For both Eqbal and Sharif-Emami, the young, self-righteous, and Western-trained economists that Ebtehaj had gathered in the Plan Organization's Division of Economic Affairs were arrogant rookies who had to be shunned. But Amini spoke their technical and cultural language and shared their economic mindset and rationale.

On 3 June 1961, Khodadad Farmanfarmayan, the Plan Organization's Financial and Economic Deputy, and his Iranian team met with reporters at *Anjoman matbou'at* (the Press Association/Club) to provide a general picture of Iran's economy and the reasons for its predicament. Farmanfarmayan blamed the political decision-makers for not listening

40 Foreign Relations of the United States, 1961–1963, Volume XVII, Near East, 1961–1962, Documents 51.

41 *Ettela'at*, 6 Khordad 1340.

42 FO 371/157625, EP 1102/20.

43 McLeod, "National Planning in Iran," pp. 135, 142, 143, 163, 212.

to the good advice of the Division of Economic Affairs and accused the "high government officials" of being "either incapable of understanding the technical issues or ill-intentioned". Economic improvement, he suggested, needed "people in authority who were both responsible and capable of understanding economic policies and their consequences".[44] With Amini in charge, Farmanfarmayan and his team believed that they were dealing with their equals in knowledge, as well as in ethics and standards.

At their meeting with the press, the Plan Organization team emphasized the comprehensive, integrated, synchronized, and coordinated aspect of the Third Five-Year Plan, beginning in September 1962 and ending in March 1968. This Plan intended to interlace every aspect of the economy, and its objectives were the rapid increase in national income (a 6% growth rate), provision of employment, and a more equitable distribution of income, in that order of priority.[45]

By June 1961, it became clear that completing the Second Seven-Year Plan projects required some additional $45 million. This figure was close to the $40 million that Ambassador Wailes had predicted as Iran's financial need in his May correspondence with the Task Force. This financial gap, which had to be funded from overseas, had to be filled before moving on to the Third Plan. The Third Five-Year Plan, which was to begin in September 1962, was dependent on the successful completion of the current Second Plan.[46] One year before the beginning of the Third Plan, the Plan Organization was short of 300 million tomans to complete the projects of the Second Plan. The problem was that it did not know where to find this sum.[47]

The US Bails Out the Second Plan

In his correspondence with the Task Force, back in on 10 May 1961, Ambassador Wailes had mentioned that once the Third Plan was ready, Plan Organization officials should approach the US and "seek [an] invitation to Washington to discuss over-all plan objectives".[48]

44 *Ettela'at*, 16 Khordad 1340.
45 *Ettela'at*, 17 Khordad 1340.
46 Foreign Relations of the United States, 1961–1963, Volume XVII, Near East, 1961–1962, Document 90.
47 *Ettela'at*, 20 Mehr 1340, 13 Aban 1340.
48 Foreign Relations of the United States, 1961–1963, Volume XVII, Near East, 1961–1962, Document 46.

On 13 July 1961, Khodadad Farmanfarmayan left for Washington. He was to be joined by Bahman Abadiyan, Mostafa 'Elm and Shapur Rasekh. The Plan Organization team was to travel to ten European countries after its visit to Washington. They had the Herculean task of addressing three major issues. First, it was to solicit financial help of some $45–50 million to fill the "gap" and finish the remaining projects of the Second Plan. Second, it had to present the first draft of the Third Plan to World Bank officials and European economists, bankers, and professionals for their professional and technical advice and feedback.[49] Finally, their longer-term objective was to secure some $732 million of credit to complete the Third Plan. Iran hoped to muster this loan through an international consortium of creditors, including American, British, and West German banks, guaranteed by the International Monetary Fund.[50]

The Iran Task Force reacted positively to the Third Plan presented by the Iranian delegation to the International Bank for Reconstruction and Development (World Bank). It assessed the Plan as "generally well-conceived" and announced that it would extend all possible encouragement and assistance in its development. The Task Force promised to "re-orient" and "direct" US "technical and economic assistance programs to fit in with the Plan".[51]

On a technical level, however, Western economists had some concerns with the Third Plan. First, the targeted average 6% growth rate per year in the gross national product during the Third Five-Year Plan period seemed optimistic to them. Second, they deemed a 7% increase in money supply as inflationary. Third, the projected deficit of 6.9 billion tomans in the Third Plan was considered an underestimate. Fourth, the Plan could not be self-financed. Fifth, the growth targeted in all sectors needed skilled personnel, which was lacking. Sixth, priority needed to be given to "core" projects and only to "non-core" projects when finances were available for them. Seventh, the Plan lacked a "foreign exchange budget".[52]

49 *Ettela'at*, 21 Tir, 15 Mordad 1340.

50 *Ettela'at*, 7 Mordad 1340. Later, the required credit gap for terminating the projects of the Third Plan was put at somewhere between $600 and 900 million. See *Ettela'at*, 13 Aban 1340.

51 Foreign Relations of the United States, 1961–1963, Volume XVII, Near East, 1961–1962, Document 90.

52 FO 371/157625, EP 1102/25; FO 371/157625, EP 1102/27; FO 371/157626, EP 1102/34.

The initial good news for financing the "gap" in the Second Plan came from Bonn, Germany, on 17 August 1961. The Kennedy administration and the Federal Republic of Germany hoped to find a solution to finance the shortfall in the Second Plan. According to the Iran Task Force, "Curtailment of this Plan [Second Plan] would throw the Third Plan out of balance, damage the Iranian government politically, and probably result in the cancellation of large Iranian contracts with American concerns".[53]

The mission to Germany headed by the Minister of Industry and Mines, Gholamali Farivar, had begun negotiations with German financial authorities on 31 July 1961. In August, the news circulated that Germany had extended a loan of $20 million to Iran and would possibly increase it to a maximum of $36 million. These credits were tied to the completion of specific projects in the Second Plan, such as the completion of the Sefid Rud Dam, the construction of a second oil pipeline from Abadan to Tehran, and the construction of the Tehran oil refinery.[54]

At the 7 September 1961 meeting of the Iran Task Force, Phillips Talbot, the Chair, who had recently returned from a trip to Tehran and had met with the Shah and Amini, reported that "the fiscal and economic situation in Iran" was "depressing". He stated that "the Army and the Shah" were pressing "for more funds for the military", and that the financing gap of the Second Plan was $60 million, with the German aid covering only "$20 million of that gap".[55] Iran was still short of another $40 million.

The US, however, was firmly committed to the completion of "the essential elements of the Second Plan" and helping Amini "surmount the political and economic difficulties" that it faced until the beginning of the Third Plan.[56] On 27 October 1961, the US authorized its ambassador, Holmes, to inform Amini that, the "United States would provide an additional $15 million Supporting Assistance cash grant, and that a further $20 million in development lending was available from FY 1962

53 Foreign Relations of the United States, 1961–1963, Volume XVII, Near East, 1961–1962, Document 90.

54 *Ettela'at*, 26 Mordad 1340; Foreign Relations of the United States, 1961–1963, Volume XVII, Near East, 1961–1962, Document 102.

55 Foreign Relations of the United States, 1961–1963, Volume XVII, Near East, 1961–1962, Document 105.

56 Foreign Relations of the United States, 1961–1963, Volume XVII, Near East, 1961–1962, Document 127.

funds."[57] Having almost filled the gap to realize the unfinished projects of the Second Plan, the US made it known to Amini that the 1962–1963 budget had to be balanced, without US assistance.

Final Touches to The Third Plan

The Farmanfarmayan team returned from its almost two-month overseas visit in September 1961. From the meetings overseas, it had become obvious that three major studies had to be undertaken to facilitate the Third Plan's implementation. Upon its return, the Plan Organization team began fine-tuning the Third Five-Year Plan.

First, if the executive functions of the Plan Organization were to be handed over to the ministries, a survey had to assess the ability of such ministries to properly implement those projects. The second study dealt with a comprehensive national budget or a survey of expenditures and revenues for all departments, government, quasi-government organizations, and the Plan Organization. Finally, to address the pressing bottleneck of technical and skilled manpower to carry out the projects of the Third Plan, "a survey had to be made of the manpower resources available".[58]

To the original three objectives of the Third Plan, namely a 6% growth rate, job creation, and equitable income distribution, two more goals were added. These were "promotion of possibilities through necessary reforms for better utilization of human resources", and "the ensuring of a continuous growth based on economic stabilization".[59] Yet, the attainment of the 6% growth rate remained the prime objective. Pledging allegiance to the continuation of economic stabilization was to guarantee the favorable decisions of the World Bank and the IMF toward obtaining foreign credit. The achievement of its prime objective of a 6% growth rate, however, was also incumbent upon an "increase in national savings", "administrative and organization improvements and reform in social relations", and family planning to control the population increase.[60]

After lengthy deliberations, the Third Plan seemed ready. The Shah paid a highly publicized visit to the Plan Organization on 3 January 1962 to hear

57 Foreign Relations of the United States, 1961–1963, Volume XVII, Near East, 1961–1962, Document 133.
58 FO 371/157626, EP 1102/48.
59 FO 371/157626, EP 1102/51.
60 FO 371/157626, EP 1102/51.

the latest updates on the Plan. Amini and his ministers, Asfia, Entezam, and the heads of Central and Melli Banks, were present at this meeting. Serious discussions took place for three hours behind closed doors. The Iranian press reported immediately that according to Asfia, the Shah had expressed satisfaction with the Third Five-Year Plan, had asked specific questions, and had subsequently "given certain orders" (*avameri sader farmudand*), which would be incorporated into the final Plan.[61]

One day after the meeting, the press reported on it. Most probably, the content appearing in the press had been scrutinized and sanitized by higher authorities before publication. It was reported that Asfia had made essential distinctions between the Second and Third Plans. He had noted that during the Second Plan, the Plan Organization had carried out its own projects, while government ministries engaged in their activities separately, and the private sector undertook its own investments without any coordination between the three, yielding unsatisfactory project implementation results.

Asfia had identified the Third Plan as fundamentally different from its predecessor, as it was a comprehensive plan coordinating and integrating the economic activities of the private and public sectors. It also balanced and synchronized action between the Plan Organization and government ministries to implement projects. The Third Plan was unique, the product of intense consultations during 100 meetings between Plan Organization experts and members of government organizations, as well as ministries. Finally, Asfia had concluded that to ensure the smooth exercise of its new responsibilities, the ministries needed to forego significant reforms, laying off incompetent staff and employing experts and professionals.

The Shah's comments after Asfia's presentation were to determine the fate of the March 1962 to March 1963 budget, Amini, and the Third Plan. The Shah's preoccupations with Iran's future security challenges and his vision of the appropriate development style once again placed Iran's overall resource allocation between military expenditures and developmental investments at the center stage.

At the 3 January 1962 meeting on the Third Plan, the Shah referred to the fact that despite Iran's neutrality during the two World Wars, it had been invaded due to its geographical location. The Shah predicted that during the next twenty years Iran would be confronted with a serious

61 *Ettela'at*, 13 Day 1340.

threat from the "Communist world" and that all "Free World" countries were preparing themselves for this eventuality.

He therefore argued that Iran needed to "improve the living standard and purchasing power" of the people in the next twenty years to resist and prevent any temptation towards "destructive hesitations", by which he probably meant, communist tendencies or attractions. Having enumerated the military budgets of the US, USSR, Turkey, Switzerland, Egypt, and Iraq, he concluded that even small countries had to prepare to defend themselves. To defend their independence, the Shah repeated his obsessional leitmotif that, "unfortunately we are obliged to increase our military expenditures".[62]

Publicizing and Popularizing the Third Plan

From 9 January 1962, Safi Asfia, Khodadad Farmanfarmayan, and Bahman Abadiyan went on the road to explain the objectives and constraints of the Third Plan to the public and the press. The Third Plan was to be a coordinated national effort. Therefore, instead of imposing it from the top, the Plan Organization intended to make it a joint effort public project. The Plan Organization was on an American-style pedagogical mission of teaching economic development to the people, a topic and language that not even all Iranian political leaders could master. Officials at the Plan Organization argued that the more people knew about the Third Plan and understood its objectives and operations, the easier its acceptance and implementation would be.[63]

Bahman Abadiyan hammered home the importance of training skilled workers, increasing the pace of infrastructural development, and increasing investment in primary education, preventive medicine in the rural sector, and rural and agricultural development. He called these the "core" programs of the Third Development Plan. This notion of "core" programs as distinct from "secondary or non-core" programs found its way into the budget presentations.

Abadiyan also addressed the critical issue of a developing economy's "absorptive capacity". He broached a sensitive topic that was inconsequential for the press but of the greatest significance for the Shah to grasp and

62 *Ettela'at*, 14 Day 1340. Information in the previous four paragraphs is based on this source. See also FO 371/164205, EP 1111/2.

63 *Ettela'at*, 20 Day 1340.

really master, which he never did. Abadiyan's lecture was straightforward. Yes, he said, economic development is a function of investment rates, but it is not limited to investment rates. In the short term, high investment rates do not necessarily translate into high economic growth rates.

If investment rates increase beyond a threshold, Abadiyan argued, the absorptive capacity of an economy, constrained by the inadequacy of other complementary factors of production such as skilled labor, roads, ports, electricity, and adequate administrative structures, would prevent the investment from efficient utilization, causing severe imbalances in the economy.[64] This was a simple economic lesson that the Shah should have been attentive to, but was not, especially after the oil price hikes of 1973.

64 *Ettela'at*, 20 Day 1340.

12

Amini's Last Five Months: The Political Economy of His Undoing

On 21 February 1962, Amini went on a four-nation European tour, primarily in search of foreign economic investment, cooperation, and financial credit. On this trip, Amini was accompanied by Batul, his wife, Ali-Asgharpur Purhomayun, the governor of the Central Bank, Khodadad Farmanfarmayan, the Economic and Financial Deputy of the Plan Organization, and Reza Fallah, a high-ranking member of the NIOC's management board.

Amini's thirteen-day trip took him to the Federal Republic of Germany, Belgium, France, and England. In Belgium, Amini met not only with the prime minister but with King Baudouin. In Germany, he met with Konrad Adenauer, the Chancellor, and Ludwig Erhard, the Vice-Chancellor and Minister of Economics. They discussed economic cooperation between the two countries, the possibility of a consortium of countries, including Germany, extending a credit package to partially finance Iran's $2.5 billion Third Plan and future cooperation with the European Common Market.[1]

Amini's three-day visit to France was unofficial and private, yet he met with Michel Debré, the French prime minister, and President Charles De Gaulle at the Élysée Palace. In Paris, Amini said that he expected France, Germany, Belgium, Italy, Canada, England, and the US to participate in a consortium of countries under the aegis of the World Bank and provide Iran with $800 million in credit towards realizing the objectives of the Third

1 *Ettela'at*, 5 Esfand 1340.

Five-Year Plan. Finally, in London, the Iranian prime minister met with Harold Macmillan, the British prime minister and with Queen Elizabeth II.[2]

Three days before his departure, Amini had explained that he was not going to Europe to beg for money, and if he were to obtain such monies, they would have to be used to speed up the country's economic development. He then made a curious comment and added that just as the Shah's trips overseas had always proven successful in demonstrating Iran's situation, he was hoping to do the same thing.[3] Intentionally or inadvertently, Amini was comparing himself to the Shah, especially as a figurehead representing Iran overseas. This was a *faux pas*.

What may have irked the Shah even more was that four days earlier, Chester Bowles, the US President's special advisor, had spoken to the press right before leaving Tehran for Cairo. In his short declaration, Bowles had praised Amini as Iran's "capable and competent Prime Minister" and spoke of his admiration for the government's land reform program. He also remembered to say that the highlight of his trip was his "long and most useful meeting with the Shah".[4]

On the day of his departure for Europe, in what sounded like a last will and testament, Amini addressed Iranians as "dear compatriots" and issued a lengthy statement. He addressed the youth, the educated and intellectuals, as well as the underprivileged and the poor, and asked them for their support. Amini pleaded with Iranians to maintain their national cohesion and speak in a single voice (*vahdat kalameh*) to arrive at the national goal of economic and cultural development and a life of leisure and freedom. He warned against "the influential and wealthy unaccustomed to the notions of law and justice".

Sounding more like a revolutionary than a liberal reformist, Amini said, "We cannot stop the inevitable march of history." Yet, he emphasized the importance of being realistic about the constraints, and promised to plant the seeds of democracy by engaging with the people directly, being honest with them, and not promising them pipe dreams. In his address, he referred to the Shah twice. Only once did he announce that "under the leadership and guidance of the Shah", his government would follow through with its objectives.[5]

2 *Ettela'at*, 14, 19 Esfand 1340.

3 *Ettela'at*, 29 Bahman 1340.

4 *Ettela'at*, 25 Bahman 1340.

5 *Ettela'at*, 1 Esfand 1340. The previous two paragraphs are based on this source.

In his meeting with Konrad Adenauer, Amini made another statement that contradicted the Shah's official position of 4 January 1962 on the persistent threat of communism. In his attempt to assure German industrialists that their investments in Iran would be safe, Amini announced that "a direct communist threat against Iran is nonexistent."[6] To make up for his "blunder", in his later speech in Berlin, Amini compared the situation in West Berlin with Iran and said, "our problems like yours, are mostly the result of Soviet policies."[7] During the rest of his European tour, he made sure he had something negative to say about the Soviet Union.

While Amini was trying to dampen the effect of his comment on the inexistence of a Soviet threat and appease the Shah, the German press and Iranian students in Germany created another embarrassing situation for him. *Die Welt* praised Amini as "the only person in Iran whose upright/correct political tendencies can be trusted". This well-known newspaper characterized Amini as a "rational and deeply understanding person who has categorically and energetically confronted the problems of his country". A student welcomed Amini to a meeting with Iranian students in Germany by addressing him as "the leader of the Iranian people and the beloved Prime Minister".[8] Such a comment portrayed Amini like a Mosaddeq.

Michel Debré, the French prime minister, praised Amini for his "courage in confronting domestic problems". The left-leaning and progressive French daily, *Le Monde* wrote, "We have seldom seen a politician as courageous and candid as Amini." Even when the French press praised the Shah for his reformist views, it highlighted his choice of Amini as prime minister.[9] In Paris, Amini discussed Iran's outstanding debts to France and promised that they would be repaid.

During his short private visit to Switzerland on his way back to Tehran, Amini had a surprise thirty-minute visit by Dean Rusk, the US Secretary of State who was in Geneva. Their discussion revolved around US economic and military aid to Iran. Rusk asked Amini whether he could balance Iran's 1962–1963 budget. The Prime Minister is reported to have responded negatively but promised that all unnecessary costs would be cut. Amini

6 *Ettela'at*, 5 Esfand 1340.
7 *Ettela'at*, 7 Esfand 1340.
8 *Ettela'at*, 7, 9 Esfand 1340.
9 *Ettela'at*, 15 Esfand 1340.

informed Rusk that he could not touch the salaries of government employees, a significant share of government expenditures.[10]

THE SHAH UNHAPPY WITH AMINI

Even though Amini was accorded a hot welcome during his tour, he returned to Tehran without any concrete economic or financial commitments from his hosts. The praise poured on Amini during his European tour, and his popularity with foreign heads of state, could not have eluded the Shah. It is quite possible that the Shah felt envious of the attention Amini had received overseas and began to worry about "free world" leaders considering his prime minister as a worthy alternative to his own rule.

It may or may not have been a coincidence that on 12 March 1962, a historical landmark for the Amini government, the Shah went to Maragheh accompanied by Arsanjani, Minister of Agriculture, and in the absence of Amini handed out the first land deeds to the new free tenants. Had he waited for one more day, Amini would have returned from his European tour on 13 March 1962. Amini missed the big day officially marking the eventual implementation of land reform in Iran, a feat for which he was widely praised in Europe and the US.

While Amini had been welcomed in France, the Shah was in a dark mood. At the Abali ski resort, he complained to the British Ambassador, "It was not enough that his prime minister should be referred to as an American nominee. If they [the US] would not take a more sympathetic view of his military requirements, they had better take over the country." He even suggested that, given his situation, he may abdicate his throne.[11]

His Majesty had hoped that by supporting Amini, America's preferred candidate for prime minister, the US would reciprocate by providing Iran with generous military aid and credit. The pressure by the World Bank, IMF, Iran's creditors, and Amini to balance the budget frustrated and depressed the Shah, who felt that in the absence of US military aid, he would have to contain his dream of an ever-expanding military budget.

The Shah was upset at the US for its "stinginess". The US Secretary of State, Dean Rusk, recalled that since the Shah "was putting more into

10 *Ettela'at*, 24 Esfand 1340.
11 FO 371/164182, EP 1015/43/G.

his military than he needed ... we were quite reserved about the kind of unlimited military assistance that he would want from us." Rusk concluded that "there was always an edge of unhappiness on his part that we weren't doing more to help him build up this glorified position based upon major armed forces there in his country."[12]

The Shah was also unhappy with his prime minister, who had stolen his thunder at home and overseas. He felt politically and economically hemmed in by policies and objectives that were not his but came from the US and Amini. The King felt restrained and overshadowed in his own country. Since he could not rupture with the US, he needed to reassert himself and take control of the country by sacking Amini.

THE SHAH'S INAUSPICIOUS VISIT TO THE US

The Shah's official visit to the US on 10 April 1962 was at his own request. It had been originally scheduled for October 1962, but the Shah's depressive mood convinced the US to speed up the state visit to boost his morale. During his US trip, the Shah raised the issue of Iran's military and financial needs with Kennedy and his men.

At their 12 April 1962 meeting at the White House, Kennedy informed the Shah that "a very large Iranian Army was not needed." Dean Rusk added that the "Iranian armed forces are too large and are not properly equipped." Rusk recommended a 25% reduction in Iran's army in return for a five-year program for the "supply of necessary equipment".

The American President and his Secretary of State told the Shah that by downsizing his army from 200,000 to 150,000, he "would save a number of million dollars annually", resolving his budget deficit problems. This was far from music to the Shah's ears. When the Shah said that "Iran would require continuing budgetary support from the United States", Kennedy bluntly told him that "Iran could expect no such aid in future from the United States."[13]

In their meeting of 13 April, Kennedy again emphasized that the Shah's prestige was largely dependent on "Iran's economic development program", reminding him that he should put economic development ahead of military

12 "The Reminiscences of Dean Rusk in an interview with William Burr," 23 May 1986, Oral History of Iran Collection of the Foundation of Iranian Studies, p. 15.
13 FRUS, 1961–1936, vol. XVII, Near East Region, 1961–1962, Document 243.

development. Kennedy also "congratulated the Shah for having found such an excellent Prime Minister and for supporting him in his efforts".[14]

THE BUDGET DEFICIT DISPUTE: GUNS VERSUS BUTTER

While the budget deficit problem persisted and the annual budget could not be determined, Iran ran on a monthly budget from 21 March 1962. The Shah returned to Iran on 18 April 1962. All hopes which had been pinned on a US budget bailout were dashed, and Amini was intent on not disguising the budget deficit, as was the custom of his predecessors. In the meantime, relations between the Shah and Amini had grown uneasy and cold. The Shah's disgruntlement with Amini primarily resulted from his disappointment with the Kennedy administration.

As the storm gathered around Iran's budget deficit and the growing need to borrow overseas to implement the Third Plan, John Guanter, the IMF's Iran man, returned to Tehran around 7 May and left on 15 May 1962. He voiced satisfaction with the stabilization program, the government's anti-inflationary policies, and price stability in the country. Guanter announced that credit would be expanded both in the private and public sectors to relieve excessive pressure on the bazaar and praised the activities of the newly formed Central Bank. However, Guanter announced that the only point of contention between him and the Central Bank was that he opposed banning and restricting import items. Guanter was optimistic about the IMF's future credit extension to Iran.[15]

While Guanter was in Tehran, Amini was out of the country. He had left for the Haj on 7 May 1962. Again, it may have been no coincidence that Amini returned home from Jeddah at 10:34 a.m. on 19 May 1962 while the Shah and the Queen inaugurated the Sefid Rud Dam (Manjil) on the same day at 10:50 a.m. without him.[16] Once again, the Shah decided to mark a significant developmental occasion without Amini.

In his report to the Shah, Safi Asfia spoke about the impressive achievements of the Second Plan and the efforts of the Plan Organization, without mentioning that Ebtehaj had signed the contract for this project on 29 February 1956. The contractors of this dam were ETCO (Franco-Iranian)

14 FRUS, 1961–1936, vol. XVII, Near East Region, 1961–1962, Document 246.

15 *Tehran Economist*, 29 Ordibehesht 1341.

16 *Ettela'at*, 29 Ordibehest 1341.

and OFER (French), and its estimated cost stood at 450 million tomans, with another 400 million tomans anticipated for future ancillary projects. The Sefid Rud Dam was to irrigate 244,355 hectares of rice paddy fields and increase rice yield by four times in Gilan. Initially, it was to provide electricity for the Gilan province and later for other Northern provinces.[17]

Two days after his return to Tehran on 21 May 1962, Amini met with the Shah at the Marble Palace. During his four-hour visit, the main topic of their discussion revolved around the budget. Amini later told reporters that he had emphasized the importance of cutting "unnecessary costs", to balance the budget. For Amini, "unnecessary costs" had become a euphemism for military expenditures. The reporter asked him about rumors of a change in government. Amini denied it, but Tehran knew that after the Shah's return from the US, it would not be long before Amini would be replaced as prime minister.[18]

On 26 May 1962, Amini met the Shah and presented Jahangir Amuzegar as his new Minister of Finance. Amuzegar's most pressing task at the Ministry of Finance was to deal with the budget deficit of about 1.1 billion tomans ($150 million). For Amuzegar, the debate revolved around how to reduce the current budget without touching on development expenditures. He proposed dividing the current budget into a "core" and a "secondary or non-core" budget. He argued that the "core budget" had to be financed by planned government revenues. Covering the "non-core budget" could be left to the realization of future revenues.[19]

Even though Amini and Amuzegar were optimistic about resolving the budget deficit, on the same day that Amini reshuffled his government, the press reported that Safi Asfia had handed his resignation to Amini and had explained his motives in a letter. On the surface, Asfia's resignation seemed related to budget issues. The press speculated that other high-ranking members of the Plan Organization had followed suit.

Amini did not accept Asfia's resignation and refused to talk to the press about the reasons for his resignation. The mini-revolt at the Plan Organization irritated Amini. After meeting with the Plan Organization's directors, he announced that the problems had been resolved. Amini's comments after his discussions may help explain the cause of discontent at the Plan Organization.

17 *Ettela'at*, 29 Ordibehesht 1341; *Tehran Economist*, 29 Ordibehesht 1341.
18 *Ettela'at*, 30 Ordibehesht 1341.
19 *Ettela'at*, 6 Khordad 1341.

Amini had told the Plan Organization directors that the government was intent on pursuing its anti-corruption campaign. His comment indicated that the resignations were related to the Ministry of Justice's constant probes into the financial affairs of the Plan Organization after Aramesh's accusations and Ebtehaj's arrest. Asfia and his directors felt besieged by Nureddin Alamuti, the Minister of Justice's crusade against corruption at the Plan Organization. They were stressed out by Amini's demands to balance the budget. At the same time, they were under scrutiny as if they were criminals.[20] To get them back to work, Amini must have promised them that the Ministry of Justice would stop harassing them.

Another issue became entangled with the Plan Organization's mini-revolt. Around May 1962, Khodadad Farmanfarmayan moved to have the whole budgeting process and function transferred from the Ministry of Finance to the Plan Organization. According to Farmanfarmayan, the Plan Organization's leadership supported the budget transfer to ensure priority to investment expenditures over current expenditures, and Amini had given his initial green light.

Farmanfarmayan believed that "the heart of the budget must be the investment program of the country and not the current budget." For Farmanfarmayan, if budgeting was in the hands of the Plan Organization, it could ensure that during the Third Plan investment expenditures would be privileged over current and defense expenditures. Farmanfarmayan was ignoring the role and priorities of the Shah. But when Farmanfarmayan presented his final proposal for the transfer, Amini discarded it.

Consequently, Farmanfarmayan resigned during the second week of June 1962 and left the Plan Organization. After the revolution, Farmanfarmayan complained that no one in the Plan Organization had supported him. He told Habib Ladjevardi, "Well, I don't think the Shah was all that excited about the whole concept of the budget going to the Plan Organization."[21] The press deplored the fact that of all the Plan Organization directors that had resigned, only Farmanfarmayan had not returned to his job. Farmanfarmayan's resignation was regretted, and he was described as "one of the best and most energetic directors of the Plan Organization", one who deserved a ministerial post.[22]

---

20 *Ettela'at*, 5, 7 Khordad 1341; *Tehran Economist*, 19 Khordad 1341.

21 Khodadad Farmanfarmayan, Iranian Oral History Collection, Harvard University, Transcript 7, Sequence 79–81. The previous three paragraphs are based on this source.

22 *Tehran Economist*, 19 Khordad 1341.

On 3 June 1962, it was announced that to help balance the budget, Amini had requested all ministries to reduce their budgets by 15%. Five days later, Amuzegar, his deputy, Cyrus Babak Sami'i, and his director-general, Ali Mostowfi, told the press that the 15% reduction was to be applied to all ministries and organizations in the country, including cultural, military, and security organizations. Such savings would reduce the budget deficit by 300 to 400 million tomans.

On the revenue side, the high authorities of the Ministry of Finance emphasized that earnings from taxes were projected to be 10% higher during 1962–1963. The increase in tax receipts came from the 4,000 companies in the country and new land and property taxes. The highlight of this press conference was the daring public statement of the young economists that reductions in the budget applied equally to military and security organizations as to the ministries.[23] Even during Amini's government, it was implicit that only the Shah could address or discuss issues about military and security organizations.

Soon, it became evident that not all ministries would comply with a 15% budget reduction. On 20 June, General Naqdi, the Minister of War, and his deputy, along with Iran's Chief of Staff, General Hejazi, met with Amini at his office. Amuzegar was also present at this meeting. The press did not report on the contents of this important ninety-minute discussion, but later events proved that Iran's top brass, representing the Shah's position, refused to accept the cut.[24]

During the three months of mid-April to mid-July 1962, Amini, Amuzegar, and Cyrus Babak Sami'i spent more than one hundred hours reviewing the bookkeeping of Iran's deficit. The crux of the problem remained the military budget. Most unusually, even the press reported on the inevitability of reducing military expenditures if the budget was to balance.[25] The old guns versus butter dilemma presented itself. Amini was not prepared to meet the Shah's military objectives, which meant reducing the country's development expenditures and retarding the country's economic growth.

23 *Ettela'at*, 19 Khordad 1341. The information in the previous two paragraphs is based on this source.
24 *Ettela'at*, 30 Khordad 1342.
25 *Tehran Economist*, 2 Tir 1341.

A GRINDING MONTH OF NEGOTIATIONS: ECONOMIC VERSUS MILITARY DEVELOPMENT

The budget marathon's last stretch began at the end of June and was the most exhausting and grueling part. On 27 June, Amini and Amuzegar flew to Nowshahr to present the Shah with the final budget and seek his support for the 15% reduction in the military budget. According to British sources, his Majesty sided with his Minister of War, General Ali-Asghar Naqdi.

After much haggling, Naqdi, who received his direct orders from the Shah and reported directly to him, agreed to "some $45 million over its appropriation" of the previous budget year.[26] While Amini and his economic team squeezed all ministries to the maximum possible, the Minister of War's budget estimate, demonstrated a 70% increase over the previous year.[27] What made matters worse was that for the budget year of 1962–1963, the US had altogether cut back its $30 million of civil and military aid to Iran.[28]

The Iranian press gave a distorted picture of what was happening with the budget and minimized the gravity of the situation. It reported that the budget was almost balanced. The actual deficit figure, however, remained between 600 and 700 million tomans, but with creative or cosmetic accounting, it was presented as 334 to 434 million tomans. Reports on the military budget were even more confusing. It was simultaneously reported that "apparently nothing has been deducted from the military budget, and it equaled the previous year's budget", and that "the army has also deducted 15 percent from its budget ... and has played its positive role in reducing the deficit."[29]

One day after meeting with the Shah at Nowshahr, Amini and Amuzegar met with the press. In his long yet articulate address, Amini evoked Ebtehaj's old complaint and reminded Iranians that 80% of all oil revenues were supposed to be spent on developmental projects. That figure, he said, had now dropped to 55%, and if proper attention were not paid, it would dwindle even more. He concluded that taking away from developmental projects to pay for current deficits in the budget was disastrous for the economy and a sin.

26 FCO 371 164184, EP 1015/98; FCO 371 164185, EP 1015/107.
27 FO 371/164205, EP 1111/10.
28 FO 371/164205, EP 1111/11.
29 *Ettela'at*, 7 Tir 1341.

Amini emphasized that public expenditures had to be financed by public revenues, necessitating cutting costs. So, where organizations failed to cut costs due to their customary profligacy, "they should be forced to do so." As for foreign aid and credit, Amini followed the same logic. He told reporters that during his European tour, he was assured that the West would support all developmental projects but was unwilling to help with the budget deficit. Without economic development, Amini argued, we are faced with a major unemployment problem in Iran, especially among the youth.[30]

Meeting the military and security budget estimates supported by the Shah meant eating into the oil revenues earmarked for development purposes. The Plan Organization would be left with little to implement new development projects. The Shah was fixated on keeping the military well-armed, well-trained, and well-housed. He feared that cutbacks in the size of the military and security forces would "endanger security".[31] Investment in security was prioritized over investment for the people whom security was supposedly intended for.

On Saturday 7 July, Amini spent two hours with the Shah at the Sa'dabad Palace discussing the budget. Later in the afternoon, he met with his cabinet to finalize the budget. Once again, the untenable stand-off over the budget of police, gendarmerie, and the Ministry of War persisted. Three days later, to no avail, Amini met with the Shah again for two hours at Sa'dabad Palace to resolve the budget problem.

Amini then met with the press and said that the budget he was trying to finalize was the first real and unfalsified one and that was why it was taking so long. He also repeated the importance of funds for developmental programs in the budget, without which the country's growth rate would stall, unemployment would climb, government revenues from taxation would decline, and the standard of living would plummet.

Amini accused a circle of "unpatriotic" elements in the "ruling class" as responsible for the ills in the country. He called them loafers, thieves, and corrupt and promised to repress them harshly after the Shah approved the budget. Amini said, "If I remain in my post, and they would pray that I do not, I will not have pity on them." As if foreseeing his own departure, Amini concluded, "I believe that if a government lacks decisiveness and fails to use its power for just and upright causes, it has no legitimacy to stay in power."[32]

30 *Ettela'at*, 9 Tir 1341.
31 FO 371/164205, EP 1111/11.
32 *Ettela'at*, 20 Tir 1341.

At 9:00 a.m. on Monday, 16 July 1962, Amini, Amuzegar, and Naqdi met with the Shah again. No details of this decisive meeting were leaked to the press. Amini later recalled that the Shah wanted an exceptional clause for the Ministry of War. He wanted all the items in the "secondary" budget of the Ministry of War to be included in the "core budget", thus preventing any cuts and, in fact, demanding an increase in the military budget. Amini believed that "the Ministry of War was an unassailable taboo for the Shah, very much like a distinct caste."[33]

Jahangir Amuzegar would later refer to the military budget impasse. In meetings with Shah in 1962, some lasting three hours, the King would try to "persuade his reluctant finance minister of the necessity of raising the military budget".[34] Amuzegar believed that, among other things, had the Shah "placed more trust in Dr. Amini's reformist government" and "agreed to a more manageable military budget" he could have created a shield protecting and prolonging the Pahlavi dynasty.[35]

On 16 July 1962, having met the Shah once in the morning and for a second time in the evening, Amini convened his cabinet for a three-and-a-half-hour session. After this meeting, Amini told reporters that "I will resign if I cannot finalize the budget with a reasonable (*ma'qul*) deficit."[36] On the next day, 17 July 1962, the press reported on the "budget cul-de-sac". Amuzegar told reporters that "certain ministries are demanding higher budgets", and the government will not accept a large budget deficit. The budget stand-off was resolved in the evening of 17 July when Amini met with the shah and "resigned". On 19 July 1962, the Shah appointed Asadollah 'Alam as prime minister.

The debate over economic development versus military development, which had pitted Ebtehaj against the Shah, was once again resolved in favor of military development. Amini was out of the political picture after a year of futile haggling over the 1962–1963 budget. The Shah had learned his lesson and would never again allow a prime minister or a minister to challenge his economic vision or his fundamental axiom of "military strength

33 Ali Amini, Iranian Oral History Collection, Harvard University, Transcript 4, Sequence 104, Transcript 5, Sequence 120, 121.

34 J. Amuzegar, *The Dynamics of the Iranian Revolution, The Pahlavis' Triumph and Tragedy*, pp. 340, 342.

35 J. Amuzegar, *The Dynamics of the Iranian Revolution*, p. 309.

36 *Ettela'at*, 25 Tir 1342.

first". In the Shah's universe, that of an aspiring militarist, opportunity costs did not apply to military expenditures, as there was no choice or alternative.

Never again would ministers, the Plan Organization or Central Bank economists, and the press be allowed to debate economic versus military development. Behind closed doors, those who dared did it at their own peril. After 19 July 1962, the definitive contours of resource allocation within the national economy, even though amended and altered at times, were set by the Shah and only executed by the ministries and the Plan Organization.

In the years to come, the Shah often alluded to the Amini years with bitterness, without mentioning his name. At the High Economic Council meeting of 12 April 1965, with Prime Minister Hoveyda, numerous ministers, and Asfia present, the Shah would say, "In 1961, the country's economy was growing rapidly, but then *they* began talking about the bankruptcy of the economy and suddenly all activities were paralyzed, and this event left a significant mark on the country."[37] The Shah spoke as if Amini had been responsible for the economic downturn of 1961–1962. All those officials present who knew better dared not say otherwise.

Yet, the issue of Iran's allocation or misallocation of resources to military expenditure continued to preoccupy Kennedy. On 14 March 1963, some eight months after Amini's departure, Kennedy brought up a fundamental issue with his top administrators, including the secretaries of state and defense and the director of the CIA. Having signed the five-year military assistance package for Iran, he expressed concern "over the fulfillment of other aspects of the basic strategy", which underlaid his "earlier approval of this military commitment". Kennedy asked, "Is there a satisfactory relationship between the ordinary budget, including military expenditures, and the development budget? Is the outlook encouraging in this respect?"[38]

At this time, the only remaining voice nagging the Shah that economic development was more important than military might was coming from the US. To the Shah's delight, this bothersome noise was silenced after Nixon's Presidency in January 1969 and especially after Nixon visited Tehran along with Henry Kissinger in May 1972.

---

37 Nikpay (gerdavarandeh) *Surat jalesat-e showray-e 'aliye eqtesad dar pishgah Shahanshah Aryamehr, az Shahrivar 1343 ta Shahrivar 1345*. Surat Jaleseh-e 23 Farvardin 1344, p. 74 (italics is mine).

38 National Security Action Memorandum No. 228. Subject: Review of the Iranian Situation, https://pdf.usaid.gov/pdf_docs/Pcaaa901.pdf (retrieved 10/6/2024).

13

Shifting Tastes, Shopping, Eating, and Drinking (1957–1962)

Between 1957 and 1962, rural Iran and its backwaters, constituting some 65–75% of the country, remained sleepy and fixed in their customary and conventional ways of life. The land reform of January 1962 fostered a change in rural Iran's relations of production, including ownership and socio-economic relations. But its impact on the transformation of rural to urban society and the everyday life in the countryside was minimal. From 1957, Iranian society bifurcated into two different worlds, moving and developing at two separate speeds: the fast-moving dynamic urban and the lethargic static rural.

The socio-economic landscape of Tehran and a few other urban centers transformed perceptibly in those five years. The mode of urban life and the face of big cities underwent change. In tune with new factories producing modern consumer goods, the service and hospitality industry began to shift into a different gear. Consumer behavior began to change as different and modern consumer goods, services, amenities, and facilities appeared on the market.

Brand promotion, selection, and identification came with a greater variety of consumer goods. Consumer tastes and preferences were being created, changed, and formed. The craving for things that were different, modern and Western, manifested itself in a change of diet, clothing, housing, shopping, laundering, transportation, recreation, entertainment, and social interaction. Urban Iranian society and its mode of life were shedding their traditional and monotonous skin and transforming in a fundamental way.

In urban Iran, producers of consumer goods and services, and importers of consumer goods, were getting their message out to their target population much more easily through the booming business of advertising firms, as well as through expanding outlets such as radio, press, cinemas, and television. Change in consumer behavior in post-1957 Iran can be traced to a loosely termed "demand shock", caused mainly by the expansion of credit to industries, and its multiplier effects from the Special Revaluation Fund. A "taste shift" was set in motion, facilitated by Iran's open economy, and exposure to the West. The one-time injection of monies from the Special Revaluation Fund increased income and business activity, reverberating throughout the country.

In this case, the notion of a "taste shift" refers to a noticeable switch in demand towards modern goods, services, and practices emanating from Western societies. It signifies a clear break with customary consumer behavior. The "taste shift" is closely associated with the movement from consuming an undistinguished traditional home product to one identified by a brand name, foreign or Iranian. From 1957, urban Iranians were suddenly exposed to an array of brand names coming onto the market successively. The long-lasting transformation in the composition of goods and services in the consumer basket of urban Iranians after 1957 is simply attributed to a "taste shift" plus an increase in income.

The "taste shift" could be partially attributed to a demonstration effect or the phenomenon of keeping up with the foreign and domestic Joneses among the upper classes. The shift to shopping at department stores or supermarkets instead of the bazaar, or attending a drive-in movie or a drive-in bank, may have been induced by competing with one's peers, more prevalent among the upper and upper-middle classes. Aside from their convenience, the use of such services imparted some degree of status, distinguishing the consumer as modern and well off as it meant affording a car and having a bank account.

Then, there were those shifts in tastes that did not necessarily impart any status. The sudden increase in consuming manufactured brand name cooking oil, soap, detergents, soft drinks, biscuits, and ice cream rather than artisanal non-differentiated goods indicated "taste shifts" among the middle and lower urban classes and even trickled into the rural areas. This switch and automatic replacement of old products and services with the new mass-produced, industrialized ones was probably because of the convenience, flavor, consistency in the quality and taste of the product, hygienic and standardized production, price advantage, or attractive packaging and presentation of such products.

OUT OF THE BOX ENTREPRENEURS

The radical change in consumer behavior after 1957 corresponded with a new wave of pioneering entrepreneurs. They thought outside the traditional box and had an eye fixed on what was going on in the West and what would appeal to Iranians. At times, they jumped into numerous projects, pursued their ideas, tried to maximize profits, and, in the process, presented consumers with new, appealing, and differentiated goods.

These enterprising individuals came from different backgrounds, provinces, social origins, and religions. Some were self-made and from humble backgrounds, some from monied families; some had roots in the bazaar, some were first-generation artisans and craftsmen, and some began their careers in family businesses and as apprentices in trading companies. They differed in levels of education, and most started with little capital. Some were Shi'i Muslims, others were Jewish, Baha'i, Zoroastrian, Christian, or belonging to the Armenian Apostolic Church. The blend and meld of business partners' religious, cultural, and geographical origins is thought-provoking and revealing in retrospect. They all had one thing in common: the urge to break new ground and the will to innovate, and succeed. As Iran transformed into a version of the capitalist mode of production, profit-seeking broke down all religious, cultural, and ethnic barriers, compelling businessmen to embrace plurality.

One well-known and successful example of this multicultural, multi-religious, and multiethnic business partnership was the Sabet P-A-Sa-L Company, dating from before 1953. The P-A-Sa-L company was already established in Iran, and its members were close friends of Habibollah Sabet, who had moved to the US in December 1941. At the time, Sabet, who lived in New York, was exporting non-bulky goods, such as men's and women's socks and stockings and pharmaceutical and cosmetic goods, to Iran in postal packages. This was a thriving business. It must have been around 1943 that Sabet partnered with the P-A-Sa-L Company as a majority shareholder to establish what was subsequently called Sabet P-A-Sa-L Company.[1]

1 H. Sabet, *Sargozasht Habib Sabet*, Los Angeles: Mazda Publishers, 1993, pp. 167–192.

The principal activities of this successful company first revolved around the sales of imported Volkswagen cars and Esso motor oil, and then the home production with General Tire and Esso motor oil in 1965. The Sabet P-A-Sa-L Company became so famous and intertwined with Habibollah Sabet that it was erroneously believed that Pasal was Sabet's surname. It is reported that the net annual receipt from the sale of Volkswagen cars in 1961 amounted to something between 10 to 15 million tomans.[2]

Habibollah Sabet was a self-made businessman. He had come from humble origins on his paternal side. On his maternal side, he belonged to the monied Arjomand family. Both families were from Kashan, and had converted to the Baha'i faith from Judaism. Sabet was born in Tehran, and his name became associated with transformative enterprises such as Pepsi-Cola and the first television station in Iran. He went on to become one of modern Iran's most esteemed business tycoons.

Ali-Asghar Panahi, the 'P' in P-A-Sa-L, who came from a prominent monied commercial and landowning Shi'i family, was born in Tabriz. Panahi studied engineering in France and began his business by founding a construction company. He was also a member of the Fourteenth Majles. Emile 'Abboud, the 'A' in P-A-Sa-L, was a Lebanese Christian merchant who had migrated to Iran and spoke Persian with an Arabic accent. The Jewish businessman Alexander Safiyan, the 'Sa' in P-A-Sa-L, was of Russian origin and had parents who had migrated to Iran. Finally, the Sorbonne-educated Mohsen Lak was from a well-established Azarbayjani Shi'i family. He was chairman of the board of directors of the General Tire company, which belonged to the Sabet P-A-Sa-L group, and the owner of Basco, a shipping service company in Bandar Abbas.

In March 1965, after some twenty-three years of friendship and lucrative partnership, Sabet, Panahi, Abboud, and Lak registered a new company called Sherkat Sahami-ye Iran Foleks (Iran Volkswagen Corporation). This new company was created to import, assemble, and produce cars in Iran. The founders of this new company were all the original members of the Sabet P-A-Sa-L company and their children. The exception was Alexander Safiyan, who had parted ways or had been excluded from the original pack. The founders of Iran Volkswagen Corporation also included Mahmud and Mas'ud Khamsi.[3] The Khamsis came from the wealthy and

2 *Tehran Economist*, 6 Aban 1340.

3 *Tehran Economist*, 14 Farvardin 1344.

modernist Baqerof family in Gilan, who had migrated to Iran from Russia. The Baqerofs had converted from Islam to the Baha'i faith. Sabet's lifelong wife, Bahereh, was of the Khamsi family.

The Pahlavi system created a conducive business environment for Iranian entrepreneurs to realize their dreams by encouraging and supporting them, especially if the Shah took a particular liking to their initiatives or person. The socio-economic transition of Iranian society from pre-modern to modern had many facets.

FROM THE BAZAAR TO FORUSHGAH-E FERDOWSI DEPARTMENT STORE

Until 1957, there reigned a peaceful coexistence between the five established department stores in Tehran's Lalehzar neighborhood and the Tehran Bazaar. This was to change abruptly with the entrance of a new store. By 1953, Tehran possessed two major clothing department stores, General Mode, and Pirayesh, with three others trailing them, Khoshpush, Pushāk, and Pushesh. These five department stores were the flagships of modern Iranian retail stores, with a variety of goods for male and female customers. At these stores, prices were fixed, pre-empting haggling, as was customary in Iranian bazaars.

Pirayesh was more than a clothing store. It was a full-fledged department store, selling various goods, from high-end cutlery to house furniture. It was founded in 1935 by Hasan Pirayesh and his wife, Mehr Saltaneh. Mehr Saltaneh was German, spoke fluent Persian, and was the manager and director of Tehran's most reputable modern department store. The goods in the store were mainly imported from Germany. The imposing Pirayesh building, constructed in a European–Iranian architectural style, was located on Lalehzar Street, the hub of Tehran's non-bazaar commerce, and frequented by Tehran's upper-middle and upper classes. General Mode, initially located on Saadi Street and subsequently located on Koucheh Berlin, was founded by Hasan Torab and operated with some 250 employees, two of whom were Germans, a couturier and a tailor.[4]

Yet Tehran got its taste of a truly modern and Westernized department store with the inauguration of Forushgah-e Ferdowsi (Ferdowsi

4 *Tehran Economist*, 18 Ordibehesht 1338.

Department Store) on 14 December 1957. The presence of the Shah, his two brothers, Gholamreza and ‘Abdolreza, and Queen Soraya, accompanied by Manuchehr Eqbal, the prime minister, the entire cabinet, and the presidents of both houses, Majles and Senate, signaled the importance of this event. On this special occasion, the smiling and delighted King and Queen were the first customers of Forushgah-e Ferdowsi. The Queen bought a ceramic statue of a warrior on horseback, and the Shah bought a black lighter.[5]

The Ferdowsi Department Store, a fifty-fifty joint venture between the Iranian government and two German retail investors, with a capital of one million tomans, was the first of its kind, boasting some 12,000 articles. On display were both foreign, mainly German, and home-produced goods. The variety and abundance of so many goods under one roof, as well as the professionalism of the sales personnel clad in uniforms, heralded a new retail era and distinguished Ferdowsi Department Store from all its predecessors.

As its name would indicate, the store was on Ferdowsi Street. The imposing, custom-built four-story building, with very high ceilings and two basement floors, housed different goods, from home furniture and food products to cosmetics, sporting goods, jewelry, kitchen utensils, bedding, and clothing, each neatly arranged on independent floors. The variety of goods available under one roof largely surpassed Pirayesh's offering. Among other novelties, the store was air-conditioned, equipped with elevators, and, for the first time in Iran, escalators connected the floors. The store also had a rooftop restaurant.[6]

The Ferdowsi Store employed 400 employees, many of whom were well-trained female sellers and clerks trained by the store's German partners. The female personnel were a novelty on their own. The first few days of its opening proved to be a happening, disrupting traffic on Ferdowsi Street and causing huge congestion on the sidewalks leading to it. Its sudden attraction as a tourist space for inquisitive Tehranis, as well as its popularity with well-off customers, led to the closing of its doors for a few hours in order to regulate the inflow of visitors and shoppers.[7]

5 *Ettela'at*, 24 Azar 1336.
6 *Ettela'at*, 21 Azar 1336, *Bours Mahaneh*, 1 Shahrivar 1342.
7 *Eftetah-e forushgah-e zanjireh-ie Ferdowsi 1336*. See https://www.youtube.com/watch?v=hetQjFJb-is (Retrieved 28/4/2024).

Not surprisingly, the advent of the Ferdowsi Store scared the Tehran bazaar and the small retailers that felt threatened by the diversity and plenitude of offerings under one modern roof and its attractive setting. Modern distribution was competing with traditional retailing. After the initial shock, bazaar and traditional retailers realized they would not lose part of their middle and entire lower-middle class and lower-class customers. They understood that the higher prices at the Ferdowsi Store, its retail culture, customer service, and its Westernized products appealed to a different type of clientele than theirs. Iran's growing class disparity demanded greater product and customer service differentiation, and the market was obliging. It would take another fifteen years before the bazaar would lose most of its middle-class customers to modern retailing.

Unfortunately, rumors of bribes and payoffs in the press surrounded the foreign purchases of the Ferdowsi Store. It was said that the two trading companies, Orient Hanzara and Europ, created as intermediaries to purchase goods for the store, had received lucrative commissions. Unnamed influential Iranians were said to be partners of the two trading companies and were suspected of having greatly benefited from exorbitant commissions.[8]

In 1961, the Iranian government bought out the private German interests and obtained full ownership. Its successive Iranian general directors were Manuchehr Nikpour and Amir Motaqi, who was close to Asadollah 'Alam. By September 1962, the crowded cafeteria at the Ferdowsi store was flagged as one of Tehran's most popular hangouts for the newly liberated youth. It was identified as a place where young people could meet, socialize, and flirt.[9]

By September 1963, the Ferdowsi Store had created a children's space on its first floor allowing parents to peacefully shop while their children played. By this time, the Store had become a member of the Diners Club, so that its modern customers who enjoyed this novel means of payment could shop freely there. Diners Club was the first charge card in the world, founded in February 1950. By September 1963, the number of Ferdowsi Store customers had swollen to between 11,000 and 15,000 per day.[10]

The next generation of department stores did not come until 30 November 1967, with the inauguration by the Shah and Queen Farah

8 *Khandaniha*, 6 Esfand 1336; *Tehran Economist*, 8 Khordad 1338.
9 *Sepid o Siyah*, 13 Mehr 1341.
10 *Bours-e Mahaneh*, 1 Shahrivar 1342.

of Hamid Kashani-Akhavan's Foroushgah-e Bozorg-e Iran (Iran Grand Department Store). This 40 million toman, ten-story building, composed of 32 departments, was located at the intersection of the Pahlavi and Shah streets. The financing of this huge department store was entirely from Iranian sources, the Kashani-Akhavan brothers. Its design and planning were contracted to the famous American Sears and Roebuck department store. The products sold at the Iran Grand Department Store were primarily produced by its own sixteen production units, employing 2,500 workers. Some 500 young employees with degrees ranging from high-school diplomas to PhDs in economics worked at this department store.[11] By the end of 1967, the Iran Grand Department Store had brought almost every conceivable consumer good under one roof for the benefit of Iran's emerging modernized middle and upper-middle class.

FROM THE OPEN-AIR SABZEH MEYDAN MARKET TO THE AIR-CONDITIONED IRAN SUPER

On 14 February 1961, while the Iranian political class eagerly awaited the results of the second election to the Twentieth Majles, Iran Super, Iran's first thoroughly Western-style supermarket, opened its doors on Takht-e Jamshid Street. An impressive array of Iranian notables and politicians were present at the inaugural ceremony.[12] The entrepreneur behind this flagship institution was Naser Cohanim.

In 1952, having finished studying Business Administration at Syracuse University in the US, Cohanim, who came from a line of Jewish businessmen, returned to Iran. He formed an initial partnership company with Habib Cohanim, which was dissolved in February 1961, right around the time of opening of Iran Super. After he got married in 1953, Eliane, his French wife, would talk to him about the inconvenience of going to several different stores to do the weekly grocery shopping. Thus, the idea of an American-style self-service supermarket in Tehran was planted in Cohanim's mind, even though his family did not look favorably upon such a venture. Cohanim did not plan to borrow money from Iranian banks and spent some six years, from 1953 to 1959, working as a merchant to save

11 *Ettela'at*, 5, 7, 9 Azar 1356.
12 *Ettela'at*, 24, 26 Bahman 1339.

enough money before launching into unchartered waters. The capital for Iran Super was put up by Cohanim and a few others who initially invested in the business. His partners later recuperated their money and left.

With no prior knowledge or experience of how to run a supermarket, he did his homework and learned how to build, equip, provide and manage. Cohanim went to the US at the end of 1959 and attended a one-month course in Dayton, Ohio, to learn the ins and outs of the supermarket business and purchase the necessary equipment. He spent the last week of his course working as an apprentice at a local Dayton supermarket, learning the practical aspects of the trade. The supermarket construction plan and design, including the storage and the cold stores, were hashed out and completed in Dayton.

On 1,500 square meters of land in fashionable Takht-e Jamshid Street, he built a congenial space where consumers could do all their grocery shopping, just as Mrs. Cohanim had wished. This new space had no resemblance to the traditional markets of Tehran, Meydan-e Aminsoltan, Sabzeh Meydan, and Bazaar-e Tehran in the south or Bazaar-e Tajrish in the north. Consumers did not have to go from one place to the next, looking for oranges, rice or meat, having to haggle for every item. Nor did they have to get their shoes muddied or their feet wet when shopping in the winter. At this new, elegant, and consumer-friendly outlet, under the supervision of an American specialist, consumers could find items such as Kellogg corn flakes and Heinz ketchup, items unfamiliar to traditional Iranian consumers and not found in any other Iranian grocery store.

Cohanim sought and obtained the help of Eskandar Arjomand, another self-made model entrepreneur, to install his Arj brand air conditioners at Iran Super. But when Cohanim was ready to open his store, with the shelves filled with domestic and imported goods, he confronted a major hurdle. Around January 1961, when Cohanim sought a working permit to begin operations, he was informed by Tehran municipality that in the absence of an official supermarket guild, proper guidelines for what constituted a supermarket did not exist. Therefore, the authorities could not advise him on which guild to apply to for a supermarket permit.

The news was surprising as numerous establishments, such as Supermarket-e pars, and Supermarket-e chahar-rāh-e Pahlavi, had already advertised themselves as supermarkets and were already operating. This meant that they were probably operating without bothering with legalities.

Without official and proper organizational specifications for supermarkets, the Tehran municipality in charge of issuing working permits stalled.

Cohanim was neighbors with Abbas Mas'udi, the influential owner of the daily *Ettela'at*. It was thanks to Mas'udi that Fatollah Forud, Tehran's Mayor, was informed of the snag and came to Cohanim's help. Once he visited Iran Super, Forud requested that Cohanim write the by-laws, specifications, and regulations for all future supermarkets. He did and thus obtained the first official supermarket permit in Iran.

After its inauguration, Iran Super became the shopping hub of Tehran's upper classes, the diplomatic corps, and expats. The latest model cars subsequently lined up in front of it. Iran Super had some 150 employees, including workers, people for maintenance, cashiers, and office staff. The cashiers at the supermarket were women. Consumers enjoyed the accessibility, variety, freshness, quality of goods, and professional service. The fact that items had price tags and that printed receipts were provided at the cash register added to the popularity of shopping at Iran Super. Another novelty for customers, and especially enjoyed by children, were the trollies.[13]

By December 1961, Iran Super had its own Westernized and upper-class clientele. When Joe Adams and his Broadway and Hollywood musicians and dancers were scheduled to perform a musical variety show for six nights at the Mohammad-Reza Shah Sports stadium in Tehran, tickets for the show were sold only at the Iran-America Cultural Society, Cohanim's Iran Super, and Mansur Jahanbani's famous café and restaurant, Hot Shop, on Vanak Square.[14]

On Thursday evening, 21 October 1965, regular customers at Iran Super were busy with their weekend shopping when they observed the Queen, Farah Pahlavi, walking up and down the long aisles of the store, doing her shopping and filling her cart.[15] Cohanim remembered that when the Queen came shopping at Iran Super, the Crown Prince, Reza would have great fun riding on the trollies, while his mother did her shopping.

13 Shahrzad Majidi/Saleh, Interview with Naser Cohanim, Los Angeles, 25 May 2023. The information on *Iran Super* is based on this source, and I am greatly indebted to Shahrzad Majidi for her gracious help. Date for the dissolution of his partnership with Habib Cohanim, see *Ettela'at*, 26 Bahman 1339.

14 *Ettela'at*, 22, 27 Azar 1340.

15 *Ettela'at*, 1 Aban 1344.

FROM JIGAR (LAMB LIVER) TO WIMPY

Tajrish Square (Meydan-e Tajrish), also known as "On the bridge of Tajrish" (Sar-e pol-e Tajrish) in the north of Tehran, was located right at the foot of the Alborz mountains. It had fresh and cool weather, served by the breeze from Tochal in the mountains and two streams that came down from the same place. These attributes made Tajrish Square the favorite hangout of Tehranis of almost all classes, especially during the long summer months. Tehran in the late 1950s possessed three substantial green spaces: Park-e shahr, Baq-e rāh ahan, and Park-e jonub or Sush. All three were in the south of Tehran, which became hot and stuffy during the summer.

So, entire families, young couples, or single young men and women in packs would gradually come to Tajrish Square, saunter, and lounge in this pleasant and spacious area. They whiled away the hours by eating, chatting, eyeing whomever they found attractive, snacking, and fanning out to its nearby, even cooler streets of Sa'dabad, Ja'farabad, and Sabt leading to Darband. The fun ambiance at Tajrish Square is well reflected in a song by Ali Nazari, called "The Bridge of Tajrish" (Pol-e Tajrish), where the singer recounts how he catches sight of his beloved in the company of another man.

One of the most popular attractions in Tajrish was its traditional Jigaraki stands and restaurants. The Jigarakis grilled lamb liver (jigar), heart (del), and kidney (gholveh) on skewers, directly over a bed of charcoal. The well-cooked food was served on traditional thin Iranian bread to their eager customers. The preparation and serving of this food were far from hygienic. Flies usually buzzed around the meat left out in the open, and customers never knew how long the lamb's intestines had been kept in unrefrigerated spaces before they were cooked. As long as it tasted delicious, and naturally it did, no one cared until they fell ill. According to one report, during one week in August 1962, some 174 people in Tehran suffered from food poisoning and were taken to hospital, and seventeen died.[16]

On 4 September 1957, Tajrish Square was exposed to a culturally alien food, served at a new restaurant on Sa'dabad Street, one of the streets to the north of Tajrish. The flashing neon lights of Wimpy attracted the curious. The main food offered for free on this opening night was a plain burger, a novelty to Iranians. Wimpy had already been advertised in the

---

16 *Sepid o Siyah*, 19 Mordad 1341.

newspapers as an innovative and hygienic type of kebab. Two owners, Hoseyn and Hasan Moqadam, borrowed the idea and name from the Wimpy fast-food chain, which had become a great success in England after its rise and fall in the US. In 1954, the British J. Lyons and Company had bought the license from the American mother company, Wimpy Grills.

This first Iranian Wimpy shop had not bought its license from J. Lyons and had just copied the name and imitated the restaurant's style, logo, and production process. The Iranian press described Wimpy as "an almost American hamburger" and tried to pass it off as a kebab. Aside from introducing a mutton meat patty between two buns, an important sales pitch of Iran's Wimpy was that it was prepared under safe, clean, and strictly hygienic conditions. Hasan Moqadam's dreadful stomach ache and illness after eating the traditional skewer treats in Tajrish had sent him to England to seek medical attention, and it was there that he discovered Wimpy and its magic.

The Iranian investors of Wimpy spent 200,000 tomans on their restaurant. The main feature of the spacious restaurant was a large square metallic grilling surface heated from beneath by seven flames on which the Wimpy patties were flipped and sizzled. The flames were powered by butane gas capsules. Over the large flattop grill stood a giant kitchen hood that sucked in the fumes allowing customers to sit comfortably on bar stools around the grill, enjoying their food. In addition to the table service seating arrangement, the counter service was also a novelty. The burgers were prepared in about one minute, and were wrapped in neat napkins, placed on a plate, and served.

There must have been a certain flavor rationale for the successful combination of hamburgers, French fries, and cola which had conquered the world. But Iran's first Wimpy was both modern and traditional, mixing tastes and opting for fusion cuisine. It did not serve French fries, as in the US and UK, or Pepsi or Coca-Cola, which was being produced in Iran. Instead it served doogh, a traditional salty yogurt drink, which went well with chelokabab (kebab and rice) but not with a burger. And the dessert was a specialty of the house, an Italian style ice-cream, almost resembling a sundae.[17]

Besides its relatively high price, Iranian Wimpy did not catch on like wildfire because it was not ready to go all the way with the culinary

17 *Ettela'at*, 14 Shahrivar 1336.

revolution. Burgers without their accommodating fries and colas did not deliver the whole package. Wimpy continued to have its clientele, mainly the upper middle and upper classes, but it failed to become a craze.

On 1 May 1960, another Wimpy shop opened on Shah Reza Street. This one, however, was an official franchise of the British J. Lyons. Even though this one did offer the classic burger, French fries, and cola, Iranians of the late 1950s and even 1960s remained mostly indifferent to the Americanization of food. Only in the mid-1970s did another branch of the official Wimpy open on Vali'ahd Square. This one did become a hit.

FROM KOLUCHEH COOKIES, TO VITANA'S PETIT BEURRE BISCUITS

Iran has a rich tradition of pastries and delicacies. A few of its varieties included Kak, Nan-e panjerhie, Nan-e gerdouie, and Kolucheh. These artisanal products were often geographically specific. Their basic ingredients were flour, sugar, butter/fat, and, in some cases, egg and milk. Even though some have bread (nan) in their names, they have nothing to do with staple bread and should not be confused with a third category of brioche-type bread, such as the elongated Nan-e shirmal (bread made with sweetened, saffron-flavored milk).

Kak, originally from Kermanshah and called Yokheh in Shiraz, is a dry, layered parallelogram-shaped confectionary that uses basic ingredients, including almond powder and cardamom. Kak is neither a cookie nor a pie. Nan-e panjerehie is a refined Persian rosette cookie that is light and crispy, with powdered sugar decorating it and rosewater as one of its main ingredients. Nan-e gerdouie, or walnut cookie, has walnuts added to the main ingredients and possesses a crispy meringue outer surface.

Kolucheh is a round and popular cookie-like pastry that is said to have been around since the seventh century. It can be soft on the inside, hard on the outside, or hard on both. Its production requires saffron, cardamom, cinnamon, and basic ingredients. In Southern Iran, Kolucheh has dates in it, while in the north, dates are replaced with walnuts and nutmeg. So, shifting the taste of Iranians from their rich and wide variety of pastries to a mass-produced simple biscuit must have seemed impossible.

Dr. Reza Tehranchi, a dentist by training and a graduate of Tehran University, decided to have a radical career change at age 35. When he began his dental practice around 1949, he became aware of his patients' malnutrition, poor health, and dental condition. His dental practice was in the densely populated and working-class neighborhood Chahar-rāh-e Mokhtari. Eager to learn about nutrition, he fell under the influence of the American nutritionist and prolific writer Gayelord Hauser, who was not a medical doctor but whose work on nutrition had become popular in the late 1940s and early 1950s.

Tehranchi is said to have become interested in producing biscuits and cookies to fight malnutrition. On 8 May 1958, Reza and his brothers, Javad, Jalil, and Jabbar Tehranchi, registered their partnership company of Vitana. The Tehranchis began their enterprise with a 30,000 toman loan. A few months later, in July 1958, Von Wakeren, an internationally renowned German specialist, was invited by Vitana to establish a biscuit factory in Iran. The factory's fully automated machinery was imported from Germany and the Netherlands. The factory was built on a 10,000-square-meter site, some 11 kilometers from Tehran, on the road to Karaj.

The flagship brand of Vitana, Madar (Mother), was a typical indented rectangular petit beurre biscuit. The trademark of Petit Beurre had been registered in France (Nantes) in 1888. Like most Iranian cookies, Madar biscuits contained wheat, sugar, butter, and milk. Its size was about 55 by 35 millimeters and they were neatly packed into rectangular boxes. It was probably the consistent flavor of Madar and the fact that one could dip it in tea like sugar cubes, something that could not be easily done with Iranian cookies, that made it a success. It was said that using wheat germ in the production of Madar provided it with a nutty flavor, adding to its attraction.

Vitana quickly earned the reputation of being a nutritious, high-calorie, tasty, attractively packaged, and affordable biscuit that stayed fresh for a long time. Furthermore, its production process operated according to safe and highly hygienic German standards, assuring mothers that the biscuits would be safe for children of all ages. Vitana's Madar was also the first processed food product in Iran to have an expiration date.

In a short time, Vitana attained widespread popularity and was found in most grocery stores. The taste shift from Iran's regional and national cookies and pastries to the dry and plain Vitana biscuits was surprising. Vitana became a supplementary staple food that appealed to the young and old. It entered the consumer basket of lower-middle, middle, upper-middle, and upper-class households in Iran's major cities.

Reassured by the success of its products, Vitana launched a new product that was alien to Iranians. Vitana's Chub-e shur, or salt sticks, came on the market in 1961, appealing to the salt rather than sweet tooth of Iranians. These long, thin breadsticks sprinkled with coarse salt soon became an attractive accompaniment to alcoholic drinks, especially beer. By 1961, three Iranian brands of beer, Shams (February 1959), Majidiyeh (August 1959), and Argo (November 1959), were on the market alongside the more expensive foreign imported beers, such as the German Becks, the Dutch Heineken, the Danish Tuborg, and the Czechoslovakian Pilsner Urquell.[18]

In 1962, Vitana employed 135 workers, 25 office staff, 7 designers and engineers, and 1 foreign expert. Its output was 7,200 kilos of biscuits per day. In addition to its most popular biscuit, Madar, Vitana produced Nazok narenji, an orange-flavored fluffy biscuit, and Khoncheh, an assortment of biscuits, the most expensive of its products at 17.5 rials.[19]

On 14 April 1962, a new biscuit brand, Gorji, came on the market. Ali Gorji, the owner of Biscoperse Company, built his factory in Robat Karim, 55 kilometers southwest of Tehran. The factory operated under the supervision of British technicians, producing orange, lemon, vanilla, and cocoa-flavored biscuits.[20] One of its products was labeled Swiss petit beurre to distinguish it from Vitana's French petit beurre, another was called Afternoon Tea, and finally a third was an assorted box of biscuits called Rangin kaman or Rainbow. Gorji became Vitana's competitor but was never able to equal its popularity. Only in 1975 did Vitana become overshadowed by the emerging biscuit and confectionary giant Minoo.

From around 1964, Minoo's miracle-makers, Ali, Hasan, and Jalil Khosrowshahi, began revolutionizing Iran's confectionery, wafer, and snack market. It was in 1975 that Minoo's biscuit production line at Khorramdareh began producing the Iranian version of the British brand McVitie's Digestives. The cylindrical-shaped, red, and gold package of the whole wheat flour biscuit, Saqeh talaie (Golden Stem) soon became a national sensation, appearing even in Iran's remote rural areas. Whereas

18 *Ettela'at*, 25 Bahman 1337, 16 Esfand 1337, 31 Farvardin 1338, 27 Mordad 1338, 15 Ordibehesht 1339, 6 Mordad 1339, 22 Aban 1339.

19 Information on Vitana is based on: *Tehran Economist*, 19 Tir and 2 Mordad 1338, 26 Azar 1339, 26 Esfand 1341; *Ettela'at*, 29 Esfand 1340, 28, 30 Farvardin 1341, 19 Ordibehesht 1341. *Ayandeh Negar*, Ordibehesht 1401, Shomareh 119. *Nabz-e Bours*, Reza Tehranchi Khaleq-e biscuit Madar kist?, 11 Esfand 1401, https://nabzebourse.com/fa/news/54610/رضا-تهرانچی-خالق-بیسکویت-مادر-کیست (retrieved 23/1/2024).

20 *Ettela'at*, 27 Farvardin 1341, 2 Ordibehesht 1341.

in 1962, Vitana produced 182 tons of biscuits per month and had 167 employees, in 1977, Minoo produced 3,540 tons of assorted products per month and employed some 2,000 workers.

FROM ALASKA ICE POPS TO KIM AND CANADA FROST

Iran had its own traditional ice cream, made of milk, sugar, and cardamom, and was well-known for its soft and creamy elastic content and the frozen cream chunks (*sa'lab*) in it. It is suggested that Nasereddin Shah introduced Iranians to ice cream after his third trip to Europe, and Mamad Rish innovated this Iranian version of ice cream. Mamad Rish is said to have been selling this type of ice cream in 1896.

Iran's traditional ice cream was either served in a dish or like a sandwich between two round, crunchy pieces of wafer, hence the name bready ice cream (*Bastani nuni*). However, this kind of ice cream became known as Akbar-Mashty ice cream. During Reza Shah's rule, Akbar Ja'fari/Mashhady Malayeri, commonly known as Akbar Mashty, opened an ice cream shop by this name around the Rāh āhan neighborhood. Akbar Mashty added saffron to the original ingredients.[21]

Popsicles, however, had a Western name in Iran. They were called Alaska. These were popular frozen delights with various colors, representing different artificial tastes, and produced by local artisans. These popsicles were easy and cheap to produce; all they needed was water, sometimes just watered-down lemon juice or colored flavors, a small wooden stick, not necessarily of a standardized length, and freezing temperatures. The finished product was sold by street vendors who roamed through neighborhoods during the summer, often pushing their three-wheeled ice boxes filled with goodies and calling out, "Bastani (ice cream), Alaska." The production of these popsicles was far from standardized or hygienic.

Every year, especially in the summer months, newspapers reported on people, especially children, getting food poisoning from eating unhygienic ice cream, being sent to hospitals, and even dying. In September 1960, during festivities at Rasht's City Park (Park-e shahr), 2,000 people suffered from food poisoning from consuming unhygienic ice cream. Two young

21 *Hamshahri*, Ashnaie ba tarikhcheh Bastani dar Iran, 5 Bahman 1391.

people died of it.[22] The absence of any health standards and the crude methods of production posed a significant risk.[23]

Iranians were informed of the advent of a new kind of modern ice cream called Kim through an advertising campaign in the press on 12 September 1959. Kim began selling on 5 October 1959. It initially entered the market with chocolate, coffee, and vanilla flavors in one-liter and half-liter boxes and as individual ice creams on sticks or popsicles. It was the individual ice-cream stick that became popular. Kim's pasteurized and homogenized ice-cream sticks, wrapped in hygienic sleeves or boxes, were sold at the dairy and confectionary stores as well as restaurants, first in Tehran.[24] Kim quickly established itself as a tasty and, most importantly, safe ice cream that parents could trust.

Kim was founded by Farrokh Panahizadi, Ali-Asghar Panahi's nephew. He had attended Michigan University and San Francisco State University. On a trip to Paris in 1956/57, Panahizadi attended a movie and was served a French ice cream cone called Kim. The idea of producing a hygienic ice cream in Iran piqued his interest. He approached the French Gervais ice cream company, which produced Kim among other products, and secured their collaboration to produce the brand in Iran. Curiously, while the logo of Gervais' Kim in France was the drawing of a smiling Eskimo female child, in Iran, its logo was a cute-looking baby polar bear smiling at the stick ice cream he held in one hand.

Kim's fully automated machinery was imported from France and installed at a factory that was custom-built for this purpose on the road to Karaj. During its initial year, the production process was supervised by French specialists, who also trained the Iranian workers. The capital for the plant was primarily from Panahizadi's mother, Raziyeh Panahi, who came from a monied family, who held large tracts of land in Ardebil and Khalkhal before the land reform.[25]

The managing director, and one of Kim's principal shareholders, was Haj Aqa Mosta'edi, and the factory's manager was Haj Aqa Mo'ini. All of

22 *Ettela'at*, 24 Shahrivar 1339, 28 Farvardin 1341.

23 *Ettela'at*, 9 Ordibehesht 1337, 14 Ordibehesht 1338.

24 *Ettela'at*, 20 Shahrivar 1338, 12 Mehr 1338.

25 Kaveh Rahnema, phone interview with Darush Panahizadi, 12 February 2023, and correspondence with Nader Panahizadi, 10 June 2024. The information in the previous two paragraphs is based on these sources, and I am greatly indebted to Kaveh Rahnema, Nader Panahizadi, and Farhad Panahi for their gracious help.

Kim's ingredients other than fresh milk and sugar were imported.[26] By 1961, Kim had eight different flavors of ice cream, including lemon, orange, blackberry, vanilla, chocolate, and coffee on sticks, as well as individual pots and boxes of half and one-liter sizes.

Between 1959 and 1961, Kim was the uncontested and most popular modern ice cream producer in Iran. But from 1961, Kim faced competition from a new series of manufactured ice creams. The Iranian market was subsequently flooded with at least five modern brands: Canada Frost and Pak ice creams appeared in 1961, followed by POP ice cream in 1962, Eldorado in June 1963, and Cowboy in April 1965.

Canada Frost belonged to the Sard Company, established in 1960. It was owned by the successful Armenian brothers, Rafik, Jebra'il, and Daniel Sahakiyan, who also produced Canada Dry.[27] Eldorado is said to have been owned by Morad Eriyeh. The Iranian urban market had warmed up to manufactured ice creams. In March 1965, Canada Frost sold its ice cream in small glasses, produced by Sahakiyan's own bottle and glass producing company. Cowboy and Eldorado followed Canada Frost's suit and produced their products in appealing small glasses. Pak ice cream failed to jump on the bandwagon of the new glass packaging, and its June 1965 advertisements posited that consumers bought an ice cream for its taste and not its packaging.

Kim launched a new product on 11 September 1963, looking for a new market. Kim's uncarbonated "natural orange juice" was advertised as abundant in vitamin C. Kim's orange juice had new packaging. It was sold in a tetrahedron or four-sided pyramid-like laminated carton with a small plastic straw attached to it. On the face of the package, a small circular area was clearly marked where consumers could insert the straw and enjoy the orange juice immediately.[28]

FROM KHIYAR SEKANJEBIN AND LIMUNADE TO PEPSI AND CANADA DRY

Iran had long been the home of sharbat, a non-carbonated fruit-based drink. Sharbats were made from any of the following fruits, plants, and flower

26 *Ettela'at*, 29 Azar 1338.
27 *Ettela'at*, 6 Shahrivar 1346.
28 *Ettela'at*, 20 Shahrivar 1342

petals: lemon, bitter orange (bahar narenj), musk willow (bidmeshk), flixweed (khakeshir), pomegranate, and sour cherry. One distinctive and refreshing sharbat, consumed mainly by the upper classes, was khiyar sekanjebin. It is said that Avicenna (Ibn Sina), the tenth-century Persian philosopher and physician, wrote a treatise on the benefits of sekanjebin, a heavenly compound of honey, grape syrup or sugar, vinegar, and water with mint added to it. To this rich and sweet drink, Iranians added cucumber or khiyar chopped into small dice and ice, a real treat during hot summers.

It is reported that by 1937, Mashhad had three artisanal workshops producing lemonade drinks. The Iranian version of lemonades was called limunade. However, the production of such drinks remained limited to households and workshops until the mid-1950s. The price of limunade around 1954 was two rials, but due to the unhygienic and polluted quality of water used in it, consumers often became sick after consuming it.[29]

On 30 August 1955, one of Tehran's leading intellectually inclined and Third Worldist weeklies, *Ferdowsi*, gave news of a new drink on the Iranian market: Pepsi-Cola. *Ferdowsi* made three references to Pepsi-Cola, which had recently arrived on the market. Its front page had a cartoon of ʻAla, the prime minister, dressed as a waiter and holding up a tray. On the platter was a huge bottle called Peyman Cola or Pact Cola, in reference to the Baghdad Pact, which Iran was considering joining at the time, and a champagne flute.

The bottle had a chained map of Iran drawn on it, surrounded by other members of the Baghdad Pact, Turkey, Iraq, and Pakistan. Predicting Iran's adherence to the Baghdad Pact, the caption underneath it read, "A new drink that will come on the market". *Ferdowsi* suggested that the idea behind both Pepsi and the Baghdad Pact came from the US. Three days later, the same cartoon was reproduced in *Khandaniha*, referencing *Ferdowsi*.[30]

Ferdowsi did not content itself with a mere political jab at Iran's imminent entrance into a military pact with the West. In its comedy section, Ghelghelak (tickle), it also played on the word Cola, which in Persian means hat. It ridiculed Pepsi as being the new cheap woolen hat (kolah) being pulled over the eyes of Iranians. *Ferdowsi* sarcastically congratulated the producers of Pepsi while describing the drink as a product prepared by American stylists and intended to deceive and empty the people's pockets.

29 *Khandaniha*, 14 Mordad 1337.
30 *Ferdowsi*, 7 Shahrivar 1334; *Khandaniha*, 10 Shahrivar 1334.

In a second piece, *Ferdowsi* wrote a funny yet telling obituary of O-So in the aftermath of Pepsi's arrival on the market. O-So had been the first modern US soft drink produced in Iran and was owned by Luven Palanchiyan. This fruit-flavored soda had been on the market since the summer of 1953.[31]

But Pepsi's widespread and aggressive advertising campaign soon brought many reluctant weekly owners, who needed revenue-generating advertisements, into the fold. Eight days after having reproduced *Ferdowsi's* cartoon of 'Ala and the Pact Cola, *Khandaniha* published a full-page advertisement for Pepsi.[32] Faced with Pepsi's instant success, within a few weeks the approximately two dozen limunade producing workshops in Tehran went bankrupt and closed their doors.[33]

On 14 September 1956, Pepsi became a topic of discussion in Iran's Eighteenth Majles. Mehdi Mirashrafi, an unscrupulous character and member of parliament, spoke about Pepsi. By exaggerating the power of Habibollah Sabet, the owner of the new Pepsi production plant in Tehran, Misashrafi contended that it was Sabet, and not 'Ala, who controlled the Iranian government. He also asserted that 'Ala was a partner in the new Pepsi factory. Mirashrafi tried to whip up public sentiments against Pepsi by announcing that Sabet was a Baha'i.[34]

Sabet, and not Sabet P-A-Sa-L, as Mirashrafi had erroneously referred to him, mixing up his name with the name of a company where he was a major shareholder, was a Baha'i, and he made no secret of it. The fact that Sabet had launched his Pepsi project less than four months after the intimidation campaign against Baha'is in May 1955 demonstrated self-confidence in his business undertaking. In his anti-Baha'i speeches, broadcast on the radio in May 1955, Mohammad Taqi Falsafi had named General Abdolkarim Ayadi, the Shah's personal physician as a Baha'i and had demanded that the Shah dismiss him, but he had made no reference to Sabet.

Shortly after Mirashrafi's interjection in the Majles, an unnamed member of parliament jested that the sale of Pepsi had increased by 20,000 bottles due to his statements. He added that if Mirashrafi kept talking about Pepsi, the new soft drink would become scarce.[35] Pepsi did turn

---

31 *Ferdowsi*, 7 Shahrivar 1334, *Ettela'at*, 4 Mordad 1339.

32 *Khandaniha*, 18 Shahrivar 1334.

33 *Khandaniha*, 14 Mordad 1337.

34 *Ruznameh-e Rasmi-ye Keshvar Shahanshahi-ye Iran*, 29 Shahrivar 1334 Mozakerat-e *Majles-e Showra-ye Melli*, 23 Shahrivar 1334, Neshast-e 149.

35 *Ferdowsi*, 28 Shahrivar 1334.

out to become a huge success with the Iranian public. There were other successful soft drinks, such Canada Dry which followed Pepsi in sales and Coca-Cola, which came in third. Neither threatened Pepsi's lead position in the Iranian market.

Pepsi was owned by Habibollah Sabet's Zamzam company, and the capital invested in it was about 7 million tomans. In the 1940s, Sabet had witnessed the production of a soft drink called Lamar on the side-streets of Tehran. The deplorably unhygienic production, bottling, and capping of Lamar left a mark on Sabet. In the US, Sabet came to appreciate soft drinks such as Pepsi and Coca-Cola, and gradually became convinced that the use of such drinks in Iran could prevent diarrhea and typhoid. In 1946, Sabet approached Pepsi, obtained its franchise and started looking into the construction of a factory in 1947.[36]

Germans and Americans designed the plant. Its fully automated small-size machine was imported from the US and installed in a factory on Eisenhower Street. Arjomand's Arj Company completed the ceiling and the pillars of the factory. The huge windows of the Pepsi production facility allowed Tehranis to watch and be entertained by the production belt inside. Pepsi was priced at 5 rials per bottle, 2.5 rials of which went to the retail stores.[37]

One year after its commercialization, Pepsi produced on average 120,000 bottles daily. It employed 180 workers and distributed its product through 5,000 retail outlets in Tehran.[38] By January 1957, Pepsi opened a second factory in Khorramshahr and sold 300,000 bottles per day in the summer months and 100,000 during the winter months.[39]

Habibollah Sabet handed over the management of Pepsi to his son Iraj Sabet, who had obtained his MBA from Harvard. Hamzeh Samimi-Ne'mati's leading advertising firm, Kanun agahi Ziba (Ziba Advertising Center) launched Pepsi's widespread and intensive advertising campaign. The soda was advertised as the drink that fostered and strengthened "friendship and comradeship" (*dousti o refaqat*).

Facing growing competition from Iran's riveting soft drink industries, in the summer of 1960, Pepsi launched a vigorous advertising campaign spearheaded by Ziba Advertising Center. Pepsi *kulak mikonad,* (Pepsi gives

36 H. Sabet, *Sargozasht Habib Sabet*, pp. 227–235.
37 H. Sabet, *Sargozasht Habib Sabet*, pp. 230–233.
38 *Ettela'at*, 6 Shahrivar 1335.
39 *Ettela'at*, 18 Day 1335.

you a surge), was the caption to an image of laughing men and women, young and old, defying gravity and rising in mid-air, holding up a Pepsi in one hand. The catchy slogan became popular very quickly. By July 1962, Pepsi was the leading soft drink in Iran, with plants in Rasht, Ahvaz, Esfahan, Kerman, and Shiraz. It was also exporting its soft drinks from its new Mashhad plant to Afghanistan.[40]

Pepsi's real competition was Coca-Cola, which began commercial distribution in Tehran on 13 October 1956 or more than a year after Pepsi's launch.[41] Less than two months before the launch of Coca-Cola, the Ministry of Industry and Mines announced that it had approved a loan of 335,000 tomans to the Coca-Cola Bottlers factory and ordered Bank Melli to make the payment.[42]

Coca-Cola, however, franchised its drink in different cities in Iran to different individuals and companies. In Tehran, the Coca-Cola factory was on Farahabad Road near Dowshan tapeh, and its franchise belonged to Gregor Mirza Touni and Mr. Sobhani. Mr. Touni's son was the plant's technical director, and his two daughters managed the laboratory. General Ahmad Khosrovani was the manager, and Mosavvar Rahmani and Farzaneh were members of its board of directors. The Abadan franchise of Coca-Cola belonged to the Kosariyeh Company, which also began operation in 1956.[43]

Coca-Cola's third automated plant was opened in Esfahan on 24 October 1957. Three brothers, Abdolali, Abolbashar, and Faruq Farmanfarmayan, founded and managed the Noush Company, with a capital of 1.8 million tomans. The Coca-Cola franchise for production in Esfahan and Rasht belonged to the Farmanfarmayans. The Esfahan factory was designed by Abdolaziz Farmanfarmayan, employed 35 workers, and produced 50,000 bottles daily.[44] In 1957, Coca-Cola also began production in Mashhad. That franchise belonged to Khoshgovar Company, owned by Mr. Yazdi.

In the middle of its tight competition with Pepsi, especially in 1961, Coca-Cola did, on occasion, try to gain an edge by presenting itself as a

40 The previous two paragraphs are based on *Ettela'at*, 6 Farvardin 1336, 14 Tir 1338; 2, 7, 21 Mehr 1339, 4 Aban 1339; *Tehran Economist*, 22 Tir 1341, *Sepid o Siyah*, 27 Khordad 1339, 3 Tir 1339.

41 *Ettela'at*, 17, 19 Mehr 1335.

42 *Ettela'at*, 6 Shahrivar 1335.

43 All information on Coca-Cola in this paragraph is based on *Tehran Economist*, 2 Tir 1335, 7 Mehr 1335, 23 Shahrivar 1336; *Ettela'at Haftegi*, 30 Azar 1335.

44 *Ettela'at*, 18 Khordad 1336, 9 Aban 1336.

drink for the pious public. After the death of Ayatollah Borujerdi, Coca-Cola printed an advertisement on the first page of *Ettela'at* extending the condolences of its employees to the Shi'i of the world, especially Iranian compatriots.[45] It was rumored that Qom's religious dignitaries had recommended that the Shi'i should desist from consuming Pepsi since it was owned by a Baha'i.

Pepsi-Cola also faced competition from Canada Dry, a fruit-based soda, particularly orange, which came onto the market in Tehran on 19 August 1957. By 1962, Canada Dry had six factories in Tehran, Tabriz, Rasht, Esfahan, Abadan, and Mashhad. Canada Dry's franchise belonged to Sasan Company owned by Rafik Sahakiyan and his brothers Jebra'il and Daniel.

Canada Dry's fully automated machinery and pre-packaged fruit syrup and extract were imported from the US. American specialists assisted in setting up and running the plant. Canada Dry began production simultaneously in Tehran and Tabriz. On its first anniversary, Canada Dry was distributed for free in around ten different locations in Tehran.[46] A comparative edge of Canada Dry over Pepsi was that by 1965, it possessed its own bottling company, *Karkhaneh shisheh va gaz*, and Pepsi did not.

An orange-flavored German soft drink, Sinalco, a rival of Canada Dry, appeared on the market in late 1959. Fanta, the orange-flavored drink produced by the manufacturers of Coca-Cola, followed suit in June 1959. Bubble Up, the American lemon-lime soft drink followed Fanta and appeared in July 1959. It belonged to Palanchiyan, who also produced O-So.

Alpine entered the soft drink market on 5 November 1960 with ten different fruit flavors. This was a British soft drink, and its franchise holder was Mir Hashem Ariyan, who launched his soda with an expensive full-page advertising campaign in leading Iranian newspapers. Vigen and Tabesh, two highly popular figures of Iranian music and cinema, promoted Alpine.[47] By 1966, Alpine was phased out and Ariyan was running the Tabriz Coca-Cola company and had a partnership with Canada Dry.[48] A year later, the Sahakiyans bought out the Tabriz Coca-Cola factory from Ariyan.

45 *Ettela'at*, 10 Farvardin 1340.
46 *Ettela'at*, 28 Khordad 1336, 24, 30 Mordad 1336, 11 Shahrivar 1337, 16 Aban 1340.
47 Information in this paragraph is based on *Ettela'at*, 8 Farvardin 1338, 18 Khordad 1338, 19 Tir 1338, 1–19 Aban 1339.
48 *Tehran Economist*, 19 Azar 1345.

One of the last soft drinks to try its luck in Iran was Mission California. This American soda was claimed to be based on natural fruits and was full of vitamin C. It entered the Iranian market on 4 April 1962. It made its debut with an orange-and-pineapple-flavored soda in two bottle sizes. The Iranian owner and franchise holder was Moshkab Company, which was owned by Rahimzadeh. The syrup for the soda was imported from the US. The plant in Iran employed 125 workers and two foreign engineers.[49]

Once the intense competition among soft drink producers subsided in 1964, four brands were left standing. Iranians had finally decided on Pepsi and Coca-Cola among the colas, and Canada Dry and Fanta, the orange-flavored drinks.[50] Yet in December 1965, 7Up, the American lemon-lime soft drink entered the soda market as "the drink of those who are not fond of ordinary drinks".

In December 1966, the rivalry between Pepsi and Coca-Cola peaked, as Tehran's Coca-Cola factory filed a complaint against Pepsi for hoarding its bottles.[51] By January 1967, the concentration of capital and mergers in Iran's soft drink industry was being finalized. In addition to Canada Dry, the Sahakiyans had obtained the franchises to Coca-Cola, Fanta, and 7Up and had become the new soft drink powerhouse. Pepsi, on the other hand, had entered a partnership with O-So and Bubble Up.[52]

49 *Ettela'at*, 19, 21 Esfand 1340.
50 *Ettela'at*, 15 Azar 1344. *Ettela'at*, 5 Azar 1346.
51 *Tehran Economist*, 3 Day 1345.
52 *Tehran Economist*, 24 Day 1345, *Ettela'at*, 4, 5 Shahrivar 1346.

14

Changing Lifestyles, Washing, Housing, and Watching (1957–1962)

A quick and random numerical glance at the Iranian economy and society between 1955 and 1962 reflects the significant transformations in the country. In 1955, some 2,902 factories, employing 108,000, were at work.[1] In 1962, Iran possessed 9,438 factories employing 136,419 people, of which 126,156 were laborers, 9,131 were office staff, and 950 were engineers. Of these total numbers, Tehran's share was 3,577 factories, 49,535 laborers, 4,411 office staff, and 549 engineers. Tehran also produced 77% of all vegetable shortening (solid vegetable oil) and 38% of all textiles produced in Iran, surpassing Esfahan (22%), the traditional lead producer of textiles in the country.[2] By 1961, Iran possessed 28 banks with a capital of 1.9 billion tomans, more than 23,000 employees and 810 branches.[3]

In 1956, approximately 8,000 private cars, 3,000 taxis, 2,500–3,000 buses, 1,500 trucks and pick-up trucks, 75,000 bicycles, and 300 motorbikes roamed the streets and roads of the country. Most of them were concentrated in the urban area. Side by side with these modern means of transportation, 811 horse-drawn carriages (*doroshkeh*) provided urban transportation, and 1,870 donkey or human-drawn carts hauled cargo.[4]

On 20 March 1959, the number of private cars officially registered in the country stood at 45,491, and the number of taxis reached 17,291.

---

1 *Khandaniha*, 21 Ordibehesht 1336; 18 Day 1338.
2 *Ettela'at*, 8 Ordibehesht 1341.
3 Mehran, *Hadafha va Siyasathay-e Bank-e Markaziy-e Iran*, p. 39.
4 *Ettela'at Haftegi*, 11 Aban 1335.

Of these total numbers, Tehran possessed some 70% of the private cars (31,538) and 56% of the taxis (9,744). Within four years, the number of cars increased rapidly. By March 1963, the number of registered private cars in the country grew to 86,960, while the number of registered taxis (*taksi va kerayeh*) reached 24,824.

The share of private cars registered in Tehran grew by some 85% from 1959 to 1963. But the staggering increase in private cars occurred in provinces such as Esfahan, Shiraz, Tabriz, and Mashhad. The increase in private cars was four-fold in Esfahan, almost three-fold in Shiraz and Mashhad, and two-and-a-half-fold in Tabriz.[5]

Most importantly, the composition of drivers was also dramatically changing. While prior to 1961, the number of women taking their driver's license test was less than 40 per week, from 1962, this number jumped to 40 per day.[6] On 18 April 1962, the traffic department of Tehran police banned the circulation of 300 horse-drawn carriages as well as the 350 donkey or human-drawn cargo carts that cluttered and slowed down the traffic on the streets of Tehran. This ruling was to pave the way for faster-moving motor vehicles in the city.[7]

Whereas in 1965 Tehran had some 120,000 motor vehicles of all kinds, including 45,242 private cars, taxis, buses, ambulances, vans, and trucks, by 1972, some 500,000 private cars roamed the streets of Tehran, and approximately 5,000 new cars matriculated every month.[8]

As Tehran grew and expanded, public services increased in tandem with it, but far from proportionately. Tehran's bus service company, *Sherkat-e vahed-e otobus rani-ye Tehran* (Tehran's Unified Bus Service Company), was launched by Tehran's municipality. The Tehran bus service united all previously private and independent bus services and began operations with 80 buses on 5 July 1956. Tehran at the time had one bus line, serving a south–north axis, from the Rāh āhan train station to Shahreza Street. Soon, it boasted nine bus lines. The fare for the complete route was one rial per passenger.[9]

By February 1962, Tehran's Unified Bus Service operated 73 bus lines and transported one and a half million passengers in the capital city.

5 *Tehran Economist*, 2 Azar 1342.
6 *Ettela'at*, 18 Tir 1341.
7 *Ettela'at*, 29, 30 Farvardin 1341.
8 *Ettela'at*, 8 Tir 1344. *Khandaniha*, 29 Mehr, 27 Aban 1351.
9 *Ettela'at*, 13, 15 Tir 1335.

Its routes had expanded to Shahr-e Ray, Shemiran, and Karaj. Within five-and-a-half years, it came to possess 1,427 buses, of which 236 were German Mercedes Benzes and 93 were Chevrolets. Tehran's Unified Bus Service employed 2,485 bus drivers, 2,273 bus attendants/assistants, 1,444 ticket sellers, 954 skilled workers, and 890 office staff members. By 1962, buses in Tehran had differentiated prices, ranging from two to eight rials, depending on the routes.[10]

As the number of private cars increased, the taste of consumers went through an interesting change. Whereas in 1956 Iranians preferred US-built cars, particularly Chevrolets, by 1960 some 50 to 70% of the cars were German: Volkswagen, Benz, DKW, or Opel.[11] The Volkswagen Beetle became popular among the Iranian middle class, while the Mercedes Benz 220 became a sudden status symbol. In January 1961, the Iranian Senate was said to have ordered some thirty to forty Mercedes Benz vehicles to be sold to the senators in installments.[12] This important shift in taste meant considerable increase in revenue for the Sabet P-A-Sa-L company, which held the franchise for Volkswagen, and the Merrikh Company belonging to the Sudavar brothers (Samad, Fereydoun, and Ahmad), who possessed the franchise for Mercedes Benz.

The number of schools and enrolled students constituted another indicator of Iran's modernization tempo. In 1953 Iran had 5,675 primary schools, in which 730,793 primary school students were enrolled, and 465 secondary schools, enrolling 101,140 secondary school students. Iran possessed twenty-five institutions of higher education, thirty teacher training institutions, and six technical and agricultural schools. Over the next nine years, most of these figures more than doubled.

In 1962, Iran had 10,852 primary schools in which 1,554,554 primary school students were enrolled, and 1,184 secondary schools, enrolling 300,885 secondary school students. Iran came to possess forty-seven institutions of higher education, eighty-six teacher training institutions, and seventy-nine technical and agricultural schools. The number of teaching staff increased from 31,696 in 1953 to 65,900 in 1962.[13]

10 *Ettela'at*, 22 Bahman 1340, 3 Ordibehesht 1341.

11 *Tehran Economist*, 25 Esfand 1335, 16 Mehr 1339.

12 *Tehran Economist*, 15 Bahman 1339.

13 All figures are from Parviz Natel Khanlari, the Minister of Education's report. *Ettela'at*, 22 Mehr 1341.

The number of Iranian students studying abroad in the academic year 1957–1958 was 8,072. Of this number 1,559 studied in the US, followed by 1,369 in Germany, 553 in the UK and 502 in France. The number of students studying abroad by January 1963 was estimated at 13,000 to 14,000 and grew to 16,000 in 1964.[14] The US continued to absorb a growing proportion of Iran's students.[15]

In 1959, Tehran had thirty-six squares (Meydan) and seventy-four statues, but only three parks. According to the Tehran municipality's classifications, Tehran had twelve luxury hotels, ten first-class hotels, sixteen luxury restaurants, thirty-five first-class and sixty-five second-class restaurants, fifty-six cinemas, six of which were luxury cinemas, and eight theaters. Its tallest building was the ten-story Agricultural Bank. Tehran had 3,293 grocery stores, 1,627 hairdressers, 996 bakeries, 42 toy stores, 227 photo shops, 93 bookstores, 22 lemonade manufacturers, 3 beer producers, and 388 confectionary shops.[16]

By 1961, Tehran had some 100 bars and cabarets. Of these, some seventy employed foreign performers, men and women, dancers, singers, and musicians. Before the Amini government's temporarily ban on foreign dancers and singers, some 400 foreign performers, mostly women, worked in Tehran. The majority of them came from France, followed by Germany, Italy, and Austria.[17]

On 15 November 1961, the Shah inaugurated the first bowling club in Tehran at Kouy-e Mekanir, Vanak. The club was owned by Ali-Mohammad Abdoh, a professional boxer who shortly after became the head of Iran's Boxing Federation. Abdoh had spent some five years in the US and was the founder of the export-import company CRC, whose shareholders included court members.

The Vanak bowling club had another prominent co-owner, Azar Ebtehaj, whose husband Abolhasan had been imprisoned four days before the club's official opening. The Shah, in his three-piece suit and tie, and his jacket buttoned, nonchalantly opened the new sports complex by rolling the first bowling ball down the lane.[18] There is no record of how many

14 FO 371 170805, EP 2881/1. *Khandaniha*, 25 Esfand 1343.
15 *Khandaniha*, 5 Bahman 1336; *Ettela'at*, 20 Day 1339; 11 Ordibehesht 1342.
16 *Ettela'at*, 23 Tir 1338.
17 *Ettela'at*, 6 Shahrivar 1340.
18 *Ettela'at*, 25 Aban 1340.

pins he knocked down or whether he had the slightest reservation about Ebtehaj being in prison, while he enjoyed the game at Mrs. Ebtehaj's club.

FROM WASHING IN SIDEWALK STREET GUTTERS WITH CHUBAK TO BARF LAUNDRY

In Iran, the arduous job of washing clothes and bed linen was the domain of women, wives, daughters, and daughters-in-law. In the upper classes, it was a chore carried out by maids. Tehrani women would spend hours handwashing clothes. Washing boards that had been around in the West since the nineteenth century did not make their way to Iran, rendering the job more trying.

First, women had to find a basin-like structure, natural or man-made, to wash their laundry in. Sidewalk street gutters (joub), and streams/creeks (nahr), were the washing place of the poor. Various sections of a famous stream/creek in Tehran's nahr-e firuzabad, stretching from the Farahzad hills in the north to the Naziabad and Firuzabad districts in the south, were used to wash clothes.

The better-off families owned round copper tubs of various sizes and washed their clothes at home. Some used the small ponds/pools (howz) in their gardens. The idea of washing in hot or lukewarm water was alien even to upper-class households, while rainy and snowy weather rendered open-air washing most irregular.

Cleaning clothes implies the use of soap or detergent. In the early 1950s, the principal detergent used in Iranian households was the powder form of chubak. Chubak was derived from the dried and crushed roots of the Acanthophyllum bracteatum plant found in Iran, Iraq, Pakistan, and Saudi Arabia. Households also used khakestar (ash wood) and lajevard (azure). All three of these natural products had cleansing and detergent properties. While squatting for long hours, women would apply these products to clothes and then rub, agitate, scrub the fabrics, and soak. This cycle would be repeated at least three times before the wash was rinsed. Long hours of crouching down caused women spinal and back injuries as well as hemorrhoids.

The unpleasant condition for Iranian women who used chubak and khakestar was somewhat alleviated as a series of washing powders and soaps appeared on the Iranian market. Such products using chemicals speeded up the wash cycle. Ray washing soap, a product of Tehran Industrial Factories, was already available for sale by March 1956.[19] Surf, an imported detergent of the British Lever Brothers, was also on the market by March 1956. It promised the "whitest and cleanest" wash and boasted of cleaning the worst of stains with its miraculous foam.[20]

Concurrently, Tim, a detergent produced by the Iranian Darugar factory, came on the market in April 1956. Tim was advertised as suitable for washing all kinds of clothes, including wool, silk, and nylon. It came in a big box size of 22 rials and a small box for 6.5 rials.[21] Darugar was one of the pioneers of toiletries in Iran and the most established one. Its logo was a palm tree with seven fronds. Gholamreza Darugar, the founder and owner of Darugar Industries, was a pharmacologist who had started his business during Reza Shah's rule, producing soap and skin creams. His sons followed in the footsteps of their father.

The year 1956 was when the market was flooded by detergents. After Ray, Tim, and Surf, it was the turn of Fab, a product of the renowned US Colgate-Palmolive company, which appeared in April 1956. Fab promoted itself as the miraculously quick cleaner and the solution to women's rough hands.[22] A German washing powder called Wipp came on the heels of Fab. In August 1956, Ali Khosrowshahi began the distribution of Wipp which, despite a long advertising campaign in the press, failed to appeal to Iranian consumers.[23] Soon, it was Fab that surpassed all other detergents in sales, imposing its name as a generic term for washing powder among Iranians.

In June 1957, Fab faced tough competition from a new import product, Tide, the flagship detergent of the US giant Procter and Gamble. Tide entered the market as the "easiest and cleanest" washing powder available. Hasan Khosrowshahi and his six sons, most of whom were US-educated, distributed Tide in Iran.[24]

It was not until May 1960 that Tide was produced in Iran. By this time, it made sense for established imported brands to avoid the increasing

19 *Ettela'at*, 9 Farvardin 1335.
20 *Ettela'at*, 11 Farvardin 1335.
21 *Ettela'at*, 1, Ordibehesht 1335, 3 Khordad 1335, 7 Khordad 1336.
22 *Ettela'at*, 1 Ordibehesht 1335.
23 A-A. Sa'idi, *Zendegi va Karnemeh-e Ali Khosrowshahi*, Tehran: Nashr-e Ney, 1398, pp. 71–73; *Ettela'at*, 5 Shahrivar 1335; 22 Farvardin 1336.
24 *Ettela'at*, 12 Khordad 1336; A-A. Sa'idi, *Zendegi va Karnemeh-e 'Ali Khosrowshahi*, p. 71; F. Shirinkam and I. Farjāmniya, *Sargozasht-e panjah koneshgar-e eqtesadi-ye Iran*, Tehran: Farhang Saba, 1398, pp. 266–269.

import duties imposed by the government and get behind the trade barriers. Tide announced that its Iranian production would be much cheaper than its imported rivals, most significantly Fab, since it would be exempt from import duties and transportation costs.[25]

The production of Tide in Iran was contracted to the Darugars who were already experienced in the production of detergents. Its distribution in Iran was transferred from Hasan Khosrowshahi's KBC company to his cousin's (Ali Khosrowshahi) company Khorāk.[26] The next phase in the washing powder war to control the market (1963–1965) came with the advent of Kazem Khosrowshahi's Darya and the Lajevardis' low-priced Barf detergent on 19 April 1964, which underpriced all competitors.[27] By 1965, Darya, Barf and Tide controlled the Iranian detergent market.

Iranian entrepreneurs were correctly aware that the domestic market was ripe for the import and even home production of washing powder. Yet, at the end of the 1950s and early 1960s, the urban Iranian market was still not fully developed enough to commercialize washing machines. In anticipation, a newly imported idea was brewed and put into effect to gradually rid the Tehrani female urban middle class of the pain of hand washing.

On 7 September 1960, a nondescript advertisement appeared in the press simply saying "barf", or snow, with no further explanation. A week later, Tehranis discovered that a new commercial laundry service with six branches, all concentrated in upper-middle- and upper-class neighborhoods, was offering its services. Tehranis were promised that if they were to take their dirty clothes to the branches on Khiyaban Shahreza, Boulevard, Vanak, Jadeh Shemiran, or Seyyed Khandan, their laundry would be returned to them "as clean as snow" as the catchy slogan of Barf Laundry Industry (*karkhaneh lebās shu-ie barf*) went.[28]

Mohammad Yazdi, the founder of Barf Laundry, correctly anticipated that middle and upper-middle-class Tehrani women were willing and able to abandon handwashing. He was proposing an alternative to those not prosperous enough or not accustomed to using washing machines at home. This idea became popular.

25 *Sepid o Siyah*, 13 Khordad 1339.
26 *Ettela'at*, 15 Ordibehesht 1341.
27 *Ettela'at*, 30, 31 Farvardin 1343.
28 *Ettela'at*, 16–24 Shahrivar 1339. With a slight alteration, this slogan was later taken over by the producers of barf detergent, which is in no way associated with Barf Laundry industry.

Yazdi was neither a businessman nor a merchant by education or training, even though his grandfather had been a successful merchant in Tehran's bazaar. He was a medical doctor who specialized in pulmonary medicine and the treatment of tuberculosis. He had received his medical education in France, Switzerland, and Italy and returned to Iran to practice his profession.

On 10 September 1946, the Shah had inaugurated Dr. Yazdi's newly built sanatorium in Niavaran. However, within a few years, Yazdi was embroiled in a dispute with the Shah as the lease for the land on which the sanatorium was built belonged to His Majesty, and the Shah wished to reclaim his land way before the lease's expiry date.

It was during a long and unwinnable legal and extralegal battle with the court that Yazdi transitioned from the medical profession to providing hygiene and sanitation to Iranians through the establishment of a modern industrial laundry. His years of professional experience with hospitals and sanatoriums in Iran, where bedding needed to be cleaned at short intervals and was still hand-washed, had convinced Yazdi that there was a market for industrial laundries. Yazdi borrowed 38,000 tomans from the Shahsavar branch of *Bank-e Saderat* in Mazandaran and a more substantial amount from Bank Melli through his friendship with Yusef Khoshkish.

The initial two-story Barf plant was in the Tehran-No district, some 8 kilometers from the city center, and its modern machinery came from Denmark. Barf's plant and operation manager was a Dane named Jensen. Male workers moved heaps of heavy bedding, drapes, and clothes from huge washing machines to rinsing machines and then to dryers, while for "ironing, pressing, and folding" Yazdi hired Armenian women, most of whom were skilled and high school graduates.

From 1957, Barf provided quality service to Tehran's hospitals, hotels, and restaurants and established itself as an uncontested and reputable enterprise. Three years later, in September 1960, Barf extended its dry-cleaning know-how and service to households. "Thousands of pieces of clothing, each in small batches belonging to individual customers, would have to be separated into laundry and dry-cleaning batches, labeled individually, and sent through the various steps and departments (washing, drying, dry cleaning, ironing, folding, packaging)."[29]

29 Fardad Yazdi, *Namehhay-e delnishin-e ou. Mokhtasari az zendegi-ye shadravan doctor Mohammad Yazdi*, unpublished manuscript, p. 16. All information on Mohammad Yazdi and Barf, other than the first paragraph, is based on this document. Fardad Yazdi graciously provided me with this manuscript, and I am grateful to him.

Within a few years, Barf succeeded in transforming the taste and lifestyle of middle and upper-middle-class Tehranis while establishing itself as the leading brand in the field. Since May 1962, Towelmaster roller towels had been available in Iran. They were produced by the British Advanced Linen Services and distributed by Moqadam. In January 1964, Towelmaster launched a major advertising campaign to rival Barf. Instead of operating through vendors, Towelmaster offered home pick-ups and deliveries of laundry by vans or motorcycles through a telephone service.[30] Competition in the laundry industry intensified, and in January 1966, Barf offered a 40% discount for a limited period at its twenty-five different branches.[31]

It was not until 1973–1974 that Barf's dry-cleaning business faced serious competition, both from an increasing number of Tehrani households owning their own washing machines and the rapidly multiplying small, local, dry-cleaning operations. By this time, old-style handwashing remained the lot of poor Tehranis, especially the newly arrived rural-urban migrants, who were brimming over in shanty towns around Tehran.

FROM LIVING IN JAVADIYEH AND MOWLAVI DISTRICTS TO TEHRAN PARS, SHAHR-ARA AND SAHEBQARANIYEH

Constructions without basic facilities, such as piped water, electricity, sewage, and adjacent tarmac streets, were characteristic of Tehran's unplanned and disorderly urban sprawl after 1953. The first phase of Tehran's pipe water project was completed in 1955, and the second was not completed until 1959. As for the provision of electricity, it was not until September 1959 that the French Alstom company began operating the fifty-megabyte factory at Tarasht in Tehran, providing some 50% of Tehran's electricity needs. Even though this electricity plant and the Karaj Dam in 1963 somewhat alleviated Tehran's electricity problem, demand in Tehran and other emerging urban centers always ran way ahead of supply.

One of the main reasons for Tehran's electricity deficit was the increase in its population, and the concomitant hectic urban growth that it implied. In a most revealing seminar on the Assessment of Tehran's Social Problems,

30 *Ettela'at*, 30 Ordibehesht 1341. *Tehran Economist*, 12 Bahman 1342.

31 *Ettela'at*, 29 Day, 5 Bahman 1344.

held on 21 April 1962 at the Institute of Social Studies and Research (*Moaseseh-e motale'at va tahqiqat-e ejtema'i*) of Tehran University, glaring facts about Tehran came to light.

Between 1927 and 1960, 100,000 people per year on average were added to Tehran's population. Between 1950 and 1956, rural-urban migration accounted for 62,000 of this number annually. Even though this 60% component abated between 1956 and 1959, it picked up exponentially after the land reform, especially during its third phase in 1967. The attraction of Tehran's city lights, anticipated employment opportunities, higher incomes, services, and cultural freedoms compared to rural and provincial Iran, made it the promised land of migrants. Faced with unfulfilled expectations, Tehran's bulging migrant population gradually built its own informal economic and housing sector.

By 1960, Tehran needed to improve the dwelling conditions of its population of almost 2 million. Of the 359,600 living residences or shelters (*ma'va*) in Tehran, 44% were one-room constructions, 28% were two-room, and 11% were five-room and more. A significant share of the one and two-room residences or shelters were made of sun-dried mud bricks (*khesht o gel*). According to Abdolhoseyn Minuchehr, the mayor of Javadiyeh, a poor southern district of Tehran, in 1960, 90% of the houses were less than thirty square meters.[32]

Tehran was also the hub of Iran's bureaucracy. Of Tehran's 580,000 working population, 120,000 were administrative staff (*karmand-e edari*). The population concentration varied substantially between the southern districts in Tehran, such as Shahpur and Mahmudiyeh Square, with some 1,000 inhabitants per hectare, and the central districts, such as Sepah Square and Naser Khosrow, with 100 inhabitants per hectare.[33]

In 1962, house number 37 on Gozar Bashi Alley, also known as Qater Bashi, in the south of Tehran (Mowlavi and Bazaar district), had an area of 600 square meters. In it lived 164 people belonging to 63 households. On average, each inhabitant lived in 3.6 square meters. Such cases were not exceptional in Tehran's southern neighborhoods. There were even cases of two households living in one room.[34] Construction in Tehran between 1959 and 1963 constituted 50% of all housing that had been built before 1959.[35]

32 *Ettela'at*, 5, 6 Ordibehesht 1341.

33 *Ettela'at*, 2 Ordibehesht 1341.

34 *Ettela'at*, 8 Ordibehesht 1341.

35 *Tehran Economist*, 10 Mehr 1344.

While government buildings, ministries, banks, commerce, sports clubs, cinemas, and cafes remained in the city center around the Ark, Bazaar, Sepah Square, Lalehzar, and Naderi streets, residential Tehran was pulling towards the north. Well-off and high-income households began building houses in large garden areas in Vanak, Qolhak, Za'faraniyeh, Qeytariyeh, Niavaran, and Darband, where inhabitants per hectare were probably around five or less. Prominent bazaar merchants who traditionally lived in the city center had also begun to find residency in northern Tehran. Gradually, in the 1960s and early 1970s, commerce, banks, cinemas, cafes, restaurants, sports clubs, and nightclubs followed and migrated to northern Tehran.

Differences in household income implied planning different housing accommodations. Yet, the Zahedi, 'Ala, Eqbal, and Sharif-Emami governments had no concrete and specific plan for population control, migration policy, rural development, or urban development. Tehran's house construction, spatial development, and urban transformation were unregulated, uncoordinated, and haphazard. General state policy was to increase housing in Tehran, but in the absence of a master plan, the how of it was largely left to chance and individual homeowners and developers.

Fortunately, on 19 August 1952, Mosaddeq had signed a bill that had become law which prohibited grabbing large unclaimed tracts of land around Tehran. According to this law, individuals were prohibited from enclosing and registering these lands as private property, and all such lands subsequently belonged to the government. This law placed somewhat of a break on usurping land and profiteering by unscrupulous influential politicians, courtiers, and notables.[36]

According to this law, seventeen large tracts of some 17.3 million square meters had become common land. They were placed under the ownership and tutelage of the state-owned Construction Bank (*Bank-e Sakhtemani*) to be used for building affordable housing. The housing project at Narmak resulted from the Construction Bank selling some 4,000 plots of land between 50 and 200 square meters on long-term and low-interest credit to public servants by the draw of the lot.

The land sale projects in Yusef-Abad, Abbas-Abad, Shahr-Ara, Tehran-No, parts of Shemiran, Shahrak Gharb, and Nazy-Abad were

36 Mohammad Saleh Moayedi, *Layeh-ye qanuniy-e tasis bank sakhtemani va asasnameh an*, http://www.moaydilawyer.com/laws/ (retrieved 18/5/2024).

also conducted under the aegis of the Construction Bank.[37] One of the unintended consequences of the government's land sale to individuals for construction of housing was an increase in the price of such plots by some 500%, due to land speculation. Financially incapable of building on the lands obtained, recipients of government land sold them to land traders. By 1960, Tehran had a thousand real estate agencies.[38]

In 1959, the Shah set the ambitious target of building three million residential units in twenty years. Housing projects around Tehran, such as Tehran-No, Narmak, Kouy-e Mekanir, Kouy-e Kan, and Nazy-Abad, mushroomed. In addition to the above government housing projects, three were spearheaded by the private sector.

The Shahr-Ara and IBEC/Sahebqaraniyeh housing projects were built on government-owned land, with the participation of the Pahlavi Foundation, and were targeted at two very different income categories. Shahr-Ara, built by the Iranian Mehdi Ebrahimi Daryani, was intended for lower-middle and middle-income groups. In contrast, the American Winthrop Rockefeller built the IBEC/Sahebqaraniyeh project for upper-income groups. The third housing project, an initiative of the Zoroastrian community, was that of Tehran Pars, which neither benefited from government lands nor the investment of the Pahlavi Foundation but, given its private resources, turned out to be the most successful.

Shahr-Ara: Private initiative with the Pahlavi Foundation

Shahr-Ara Company (*Sherkat-e Shahr-Ara*) was created on 7 October 1957 to build modern and affordable housing in northwest Tehran, an isolated, uninhabited, and desolate area. The company committed itself to building modern housing and apartments and was the brainchild of Mehdi Ebrahimi Daryani, a prominent tea merchant from Azarbayjan. Daryani was the producer and distributor of his brand of tea, Chai ʻOqab (Eagle Tea). Daryani and his influential partners, such as the Pahlavi Foundation and General Haj Ali Kia, created a limited liability partnership and sold 45% of the company shares to the public. The company's capital was 125,000,000 tomans.

37 *Tehran Nameh*, Sabt-e arāzi-ye mavat-e atraf-e Tehran, https://tehrannameh.com/list-category/%d8%ab/ (retrieved 18/5/2024).
38 *Ettelaʻat*, 2 Ordibehesht 1341.

On 25 November 1957, Daryani, who was well-connected and very fond of press interviews and publicity stunts, held the first general assembly of his company's shareholders at Amjadiyeh Stadium, Tehran's biggest arena. He informed some 8,000 potential homeowners that construction work would begin in March 1958 and promised that some 2,000 modern housing units would be built within a year. After the shareholders' meeting, Daryani told reporters that he had met with the Shah and given him a progress report. According to Daryani, the idea of his housing project had come from His Majesty. The housing project was contracted to six Iranian contractors: Alep, Etude, Pirooz, Jasar, Khakriz, and Nav.[39]

Daryani could not deliver housing to all his clients at once, yet they, eager to move into their new residences, felt entitled to receive the first finished units. The manner of allocating the finished units among shareholders created problems. As of 20 March 1958, some 2,000 disgruntled shareholders gathered at the company's headquarters on Pasteur Street, seeking clarifications over the distribution procedure for homes as they became available. It was finally decided that, as each series of apartments was finished, they would first be allocated to shareholders, who were tenants/renters, by drawing lots.

A year and a half later, tension again mounted between the directors of Shahr-Ara and the small shareholders of the housing project when, on 19 October 1959, the new terms for allocating the finished housing units and their prices were announced. A large crowd gathered in front of Shahr-Ara's central office and protested the changes in terms and conditions. Their main objection was the sudden price increase of two-bedroom units from 10,000 to 30,000 tomans. They also protested the rise in monthly instalment payments from 100 to 304 tomans.

It was not until November 1960 that 1,200 residential units, 800 of which were apartments, were ready. Shahr-Ara was equipped with a sewage system, piped water, electricity, a public bath, shopping facilities, a park, primary and secondary schools, a dispensary, and a police outpost. The Shah's interest in the Shar-Ara construction project was important in its progress. The Shah was aware of the housing shortage in Tehran, had long been interested in constructing low-cost housing, and took a keen interest in Daryani's housing project. He visited Shahr-Ara at least three

39 All information in the previous three paragraphs is based on: *Ettela'at*, 25, 27 Aban 1336; 5, 7 Azar 1336; 13 Ordibehesht 1337. Amordadnews.com, https://amordadnews.com/69091/ (retrieved 17/5/2024).

times. The Shah was also interested in Daryani's project since the Pahlavi Foundation held one-fourth of all shares in the company.

In the middle of completing the second series of houses at Shahr-Ara, Mehdi Ebrahimi Daryani entered the winter elections of the Twentieth Majles in February 1961. As a candidate of Asadollah 'Alam's *Hezb-e Mardom* (People's Party) he stood for election from Tabriz and entered the short-lived Majles, which lasted only twenty sessions and was dissolved by the Shah's royal edict on 9 May 1961. Like many others who had tried hard and spent much on their election campaign to become deputies, Daryani was unsuccessful at obtaining political power.

During Amini's office, Daryani's fortune took a turn for the worse when, on 21 August 1961, he was arrested on charges of misconduct concerning the sale of Shahr-Ara shares, tampering with the company's financial books, and making false promises. His company's assets were subsequently frozen, and its accounts were blocked. On 20 March 1962, he was released from prison on a 20 million toman bail.[40]

The homeowners in Shahr-Ara were not happy campers. They wrote several open letters to the press complaining about the unpaved primary and secondary streets making their lives miserable due to the daily dust kicked up by vehicles traveling on them. Shahr-Ara's unfinished streets were contracted to the Shahr-Saz Construction Company. The inability of the housing project to provide necessary utilities and services such as garbage collectors, sweepers, and maintenance personnel led the inhabitants of Shahr-Ara to petition for a municipality of their own.[41] On 29 June 1962, Amini, accompanied by the mayor, Ahmad Nafisi, paid Shahr-Ara a quick visit. The Prime Minister listened to the resident's complaints and asked Nafisi to resolve their problems.[42]

Despite its construction, financial, and managerial problems, in the early 1960s, Shahr-Ara was a modern building project with some basic services though without all the complementary amenities of a flourishing modern suburb or district. A regular bus service between Shahr-Ara and the city center, Meydan Sepah, would not be established until April 1963, and it was not until 1965 that a mosque was built. Yet Shahr-Ara was free of the narrow and congested streets and alleys of old central Tehran; the

---

40 *Ettela'at*, 30, 31 Mordad 1340; 2 Shahrivar 1340; 29 Esfand 1340.

41 *Ettela'at*, 20 Khordad 1341.

42 *Ettela'at*, 10 Tir 1341.

streets were wide, two to three-story buildings were well spaced out, and open spaces were abundant.

The Shahr-Ara project was successful in transforming middle and lower-middle class tenants into homeowners. Shahr-Ara housed Tehran's junior level civil servants, schoolteachers, staff of government ministries, and employees of the national railroad and tobacco company. But Shahr-Ara did not have the zest, community spirit, and serenity of the two other housing projects.

Winthrop Rockefeller's Houses

Winthrop Rockefeller, general director of the IBEC Housing Corporation, arrived in Tehran for a four-day business trip on 22 May 1956. The grandson of Standard Oil co-founder John D. Rockefeller and brother to David Rockefeller, the chairman and chief executive of Chase Manhattan Bank, flew in on his private plane, accompanied by directors and managers of his real estate firm. Upon arrival, he announced that the purpose of his trip was to sign a contract to build houses in Iran.[43]

International Basic Economy Corporation (IBEC) was founded by Nelson Rockefeller, Winthrop's older brother, in 1947 to foster economic well-being in less-developed countries. IBEC also had a housing activity called the International Housing Corporation (IHC), and after Nelson Rockefeller entered politics in 1953, the leadership of IBEC was entrusted to Winthrop.

On 3 March 1958, IBEC signed a contract to build houses in Tehran.[44] IBEC officially registered itself on 28 September 1958. The activities of this American company in Iran involved designing, planning, and constructing residential, commercial, and industrial buildings, as well as the purchase and sale of all construction materials in Iran.[45]

The Iranian partner of IBEC was *Bank-e Omran* of the Pahlavi Foundation. To conclude this contract, *Bank-e Omran* had obtained a $5 million loan from Chase Manhattan and a 15-million-toman credit from *Bank-e Melli*. The monies borrowed from *Bank-e Melli* were explicitly

43 *Ettela'at*, 1 Khordad 1335.

44 Dalal Musaed Alsayer, *System and Experimental Housing in Baghdad, Iraq, 1953-58*, Rockefeller Archive Center Research Reports, p. 10, https://rockarch.issuelab.org/resources/35486/35486.pdf (retrieved 20/5/2024).

45 *Tehran Economist*, 5 Mehr 1337.

earmarked to build housing for *Bank-e Omran's* employees. Later, however, the houses were sold to others.

IBEC outsourced the building project to Iranian contractors. On 4 July 1959, work began on a 300,000 square meter modern housing complex of 200 units in Sahebqaraniyeh, located north of Tehran. The three-to-four-bedroom villas were built on one- and two-floor buildings, with central heating. The modern buildings were intentionally referred to as villas to impart their prestigious style and architecture. They were built on two plot sizes of 1,250 and 850 square meters, and their prices varied between 350,000 and 450,000 tomans. The price and the fact that the four-bedroom constructions had two servant quarters on the first floor indicated that IBEC houses were reserved for the upper classes. The building complex had electricity, telephone lines, running water, and sewage.

On 25 June 1960, Winthrop Rockefeller inaugurated the IBEC housing project. At the cocktail party organized in his honor by Hushang Rām, the general director of *Bank-e Omran*, many Iranian dignitaries, businessmen, members of parliament, and political figures such as 'Ala, the Minister of Court, were present. Rockefeller had travelled to Tehran at the invitation of *Bank-e Omran*, and he had met with the Shah at his summer residence on the Caspian Sea in Nowshahr (Mazandaran).

It was not until April 1962 that Sahebqaraniyeh's homeowners gradually began to move into their new residences. The proximity of this new building complex to the Shah's Sahebqaraniyeh Palace (Niavaran) was an indicator of its standing and status. It also meant that for security reasons, not everyone could buy a house there. This US-style modern suburban housing project was luxurious by Iranian standards, and the press referred to the constructions as "technically unmatchable" and "faultless". The IBEC project attracted the modern and not the traditional Iranian upper classes. Its residents were successful and Westernized businessmen, doctors, lawyers, architects, senior civil servants, and high military officials attracted to the idea of living in a modern suburban space.[46]

The security of the gated area, and the common green space between every few adjacent villas created an ideal and safe environment for children to play and socialize. Sahebqaraniyeh's location on an elevation provided an exceptional view of the Alborz mountains to the north and Tehran's

46 *Ettela'at*, 18 Aban 1337, 1 Tir 1338, 4 Tir 1339; *Tehran Economist*, 19 Tir 1338, 2 Mordad 1338, 11 Tir 1339. Information in the four previous paragraphs is based on these sources.

spread to the south. The spacious and sunlit rooms, modern imported kitchen and bathroom equipment and facilities, and the free availability of plumbers, electricians, and handymen in case of any mishaps provided ease of mind for IBEC's well-off residents.

The distance between Sahebqaraniyeh and the city center was about 20 minutes, and all residents had private cars. By October 1962, the Sahebqaraniyeh complex had a supermarket, laundry, flower shop, pharmacy, women's hairdressing parlor, and restaurants within walking distance. The new homeowners did not hide their pride in being members of an elite community. One new homeowner told the press, "What is most important here is that the inhabitants belong to one class." Heads of households soon bought units for their children in the IBEC compound, assuring community spirit and class homogeneity.[47]

Tehran Pars: The Special Housing Initiative

The project of a new middle and upper-middle-class suburb some 8 kilometers east of Tehran was started in December 1955 by a group of eighteen Zoroastrians. The Tehran Pars Development Organization (*Sazeman-e Abadani-ye Tehran Pars*) was a private company whose principal shareholders were Hormoz Arash (Arbab Hormoz) and his wife Parvin (Pari) Banu Agahi. Arbab Hormoz had made his fortune in India, where he had an ice manufacturing factory. He subsequently returned to Iran and bought the land on which Tehran Pars was built. Arbab Vafadar Tafti and Arbab Rostam Diniyar Marzban partnered with him to build and develop the new suburb.

The company's original capital was 17 million tomans. The developers of Tehran Pars bought 7 million square meters of land in an undeveloped and desolate area outside Tehran. To realize their vision of a modern, well-spaced-out, quiet, peaceful, enjoyable, and vibrant suburb, they allocated 2 million meters to wide streets and squares, 2 million meters to communal spaces and amenities, and the remaining 3 million meters to home building.

The developers divided the residential land for sale into two categories: land on which the Tehran Pars Development Organization built houses and unconstructed land on which individuals could build their own homes.

47 *Ettela'at*, 12 Mehr 1341, 17 Aban 1341.

The unconstructed land was sold conditional upon the purchaser building a housing unit within eight months, and according to strict and defined housing standards and specifications set by Tehran Pars' city planners and architects, one of whom was the young and talented, French-educated Mohammad-Reza (Manu) Moqtader. The three- to five-room houses with all the amenities built by Tehran Pars developers were priced at 50,000 to 60,000 tomans. The buyers were obliged to pay one-third of the price upon signing the purchase contract, and the rest was to be paid over thirty-six months.

Tehran Pars was planned and constructed by French urban developers based on modern Western standards, hence its nickname "Tehran Paris." Its Western-style houses were built on plots of land anywhere between 300 and 1,000 square meters. Tehran Pars became a model suburban area with modern buildings, wide, tree-studded asphalt streets, decorative water basins with fountains, piped water, a sewer system, electricity, telephone lines, green space, schools, a mosque, public baths, public phones, hair-dressing shops, grocery stores, a hospital, and sports facilities. Tehran Pars had its own ice, electricity, and asphalt-producing plants.

Arbab Rostam Giv, a philanthropist and the Zoroastrian representative at the Majles, donated the primary and secondary schools as well as the hospital in Tehran Pars. He bought 100,000 square meters at Tehran Pars and paid the cost of building the educational and health facilities. The two-story brick primary school building, with seventeen spacious and luminous rooms, was opened in September 1958.

One of the distinguishing features of Tehran Pars was that services such as electricity, water, security, transportation, sanitation, and municipal services were provided by the original developers in cooperation with the inhabitants. At night, private security personnel, along with gendarmes, roamed the well-lit streets, making it a haven for families and children. Transportation to and from Tehran Pars was guaranteed by ten readily distinguishable red and comfortable buses, connecting the suburb to Fowziyeh Square in Tehran. Tehran Pars stood out as a tidy, comfortable, and jolly Westernized suburb, an exception to Tehran's usually shady housing developments. A reporter visiting Tehran Pars in January 1958 described it as "a beautiful and modern European city".

At the entrance of Tehran Pars, a billboard reading "good thoughts, good words, good deeds", promoting the three ethical axioms of Zoroastrianism, drew particular attention. Tehran Pars attracted not only the Zoroastrian community but also the upper-middle echelons of bureaucrats, technocrats, businessmen, lawyers, doctors, military officers, and American expatriates. Prince Hamid Reza Pahlavi was said to have had a house there.

Another distinguishing feature of Tehran Pars was that it housed the first drive-in movie in Iran. This novel concept cost 3 million tomans and had the capacity of 284 cars. The entrance fee for each car was 15 tomans, and each car was allowed to have a maximum of six passengers. This modern facility opened on 27 April 1960, screening a dubbed German film called *Peter Voss, Thief of Millions*, a comedy and detective movie in color. The drive-in had a food service, where snacks and beverages were brought to the cars in trolleys operated by uniformed attendants.

By 1961, Tehran Pars had 2,000 housing units, a swimming club, a nightclub (Tehran Pars Club) with live music and three dance floors next to an open swimming pool. The casino and club were designed by Heydar Ghiyai and were located near a huge man-made lake with boating facilities. The regular performers at the club were popular Iranian singers and showmen such as Vigen, ʻAtaollah Khorram, and Hamid Qanbari, as well as foreign musical bands and singers.

On 29 July 1965, the Shah, accompanied by the Queen and their children, Crown Prince Reza and Farahnaz, inaugurated the Farahnaz Sports Stadium at Tehran Pars. This impressive sports complex housed a football, volleyball, and basketball field, along with tennis courts and a swimming pool.[48]

The three late 1950s and early 1960s housing projects introduced Tehranis to a modern housing concept. Among them, Tehran Pars was probably unique in terms of its purely private initiative, the heterogeneity of its residents, the smooth operation and timeliness of its housing construction, and the breadth of services it provided. Tehran Pars was more than just a suburb; it was a well-thought-out, pleasant, middle and upper-middle-class village. Along with IBEC, it could boast a low or nonexistent level of resident dissatisfaction.

48 *Ettelaʻat*, 28 Aban 1336, 21, 26 Day 1336; 9 Bahman 1336; 4 Aban 1337; 5, 6 Ordibehesht 1339; 9 Mordad 1339; 23 Azar 1339; 20 Ordibehesht 1340; 5, 7 Mordad 1340; 9 Mordad 1344. *Tehran Economist*, 11, 25 Azar 1340. Atlas Aqaliyathay-e diniy-e Iran, Arbab Hormoz Arash, https://adyan-iran.com/1400/1/11/ارباب-هرمز-آرش/ (retrieved 8/10/2023). All information on Tehran Paris is based on these sources.

FROM SHAHR-E FARANG PEEP BOX TO SABET'S TELEVISION BOX

The peep box, or peep show, was a box-shaped entertainment device with usually three eyeholes through which youngsters and even grown-ups watched a series of successive images, paintings, or pictures. The peep box operator, the itinerant showman, provided the narrative for the show. He carried the box on his shoulders, set it up on its four legs on a street corner, and charged a fee for each peep.

It is said that just as Nasereddin Shah Qajar brought ice cream to Iran, Mozafareddin Shah brought the peep box into the country, probably after his July–August 1900 visit to the Paris Exhibition. In Iran, the peep box was called *Shahr-e Farang* (European city), and its outward appearance was more elaborate than a simple box. The part of the device above the eyeholes had an attractive fortress or domelike structure made of shining tin.

The images portrayed inside *Shahr-e Farang* told both European and Iranian stories. Through *Shahr-e Farang*, Iranian children were exposed to pictures and paintings of the Eiffel Tower or European buildings and locations, and also tales of ancient Iranian heroes such as Rostam and Sohrab as well as Qajar era folktales, such as Amir Arsalan Namdar and his beautiful foreign beloved Farrokhlaqa.

Shahr-e Farang was a portal to a different experience and understanding than the everyday life of Iranians in the 1930s and 1940s. It was a "magical mystery tour" of distant worlds and fantasies for the young but also the curious old. A world of dreams that could be obtained for only one qaran, or a tenth of a toman. Like the muezzin calling the pious to prayers, the itinerant box operator would call the inquisitive to a show of thirty images.

His voice would ring out, "This is a European city. It is of all colors. Look closely. This is Paris, Faraneseh's [how he mispronounced "France"] capital. The celebration you see is called the festivity of flowers [reference to Fête des Fleurs]. This is the daughter of King Petros [reference to Farrokhlaqa]. Watch carefully, sit, and explore. European nights are alight until daybreak. This city is a European city. It is of all colors."[49] In December 1956, Habibollah Sabet announced the arrival of a new kind of *Shahr-e Farang*. In a press conference, Sabet informed the public that

49 Negar Jamshidnejad, *Shahr farang az hameh rang*, amordadanews.com, https://amordadnews.com/81246/ (retrieved 24/5/2024).

he had been given the right to establish a television station serving only Tehran and its vicinities.

Sabet's television tells the tale of serendipity in the lives of successful entrepreneurs. It must have been between June and 16 August 1953 that Sabet, who then lived in New York with his family, was informed that the Queen Mother (Taj ol-moluk Ayromlu) was coming to New York by boat from Europe. At the time, because of political tensions between Mosaddeq and the Court, officials overseas preferred to distance themselves from the Pahlavis. Sabet, however, chose to go to the Hoboken docks to welcome the Queen Mother.

As Taj ol-moluk descended the ship's stairs, she slipped, broke her leg, and was hospitalized. For twenty-nine days, Mrs. Sabet cooked Taj ol-moluk Iranian food and had her sons deliver it to the hospital, while she and Sabet visited the Queen Mother regularly. After the 1953 coup and her return to Iran, the Queen Mother felt a great debt towards the Sabets, and a strong bond of friendship developed between them.

It was probably in the summer of 1956 that Iraj Sabet brought a small and portable transmission and receiver closed-circuit television set from the US to Iran. The young Sabet proposed arranging a musical performance by the ten-year-old child prodigy Gogoush at the Queen Mother's Marmar Palace garden. He placed the television receiver in Taj ol-moluk's sleeping room, where she would watch the performance.

Just as the Queen Mother was thoroughly enjoying the show on the magical box, the Shah entered the room unexpectedly to visit his mother. He, too, was mesmerized by the box. The Shah became so interested in having a television system in Iran that he promised Sabet to help him launch the first television station. Subsequently he ordered Manuchehr Eqbal, the Minister of Court at the time, and Amir-Qasem Eshraqi, the Minister of Post, Telegram and Telephone, to facilitate Sabet's efforts.[50]

In his December 1956 interview, Sabet announced that the goal of his television network was to provide a service for the general benefit of the public which would include cultural, health, sports, and agricultural programs, as well as musical and dance shows. He hoped that his television would provide a platform for Iranian artists, performers, and debutant stars to present their talents. Sabet emphasized that political programs,

50 H. Sabet, *Sargozasht Habib Sabet*, pp. 239–248. All information in the previous four paragraphs is based on this source.

as well as domestic and international news, would be under the strict supervision of the Office of Propaganda and Publication. This office was the government watchdog over civil duties, protecting and promoting national, moral, and religious principles of the state.

Sabet anticipated that the cost of real estate, construction, and equipment, including the broadcasting network for his television, would be five to seven million tomans. The architectural plan, equipment, technical engineering, initial launch, and training of Iranian technicians were contracted to the Radio Corporation of America. RCA was a major American electronics company officially represented in Iran by Sabet. According to Sabet, the price of a television set would be between 1,500 to 2,000 tomans.[51]

The first reaction in the soft opposition press to the news of Iran's television station, on 1 January 1957, was complicated. Ne'matollah Jahanbanui's *Ferdowsi* published a long history of television and from there it came to familiarize readers with what it called *Jam-e jahan nama* or the mythical Persian chalice in which the activities of the whole world, good and evil, could be seen.

It pointed out that Sabet's television would cause substantial financial damage to movies and theaters. In one line hidden amidst volumes of encyclopedic information about the operation and impact of television in Western societies, the author wrote, "Most certainly Sabet P-A-Sa-L must carry a lot of clout to neutralize the opposition of movie owners and obtain a television contract from the government." The article ended sarcastically by wishing that the government would allow "beautiful and shapely [*ziba va khosh peykar*] women artists to sing on television" and accept that Iran, too, needs to advance in step with other countries.[52]

Another weekly published criticism aimed at Sabet's politico-financial power and implied that the regime's hidden hands were favoring Baha'is. First, *Sepid o Siyah* (White and Black) expressed surprise that the television contract was handed over to Sabet instead of being sent to tender. The weekly argued that since the Dutch Philips Company and the French Radio and Television Company were also interested in the contract, competition in a public tender should have determined the winning bidder.

Ali Behzadi's *Sepid o Siyah* lamented that Sabet would use his television station to promote the goods he produced, such as Pepsi Cola, or the ones

---

51 *Ettela'at*, 4 Day 1335. *Tehran Economist*, 8 Day 1335. All information in the previous two paragraphs is based on these sources.

52 *Ferdowsi*, 11 Day 1335.

he held a franchise for, such as Volkswagen and Studebaker cars. Finally, the tone of the weekly became personal, smacking of old Baha'i conspiracy theory. It expressed surprise at the fact that while at the beginning of 'Ala's premiership, Iranian radio constantly attacked "a particular group" (*dasteh makhsusi*), the Prime Minister was now handing over the country's television network to a member of that same group. By referring to a double standard in the government's approach to Baha'is, without naming them, *Sepid o Siyah*, was implicitly questioning the regime's choice of leaving Iran's television network to a Baha'i.[53]

Criticism of Sabet's financial success never abated in the Iranian press. In 1965, he was regularly attacked for the number of businesses he owned, his powerful connections, his unfair competition strategies, and his claims that he was a self-made man who had started his business with thirty shahis. The press claimed that the land on which the Tehran and, later, the Abadan television facilities were built was government-owned and that Sabet did not pay his municipal duties, import duties, and taxes. Often, in the tone of such criticisms, a dash of jealousy could be felt.[54]

On a 10,000 square meter piece of land on 'Abbas-Abad hills, close to Pahlavi Street, with the help of RCA specialists, Sabet built a modern, spacious, and state-of-the-art four-story building with some 200 offices and two fully equipped television studios. Sabet's television station was equipped with a mobile transmitter installed in a bus to cover news and report on sports and social and cultural activities around the city.

On 2 October 1958, the Shah was given the first viewing of programs on Sabet's Iran Television (ITV) at the Marble Palace. The broadcasting commenced with the concurrent display of the Iranian flag, and the playing of the national anthem (*Soroud-e shahanshai*), followed by the Shah's message. On the next day, Sabet began daily broadcasts for four hours, from 18:00 to 22:00, and Tehranis watched their first black and white television shows.

Sabet's television station followed the first Middle East television service in Iraq by 27 months. Within a month and a half of its launch, some 120,000 people were watching television in Tehran. By September 1960, Iran Television Station was broadcasting six hours per day, and its transmitters reached a radius of 150 kilometers. A second television station,

53 *Khandaniha*, 22 Day 1335.
54 *Khandaniha*, 24 Mehr 1344; 1 Aban 1344.

owned by Sabet, was built in Abadan in the summer of 1959, providing coverage to Abadan and its vicinities, Ahvaz, Khorramshahr and Bandar Ma'shur.[55] Yet, it was not until January 1964 that the Iran Television Corporation (*Sherkat Sahami Television Iran*) was registered. Its founders were Iraj and Hormoz Sabet, Kambiz Mahmudi, Ali-Asghar Rasekh, and Mas'ud Khamsi.[56]

Sabet's television was a gateway to a new kind of entertainment, introducing aspects of Western culture, life, and entertainment to a broad audience. By October 1962, or within four years, broadcasting began at 18:00 and finished at 23:00. On Fridays, a special morning program began at 10:00 and ended at 13:00 in addition to the regular evening broadcast. The Abadan program was broadcast on Fridays from 16:00 to 22:00.

Programs were more inclined towards entertainment and recreation than political propaganda or social and civil education. Every night, the news was covered in just fifteen minutes from 21:00 to 21:15. Regular programs were either directed specifically at children, youth, and women or were for public amusement, consisting of musical performances—Iranian and Western—variety shows, games, and quiz shows, and dubbed Western movies.

Iranians were thus exposed to American-made cartoons and popular American television series, such as Annie Oakley, a Western featuring a pigtailed blond female sharpshooter as a hero, or Whirlybirds (*parandeh ahanin*), a production about the adventures of two helicopter pilots. Western brands, which sold their goods in Iran, such as the German Blendax (toothpaste and shampoo), the German Margaret Astor (cosmetics), and Sabet's Pepsi, had their own sponsored variety, sketch, game, talk, and musical shows.[57]

By November 1963, Sabet's television had some 200,000 viewers per night. A minute of advertising between 20:30 and 22:00 cost 1,500 tomans, and Sabet's television earned 15,000 to 20,000 tomans per night from its commercials. The 15 to 30-minute sponsored programs, ranging from cooking and sewing classes to various quiz and game shows, had a price tag of 2,000 tomans.[58]

---

55 *Khandaniha* 28 Day, 1336. *Ettela'at*, 12, 13 Mehr 1337; 3 Azar 1337; 21 Mehr 1339. The information in the previous three paragraphs is based on these sources.

56 *Tehran Economist*, 28 Day 1342.

57 *Ettela'at*, 29 Azar 1341, 3 Day 1341. *Sepid o Siyah*, 20 Mehr 1341.

58 *Tehran Economist*, 2 Azar 1342.

However, the comprehensive peep into various aspects of American life came after the launch of the American Armed Forces Radio and Television Services (AFRTS), which started broadcasting on 24 December 1959. Fourteen months after Sabet's television appeared, this English-language television targeted some 2,000 military personnel stationed in Iran and brought real American television into Iranian homes.

But AFRT programs broadcast on Channel 8 were a free good, enabling Tehranis with a television set to watch and bathe in the American culture and way of life. The programs were produced by CBS (Columbia Broadcasting System) and NBC (National Broadcasting Company). Those who knew English appreciated the dialogues and followed the plot, and those who did not, just watched the players, how they dressed, their make-up, their body language, their behavior towards one another, and finally, the action. Aside from the Westerns, epics, and historical series and movies, Iranians were exposed to American life, offices and houses and their furniture and gadgets, the American judicial and political system, and American cities, streets, bars, jazz clubs, and shops. To most Iranians, AFRT was the genuine *Shahr-e Farang.*

By April 1962, Tehranis could plunge into what New Yorkers were watching, albeit with a short delay. For New Yorkers, the shows reflected dramatized versions of their own situations, with their own mores, customs, and traditions. However, for the Iranians watching them, most of what they saw were unconventional novelties and even taboos.

At this time, AFRT's nightly series included westerns, detective stories, legal drama, science fiction, and sitcoms. Host and comedy shows, such as Jack Benny and Ed Sullivan, were meant to entertain average American families with a mix of comedians, singers, actors, actresses, musicians, and puppeteers. It does not require a psychologist to speculate what kind of fantasy young Tehranis conjured up when watching a December 1961 sketch where the blond sex symbol actress and singer Mamie Van Doren tried to seduce Jack Benny and Dennis Day to let her sing on the show.[59] The new *Shahr-e Farang* was truly revolutionizing urban culture and lifestyle.

59 *Ettela'at*, 3 Day 1337; 23, 30 Farvardin 1341, 2 Ordibehesht 1341. To see the sketch mentioned in the text: https://www.youtube.com/watch?v=g562WYoSezA&ab_channel=ChuckPenn3 (retrieved 25/5/2024).

15

'Alam Sailing Against Stagnation, Hampered by Political Headwinds

With the departure of Amini, the Shah, unfettered, resumed his uncontested decision-making role. From 'Alam's cabinet onwards, the executive was exclusively the Shah, and "ministers were more or less (*taqriban*) solely involved with their own technical and specialized activities, and their work involved the management and administration of their respective ministries."[1]

When 'Alam came to power on 19 July 1962, Iran's economic, political, and foreign policy were in transition, unsettled and unsteady, with challenges looming. It was as if a hefty London fog had settled over the country's political, economic, and foreign policy conditions. On 7 March 1964, after almost twenty months in office, 'Alam reluctantly handed power to Hasan-Ali Mansur. By the time he left, the fog had lifted on the political scene and was on its way to clear on foreign policy, but it remained unsettled in the economic realm.

Part of 'Alam's success had been the Shah's complete trust in him and 'Alam's total and unquestionable devotion to implementing the Shah's wishes and looking after his political interests. The two complemented one another and worked in unison. When the Shah led in the domain of foreign policy, 'Alam followed, and when the Shah hesitated, as in the case of repressing the 5 June 1963 revolt, Alam took the lead, and the Shah followed. In matters of domestic economy, inertia prevailed when

1 Interview with Abdol-Majid Majidi, Foundation for Iranian Studies, BPT-II, p. 55.

the two hesitated or were distracted by other issues and the US refused to be as generous as before.

'ALAM'S DOMESTIC POLITICAL HEADACHES

'Alam's premiership was concurrent with the US-prompted and Arsanjani-driven land reform initiative. This push to jolt Iran out of its feudal/Asiatic mode of production subsequently transitioned into the Shah's top-down White Revolution. The six principles of the Shah and Peoples' Revolution not only included the abolition of the landowner-tenant system but also the nationalization of forests, the sale of shares in state-owned factories, benefit/profit sharing of workers in industries, reform of the electoral law, and the establishment of the literacy corps.

The six principles were put to a vote in a referendum on 26 January 1963. 'Alam's government announced that 99% of the Iranians who participated in the referendum approved the Shah's White Revolution. These principles were essentially social, but the proper realization of at least three of them, land reform, profit sharing, and selling shares of government-owned factories, had significant economic ramifications.

Within a few months of the success of the referendum on the White Revolution, a one-day bloody upheaval by the devout followers of Ayatollah Ruhollah Khomeyni shook the country. This pivotal political event changed the course of Iran in one direction in the short run and then the opposite in the long run. The 5 June 1963 uprising was the boiling point of a brewing eight-month struggle during which 'Alam and the Shah found themselves in confrontation with the representatives of Iran's religious establishment, led by Khomeyni. The main point of contention was the rights of women and, tangentially, the social and political participation of religious minorities.

The tug of war began on 7 October 1962, when the Sources of Imitation (*maraje' taqlid*), including Khomeyni, made known their soft opposition to 'Alam's decree on Regional and Provincial Councils. The Regional and Provincial Councils Law (*Qanun-e anjomanhay-e ayalati va velayati*) had been a product of the Constitutional Revolution and was voted on by the Majlis in May 1907. Articles seven and eight of the law, under the rubric of eligibility of voters and those standing for election, specified that women (*nesvan*) were ineligible to participate, but did not specify that Iran's non-Muslim religious minorities were barred from voting or standing for election.[2]

Article three of 'Alam's 8 October 1962 decree on Regional and Provincial Councils, however, did not specify women as ineligible to be become candidates or be elected, effectively allowing them participation. Article 49 also stipulated that those elected had to swear on the "heavenly book" (*ketab-e asemani*) without referencing the Qur'an. This implied that Iran's non-Muslim religious minorities could participate in such Councils and take their oath of office on their respective holy/heavenly books, and not necessarily the Qur'an.[3]

So long as Amini was in power, Khomeyni appreciated his high respect for religious matters, religious rites, and the input of the high religious authorities. Khomeyni did not oppose land reform implemented during Amini's tenure. In stark contrast, Khomeyni disliked 'Alam because of the latter's social views.

The four axes of 'Alam's People's Party (*Hezb-e Mardom*) back in May 1957 were the distribution of large landholdings among peasants, equitable distribution of income, worker profit-sharing in large factories, and, most importantly, allowing women to participate in elections. Article 45 of his Party's Charter read, "The provision/safeguarding of women's social and political rights according to the U.N. Charter and the [Universal] Declaration of Human Rights".[4]

Khomeyni quickly and astutely appropriated the clash between the clergy and 'Alam over Regional and Provincial Councils and, primarily, the women's issue. To gain political traction, Khomeyni transformed the clerical objection into an anti-corruption, anti-immorality, anti-despotic, anti-imperialistic, and anti-Zionist platform. Khomeyni warned against the eradication of the faith and Iran's subservience to Israel and the US. The crushing of the 5 June 1963 religious revolt by 'Alam paved the road for Iranian women's right to vote even in the Islamic Republic. For the next fifteen years, the question of who held ultimate power and authority in the land, the Shah or the clergy, was also settled in favor of the former.

2 *Qanun-e anjomanhay-e ayalati va velayati*, Markaz pajuheshhay-e majles showray-e Eslami, https://web.archive.org/web/20190624133759/http://rc.majlis.ir/fa/law/show/90097 (retrieved 4/11/2024).

3 *Ettela'at*, 16 Mehr 1341.

4 *Ettela'at*, 26, 28 Ordibehesht 1336.

CHANGING INTERNATIONAL POLITICS

In international politics, instructed and guided by the Shah, 'Alam's government buried the hatchet with the Soviet Union and established closer economic ties. Once the Shah guaranteed that there would be no US missile bases established in Iran, the Soviets reciprocated with normalization of relations and economic offerings. This new equilibrium of reciprocal economic benefits with the Soviet Union, in September 1962, was achieved without the slightest political, economic, and military crack in the solid US–Iran strategic alliance or Iran's commitment to the anti-communist camp and cause. For Iran's Third Five-Year Plan, the US pledged $300 million in military assistance, a long-term commitment.[5]

The Shah had witnessed the thaw between the US and the Soviet Union after the October 1962 Cuban missile crisis. Having been under heavy Soviet propaganda attacks and weary of their military threat and agitations, the Shah embarked on befriending his communist northern neighbor. On 30 May 1963, a substantial barter trade agreement was signed between the Soviet Union and Iran, according to which Iran would receive 40 million tomans worth of agricultural machinery, tractors, bicycles, and motorbikes, among others things, in return for cotton, galena (lead ore), zinc stone, carpets, and rice, among other items.[6]

Less than two months later (24 June 1963), Iran and the USSR signed a technical and economic cooperation agreement to build a dam on the Aras River and to share its electricity and water. The Soviets extended 35 million rubles of credit to Iran on favorable terms and pledged machinery, equipment, construction material, and experts to build eleven grain silos in Iran.[7] On 16 November 1963, the Soviet chief of state, Leonid Brezhnev, and his wife came to Tehran at the Shah's official invitation for a state visit.

Three months before the royal trip to Moscow, while on a private visit to England (4 March 1965), the Shah announced that he made a distinction between Communism and the Soviet Union. He argued that the Soviet Union believed in peaceful coexistence and a good neighbor policy, while communism remained a problem. These were necessary preliminary steps leading to the historic visit of the Royals to the Soviet Union

---

5 FRUS, 1961–1963, vol. XVIII, Near East, 1962–1963, Document 85.

6 *Ettela'at*, 9 Khordad 1342.

7 *Ettela'at*, 5 Mordad 1342.

on 21 June 1965.[8] Political pragmatism and pursuing national economic interests overcame ideological schisms and paid off. In 1966, "the USSR extended more than $305 million in new credit" to Iran.[9]

ʻALAM'S ECONOMIC WOES

In the economic realm, however, uncertainty and fogginess continued throughout most of ʻAlam's tenure. One reason may have been ʻAlam's lack of insight and interest in economic matters. Khodadad Farmanfarmayan recalled that "He [ʻAlam] had no real understanding of economic development, [and] financial aspect of government at all."[10] ʻAlam was not an economist. However, he was intelligent enough to delegate economic matters to experts, most of whom were young and not US-trained. Moreover, he left them a free hand to choose their team. At the Plan Organization, Asfia was reinstated as director general, and he appointed three capable and well-educated deputies, Cyrus Babak Samiʻi, Abdolmajid Majidi and Hasan Sedehi.[11]

At the governmental level, ʻAlam merged the two ministries of Industry and Mines and Commerce, often at loggerheads, and formed the new Ministry of Economy. On 18 February 1963, the responsibility of this new ministerial powerhouse was given to the thirty-four-year-old, French-educated Ali-Naqi ʻAlikhani. He, too, changed all the old-guard vice ministers and appointed the French-educated Ahmad Ziai and the Iranian-educated Gholamreza Kiyanpur, both around thirty-four years old. On 13 May 1963, ʻAlam appointed the British-educated Mehdi Samiʻi as the governor of the Central Bank, and Samiʻi chose Khodadad Farmanfarmayan as his vice-governor. Samiʻi was intent on keeping the Central Bank out of politics and maintaining its independence. While he was at the Central Bank, Samiʻi did not recall ever being told by the Shah what to do or not

8 *Ettelaʻat*, 13 Esfand 1343.

9 Central Intelligence Agency, "The Character of Soviet and Eastern European Economic Involvement in Iran," July 1971, https://www.cia.gov/readingroom/docs/CIA-RDP85T00875R001700010077-5.pdf (retrieved 21/6/2024).

10 Khodadad Farman Farmaian, Iranian Oral History Collection, Harvard University, Transcript 9, Sequence 115.

11 Ettelaʻat, 2 Mehr 1341.

to do.[12] For Sami'i, the main job of the Central Bank was to adjust the money supply and credit to the realities of the economy, contraction in case of inflation and expansion in case of deflation.[13]

Economic dilemmas during 'Alam's premiership had other causes as well. The economic uncertainty caused by land reform, workers' profit-sharing, and the June 1963 revolt were not conducive to a secure business environment and did not help private investment. The prevailing recession, the government's continued austerity program, and tight credit policy placed a further damper on private sector profit expectations. Without significant government spending, which was reined in by reducing developmental expenditures to balance the budget, the economy remained in the doldrums, with "unused productive capacity". According to the World Bank (International Bank for Reconstruction and Development) Iran's recession and "unresponsive investment climate" had prevailed "since the end of the inflationary crisis in 1960/1961".[14]

Iran experienced high unemployment and considerable hidden unemployment rates in the civil services. According to one account, out of some 300,000 government employees, approximately 50,000 were redundant.[15] Iran's structural problems, such as high illiteracy rates, reported to be as high as 70% at the time, translated into uneducated workers and low productivity, adding to its economic woes.[16] The establishment of the literacy corps, the sixth point of the White Revolution, was to address this problem.

On the bright side, Iran's oil revenues increased by about 18% during 1962–1963 compared to 1961–1962, the balance of payments improved, and foreign reserves increased from $190 million in March 1961 to $246 million in September 1963. Foreign debts were repaid.[17] Domestic savings

---

12 Mehran, *Hadafha va Siyasathay-e Bank-e Markaziy-e Iran*, pp. 50, 55. This statement becomes complicated when Mehran notes that Sami'i was also responsible for "the loan accounts of military hardware purchases, and the coronation ceremonies" of 1967. See Mehran, p. 55.

13 *Ettela'at*, 23 Tir 1342.

14 International Bank for Reconstruction and Development, *Recent Economic Developments in Iran and Progress of the Third Plan*. February 6, 1964, Department of Operations, South Asia & Middle East, https://documents1.worldbank.org/curated/en/164571468262763269/pdf/multiopage.pdf (retrieved 4/6/2024), p. 5.

15 FO 371/170805, EP 2181/3.

16 FO 371/170805, EP 2181/1. FO 371/170805, EP 2181/4.

17 International Bank for Reconstruction and Development, *Recent Economic Developments in Iran and Progress of the Third Plan*, pp. ii, 8.

increased and inflation was brought under control, but there were no signs of economic growth.

In November 1962, the Money and Credit Council (*Showray-e poul va e'tebar*) allowed the Central Bank to extend 200 million tomans of credit to the banking system to stimulate private investment. However, between March 1961 and September 1963, the increase in credit to the private sector was largely offset by a reduction in credit to the public sector. On 26 October 1963, the Central Bank reduced interest rates from 6% to 4%. Yet the economy did not pick up immediately, and the private sector remained unresponsive.[18] It was becoming evident that appropriate fiscal policies were needed to support the expansionary monetary policies.

'Alam's Priorities: Budget and the Third Five-Year Plan

In August 1962, 'Alam finally presented the budget for the financial year March 1962 to March 1963. Amini had clashed with the Shah over the size of the 600 to 700 million budget deficit and Amini's refusal to cut back developmental expenditures for the benefit of the military budget. On the face of it, 'Alam's budget had a reasonable 220 million toman deficit.

However, the Plan Organization had forfeited 346 million tomans of its share of oil revenues for developmental expenditures to the Ministry of Finance for current expenditures, and the National Iranian Oil Company had transferred an additional 150 million tomans to the government. A rough estimate of the budget deficit, if the monies from the Plan Organization and NIOC had not been transferred to the government, would have put the deficit figure at 600–700 million, initially announced by Amini. While the budget of the Ministry of Defense increased from 1.13 billion to 1.25 billion tomans, the Plan Organization's budget was reduced by 1.5 billion tomans. And while the budget of the Ministry of Education increased from 859 million tomans to 937 million, the budget of the Ministry of Health decreased from 157 million tomans to 127 million.[19]

---

18 *Ettela'at*, 19 Shahrivar 1341; 6 Aban 1342. FO 371 172359, UEE 103134/3. International Bank for Reconstruction and Development, *Recent Economic Developments in Iran and Progress of the Third Plan*, pp. 6, 9.

19 FO 371/170389, EP 1102/10. *Ettela'at*, 29, 30 Mehr 1341, 4 Shahrivar 1341. *Sepid o Siyah*, 2, 9 Shahrivar 1341. International Bank for Reconstruction and Development, *Recent Economic Developments in Iran and Progress of the Third Plan*, Annex, Table 9.

One of the most important tasks of the 'Alam government was to finalize and ratify the Third Five-Year Plan on 9 September 1962, which was to begin on 23 September 1962 and end on 20 March 1968. This plan, in contrast to the Second Plan, was to emphasize education and manpower training, social programs, public health, urban development, and the provision of agricultural and industrial credit.[20]

The Third Plan that the Plan Organization had been working on since mid-1959 was very different from the one approved by 'Alam's government. The Plan Organization had planned for the government to invest 19.9 billion toman ($2.6 billion) during the Five-Year plan. This figure was subsequently reduced to 14.5 billion toman ($1.92 billion), parts of which were earmarked to repay past debts. The Plan Organization had also anticipated 15.8 billion tomans of private-sector investment. The bleak macro-economic conditions and the continuing recession made the realization of this sum highly suspect.

The government also announced that the average growth rate, projected to be about 6% per annum during the Third Five-Year plan, would be revised downwards to about 3%. Given a 2.5% population rate of growth, per capita growth was anticipated at a meager 0.5%.[21] One day after the government's report on the coming Third Plan was published, Safi Asfia, the director general of the Plan Organization announced an upward revision of the growth rate to 6% during the Third Plan.[22]

Aside from changing the content of the Third Plan, the 'Alam government redefined the Plan Organization's role and responsibilities in implementing the Third Plan. The Plan Organization became a technical and economic office responsible for preparing and presenting economic policies and reports, approving and supervising developmental projects, keeping accounts of the projects, and taking charge of all foreign borrowings and grants, including negotiations concerning such foreign aid.

The implementation and execution of projects were handed over to relevant ministries, which lacked the technical expertise and "administrative capabilities" to carry out such tasks.[23] Consequently, the Plan

---

20 International Bank for Reconstruction and Development, *Recent Economic Developments in Iran and Progress of the Third Plan*, pp. 11, 15.

21 *Ettela'at*, 19 Shahrivar 1341. For the full law, see *Ettela'at*, 20 Shahrivar 1341.

22 *Ettela'at*, 20 Shahrivar 1341.

23 International Bank for Reconstruction and Development, *Recent Economic Developments in Iran and Progress of the Third Plan*, pp. 3–5.

Organization's budget, as well as its employees, were reduced. Some 200 employees were cut back on severance pay, and another significant number were transferred to other ministries. The Plan Organization's employees were to drop from around 1,000 to about 650.[24]

A new body was created to supervise and administer the development process. The "High Plan Board" (*Hey'at 'aliy-e barnameh*) composed of the prime minister, the ministers of commerce and finance, the governor of the Central Bank, and three members of the Plan Organization, was tasked with ratifying annual developmental expenditures and coordination of activities between ministries and the Plan Organization.[25]

On 11 September 1962, or two days after the ratification of the Third Plan, Abdolhoseyn Behnia, the Minister of Finance, left Tehran for Washington to attend the annual World Bank and International Monetary Fund Conference, and meet with World Bank and IMF leaders. His prime objective was to obtain loans to finance the Five-Year Plan, which now required foreign borrowings of some $450 to $500 million.[26]

A few key issues arose during Behnia's meeting with World Bank authorities. First, the World Bank insisted that to officialize and legalize a loan from this body, the Iranian Constitution required the parliament's ratification of loan agreements. The Iranian Majles, however, remained closed since Amini had dissolved it. The World Bank also reproached Behnia for gutting the Plan Organization of its senior, well-educated, and expert economists.[27] At this time, Khodadad Farmanfarmayan, Manuchehr Gudarzi, Bahman Abadiyan, and Gholamreza Moqadam had all left the Plan Organization for different reasons.

Even though the Third Plan was officially launched on 23 September 1962, it was still being fine-tuned and revised by 23 March 1963. The modifications were made necessary by the spin-offs of the land reform and the Shah's emphasis on developing and funding rural cooperatives to aid new freeholders, or the beneficiaries of the land reform, which now required more funds.[28]

The Third Plan had allocated 440 million tomans ($57 million) for land purchases related to land reform and 680 million tomans for agricultural

24 *Ettela'at*, 6, 22 Shahrivar 1341; 1, 7 Mehr 1341.
25 *Ettela'at*, 20 Shahrivar 1341.
26 FO 371/170389, EP 1102/13. *Khandaniha*, 20 Shahrivar 1341.
27 FO 371/170389, EP 1102/1.
28 FO 371/170389, EP 1102/13.

credit to the new smallholders. By September 1963, the 440 million tomans allocated for land purchase from landlords during the first phase of the land reform was exhausted, while the second phase of land reform was to start in July 1964. From monies earmarked for agricultural credit (680 million tomans), 500 million had gone directly to increase the capital of the Agricultural Bank, to be eventually distributed mainly through the rural cooperatives to the new smallholders. The remainder was again loaned through the Agricultural Bank for special projects such as deep wells selected by the Plan Organization.[29]

The Shah's Changing Attitude

While Iran was still caught in a two-year stagnation doldrum, on 27 February 1963, the Economic Stabilization Conference opened in the new senate building with 700 attendants and the Shah as its keynote speaker. The purpose of the Conference was to re-establish business confidence, create economic stability, and encourage private-sector investment. Horace Phillips of the British Embassy in Iran noted that one hour out of the Shah's one-and-a-half-hour speech was "in fact a political review of his reign, of little direct interest to a Conference called for the reappraisal of the country's economy".

Phillips' remarks revealed an ongoing evolution in the Shah's demeanor and conduct. In his opinion, the Shah's economic comments were general and uninspiring. The Shah, however, "concentrated on his own personal and superior role in the direction of social and economic reforms". This was the beginning of the Shah's overflowing self-infatuation and grandeur, leading to what Phillips identified as "a somewhat cavalier treatment of his audience".[30]

The Shah's sense of self-importance was rooted in three factors. First, he received positive feedback from the land reform beneficiaries during his September and November 1962 provincial tours. For eighteen days, the Shah experienced the genuine warmth and appreciation of the new freeholders who had benefited from land reform. The Shah interacted with them, cherished their enthusiasm, spoke to them, and attended their marriages. He felt elated and loved as he walked freely among his people.[31]

29 International Bank for Reconstruction and Development, *Recent Economic Developments in Iran and Progress of the Third Plan*, Annex, p. 1.

30 FO 371 170389, EP 1102/15.

31 *Ettela'at*, 31 Shahrivar 1341; 1, 2, 3, 4, 5, 7, 8, 9, 10, 11, 15, 16 Mehr 1341.

The Shah's increasing self-confidence was also rooted in the 26 January 1963 referendum and the bloody repression of the 5 June 1963 uprising. The first validated and legitimized him. The second empowered him as he was left with no real opposition. The Shah felt that no one other than him knew what was best for the country and therefore no constraints could be placed on his right to rule as he pleased. He articulated his ideas and goals as he went along and expressed his views and theories (*nazariyat*) in his 1967 publication, *The White Revolution*.

According to Abdolmajid Majidi: "the Shah had clearly stated his views on just about all issues and aspects of the country. Regularly, at meetings of the High Economic Council, when one raised an issue that was out of the context of the ideas established by him, the Shah would say, 'Haven't you read my book?'... therefore, no one could suggest a different/new path."[32]

Towing the Economy Out of Recession

'Alam's appointees to the country's three key economic posts, the Plan Organization, the Ministry of Economy, and the Central Bank, were committed to pulling the economy out of its stagnant state and worked well together. However, the country needed time to reel back from the shock of 5 June 1963, regain its stability, and then get along with the economic problems at hand. Political turmoil had not only alarmed the private sector, which was already cautious with investment given the Shah's profit-sharing scheme, but also scared away potential foreign investment. The first economic news after the 5 June uprising was not very comforting.

The Americans were cutting back on their economic aid and credit to Iran. Robert Macey, USAID mission director to Iran, announced that USAID had approved $74 million of economic assistance to Iran. The bulk of this package, or $50.8 million, was for agricultural goods (PL 480). Public Law 480 permitted the US president to dispatch surplus agricultural goods to "friendly" nations. Technical and administrative assistance to Iran came to $4.4 million. The US economic aid component of this package was only $1.3 million, while loans constituted $17.4 million. These loans were earmarked for the construction and development of port facilities at Bandar Abbas ($15 million) and the planning of electricity grids for six provinces, including Tehran, Shiraz, and Esfahan ($2.4 million). The

32 Interview with Abdol-Majid Majidi, Foundation for Iranian Studies, BPT-II, p. 54.

project at Bandar Abbas was a major investment and included three piers for commercial goods and one for minerals.

On top of the $74 million economic package, Iran was to receive $75 million in military aid. It is noteworthy that the level of US economic aid and loans for 1963 had dramatically decreased since the Amini period of 1961 and 1962. In 1961, US economic aid was $22.1 million and it had increased to $30 million in 1962, while loans were $62.9 million in 1961 and $39.1 in 1962.[33]

From the summer of 1963, 'Alam's speeches on the state of the economy transitioned from optimism to realism. In his positive and encouraging public speeches, 'Alam would thank the army for ending the 5 June uprising and then promise that the recession would soon be over and that economic activities would resume quickly. He would even imply the end of unemployment in two to three months.[34]

On 11 July 1963, 'Alam inaugurated the new Farahzad highway and assured the people that new development projects and public works such as home construction, roadbuilding, and dams were coming. He mentioned that the White Revolution had not impeded development, economic, and construction activities. 'Alam then modified his statement, saying, "Even if it had, the economic lull was temporary." He finally warned against everyday activities coming to a halt.[35]

By the end of the summer, preparations and political maneuvers for the Twenty-First Majles, which began on 17 September 1963, started to overshadow the economy. Almost two-and-a-half years (twenty-eight months) after dissolving the Twentieth Majles and running the country by fiat, Iran was to have a new parliament. The candidates for the new Majles were selected by some sort of "people's congress" embodied in "The Congress of Free Men and Women", which had begun work on 27 August 1963.[36] For the first time, women were allowed to vote and stand for election during the September 1963 parliamentary elections.

Once again, in October 1963, the government tried to present an image of an economy gradually picking up. 'Alam was reported in newspapers as being on the move, breaking ground with a pickaxe, and participating

33 *Ettela'at*, 5, 6 Tir 1342.
34 *Ettela'at*, 10 Tir 1342.
35 *Ettela'at*, 20 Tir 1342.
36 A. Rahnema, *The Rise of Modern Despotism in Iran*, London: Oneworld Academic, 2021, pp. 419–422.

in ceremonies commencing construction work on factories, schools, hospitals, and housing projects. The popular satirical weekly, *Towfiq*, picked up on the show and began referring to him as "the pickaxe grand vizir" (*sadr-e a'zam kolangi*). 'Alam was illustrated in cartoons flying on a pickaxe, delivering a speech at the podium with an axe in one hand, or standing on an elephant breaking the ground with a pickaxe.[37]

On 15 December 1963, the Shah held his annual audience (*salam*) at the Golestan Palace, marking the day when the Prophet Mohammad received his first revelation (*mab'as*) in 609/610. On this day of festivity, the country's prominent political, economic, social, military, and cultural leaders paid respect to the Shah. They gave him a progress report on the activities of their respective fields.

Mehdi Sami'i, the Governor of the Central Bank, reported on the state of the economy. He pointed out that steps had been taken to initiate an economic upswing, such as reducing the discount rate and extending 200,000,000 tomans of credit to the Plan Organization to undertake developmental and industrial investments. Sami'i informed the Shah that the expansionary measures had not yielded the expected results, and despite an increase in investment in the construction industry, economic activities remained sluggish. Sami'i concluded by hoping that the Shah's wish for an economic recovery would soon be realized.[38]

Despite Sami'i's promises, the market remained anxious and uncertain, transactions were slow, and investments were not forthcoming. Money was being held and not invested, and by the end of 1963, the government seemed unable to convince businessmen to spend. Aside from the unknown large amounts of money that the traditional Iranian merchants and bazaaris held in their safes and under their mattresses, during October and November 1963, saving deposits had increased by 130,000,000 tomans and demand deposits by 100,000,000.[39]

The first signs of optimism, signaling the end of the recession, appeared in January 1964. In the real estate and undeveloped land market, transactions were picking up, construction was increasing, import orders were higher than in the first nine months of March 1963 to November 1963, the inventory of textiles and cement was decreasing, sales at retail clothing

37 *Towfiq*, nos. 30, 31, 32, 1342.
38 *Ettela'at*, 24 Azar 1342.
39 *Tehran Economist*, 30 Azar 1342.

stores increased, and more businessmen were approaching the Industrial and Mining Development Bank of Iran to set up factories. [40]

On 1 March 1964, the Shah returned from a forty-day European vacation. During his absence, the government was busy preparing the budget for 21 March 1964 to 20 March 1965. But before it had the chance to present this budget, which was said to have a 400 million toman deficit. 'Alam was replaced by Hasan-Ali Mansur on 7 March 1964.[41] Signs of an economic upturn had surfaced some two months before 'Alam was laid off.

40 *Tehran Economist*, 5, 12, 19 Bahman 1342.

41 *Tehran Economist*, 5 Bahman 1342. *Ettela'at*, 17 Esfand 1342.

16

Hasan-Ali Mansur's Economic Repair

The Shah mandated Mansur's government to bring the White Revolution to fruition. Mansur's ministers were overwhelmingly French-educated, and their average age was forty. A distinguishing feature of this cabinet was that most members, even those in non-economic positions, had a degree in economics. Two of the three ministers of state, the Minister of Roads (Mahmud Kashfiyan), the Minister of Interior (Javad Sadr), and the Minister of Education (Abdolali Jahanshahi), had degrees in economics. This was a veritable "economic cabinet", and Mansur was to put his young and technocratically minded economists at the service of fulfilling His Majesty's designs.

On 29 May 1963, some ten months before appointing Mansur as prime minister, the Shah had issued a royal edict announcing that Mansur's Progressive Center (*kanun-e moteraqi*) was also the Shah's Bureau of Economic Studies. In intimate terms, the Shah added that members of the Centre "enjoy our special favor and attention".[1] It was not surprising that many of the newly appointed ministers were members of Mansur's Progressive Centre.

The key economically related positions in the new cabinet were occupied by 'Alikhani, Minister of Economy, and three newcomers, Amir-Abbas Hoveyda, Minister of Finance, Hushang Nahavandi at the new Ministry of Development and Housing (*abadani va maskan*) and Mansur Rowhani, at the new Ministry of Water and Electricity. Ironically, Hoveyda, the Minister of Finance, had no higher education background in economics or even the French-style political economy.

---

1 *Ettela'at*, 15 Khordad 1342.

Like his Minister of Finance, Mansur had not received any formal education in economics. Yet he had a long economic-related career. He had been a member of the High Economic Council and its Secretary-General since 1957 and became Minister of Labor in October 1959 and subsequently Minister of Commerce in January 1960. Mansur was the first post-1953 prime minister who came to power with an economic plan and program and a carefully chosen and well-prepared team. Contrary to his predecessors, nothing was ad hoc about his ascendence to power or economic program.

The Shah received Mansur and his ministers in the afternoon of 7 March 1964 at the Marble Palace. In his address, which was somewhat convoluted, he repeated his usual *tour d'horizon* of Iranian contemporary history by revisiting the miracles that secured his throne, especially that of 19 August 1953. He then engaged in his newly acquired, unabashed practice of self-praise. About the White Revolution, he noted, "Without wanting to exaggerate, we [the royal we] took an action that has been accepted in the whole world as the most genuine of revolutions." The Shah outlined the responsibility of Mansur's government as twofold. First, the government was to redo the country's civil and administrative organizations to best implement the White Revolution. Second, it was tasked to "prepare all classes of people to further the cause of this revolution."

As for economic priorities, the Shah's comments were general, fragmented, and bereft of statistical information. He identified the founding of steel and petrochemical industries as a prime and urgent objective. He hoped that through industrialization over twenty years the percentage of the rural population to the urban, without citing the actual percentages, would be reversed. The Shah acknowledged that housing was necessary for the people and that the creation of the Ministry of Development and Housing was for this purpose as well as to help economic recovery and generate employment. The Shah was in a hurry to see the country develop and insisted that the new government should not waste a minute.

Mansur's response to the Shah's speech established an unhealthy relationship long in the making between the monarch and his prime ministers. Mansur's response was eulogistic and not professional. He said, "Your royal words are truly so exciting and instructive that they leave no room for a rejoinder." He attributed all achievements to the Shah's White Revolution and promised to implement national reconstruction and modernization within the framework of that revolution. Referring to himself and his team,

Mansur added, "We are soldiers wishing the Shah's support and ready for sacrifices in the path of serving [him]."[2]

On 8 March 1964, Mansur, accompanied by his ministers, went to the Majles, holding his 53-page program neatly tucked into an orange folder. In his first speech as prime minister, he delivered a clear, systematic, and coherent message outlining the main contours of his reform program centered around economic issues. He identified the rapid ending of economic stagnation, job creation, and reviving economic activities as his prime objectives, along with improving the people's daily livelihood.

Mansur intended to bring about economic recovery through widespread public works such as government investment in housing projects, road building, rural development, and credit extension to rural areas. He assured the private sector of the government's assistance and pledged to support and develop home industries with an eye to consumers' interests. Industrialization, overcoming underdevelopment, and attaining high growth rates were also announced as long-term goals.

The new prime minister was unhappy with the achievements of the Third Five-Year Plan in the eighteen months since its beginning. He enumerated the economic tasks ahead: reviewing the Third Five-Year Plan, immediately implementing a comprehensive rural development program, and launching a comprehensive housing project in urban areas. Regarding agricultural policy, Mansur promised to review the regulations and bylaws for the second phase of land reform. He reiterated the importance of increasing agricultural output and using new production methods. He placed a study of mechanized agriculture on the government's agenda.

Mansur then turned to the crucial task of finalizing the further reorganization of the Plan Organization, which had been left in limbo since Ebtehaj's departure. First, drawing up annual budgets would be transferred from the Ministry of Finance to the Plan Organization to coordinate planning and budgeting. The new budgeting procedures would differ from accounting for government revenues and expenditures, allocating resources among various ministries, and developmental plans. Henceforth, budgets would become instruments of fiscal policy, stabilizing the economy. Mansur introduced Abdolmajid Majidi as the deputy general director of the Plan and Budget Organization and the director of the newly created Budget Office. Second, Mansur announced the creation of the country's Statistical

2 *Ettela'at*, 18 Esfand 1342.

Center under the jurisdiction of the Plan Organization. Its crucial responsibility was to regularly compile data and statistics, without which proper planning was in vain.

Mansur announced that the Plan Organization would henceforth become the hub of producing economic, social, and technical studies, the designer and supervisor of developmental programs, and the formulator of the national budget. The Plan Organization would, in turn, relegate its executive tasks in the realm of rural and urban development as well as electricity and water projects to the newly created ministries of Development and Housing and Water and Electricity.[3]

MANSUR'S ECONOMIC POLICIES (MARCH 1964–JANUARY 1965)

On 28 March 1964, immediately after returning from the Nowruz holidays, the Ministry of Economy published the import and export regulations for the year. Contrary to the very long and detailed item-by-item list of import duties or commercial taxes between 1959 and 1963, the list suddenly became short and simple.

Back in 1961 and 1962, Amini had prohibited the import of 210 articles and applied high import duties on some 1,400 items to prevent a foreign exchange reserve crisis. In 1964, the foreign exchange crunch was over. The IMF and the World Bank were no longer worried about Iran's very low reserves and had, therefore, reverted to their policy of free trade promotion.

Mansur gave the green light to import all goods and reduced or removed import duties on raw materials used in factories to support home industries. Import duties on detached parts of refrigerators and air coolers, for example, were reduced to encourage home assembly. On the one hand, the import of car chassis, for example, was freed while import duties were reduced on car engines, detached motor vehicle parts, ignition systems, and spare motor vehicle parts. On the other hand, the government freed up the import of cars and coolers, which was prohibited before, but placed import duties on them. The argument behind this policy was to prevent home monopolies and encourage competition to benefit consumers.

3 *Ettela'at*, 19, 20 Esfand 1342; 17 Farvardin 1343.

The 1964 commercial policies included articles favoring specific groups. For instance, musicians benefited from lower import duties on different musical instruments, from pianos to harmonicas. Import duties on various sporting goods, from ski boots and gym shoes to billiard and bowling balls, were either reduced or removed. Higher-income categories were also favored by reducing import duties on personal luxury items from 200% to 50%. One of the most trumpeted articles of the new policies was the abolition of state monopoly over the international trade of sugar and sugar loaves, allowing the private sector to engage in its import and export.[4]

By the autumn of 1964, Mansur's drive to jump-start economic recovery was proceeding, though slower than expected. Lower interest rates, the resumption of building activities, the inauguration of a few factories, and the return of business confidence were promising signs. Nevertheless, the economy came under substantial pressure as the country faced one of its worst droughts, forcing the government to import 600,000 tons of wheat from the US, Soviet Union, and France.[5] Then suddenly, in November 1964, Mansur delivered a severe blow to the gradually recuperating economy.

A PRICKLY BILL: "SECURING FUNDS FOR DEVELOPMENT AND PUBLIC EXPENDITURES"

Mansur had been emboldened by his success in getting the controversial "Status of Forces Agreement" through the Majles on 13 October 1964. The Bill exempted US military personnel from being held accountable for crimes committed in Iran. Thirteen days later, Khomeyni, the instigator of the 5 June 1963 revolt, strongly objected to the "Status of Forces Agreement", calling it shameless, traitorous, and a "capitulation agreement". On 4 November 1964, or nine days after his inflammatory remarks, Khomeyni was sent to exile without so much as a whimper, let alone an uprising. The mute political reaction must have convinced the Shah and Mansur that Iranians were in a subdued mood.

Meanwhile, on the economic front, the Mansur government was doing its due diligence to prepare the March 1965–March 1966 budget by January 1965. Preparing and presenting the budget before March 1965

4 *Ettela'at*, 8, 9 Farvardin 1343.
5 FO 371/175726, EP 1011/1.

would have been a feat, as the ratification of the budget usually occurred a few months into the new Iranian year. The Plan Organization had begun work on it, and once again, the old problem of financing the budget, with the Shah's push for higher military expenditure, reared its head. The Shah's insistence on prioritizing the military budget meant that developmental projects would have to be slashed unless the government found new revenue sources.[6]

The Mansur government was faced with two unnegotiable and done deals. First, the Iranian government was obliged to pay for "spare parts and replacements for military equipment hitherto supplied free of charge by the US government". Second, it had to finance the pay increase in the army, which the British Embassy estimated to be around £8 million.[7]

The structural problem of the government's inability to collect income taxes from the rich was compounded by the unprecedented drought of 1964. The drought necessitated emergency imports, subsidized sales of grain to the afflicted rural areas, and the provision of credit to adversely impacted farmers. The Mansur government was caught in the same bind as most of the previous governments. Unable to oppose or attenuate the Shah's military ambitions and determined to impress the King with his cabinet's technical and economic know-how, Mansur rushed into an unexpected political morass to avoid an economic one. At noon on 23 November 1964, the Prime Minister presented the Majles with a government bill called "Securing Funds for Development and Public Expenditures" (*ta'min-e e'tebarat-e 'omrani va 'omumi*). The bill stipulated an immediate doubling in the price of gasoline, from 5 to 10 rials per liter, and a steep price hike of kerosene from 2.5 to 3.5 rials per liter.

This measure took the country by surprise. Among other indirect taxes in this bill, the government announced a 1,000 toman per head tax on exit permits for Iranians travelling abroad as well as a 1.75 rial tax per liter on all non-alcoholic beverages.[8] This hefty package of indirect taxes was said to generate 1.1 billion tomans in government revenue to finance the 1.7 billion toman budget deficit of 1965–1966.[9]

---

6 Ali-Naghi Alikhani, Iranian Oral History Collection, Harvard University, Transcript 10, Sequence 188–189.
7 FO 371/175727, EP 1102/6.
8 *Ettela'at*, 4, 7 Azar 1343.
9 *Ettela'at*, 12 Azar 1343.

The only opponents of this provocative measure were the mature and politically experienced figures, such as the National Iranian Oil Company's Manuchehr Eqbal and SAVAK's sagacious Hasan Pakravan, who implored the government to desist from increasing fuel prices.[10] Pakravan tried and failed to persuade the Shah that the new taxes would cause great hardship on the people in the winter and could have adverse political consequences.[11]

An increase in the price of kerosene, a necessity for the urban population and a growing number of rural households, was to the detriment of the lower and middle-income population, with little impact on higher income categories. The petroleum price increases, other than its adverse impact on taxi-owners/drivers and taxi riders, once again penalized lower income car owners as compared to higher income owners. The Mansur government's package of indirect taxes was a textbook example of regressive taxes, taking a more significant percentage of income from low-income earners than higher income earners.

The lack of political acumen demonstrated by the Mansur government to solve a problem created by the Shah's hubris was glaring. At a time when urban Iranians did their cooking and warmed their homes with kerosene, placing taxes on gasoline and kerosene as Iran experienced its coldest days in nineteen years, with night temperatures dropping to minus six degrees Celsius in Tehran and with snowstorms that damaged hundreds of homes in the north of the country, revealed a significant degree of insensitivity by the Shah and his Prime Minister to the people's needs.[12]

On 26 November 1964, Mansur went on television to explain the measures taken by his government. He told Iranians he would follow his objectives with courage and reminded Iranians how beholden they were to the Shah. The Prime Minister told his audience that "if you are comfortably sitting near a warm heater" and thinking about "the extra 2 rials" that you would now have to pay, you should know "that these rials put together will be spent for the welfare of the Iranian people, and the implementation of developmental projects".[13] Mansur knew that this was

10 Ali-Naghi Alikhani, Iranian Oral History Collection, Harvard University, Transcript 10, sequence 189–191.

11 FO 371/175727, EP 1102/6.

12 *Ettela'at*, 7, 8 Azar 1343.

13 *Ettela'at*, 7 Azar 1343.

not the case and the increase in taxes had become necessary since the Shah would not compromise on a reduced military budget.[14]

On Friday, the day after Mansur's television speech, Tehran's taxi drivers congregated at the Truck Drivers' Syndicate to protest the hike in the price of petroleum. They petitioned the Shah through General Ne'matollah Nasiri, Tehran's Chief of Police. From Saturday 28 November, some 16,000 taxi drivers went on strike leaving Tehranis to scramble for taxis in the snow-covered streets. The taxi drivers, in turn, huddled in various coffee houses of Tehran in Sarcheshmeh, Shapur, Meydan E'dam, Shahbaz, Cyrus and elsewhere, discussing the situation.

The deployment of army trucks and buses to take over the city transportation did not help the crisis. The two official declarations issued by the Board of Management of the Taxi Syndicate and Tehran's Syndicate of Taxi-owners, inviting taxi drivers to resume work, fell on deaf ears. The streets of Tehran were empty of cars and taxis. Waiting to catch a bus could take up to forty-five minutes, and citizens walked to get to work, go shopping, or even rush to the doctor.[15]

Iranians were unhappy with the rise in the price of fuel and its impact on their purchasing power and life. Faced with a general wave of discontent and the taxi strike, the regime responded in three ways, justifying the necessity of the unpopular bill. First, on Sunday 29 November, Mansur defended his Bill, "Securing funds for development and public expenditures" at the Senate. The press, under pressure, did not publish the speeches of five senators, Ahmad Matin-Daftari, Jahanshah Samsam, Sadeq Rezazadeh Shafaq, Issa Sadiq-A'lam, and Mohammad-Ali Momtaz, who spoke against the bill. The first three were appointed senators, and the latter two were elected.

Shafaq called the bill "a big disaster", Samsam considered it "unjust", Matin-Daftari spoke of the "deplorable" effects of the bill on the "dispossessed classes", and Sadiq-A'lam questioned the legality of the government's attempt to increase taxes. Momtaz, whose speech was the most scathing, characterized the bill as "a rushed act against national interests" that "no one was satisfied with". Matin-Daftari and Momtaz questioned

---

14 Ali-Naghi Alikhani, Iranian Oral History Collection, Harvard University, Transcript 10, Sequence 188–189.

15 *Ettela'at*, 8, 9 Azar 1343. *Khandaniha*, 10 Azar 1343.

the government's economic justification of its claim that the bill will not cause a general increase in prices.[16]

Mansur's speech was stern and aggressive, presenting a bold and fearless prime minister facing all dangers. Mansur donned the hat of a revolutionary social equalizer, claiming that Iran did not belong to its urban population and that his bill took from urbanites and gave to the rural folk. He claimed that he had saved the rural people from hunger and famine during a year of drought, and revenues had to be found for those expenditures. Mansur hammered that sacrifices were necessary and that paying taxes was a social obligation.

He made no concessions and took cover behind the shield of the Shah and the White Revolution. Mansur insisted and repeated that he and his team were "selfless soldiers of the [White] Revolution", "serving a bitter medicine", namely his bill, "to a sick people unwilling to take it". The Prime Minister said, "We started this work and the Shahanshah supports us." Mansur told the senators, "It is the Shahanshah who discerns who can serve the people and when, and it is His Majesty ... who will interrogate should there be a shortcoming." Mansur was telling the senators to stand back, that the legislative had no power over the executive, for it was in the service of the Shah.[17]

Second, as the strikes continued, on Tuesday 1 December 1964, explaining the economics of the "bitter medicine" was left to Safi Asfia. In a radio and press conference, Asfia presented the bill as necessary for balancing the 1964–1965 budget. He said, "The recent increase in indirect taxes and government frugality will eliminate Iran's budget deficit" of 1.7 billion tomans. He emphasized the necessity of sacrifices by the people or the payment of taxes to allow for current and developmental expenditures to attain the standard of living of economically advanced countries.[18]

The third justification for the bill came from the Shah. On Thursday, 3 December 1964, the Shah held his annual court ceremony on the day the Prophet received his first revelation (*mab'as*). He heard rounds and rounds of unprecedented servile flattery and adulation by different social,

16 *Mozakerat-e Majles-e Sena*, Hashtad o dovvommin Jaleseh, az doreh chaharom taqaniniyeh Majles-e Sena (dowreh davazdahom ejlasiyeh), 7 Azar 1343.

17 *Ettela'at*, 8 Azar 1343. *Mozakerat-e Majles-e Sena*, Hashtad o dovvommin Jaleseh, az doreh chaharom taqaniniyeh Majles-e Sena (dowreh davazdahom ejlasiyeh). 7 Azar 1343. All quotes in the three previous paragraphs are based on these sources.

18 *Ettela'at*, 12 Azar 1342.

political, economic, and military representatives. Mansur told him, "Today Iran and its Muslim people are ruled by a just commander (*qa'ed*) and a capable leader, whom the Prophet has inspired ..."

In his response, the Shah supported the government's bill. However, to get to the heart of the matter, he laid out a well-articulated plan for Iran's economy. He argued that to attain progress, Iran's rural population needed to be reduced from 75% to 25%, resembling rural-urban ratios in economically advanced countries. To attain this objective, he insisted that agricultural productivity would have to increase substantially by modernizing and mechanizing the agricultural sector. The Shah hoped that by investing 30 billion tomans in rural areas in the next 30 years, the 15 million engaged in agriculture would dwindle to some 5 to 6 million.

The financing of this project, he argued, would not need foreign exchange, as Iran would soon have its own steel mill and would produce its own tractors and agricultural machinery. Foreign exchange, he stated, would be used for those goods which could not be produced at home such as huge electric turbines.

The Shah finally got to the point and rhetorically asked, "But how can we mobilize the rials at home?" He rejected taxing the well-off as counterproductive, and argued in favor of encouraging and assisting them to industrialize the country and provide jobs for the excess rural population which would soon be leaving the agricultural sector. The Shah concluded that to ensure progress, all Iranians needed to pitch in, and the burden of taxes would have to be shared by all. The Shah commanded and threatened that "Iranians, irrespective of their class and education, have an important share in this [tax payment] endeavor and are not permitted (*haq nadarand*) to shirk this responsibility."[19]

The statements by the Shah, his Prime Minister Mansur, and the director general of the Plan Organization, who must have known better, demonstrated that all three failed to grasp the dire social consequences of the bill on low-income earners as compared to high-income earners. It should have seemed evident that those adversely affected would push back.

Even though the Ministry of Labor and the police threatened taxi drivers with the annulment of their work permits, the strike continued. On 3 December, after the Shah commanded Iranians to share the tax burden, rumors of a strike by grocers, butchers, and bakers caused long queues

19 *Ettela'at*, 12 Azar 1343.

throughout Tehran. By 6 December or twelve days after the government introduced its bill, some 90% of the taxis returned to work.[20] The freezing winter, however, continued to make life miserable for those lower income households who needed to keep warm with the higher price of kerosene. Even though the press towed the official government line of avoiding any reports on the hardship caused by increased fuel prices, social discontent and malaise were palpable.

On 12 January 1965, some one-and-a-half months after announcing the sudden rise in the price of fuel, Mansur went to the Majles. He said, "Last night, the Shahanshah willed that kerosene prices should revert to their previous price and that petroleum prices should be reduced by 2 rials per liter." This meant gasoline prices that had doubled from 5 to 10 rials per liter would now be sold at 8 rials per liter.

Mansur praised the King and said, "The person concerned with the wellbeing of the people is our Shahanshah, and the spiteful (*moghrezin*) should know that if some day necessity should dictate, Iranians would forego their daily bread." Having stated that it was the Shah's wish to reverse the economic decisions, Mansur made it clear that His Majesty had initiated it. He tried to further justify the decision and explained that the rainfall in the past few days had dissipated the danger of drought and that Iran's oil revenues were to increase in the three coming years.[21] A week after announcing the reduction in fuel prices, the government had to go back to the drawing board, reassessing and tweaking the 1965–1966 budget to reduce the deficit.

The rise and fall of fuel prices pointed to two issues in terms of economic decision-making by the executive and Iran's watchdogs of democracy, namely the legislative and the press. First, the same Majles that wholeheartedly supported the increase in prices also wholeheartedly supported the decrease. Senators who had voted in favor of the price increase did not feel conflicted about subsequently expressing the people's satisfaction with the reduction in the price of fuel.

Second, once the Prime Minister announced the reversals of prices, the press, which had either justified or remained silent on the price hikes, suddenly reported on how the increase in prices had caused hardship for the working classes and how Iranians were now relieved and happy. After

20 *Ettela'at*, 14–16 Azar 1342.
21 *Ettela'at*, 22 Day 1343.

fuel prices were reduced, the press gave news of how consumption of kerosene had doubled. Yet for one-and-a-half months, the press had either been prevented from reporting or had chosen not to report that due to the increase in prices, consumption of kerosene was halved.[22] The executive was becoming unbound, and the genie of despotism was exiting the bottle.

No one, however, dared to address the real reason behind the indirect tax package. The Shah would not relent on his demands for higher military expenditures. Unable to say no to his wishes, the government tried to minimize the misallocation of funds from developmental projects to the military by whipping up receipts from indirect taxes. The measure back-fired; the Shah came out looking like the savior of the people, and Mansur was forced to deal with or accept the deficit. The Shah's obstructionist role in the economic development of Iran was revealed twenty-one years later by the Shah's Minister of Economy, 'Alikhani.[23]

On 21 January 1965, only nine days after Mansur proudly announced that his government was retreating from the fuel price hikes, he was gunned down by Mohammad Bokara'i, a partisan of Khomeyni. Iran's Prime Minister passed away on 26 January 1965 at age forty-one. The next day, Mansur was replaced by his close friend and Minister of Finance, the almost forty-six-year-old Amir-Abbas Hoveyda.

22 *Ettela'at*, 22, 23 Day 1343. *Tehran Economist*, 26 Day 1343; 10 Bahman 1343. *Towfiq*, 1 Bahman 1343.

23 Ali-Naghi Alikhani, Iranian Oral History Collection, Harvard University, Transcript 10, Sequence 188.

17

Hoveyda's First Year in Office: The Shah and the People Whisperer

Hoveyda and Mansur had been friends since 1946 when they met in Paris. In February 1961, the two Westernized liberals formed the Progressive Circle (*kanun-e moteraqi*). On 15 December 1963, the flamboyant Mansur, who always enjoyed the limelight, and the pensive Hoveyda, who preferred to remain in the shadows, launched the New Iran Party (*Hezb-e Iran-e Novin*). The New Iran Party would prove to be the longest ruling party in Iran (1963–1975).

The temperament, style, and politicking of Mansur and Hoveyda at the start of each of their careers as prime minister were different. Mansur was dashing, overbearing, and vocal but came across as arrogant and brash. One of his ministers characterized him as haughty and disdainful and believed that the public had gradually become "allergic to his speeches".[1]

As prime minister, Hoveyda had a knack for understanding and connecting with people. He put them at ease and pleased them. He was not conceited and did not come off as snobbish. He listened to and showed interest in other people's opinions, even dissenting ones. Hoveyda knew how to win the hearts of the gadflies of his own generation and elders. He pandered to them, deferred to them, and made them feel special.

To the senators criticizing his first budget, he would say, "I am but a student ... standing before a treasure chest of art and science ... I know that your guidance will help me and my team attain progress in the tasks

1 Ali-Naghi Alikhani, Iranian Oral History Collection, Harvard University, Transcript 10, Sequences 188–189.

ahead of us."[2] On 18 March 1965, three days before the new Iranian year of 1344, with 127 votes in favor and 16 opposed, the Majles ratified the 1965–1966 budget presented by Hoveyda's new government. Hoveyda thanked the members of the parliament for their vote of confidence and added, "We are thankful to the gentlemen who voted against the budget, for this will prompt us to try harder, serve better, and do a better job."[3]

His tone in public was usually mild, caring, and considerate. The Iranian political scene was not used to this kind of soft approach. In Hoveyda's first official meeting with Tehran's Chamber of Commerce after he became prime minister, Hoveyda called on members to share their economic and commercial ideas and recommendations with the government. Bozorg Abuhoseyn, the highly respected and influential figure among Tehran's merchants, remarked that it was difficult to get appointments with high officials to conduct discussions. Hoveyda's reaction was simple. "Why should you come to our offices? We will come to you whenever you call on us."[4]

Hoveyda's initial uphill battle to endear himself to the people was difficult. Once Hoveyda was nominated by Mansur as Minister of Finance, a flurry of unsigned pamphlets and a parallel chorus of rumors had begun circulating that Hoveyda's grandfather, Mirza Reza Qanad, and father, Habibollah 'Eyn al-molk, were Baha'is.[5] Once Hoveyda became prime minister, more direct comments were made. A senator contended that his appointment was to the country's detriment as he was a Baha'i.[6]

The reaction of both American and British ambassadors to Hoveyda's appointment as prime minister was lukewarm. They too, argued that the Prime Minister's affiliation with the Baha'i faith would put him at a disadvantage. The British Ambassador, Dennis Wright, went as far as predicting that he was unlikely to remain in office for long.[7]

Even though Hoveyda's grandfather and father were Baha'is, his mother, Afsar al-moluk Sardari, was a pious Shi'i who meticulously performed all her religious rites and rituals. Amir-Abbas, who had lost his father at the age of seventeen, recalled that he felt much closer to his

---

2 *Ettela'at*, 27 Esfand 1343.

3 *Ettela'at*, 29 Esfand 1343.

4 *Ettela'at*, 18 Esfand 1343.

5 Be ravayat-e asnad-e savak, *Amir-Abbas Hoveyda*, vol. 1. Tehran: Markaz-e barrasi-e asnad-e tarikhi-e vezerat-e ettela'at, 1382, pp. 98, 108.

6 Be ravayat-e asnad-e savak, *Amir-Abbas Hoveyda*, vol. 1, pp. 142, 144, 148, 154.

7 FO 371/175726, EP 1011/2. FRUS, 1964–1968, vol. XXII, Iran, Document 67.

mother, who was for many years "both his father and mother". According to Hoveyda, his father was always traveling on various foreign service missions and was not at ease demonstrating his affection once at home.[8] It would be safe to say that both Amir-Abbas and his brother, Fereydun, were essentially secular.

To discredit the propaganda around the Prime Minister being a Baha'i, measures were taken to present Hoveyda as a Shi'i. At the meeting with Tehran's Chamber of Commerce, Abuhoseyn requested that mosques and holy shrines be given a substantial discount on their water and electricity bills, and Hoveyda immediately acquiesced. He bantered with Iran's business representatives and said, since he was among merchants for whom money had a particular place, he could not be disrespectful towards it and agreed to only an 80% discount. In response to Hoveyda's offer, Abuhoseyn replied approvingly, *al-ehsan bel-etmam*, meaning "goodness is in the completion of an affair." This whole act, however, had been pre-planned by SAVAK to display Hoveyda's Shi'i proclivities.[9]

Six months after his appointment, Hoveyda went to the new building of Tehran's Chamber of Commerce, flanked by a few of his ministers. The building's large courtyard was packed with more than a thousand merchants, industrialists, and businessmen. The old, upcoming, and new Tehrani bourgeoisie were all gathered. Before his arrival, Hoveyda had sent a special package, which was opened on his arrival. The Prime Minister's subtle gift was a Qur'an, a flag of Iran, and a mirror. A mirror, a pre-Islamic symbol in Iranian culture, represented light and auspiciousness. Iranians moving into a new house would first bring with them a mirror and the Qur'an. Hoveyda's gift of religiosity, nationalism, and Iranianness was warmly and enthusiastically received. There is no evidence that any prime minister before him had such tactfulness and finesse.

Hoveyda was what Iranians called "*mardomdar*", the keeper of people, or one who charms people with his kindness. One of Hoveyda's astute moves was that from the beginning of his office, he held weekly meetings with newspaper and weekly publishers, and journalists, during which he would engage in social, political, and philosophical conversations. In

8 Be ravayat-e asnad-e savak, *Amir-Abbas Hoveyda*, vol.2. Tehran: Markaz-e barrasi-e asnad-e tarikhi-e vezerat-e ettela'at, 1383, pp. 16, 18.

9 *Ettela'at*, 18 Esfand 1343. Be ravayat-e asnad-e savak, *Amir-Abbas Hoveyda*, vol. 1, p. 180.

one such meeting, Hoveyda would ask, "Why do you think people are unhappy and sad?"

In the first months of his premiership, the press characterized him as calm, fair, democratic, open to advice, eager to know, patient, capable of speaking the people's language, and honest. One journalist who had fallen under his spell wrote, "According to Hoveyda's doctrine, ensuring the happiness and gratification of those whom he deals with is a duty (*vazifeh*)", and another influential one wrote, "Hoveyda has set foot on a path directly leading to people's heart."[10]

Whereas the reports on Hoveyda, received by Iran's secret police, SAVAK, or the Bureau for Intelligence and Security of the State, were predominantly negative at first, he was later applauded for calming and soothing public opinion, playing the role of an impartial arbitrator and establishing confidence between the people and the government.[11] The *Tehran Economist*, Iran's most established financial weekly, which was cautious about the arrival of Hoveyda and his team, finally passed judgment on him after five months. The weekly praised Hoveyda and his team for listening to the people, responding favorably to their demands, being a realist, and creating an atmosphere of serenity and confidence that was conducive to business confidence and investment.[12]

Some eight months into Hoveyda's office, Ali Sha'bani wrote that prime ministers usually begin their office with a sweet honeymoon period, which gradually becomes bitter and finally toxic. Hoveyda's, he argued, began amidst rumors, and after a toxic period, it is becoming sweeter and sweeter by the day.[13] Hoveyda had the special gift of not only engaging, bantering, philosophizing, and exchanging ideas with people on the streets of Zanjan, Kermanshah, and Tehran, but he did the same with Iranian politicians, journalists, lawmakers, and businessmen as well as foreign leaders and dignitaries.

Most importantly, he also knew how to deal with the Shah. A year into Hoveyda's premiership, the Shah told the French left-leaning newspaper *Le Monde* that, "Mr. Hoveyda's government, which is following the programs

10 *Khandaniha*, 15, 25, 29 Esfand 1343, 14 Farvardin 1344, 9 Mordad 1344, 3 Mehr 1344, 4 Aban 1344. The previous two paragraphs are based on these sources.

11 *Ettela'at*, 18 Esfand 1343. Be ravayat-e asnad-e savak, *Amir-Abbas Hoveyda*, vol. 1. pp. 207, 227, 237.

12 *Tehran Economist*, 1 Khordad 1344.

13 Khandaniha, 8 Aban 1334. Some thirteen years later, Ali Sha'bani would write the game-changing article against Khomeyni under the name of Rashidi Motlaq in *Ettela'at*.

of the previous government [Mansur's] is to my perfect satisfaction, and I am pleased with this matter."[14] Even though Hoveyda began to lose some of his skills at *mardomdari*, for some time he was the attenuating and reconciling force between an increasingly arrogant and aloof King and the Iranian people.

PUTTING THE ECONOMIC HOUSE IN ORDER

From day one, Hoveyda consistently reiterated that his government's plans, objectives, and methods were the same as those of Mansur's. The Shah's broad economic mandate to both Mansur and Hoveyda was to ensure Iran's rapid ascent to the ranks of the advanced countries through industrialization and increased agricultural productivity. The Shah tied the attainment of these two objectives to the success of his White Revolution. To measure success in attaining those two targets, the Shah identified two major yardsticks: the annual rate of growth of Iran's gross domestic product and how quickly the rate of Iran's rural-to-urban population ratio (70 to 30) was changing in favor of the urban.

However, to move effectively towards obtaining those objectives, Hoveyda and his team needed first to bring some stability and security back to the country, which had been rocked by the assassination of Hasan-Ali Mansur, the prime minister, and an attempt on the Shah's life in April 1965. Hoveyda's tasks when he came to power were manifold. He needed to finalize and get the 1965–1966 budget ratified by the Majles, establish an industrial policy and coordinate it with the country's commercial policy, assure economic recovery and growth, and finally learn how to appease the Shah and keep his position while pleasing the people.

The New Budget

On 28 February 1965, Hoveyda presented the 21 March 1965 to 20 March 1966 budget to the Majles. The budget had a 139 million toman deficit, with expenditures at 5.969 billion tomans and revenues at 5.830 billion tomans. The lion's share of revenues, or some 3.8 billion tomans

14 *Ettela'at*, 21 Azar 1344; 23 Bahman 1344.

($552 million), came from oil revenues. This budget, formulated for the first time by the experts at the Plan Organization, under the auspices of Abdolmajid Majidi, contained more than one novelty. It represented a landmark advance over what the Ministry of Finance had formulated in the past. For the first time the budget was ready and presented to the Majles before the start of the Iranian new year of 21 March 1965.

The budget had numerous new features. First, it was more than a simple aggregated accounting budget with revenues and expenditures. It was a comprehensive and interlaced budget with 140 targets. Each target had an activity rubric in the current budget and a project rubric in the developmental budget. The new budget included three different sets of figures: realized activities of 1963–1964, forecast figures for 1964–1965, and projected figures for 1965–1966, facilitating comparative analyses.

Second, each ministry had its detailed and itemized budget. In the past, money was allocated to ministers. The new budget allotted funds to ministries for a specific purpose and with a particular plan. The ministries were held responsible for spending their budgets to realize the specific projects assigned to them. Ministries were also obliged to provide regular progress reports, facilitating the tracking and auditing of their activities. The budget also included a detailed account of the revenues and expenditures of government-owned commercial and financial organizations, such as banks and factories and government-financed public utility companies. The three ministries with the highest budget allocations were the Ministry of War (1.7 billion tomans), the Ministry of Education (1.1 billion tomans), and the Ministry of Health (278 million tomans).

Third, the budget was intended to affect the overall economy, relieve problems, and realize the goals of the White Revolution. Hoveyda identified four main goals in the coming fiscal year that shaped the budget's economic, financial, and commercial contours. They included "accelerating private investments and generating employment", "bolstering the country's defense capabilities", "securing the people's welfare, especially through stabilizing prices", and "stabilizing and improving the balance of payments".[15]

An essential aspect of the new budget was its developmental (*'omrani*) component of 4.5 billion tomans earmarked for infrastructure, industry, mines, and agriculture. The significance of this figure makes more sense

15 *Ettela'at*, 10 Esfand 1343.

when compared to the 8.4 billion tomans that the country had spent for the same purpose during the seven years of the Second Plan (1955–1962). The new budget aimed to expedite economic recovery and pave the way for a new and accelerated industrialization phase. Aside from promoting private investments, the government was also committed to investing in heavy industries such as steel, the Tehran Oil Refinery, and petrochemicals. Hoveyda spoke about a veritable "economic jihad".[16]

The new budget also greatly emphasized rural development by allocating substantial amounts to the literacy, health, and construction and development corps. The most important source of domestic financing in the budget was indirect taxes (about 2.2 billion tomans), which Hoveyda characterized as unfair and promised that greater reliance would be placed on direct taxes in the future. The new budget relied on obtaining 946 million tomans of foreign credit in its revenues. Whereas Hoveyda presented a long list of savings by ministries to finance the deficit, the only budget item increase in 1965–1966 was that of the military, police, and gendarmerie, which went up by more than 400 million tomans.[17]

Coordinating Commercial and Industrial Policies

On the heels of a comprehensive and detailed budget, aimed at the integrated development of the country, came Hoveyda's policies to regulate foreign trade from March 1965 to March 1966. On 27 March 1965, the details drawn up by ʿAlikhani's Ministry of Economy demonstrated the merits of merging the Ministries of Commerce and Industry and Mines.

For the first time, the objectives of a foreign trade policy were coordinated and integrated with an industrial policy based on an infant industry strategy of import substitution, and both aligned with a national development policy. In contrast to previous annual foreign trade regulations, which were subject to alteration more than once within the specified year, a vital feature of this government ordinance was that its general guidelines were to remain unchanged and in place until the end of the Third Five-Year Plan in March 1968. This critical decision provided clarity and predictability to both importers and home industrialists in making long-term financial and commercial decisions.

16 *Ettelaʿat*, 10 Esfand 1343.

17 *Ettelaʿat*, 10, 12, 15, 16, 17, 26 Esfand 1343. *Khandaniha*, 11, 15 Esfand 1343. All information in the previous 6 paragraphs is based on these sources.

The rates of import duties were mostly kept the same as in the previous year. Items such as metal doors, windows, and shades that were produced at home were prohibited from being imported, while tractors, ambulances, and refrigerator trucks were exempt from import duties. Import duties on boilers, pumps, nuts and bolts, and gaskets were substantially increased to protect the emerging home machinery manufacturing industry.

The government pushed home industries assembling imported parts to increase the home component of their final products. This time, the government was setting down firm regulations. New assembly factories were allowed only with the consent of the Ministry of Economy, and licenses were issued based on strict adherence to the schedule for increasing the number of home-produced components. Assembly plants were eligible for exemptions from import and customs duties based on the percentage to which the final good was composed of home-produced parts.

The Ministry of Economy wished to weed out non-viable and uneconomic industries or those that hoped to remain fundamentally assembly plants, benefitting from handsome import and custom duty exemptions, without generating much value-added at home. 'Alikhani used the new foreign trade regulations to announce that, while supporting the private sector, Iran's industrial transition would be planned and orderly, and that his Ministry would have the final say on which industries benefited the country. The Minister of Economy's new powers meant that he could privilege some industrialists over others.

To avoid one of the pitfalls of the infant industry/import substitution strategy, namely the fall in quality and the rise in the price of protected goods in the absence of competition from imports, the government took a strong position. It threatened industries that failed to maintain international standards and engaged in price gouging with sanctions, such as the removal of protections and the free import of protected goods.

Importing goods not produced at home or produced but not enough to meet demand was announced to be free. To ensure a balance in external payments and the maintenance of a sound foreign exchange reserve, limitations on non-necessities were maintained. The new regulations also incorporated elements of export promotion. 'Alikhani knew that Iran was far from having a solid industrial base to become a serious exporter of manufactured goods, but he wished to nudge Iranian industrialists in that direction. The new foreign trade regulations promoted exports by reimbursing producers for the import and customs duties paid on the import of their assembled pieces.[18]

The private sector was quick to pick up the new signals. On 1 April 1965, Cyrus Arjomand of Arj Industries announced the creation of a powerful industrial conglomerate, the Constructors of Industrial Factories Corporation. This first-of-its-kind formation pooled together the know-how, experience, and capacities of five reputable firms in the metal industries to design, construct, and install industrial factories in Iran. The participating members of this corporation were Cyrus Arjomand of Arj Industries, Mohsen Azmayesh of Azmayesh Industries, Shapour Behbehani of the General Mekanik Company, Mahmud Darvish of the Iran Nail Company, and Alidad Farmanfarmayan of Nir Pars Company. This new entity negotiated with the government and foreign investors to participate in constructing new installations in Iran. In April 1965, the foreign constructor of two sugarloaf factories in Mamasani and Yasuj, both located in the Fars province, outsourced 25% of their works to the Constructors of Industrial Factories Corporation. The same foreign constructor promised that 60% of the activities of a new plant in Kordestan would be subcontracted to Iranian installation companies.[19]

Reviving the Economy

To help economic recovery and encourage investment, on 3 January 1965, the Central Bank further reduced interest rates on savings accounts by 1.5%.[20] Gradually, commercial activities rebounded, and the number of licenses issued by the Ministry of Economy for the construction of factories began to increase along with prices. From February to April 1965, construction activities and the sale of construction materials increased by 60%, leading to an increase in the prices of cement and tiles.[21] On 23 May 1965, 'Alikhani announced the end of the economic recession.[22]

One by one, the helmsmen of the Iranian economy, announced that recovery was underway, showing signs of improved business activity

18 *Ettela'at*, 7, 8, 9 Farvardin 1344; 18 Ordibehesht 1344. The information in the previous six paragraphs is based on these sources.
19 *Ettela'at*, 14, 18 Farvardin 1344.
20 *Ettela'at*, 13 Day 1343.
21 *Ettela'at*, 15 Farvardin 1344.
22 *Ettela'at*, 3 Khordad 1344.

and economic expansion. At the 5th annual General Assembly of the Industrial and Mining Development Bank of Iran held on 17 June 1965, Sharif-Emami, the bank's chairman of the board, reported on the activities of the bank. He confirmed that in 1964, the bank loaned out 108 million tomans to various industries compared to 65.8 million in 1963. Sharif-Emami added that the economic prospects for 1965 were promising since industrial production was reaching its full capacity, and industrialists were putting in requests for credit to order more machinery.[23]

In September 1965, the Shah laid out his economic priorities for the country. He believed that "Iran's epoch of real economic construction" had only begun after the White Revolution of 26 January 1963. The Shah set his sights on an annual growth rate of 8% to 10% and promised to combat inflation and eradicate "artificial price hikes". He hoped for rapid increases in income and savings and looked forward to creating a stock market, which could channel savings into industrial investments.

In agriculture, the Shah argued that some 20 to 30 hectares of land, on average, were necessary to provide the farmers with a decent standard of living. He provided the economic philosophy for the second phase of land reform beginning in 1965. The Shah posited that having overthrown "the unjust, old and middle-aged system of landlord and peasants", Iranian farmers were now poised to increase their productivity and move towards mechanized agriculture on larger plots of land, thereby increasing their individual profits and also benefitting the country. The Shah spoke of agricultural workers and agribusinesses, which he called farming along the lines of industrial activities.

The Shah elaborated on his new-found theory that real democracy was nothing but economic democracy. His definition of economic democracy, which now took center stage in his speeches, replacing political democracy, which he could not deliver, had two parts: one dealing with labor, which was opaque and difficult to grasp, and the other with capital, which was understandable but vague on the specifics. The Shah maintained that economic democracy prevailed where "exploitation would be replaced by the maximum use of work done (*este'mar jay-e khod ra be hadd-e aksar-e estefadeh as kar-e anjam shodeh bedahad*)". The second part of his definition posited that "investors would be able to reap the benefits of their capital and innovation", while "respecting progressive socio-economic

23 *Ettela'at*, 1 Tir 1344.

laws such as the payment of the workers' rightful dues (*huquq-e haqeh*) and government taxes".

In international economics, the Shah opposed the idea of peripheral countries being condemned to producing raw materials while core countries monopolized the production of industrial goods. Without naming him, the Shah referred to Raul Prebisch's theory of deteriorating terms of trade but noted that Iran's situation was different because it had substantial oil deposits, and that oil was a commodity that was in demand and that it lent itself to industrialization through the creation of petrochemical industries.[24]

The Iranian year 1344 (March 1965–March 1966) proved economically miraculous. The Shah's dream of a 10% rate of GDP growth was surpassed, as Iran obtained an unprecedented rate of growth of 17%.[25] This one-time spectacular rate of growth makes more sense when compared to the world average (5.6%), South Korea (7.3%), Venezuela (4.2%), Japan (5.8%), and Taiwan (6.4%). During this year, Iran's oil output grew from 98 million cubic meters to 110, increasing government revenue by 200 million over the preceding year.[26]

Hoveyda presented the detailed Iranian budget for 1345 (21 March 1966–20 March 1967) to the Majles a month before 21 March 1966, as he had done the preceding year. Gone were the days of aggregated and blurred budgets presented sometimes several months into the year. In his presentation of the 19.2 billion toman budget, more than three times that of the previous year, Hoveyda reported a deficit of 164 million tomans, almost the same as the previous year (139 million). He boasted of a 12% increase in foreign exchange earnings and almost stable prices. Hoveyda proudly reported that 13,000 members of the literacy corps were instructing some 200,000 rural children.

The Majles' Budget Committee identified a 500 million tomans ($66.6 million) increase in the preceding year's 1965–1966 budget expenditures. It pointed out that a substantial share (*qesmat-e a'zam*) of the increase was due to military and defense expenditures.[27] Mir-Asadollah Musavi-Makuie,

24 *Tehran Economist*, 25 Shahrivar 1344.

25 World Bank national accounts data, and OECD National Accounts data files, https://data.worldbank.org/indicator/NY.GDP.MKTP.KD.ZG?end=1971&locations=IR&start=1961 (retrieved 24/7/2024). Iranian sources at the time quoted a 10% growth rate in GDP.

26 *Ettela'at*, 29 Esfand 1344.

27 *Ettela'at*, 10 Esfand 1344

a member of parliament, drew attention to the abysmal salary of the country's 80,000 teachers, 66% of whom received less than 500 tomans ($67) per month; the other third received a maximum of 2,000 tomans per month. He implored Hoveyda to raise their salaries.

Another member of parliament, Mohammad Shafi'-Amin, spoke about the need to increase the low salaries of government employees and pensioners. He pointed out that their present incomes did not cover their costs. Hoveyda's comments on the issues raised by both parliamentarians were compassionate and sympathetic. He agreed that these were real problems.

His full response, however, reflected how well Hoveyda and his ministers had internalized the Shah's fundamental axiom: the military budget has priority in national resource allocation. At the Majles, Hoveyda evoked the Shah's argument that until world disarmament were to come about, Iran had to privilege and champion military expenditures. Ignoring the possibility of reducing military expenditures, Hoveyda responded, "What can I do? To pay out increased salaries, we would have to substantially reduce our developmental programs by some 500 to 600 million tomans, which would mean no more dams and development projects."[28] According to the press, the official military budget for March 1966–1967 stood at 2.1 billion tomans as compared to the education budget of 703 million tomans and the health budget of 403 million tomans.[29]

In the High Economic Council meeting of 8 January 1968, the Shah informed his close circle of ministers, bankers and planners that the military budget was around 3.4 billion tomans annually, and that it would increase every year. The Shah pointed out that the cost of one fighter jet was about $3 million or the equivalent of two hospitals, each with 360 beds. He said, "With all our heart, we wish we could build the two hospitals instead of buying the fighter plane, but if we are negligent, we may not be able to build even one hospital. Therefore, the defense of the country has precedence for Iran." Hoveyda immediately responded that "the Shah's orders

28 *Ettela'at*, 3, 4 Esfand 1344. *Ruznameh-e Rasmi-ye Keshvar Shahanshahi-ye Iran*, 11 Esfand 1344, *Mozakerat-e Majles showray-e melli*, 11 Esfand 1344, Neshast-e 244.
29 *Ettela'at*, 22 Esfand 1344.

(*avamer*) will be obediently followed."[30] The Shah understood opportunity cost, and his priorities were clear.

By 1968, the Shah had made it perfectly clear that keeping the military budget constant, let alone decreasing it, was out of the question. His political and economic advisers came to realize that discussing or disagreeing over military expenditures was not within their brief if they wanted to keep their jobs.

30 Gholamreza Nikpay (gerdavarandeh) *Surat jalesat-e showray-e 'aliye eqtesad dar pishgah Shahanshah Aryamehr, az Shahrivar 1345 ta Shahrivar 1347*. Surat jaleseh-e 18 Day 1346, Tehran: Chapkhaneh-e vezarat-e farhang va honar, n.d.

18

The Shah's Economic Challenges: Arms and Oil

The years 1965 to 1968 witnessed important disagreements, negotiations, and compromises between Iran, the US, and the oil consortium. The public was not always privy to the ongoing disputes in the domains of oil and arms. They were exposed to oil negotiations, especially when Iran was triumphant, but the details of how the ends were reached remained largely unknown.

These two challenging domains and their spin-off consequences continuously marked the Iranian economy and was to overshadow its economic history until the 1979 revolution. It would be fair to say that broad macroeconomic and social crises that brought the Pahlavi regime to its knees were largely, but not entirely, a function of the interplay of these issues and the system's inability to resolve them.

These closely interrelated spheres were under the Shah's indisputable control, and he worked on them incessantly. Oil revenues, Iran's major source of national income, determined the pace at which the Shah could realize his two major objectives: becoming a strong military force in the region through a steady rearmament program while attaining economic prosperity and growth. In tough oil negotiations, the Shah locked horns with the world's most powerful oil companies, the major shareholders of which were American and British companies, with 40% each.

The Shah's nationalist vision of pushing to obtain a larger share of output and greater revenues for Iran clashed with the Consortium's international position and agenda, which operated in numerous oil-producing countries. What frustrated the Shah was that he was confined to the 1954

Page–Amini Agreement between the Consortium and Iran, which he had supported at the time.

To realize his military objectives, the Shah, who could now pay for his arms, needed to convince the US, his main arms supplier since 1953, to sell Iran the arms he required. The Johnson Administration, like all previous US administrations since Eisenhower, believed that the Shah was obsessing over Iran's military and defense needs and preferred to see Iran moderate its arms expenditures and spend more on economic growth and development. The fact that the US was telling the Shah not to overly indulge in arms purchases frustrated him.

The Shah viewed the Johnson Administration's posture in this regard as patronizing and condescending. Nevertheless, he remained committed and loyal to the US and believed that Iran's fate was intertwined with that of the anti-communist "Free World" led by the US. After the White Revolution, however, the Shah wished to be recognized as a strong, nationalistic, and independent leader with a say on the international scene. In 1966, the Shah exercised brinkmanship by leveraging his newly found détente with the Soviet Union to impose his will on US arms sales to Iran. By 1967, the Shah had changed the paternalistic and hegemonic US–Iran balance of power to benefit his own world outlook.

ARMS

With time, the Shah's firm belief that "successful economic development of Iran is useless unless Iran has adequate military security" hardened and became an axial national strategy.[1] From 1964, anticipating higher oil revenues, the Shah turned to the US to purchase modern arms on credit. During his July 1964 visit to the US, a "Cooperative Logistics Agreement" was drawn up to promise the "Shah good credit terms for some $250 million in sales" of modern armaments.[2]

On 25 October 1964, the Majles approved a $200 million US loan to Iran, and negotiated with American banks to purchase military supplies. The bill presented by Mansur had come 12 days after ratifying the "Status of Forces Agreement". The timing of the bills raised suspicions

1 FRUS, 1964–1968, vol. XXII, Iran, Document 105.
2 FRUS, 1964–1968, vol. XXII, Iran, Document 45.

that the government was being rewarded by the US for getting the highly unpopular immunity bill for US personnel in Iran through parliament. The Shah's $200 million credit for the purchase of sophisticated arms included M–60 tanks for the army, C-130 military transport aircraft, F–5 supersonic fighter jets, and Hawk surface-to-air missiles for the Air Force.[3]

Concurrently, high-level American policymakers were complaining that "it is a constant struggle to keep the Shah's appetite within bounds."[4] In April 1965, Robert Komer of the National Security Council, wrote to President Johnson that "With rapidly rising oil revenues ($750 million last year), he's [the Shah] tempted to spend far too much on fancy military hardware and not enough on meeting his own people's rising expectations." According to Kromer, "he [the Shah] doesn't pay enough attention to his own economy but loves (now that we've stopped the Soviets for him) to worry about the piddling Arab threat."[5]

Kromer was referring to the Shah's new shift in perception of Iran's most pressing enemy. Having concluded that the Soviet Union did not pose an imminent military threat, the Shah clamored for more weapons to defend Iran against potential threats from Egypt and Iraq. The British assessment of the Shah's misplaced anxiety over the threat of pro-Naser forces in the region resembled that of the US. The British Military Attaché in Tehran reported that "Throughout 1965, his [the Shah's] obsession with this threat [Egypt and Iraq] continued unabated."[6]

The Shah's re-armament drive in 1965 was also due to his disappointment with CENTO's (Central Treaty Organization) inability to protect regional members against military attacks, as was revealed in the India–Pakistan War (Second Kashmir War) of April to September 1965. Finally, the Shah was anxious about the planned departure of the British from the Persian Gulf, and felt that Iran needed to beef up its naval power before the eventual British withdrawal. The growing economic importance of Khark Island and its naval defense added to the Shah's concern for building up Iran's navy.[7]

3 FRUS, 1964–1968, vol. XXII, Iran, Documents 45, 54. FO 371/186705, EP 1205/1.
4 FRUS, 1964–1968, vol. XXII, Iran, Document 80.
5 FRUS, 1964–1968, vol. XXII, Iran, Document 77.
6 FO 371/186705, EP 1205/1.
7 FO 371/186705, EP 1205/1. FRUS, 1964–1968, vol. XXII, Iran, Document 110.

In June 1965, US Ambassador Armin Meyer pressed the US administration to reconsider the ceiling on Iranian Armed Forces and agree to its increase from 160,000 to 172,000. He argued that the additional personnel were largely necessary for the new arms purchases and the reorganization of the 8th Armor Division.[8] It is not clear if the US administration conceded to the increase in the number of Iranian Armed Forces.

About a year later, on 9 November 1965, the Majles ratified another bill by Hoveyda, allowing the government to raise $200 million abroad for arms purchases from any country. Hoveyda argued that Iran needed to be self-reliant and that the country needed to be armed with the latest aerial defense systems and naval weaponry.[9] Sensing US reluctance to sell $200 million of military equipment, the Shah first approached European countries and then the Soviet Union.

On 17 November 1965, the Shah dispatched Airforce General Hasan Tufaniyan, the Chief of Plans of the Iranian Armed Forces, to the UK to negotiate the conditions of an arms deal, including destroyers or frigates, antiaircraft weapons, and light tanks.[10] Iran ended up purchasing the following items from the UK: four Vosper Mark 5 destroyers, eight SRN 6 Hovercrafts, six BH 7 Hovercrafts, a refitted destroyer, eighteen Tigercat and six Seacat antiaircraft missiles, a re-conditioned destroyer, and appropriate missiles at a total estimated cost of £26 million.[11]

The Shah wanted to tell the Americans that if they did not give Iran the sophisticated arms it desired, it would buy them elsewhere. Meyer supported the Shah's military build-up and urged Washington to comply with his demands for more sophisticated weapons.[12]

On the last day of January 1966, the Shah repeated his favorite line that Iran could not abandon its military build-up until all countries reached a disarmament agreement. The Shah presented his vision for Iran's economic future as such, "This economic rate of growth must continue. We can neither reduce our programs for industrial and economic development and slow down our infrastructural investments and rate of growth, nor

8 FRUS, 1964–1968, vol. XXII, Iran, Document 91.

9 FO 371/175726, EP 1011/2. *Ettela'at*, 18 Aban 1344.

10 FO 371/180794, EP 1193/15.

11 FCO 17 351, EP 1/4. US sources put the figure at $60 million. See FRUS, 1964–1968, vol. XXII, Iran, Document 186. FCO 17 400, EP 10/17.

12 FRUS, 1964–1968, vol. XXII, Iran, Document 110.

are we able, even for a second, to neglect the rational provision of our defensive needs."[13]

After twelve years (1953–1965) of economic, political, and military reliance and dependence on the US, the Shah wished to ascertain his independence and demonstrate Iran's veritable self-reliance. The Shah was turning a historical page and felt confident sending an important message to the US. The issue that triggered his new posture was President Johnson's reluctance to provide him with the arms he asked for.

On 2 March 1966, the Shah announced, "We have friends, but we cannot leave our fate only in the hands of others, so that if one day they decided to help us, they would, and if another day they did not, they would withhold their help. This [situation] would not only be humiliating from a nationalistic point of view but would be unreliable from a foreign policy perspective."[14]

The US continued to maintain that the Shah's purchase of $200 million would "have an adverse impact on Iran's economic development". Yet, they knew that they could not prevent him from purchasing arms elsewhere and worried that their refusal would hurt their national interests in Iran.[15]

Walt Rostow, President Johnson's Special Assistant, wrote candidly to the President on the US administration's general view of the Shah's insistence on arms purchases. He wrote, "Most of us believe the Shah is foolish to spend his money this way." This said, he added, "Anyway, if we cannot dissuade him, no point in losing a good sale."[16]

On 4 May 1966, or after less than six months of friction and jostling, the US warmed up to Iran's purchase of arms up to a ceiling of $400 million, including the $200 million envisaged in 1964 plus $200 million authorized in November 1965 by the Iranian Parliament. The approval of arms purchases was contingent upon "an annual joint review of the Iranian economy". This review aimed "to determine whether Iran could afford increased military expenditures and still maintain rapid economic development".[17] This clause was intended for the US to save face and had no real teeth.

---

13 *Ettela'at*, 11 Bahman 1344.
14 *Ettela'at*, 11 Esfand 1344.
15 FRUS, 1964–1968, vol. XXII, Iran, Document 118.
16 FRUS, 1964–1968, vol. XXII, Iran, Document 141.
17 FRUS, 1964–1968, vol. XXII, Iran, Document 134, 135.

On 23 May 1966, President Johnson officially approved the $200 million military purchase loan for Iran that the Iranian parliament had authorized. The Shah's list of new arms included two squadrons of 12–16 F-4 fighter planes, 209 M-60 tanks, a thirty-day war reserve for the three services, and the Blue Shark radar system.[18] By this time, the Shah had approached the Soviets for the purchase of arms. Talk of Iran purchasing Soviet SAM missiles rendered the US nervous, forcing them to offer better terms to Iran as well as more arms. This worked, and the Shah abandoned the idea of SAM missiles, which the Soviets were not eager to sell either. The Iran–US arms sale went through, and on 15 August 1966, the Shah informed President Johnson that he had instructed his government "to sign the necessary documents for the 200 million dollars credit".[19]

Thirteen years, almost to the day, after a humiliated Shah was returned to the throne, a more self-confident *Aryamehr*, or the Light of the Aryans, forced his savior to comply with his demands for a military build-up. The son, who since 1950 had received a total of $1.4 billion from the US in economic, technical, and military assistance, seemed to have outgrown the authority of his father.[20]

Events, however, were to demonstrate that even though the Shah wished to be seen as his own independent and self-reliant man vis-à-vis the US, he also wished to be the most privileged, honored and favored ally of the US in the Middle East. The Shah's momentary fallings-out with the US went hand in hand with his need for special reassurances and consolations that he could count on the Americans.[21] This dual and conflicting posture of needing the Americans and wanting to seek independence from them shaped the Shah's attitude until the 1979 revolution.

In January 1967 came the news of a Soviet–Iranian arms deal, which was more symbolic than substantial. The Soviets extended a $110-million credit to Iran for the purchase of armored personnel carriers, antiaircraft weapons, and trucks.[22] Yet after the Shah's successful two-day visit to Washington on 22 August 1967, very warm relations and confidence were once again reestablished between the two countries. But then, the news,

18 FRUS, 1964–1968, vol. XXII, Iran, Document 148.
19 FRUS, 1964–1968, vol. XXII, Iran, Document 173.
20 $706 million economic, $757.5 military, through FY 66, FRUS, 1964–1968, Volume XXII, Iran, Document 186.
21 FRUS, 1964–1968, vol. XXII, Iran, Document 266.
22 FRUS, 1964–1968, vol. XXII, Iran, Document 206.

in early November 1967, that the Congress and the Senate had decided to end the Defense Department's overseas arms sales by 30 June 1968 alarmed the Shah.[23]

On 23 November 1967, some five months after the sudden increase in Iranian oil output and revenues during June 1967, the government sought another 2 billion tomans or around $285 million of credit for "boosting the country's military capacity". The bill presented to the Majles stipulated that the government could obtain this credit from whatever source at an interest rate "not in excess" of the prevalent rate. The fact that the Prime Minister was not presenting this important bill indicated that the relatively high military expenditures and related debt for purchasing arms had become normalized. It also implied that over the issue of arms purchases, the Shah's private domain, the government did not expect any opposition from the newly elected 22nd Majles, fully controlled by Hoveyda and his Iran Novin Party.[24]

By March 1968, the Shah was getting impatient with the US as he was not sure whether the Congress and Senate would allow Iran to buy the arms he coveted. He was brooding, and Meyer, the US Ambassador in Iran, correctly observed that "Key to US-Iran relationship is, of course, arms supplies."[25] The Shah's anxiety was partially alleviated when, on 18 May 1968, he was given assurances that contingent upon Congressional approval, and on an annual basis, he would be able to buy up to $100 million of arms on credit for five years. Yet, as soon as he received the assurances he had sought, he made it known to the American Ambassador that "Iran's immediate military needs would exceed 100 million."[26]

On 12 June 1968, the Shah was in Washington, on his way to receive an honorary degree from Harvard University. In his meetings with the President and US officials, the Shah addressed his main concern, namely the "need to bolster Iran's defense capabilities". In preparation for withdrawing British troops from the Persian Gulf, the Shah's new shopping list included, "a combination of naval craft, aircraft and land-based missiles". The Shah also asked for US technicians to maintain the F-4 fighter planes that he was to receive soon.[27]

23 FRUS, 1964–1968, vol. XXII, Iran, Document 241.
24 *Ettela'at*, 2 Azar 1346.
25 FRUS, 1964–1968, vol. XXII, Iran, Document 264.
26 FRUS, 1964–1968, vol. XXII, Iran, Documents 283, 284.
27 FRUS, 1964–1968, vol. XXII, Iran, Documents 295, 297.

Between 1965 and 1968, the Shah encountered turbulent patches of uncertainty and anxiety over where the US stood on selling him the arms he wished on credit. Every time, after some internal discussions, the Johnson Administration responded positively. The Shah was, in turn, grateful to Johnson and trusted him, but he knew that many of the President's men did not look favorably on his incessant re-armament fixation.

With the election of Richard Nixon in November 1968 and the formalization of his Nixon Doctrine in November 1969 came a paradigm shift in Iran–US arms relations. Nixon became the Shah's dream-maker. When, on 1 June 1972, Nixon gave the Shah the poisoned apple to purchase all the conventional weapons available in the US arsenal, the Shah was freed from Washington's liberal establishment, which had been resisting arms sales and moralizing to him about prioritizing development over re-armament. The Shah now faced an enchanting, unlimited choice of arms, recklessly dispensing with the reality of his continuously limited budget.

OIL

The Shah's rearmament program was closely tied to his expectation of increased oil revenues through negotiation with the Oil Consortium. In May 1966, the Shah pushed the Oil Consortium to increase Iran's oil production by 17.5% annually for the next four years to finance his military expenditures and economic programs. The Oil Consortium was thinking of a maximum increase of 12%.[28]

The first round of the annual Oil Consortium conference, which began in London on 3 October 1966, proved disappointing to the Shah. Iran was told that its production would increase by 10% to 11%. Its request to market its own oil was refused.[29] Manuchehr Eqbal, the director general of NIOC, representing Iran at the London conference, expressed his dissatisfaction with the Consortium's inflexibility and accused it of "ignoring Iran's vital interests". A second round of discussions was held on 21 October 1966 to make headway.

On the day of Eqbal's departure for London, Hoveyda had delivered a harsh speech at the Majles, warning the Consortium that Iran needed to use

28 FRUS, 1964–1968, vol. XXII, Iran, Document 135.

29 FRUS, 1964–1968, vol. XXII, Iran, Document 179. Iranian sources reported that Iran was told that oil production would increase by 9% to 10%. See *Ettela'at*, 13 Mehr 1345.

its oil to attain the objectives of the White Revolution and secure the welfare and economic prosperity of the country. Hoveyda placed the Consortium on its guard and heeded that Iran would not remain indifferent to its rights and would not allow its fate "to be unilaterally decided by foreign boards of directors behind closed doors". Hoveyda threatened the Consortium with his government's "appropriate actions to be announced later".

While negotiations were underway, the Shah repeated Hoveyda's position. In an interview with the *Sunday Times*, he threatened that unless an acceptable settlement was reached with the Consortium, he would "act unilaterally and violate the agreement". When the Consortium did not relent, the Shah announced that Iran's "demands were both just and logical". He announced that Iran was not bluffing and that the government and the people "were ready for all kinds of sacrifices". The Consortium subsequently delayed its response for another month.[30]

The oil issue suddenly became a matter of national pride and honor, pitting Iran against the Consortium, Britain, and the US to a lesser extent. It was as if an old wound, that of the reasons for Iran's oil nationalization of 1951 had been once again opened. The Consortium's resistance to agree with Iran received wide and angry reactions in the Iranian press, whipping up nationalistic feelings. Daily accounts of the British press, news agencies, and BBC Radio London were translated and published in the Iranian press, commented on their bias towards the Consortium and rebutted. References were made to Iran's history of standing up to the "colonial and world mongering oil interests" and how the intransigence of the Anglo-Iranian Oil Company, which became BP in 1954 and a member of the Consortium, had led to their eviction in October 1951.[31]

After a week of strong words and lashing out against the Consortium and Britain, at the end of October 1966, breaks were put on the press not to cross the point of no return, and attacks and even comments on the oil issue fell silent. While negotiations with the Consortium became long and drawn out, the Shah articulated his "independent and nationalistic politics" (*siyasat-e mostaqel-e melli*) and met with four key figures of the Consortium's board of directors who had come to Tehran for five days. Howard Page, of the Standard Oil Company of New Jersey, and the leading negotiator of the 1954 agreement with Amini, was among them.

30 *Ettela'at*, 13, 28 Mehr 1345; 5 Aban 1355. Information in the three previous paragraphs is based on these sources.

31 *Ettela'at*, 3, 4, 5 Aban 1345. *Khandaniha* 3, 7, 10, Aban 1345.

On 11 December 1966, Hoveyda informed the Majles that the Consortium had accepted the Shah's terms, and Iran had prevailed in the negotiations. Exuding triumphalism, Hoveyda claimed that Iran had obtained the right to take charge of one-fourth of the concession area stipulated in the 1954 agreement, market a certain amount of the oil extracted from the newly acquired areas to Eastern Europe, and increase its output by a considerable amount. Hoveyda's vague and unspecific statements were mainly for domestic political purposes.[32]

Two days later, in his press conference, Eqbal, who had led the two oil negotiations, announced that with the Shah's permission, he would discuss the agreement within certain limits (*ta anja ke emkan darad*). He clarified that by the end of 1966, Iran could increase output by 12% and that for 1967 and 1968, the increase would be considerable. Eqbal confirmed that 25% of the exploitation area under contract to the Consortium would be transferred to Iran within three months. Finally, between 1967 and 1971, the Consortium would sell Iran 20 million tons of crude oil at a special price for sale to Eastern European countries.[33]

The British authorities had a different take on one crucial issue of the deal than the Iranians. The Consortium had not compromised much on the sensitive issue of increasing Iranian output. The settlement stipulated that output would increase by 12% in 1967 and 13% in 1968. A minor detail was that the 20 million tons of crude oil were earmarked for barter with Eastern European countries and not for sale.[34] The Shah and Iran, however, could claim victory. However, oil revenues were not increasing fast enough to satisfy the Shah's military and developmental ambitions.

The year 1967 was one of transformation. The Shah replaced the old guard Eqbal with the young, US-educated Jamshid Amuzegar as Iran's lead oil negotiator. He anticipated intense negotiations with the Consortium and within the Organization of Petroleum Producing Countries (OPEC). Iran had been one of the founders of OPEC. By the mid-1960s, this body became a key player in the international oil market as it hammered at the "inalienable right of all countries to exercise permanent sovereignty over their natural resources in the interest of their national development". From 1967, Jamshid Amuzegar became the cool-headed and energetic face of oil negotiations, one who only reported to the Shah.

32 *Ettela'at*, 20 Azar 1345.

33 *Ettela'at*, 22 Azar 1345.

34 FCO 37 351, EP 1/4.

At the end of 1966 and during 1967, two unexpected regional political crises presented the Shah with enormous economic opportunities, providing fortuitous windfall gains. On 9 December 1966, while negotiations were underway between the Consortium and Iran, the Syrian government closed the Iraqi pipeline through Syria to the Baniyas Port on the Mediterranean. A few days later, the Syrians closed the oil pipeline to the Port of Tripoli in Lebanon.[35]

The Syrian government's actions followed an unresolved financial dispute over pipeline transit dues with the Iraqi Petroleum Company (IPC), a consortium whose dominant partners were British Petroleum, Royal Dutch Shell, and Esso (Exxon). The Syrian–IPC conflict resulted in the stoppage of about 1.4 million barrels of Iraqi oil per day to the world markets.[36]

The mini oil crisis of late 1966 was followed by the decision of the Middle East oil-producing countries to ban oil shipments to the US, UK, and West Germany following the Arab-Israeli war of June 1967. The Shah adopted a neutral stance. He did not participate in the oil boycott and continued the sale of oil to the West and Israel through third-party intermediaries. From June to August 1967, another 1.5 million barrels of oil per day were removed from the market. While the United States made up for 1 million barrels per day, it was Venezuela and Iran that made up the rest.[37]

The Iraqi-Syrian crisis and the Shah's decision not to join the oil boycott enabled the country to increase its oil production much higher than had been negotiated with the Consortium. In 1966, output grew by 13% instead of the settled 10 to 11%, and in 1967, it jumped by 22% from the 12% agreed with the Consortium, providing Iran with substantial unanticipated revenues. The 1967 jump in output generated $857 million in revenues, almost $100 million over Iran's 1966 oil revenues.[38]

This handsome windfall gain raised the Shah's expectations that greater oil incomes could finance his military and developmental plans. By November 1967, the Shah was pushing the US government and

35 *Ettela'at*, 20, 23 Azar 1345.

36 Brandon Roy Wolfe-Hunnicutt, "The end of the concessionary regime: oil and American power in Iraq, 1958–1972". PhD. Thesis, Stanford University 2011, pp. 177, 181, https://purl.stanford.edu/tm772zz7352 (retrieved 31/7/2024).

37 Samantha Gross, "The 1967 War and the 'Oil Weapon,'" June 5 2017, Brookings, https://www.brookings.edu/articles/the-1967-war-and-the-oil-weapon/ (retrieved 31/7/2024)

38 Foreign Relations of the United States, 1969–1976, Volume E–4, Documents on Iran and Iraq, 1969–1972. Document 165.

President Johnson to exert pressure on the American companies in the Consortium "to insure greatly increased petroleum exports from Iran".[39]

The Shah claimed that Iran needed $6 billion to realize its Fourth Five-Year Development Plan (March 1968–March 1973). The Consortium's production plans for this period and a "steady growth rate of about 10% per year would give Iran only about $4.5 billion during this period."[40] The Shah was also concerned with financing a Five-Year Military Plan (1968–1973) of initially $800 million, which was finally reduced to $600 million.[41]

The Shah's oil revenue expectations from greater oil output exceeded the Consortium's willingness to allow Iran to produce. The 22% increase in 1967 oil output had been due to exceptional circumstances, yet it had put into motion a ratchet effect in the Shah's mind. The Consortium's decision to set the 1968 increase in oil output at 9% over the 1967 level, flustered the Shah.

On 29 November 1967, less than a week after Hoveyda's government asked the Majles to ratify $266 million to purchase more arms, talks between Iran and the Consortium began in Tehran for increased production. Once more, the familiar cycle of demanding higher oil production to generate higher revenues to finance more arms purchases, as well as developmental expenditures, was at work.[42]

Since December 1967, the Shah had grown frustrated with the Iran–Consortium negotiations, which were not going in his direction. He expressed his indignation at the Consortium's increasing output in small countries like Abu Dhabi, Kuwait, Saudi Arabia, and Libya, as compared to Iran's 26 million people. In need of money for arms and developmental purposes, the Shah was clearly on a war path with the Consortium, which he derided as "thieves".[43]

Three months later, in March 1968, the Shah threatened the oil companies that the time of unilateral decisions was over. He said that just because of a "mere contract", the Consortium could not tell us to forego using our own resources and wealth. The Shah must have realized how much he sounded like Mosaddeq and immediately jabbed at his dead Prime

39 FRUS, 1964–1968, vol. XXII, Iran, Documents 240, 242.
40 FRUS, 1964–1968, vol. XXII, Iran, Document 252.
41 FRUS, 1964–1968, vol. XXII, Iran, Documents 242, 273, 277.
42 *Ettela'at*, 8, 9, 27 Azar 1346.
43 FRUS, 1964–1968, vol. XXII, Iran, Document 255.

Minister, "We are not addressing you from our bed or under our blanket ... but these are the heartfelt words of the Iranian people."[44]

As much as the Shah loathed Mosaddeq, he was taking on his mantle of fighting against vested oil corporations, even if it was for a different reason. But, whereas Mosaddeq was prepared to live without the Anglo-Iranian Oil Company, the Shah needed the Consortium, which provided more than 50% of the government's income, estimated at $800 million in 1968.[45] Without this income, the Shah's military designs, which almost defined him, could not be realized. Mosaddeq had had no such dreams.

The Shah got into the routine of succumbing to the temptation of acquiring more sophisticated weapons and financing ever more industrial projects, even when he did not have the resources. His fallback was putting pressure on the US government and the Consortium. A CIA's "Intelligence Memorandum" noted, "Since the mid-1960s, Iran has incurred generally increasing current account deficits. Although receipts rose from some $700 million in FY 1964 to $1.7 billion in FY 1970, imports increased even faster, and the current account deficit mounted from $45 million to $762 million."[46]

The same report contended that the growing current account deficit had placed periodic pressure on Iran's foreign exchange reserves since the mid-1960s, even though the country had growing recourse to foreign credits. "Even greater borrowing abroad—or a disastrous drop in reserves—was avoided only by obtaining special payments from the oil companies in the mid-1960s."[47]

According to a report by the Commercial Department of the British Embassy, by 1970 the Shah's arms purchases "on relatively short-term credit" created foreign exchange difficulties for the country.[48] Iran's external debt grew from $370 million in 1966 to over $2.9 billion in 1972. The debt service repayment increased from $55 million to $550 million during the same period. One of the main reasons for both these increases was the

44 *Ettela'at*, 23 Esfand 1346.

45 FRUS, 1964–1968, vol. XXII, Iran, Document 264.

46 FRUS, 1969–1976, vol. E–4, Documents on Iran and Iraq, 1969–1972. Document 165.

47 FRUS, 1969–1976, vol. E–4, Documents on Iran and Iraq, 1969–1972. Document 165.

48 FCO 17 1225. NEP 5/2.

rise in defense spending, which had grown to $1.95 billion or 28% of the budgeted expenditure in 1973–1974.[49]

Yet Iran's economic position had radically changed on 14 February 1971, when Iran and OPEC's five other Persian Gulf members obliged the oil companies to pay substantially more significant revenues through to 1975. The immediate revenue increase of almost 30% for the oil producers was primarily the work of the Shah's hard bargaining and the collective power of the Persian Gulf OPEC members, producing almost all of the region's oil.[50] However, from this date, the consecutive increases in Iran's oil revenues, while helping Iran's economy, also fueled Iran's military and developmental expenditure binge. The 1972 and 1973 leaps in Iran's oil revenues, partially spearheaded by the Shah, took the vicious cycle of re-armament to a stratospheric level.

With its exponentially growing oil income, the oil boom gave the Shah the impression that the gates of the "Great Civilization" were within reach. That illusion made the Shah even more oblivious that his country's infrastructure, human and managerial resources, and absorptive capacity remained limited in relation to his wants.

49 FCO 51 298. RR 6/7.

50 FRUS, 1969–1976, vol. E-4, Documents on Iran and Iraq, 1969–1972. Documents 115, 117.

19

The Curse and Blessing of The Royal Hand Instead of the Invisible Hand

From 1965 to 1968 the Shah's economic advisors came to grips with his economic mindset. The topic of guns versus butter, which had been going on at intervals since Ebtehaj and Amini, was quickly resolved in favor of the Shah's preference. By 1966, the executive, led by Hoveyda, and the legislative, led by 'Abdollah Riazi (Majles) and Ja'far Sharif-Emami (Senate), as well as all parliamentarians and government officials, were all of the same voice. The consensus was that military expenditures were not up for negotiation, and an unswerving support for its constant increase was a simple act of patriotism and nationalism.

The Shah had developed a reckless approach to government expenditure as a means of expediting economic growth. His economic lieutenants did not always concur with him, causing some irritation. Dissonances sometimes bubbled below the surface during the High Economic Council meetings presided over by the Shah. More substantial differences of opinion surfaced when drafting and presenting annual budgets or Five-Year Plans. With the passing of time, the gap between the Shah's economic goals and what the economists considered realistic grew even wider. At the same time, the Shah's economic advisors learnt to dissimulate and sugar-coat even their mildest counterarguments.

In coded language, economic experts expressed their disapproval, and the Shah would nonchalantly discard them and proceed by saying, "now it is up to you to adjust your reports to what I have just said."[1]

---

1 *Ettela'at*, 16 Aban 1351.

Thus, disagreements on economic policy were resolved not by measured theoretical discussions but by fiat. The Shah's well-educated neo-classical economists gave him sound advice, and he overruled them at his own peril.

FIGHTING INFLATION

From May 1965, the press reported on the rise in prices, especially for foodstuff, and even the senators began to mildly criticize the price increases.[2] During the 7 June 1965 meeting of the High Economic Council, Hoveyda reported to the Shah that, per his command, the government had come up with a series of measures to reduce the cost of living. The Shah, in turn, reminded Hoveyda that he had commanded (*dastur dadeh budam*) "some months ago" that he should "seriously look into reducing the cost of living", "neutralize the artificial and unfounded price increases", and report to him in the shortest delay.[3]

The ad hoc command to decrease certain prices in June 1965 was reminiscent of the order to increase the price of gasoline and kerosine in November 1964 and then partially reverse it in January 1965. What occurred between the Shah's order to reduce the cost of living in June 1965 and how Hoveyda and his team came up with the announced solutions is anyone's guess. The following hypothetical scenario is a privileged one.

At the Shah's command, Hoveyda summoned his economic team, including the Plan Organization and Central Bank economists, and passed on the Shah's message. Even though the free-marketeer problem-solvers may not have believed in the economic merit or feasibility of the mandate or its problematic economic consequences, they were politically obliged to make it happen. The Shah was demanding it. In the absence of an immediate optimal solution to the task set by the Shah, Hoveyda's economists had to settle with a second-best solution with shortcomings and adverse consequences of its own. The adverse consequences also had to be tackled within the constraints established by the Shah.

As soon as Hoveyda's economic team came up with "a solution" to price increases acceptable to the Shah, they knew their way out would

---

2 *Tehran Economist*, 15 Khordad 1344.

3 Nikpay (gerdavarandeh), *Surat jalesat-e showray-e' aliye eqtesad dar pishgah Shahanshah Aryamehr az Shahrivar 1343 ta 1345*. Surat jaleseh-e, 17 Khordad 1344, p. 95.

have negative repercussions. Hoveyda's team would soon learn that what seemed like rational solutions to the resulting problem caused by trying to resolve the first problem flagged by the Shah would again not be acceptable to the Shah. The economists would find themselves caught in an interminable vicious circle of economic paradoxes created by the Shah, with solutions acceptable to the Shah that would eventually take away from the developmental budget to fill the gaps created in the current budget, adversely affecting the rate of growth, one of the two primary economic objectives of the Shah.

During the 7 June 1965 meeting of the High Economic Council, Hoveyda enumerated the measures his government had devised. First, the government would enter negotiations with various guilds supplying foodstuff and encourage them to cut out the intermediaries to cut costs. Through the medium of producers and consumer cooperatives, directly connecting producers to consumers, the guilds were expected to supervise the decrease in the price of foodstuffs. Hoveyda added that since the guilds had become aware of the Shah's emphatic orders, they had come forward to ensure that prices would not increase.[4]

This first measure was more symbolic than anything else. The guild bosses, who were to ensure price reductions, were streetwise men wielding vested economic interests and powerful political connections. They knew full well that they could lower prices for a short period, then return to their old ways once the heat was off.

On 10 June 1965, Tehran's noteworthy guild representatives visited the Shah at Sa'dabad Palace and pledged their commitment to reducing prices. Two of the most prominent figures leading the group were the Rashidiyan brothers, Asadollah and Seyfollah, who had a long-standing and solid relationship with Tehran's guilds. Also present was Arbab Zeynolabeddin Tehrani, the powerful boss of Tehran's fruit, vegetable, and meat market (*meydan*). The two Rashidiyans and Arbab Zeynolabeddin were known for their instrumental role in toppling Mosaddeq on 19 August 1953.[5]

Hoveyda's second measure to decrease the cost of living involved reducing the prices of those goods and services over which the government had

4 Nikpay (gerdavarandeh), *Surat jalesat-e showray-e 'aliye eqtesad dar pishgah Shahanshah Aryamehr az Shahrivar 1343 ta 1345*. Surat jaleseh-e, 17 Khordad 1344, pp. 94–96.

5 *Ettela'at*, 20 Khordad 1344.

a monopoly. Hoveyda proposed reducing the price of petroleum by 2 rials per liter, electricity by an average of 20%, sugarloaf by 1 rial per kilogram, and sugar by 2 rials per kilogram. The Shah welcomed these measures and added that to improve the living conditions of Iranians, in the future, the government should further reduce the price of goods it had a monopoly over. In the same breath, he turned to Jamshid Amuzegar, his new Minister of Finance and commanded him to find a solution for the reduction in government revenues due to the decrease in the prices announced.[6]

The press reported a national euphoria in the few days following the announcement of price reductions. The price decreases were hailed as "the government's sweet policy".[7] Every day, news of plummeting prices spread like wildfire. In such reports, decreased prices and projected price reductions were getting confused, and the general impression imparted was that the Shah's edict had caused an overnight general decrease in prices. The seemingly tumbling price reductions applied to taxi and bus fares, housing, water, telephone, soda, sandwiches, pasteurized milk, chicken, eggs, medical expenses, and even *chelokabab*. However, before the end of the week, enthusiastic expectations subsided, and the press reported on price gaugers who were profiteering and warned that their permits could be suspended.[8]

At the 23 August 1965 meeting of the High Economic Council, Mehdi Sami'i, the Governor of the Central Bank reported to the Shah that price levels in June/July 1965 had decreased by 3% as compared to May/June.[9] However, the Central Bank's mid-year report (21 September 1965) indicated that the cost of living had increased by 1.2% as compared to September 1964.[10]

---

6 Nikpay (gerdavarandeh), *Surat jalesat-e showray-e 'aliye eqtesad dar pishgah Shahanshah Aryamehr, az Shahrivar 1343 ta 1345*. Surat jaleseh-e, 17 Khordad 1344, p. 95.

7 *Tehran Economist*, 29 Khordad 1344.

8 *Ettela'at*, 22–25, 27 Khordad 1344.

9 Gholamreza Nikpay (gerdavarandeh), *Surat jalesat-e showray-e 'aliye eqtesad dar pishgah Shahanshah Aryamehr, az Shahrivar 1343 ta 1345*. Surat jaleseh-e, 17 Khordad 1344, p. 95

10 *Ettela'at*, 21 Azar 1344.

HOVEYDA'S CRASH COURSE ON THE SHAH'S ECONOMICS

The reduction in the prices of sugar, sugarloaf, and gasoline alone had unexpectedly caused the government to lose 200 million tomans.[11] The Shah's edict to suddenly reduce the cost of living had caused a significant unplanned hole in the government budget. Hoveyda's economists knew that this was inevitable if they were bound to follow the Shah's orders. Politically averse to or incapable of taxing high-income groups to generate government revenue, the only solution was to transfer monies earmarked for developmental expenditures to current expenditures.

At the same High Economic Council that the Prime Minister proposed the government's solutions for realizing the Shah's command to "reduce the cost of living", an additional problem came to the fore. The woes of Hoveyda's economic team, faced with the problem of finding finances to pay for their own suggested solution, were further amplified. The Shah must have heard about the uneasiness of his economists with the deficit in the budget caused by the reduction in what was effectively indirect taxes on gasoline, sugar, sugar loaves, and electricity.

The Shah therefore interjected that "some have expressed anxiety over our treasury position." Jamshid Amuzegar explained that the government had to pay certain commitments made in the previous year, and the issue was resolved by drawing down on government reserves and borrowing from the Central Bank and the National Iranian Oil Company. However, he added, "Our main problem is that the army is demanding immediate payment of 52 million tomans for the purchase of spare parts."

The Shah replied, "If they have foreign commitments, payments should be made. Go discuss it with the army." The Shah also emphasized that "maximum savings and economies should take place in the expenditure of all governmental bodies and to implement this goal no measure of severity should be overlooked."[12] Now Hoveyda's economic team was faced with the additional problem of finding funds for the army's unplanned expenditure of 52 million tomans.

11 *Ettela'at*, 24 Khordad 1344.

12 Nikpay, G. (gerdavarandeh), *Surat jalesat-e showray-e' aliye eqtesad dar pishgah Shahanshah Aryamehr az Shahrivar 1343 ta 1345*. Surat jaleseh-e, 17 Khordad 1344, p. 96.

Hoveyda was learning about the red lines of negotiation and reasoning with the Shah. He mentioned that unless "revolutionary ways" were found to address the deficiency of funds, problems would be looming ahead. Asfia concurred and added that a significant problem with the revenue shortfall was that monies had to be transferred from developmental funds to fill the budget deficit. He warned that the budget deficit for the coming three years would be significant with the ongoing situation where government revenues fail to cover expenditures. Both men were trying to tell the Shah that his sudden decisions to impose additional costs on the tight budget would jeopardize the economy.

The Shah's response to their concerns reflected his indifference to the dangers of his erratic cost-imposing decisions. Instead of trying to understand their warning, he gave a lesson on where the government could find more money to finance the deficits he was causing. His five instructions on dealing with the deficits included obtaining foreign credit, encouraging foreign investment, imposing rigid economies on the ministries and government organizations, taking advantage of unexpected oil revenues, and promoting private domestic investment.[13] His prescriptions were broad and long-term instructions. None were magic potions.

The Shah's instructions on dealing with the deficit relied on what should be done, without any certainty that they would be achieved. He was telling his economists to accept on face value that the non-guaranteed measures he was proposing would resolve the government deficit. Hoveyda's economic team could not plan based on unknown factors such as "unexpected oil revenues". They were trained in positive economics, which meant an analysis based on facts at hand, relying on what had happened and what was happening in the Iranian economy. The Shah's economic recommendations did not respond to the immediate problems of his planners and economists. The government had to cope with the consequences of His Majesty's erratic economic orders by abandoning consistent economic policy and becoming accustomed to adjusting to ad hoc decisions.

The government economists had to get used to what seemed to be economically inconsistent instructions, such as the Shah's order to reduce the cost of living by reducing government revenues while paying unplanned extra military expenditures. With no margin of maneuver, contradictory

13 Gholamreza Nikpay (gerdavarandeh), *Surat jalesat-e showray-e 'aliye eqtesad dar pishgah Shahanshah Aryamehr az Shahrivar 1343 ta 1345*. Surat jaleseh-e, 17 Khordad 1344, p. 97.

economic instructions drove Shah's principled economists to the point of madness. The Shah could not respect an annual budget, let alone a Five-Year Plan. He believed in soft budgets[14] for his pet projects within the tight national budgets he had committed to.

The Shah's economists gradually realized that the Shah was not interested in their expert advice based on the workings of economic theory, causal relations, and trade-offs. Just as he had invented his own concept of "democracy" for Iran, he was now concocting his own appropriate economics for Iran. The Shah no longer needed economists and technocrats but functionaries who could best use their technical knowledge to improvise and dress up his ideas in economic terms and jargon, giving a seemingly scientific gloss to his erratic whims.

THE SHAH FALLS OUT WITH HIS ECONOMISTS

On 10 June 1965, three days after Hoveyda presented his government's solutions to price increases at the High Economic Council, he went to report to the Shah on the operational details of implementing his edict. Hoveyda reiterated that the government had relied on "economic principles" to prevent the undermining of social justice that may have been threatened by economic realities. Second, Hoveyda announced that in coming up with solutions for decreasing the cost of living and increasing purchasing power, the government had not lost sight of rapid economic growth and development.[15]

Hoveyda was telling the Shah that economics mattered, and it could not be bullied as politics could. His subtle message was that if economics is forced to act against its "natural laws" in one domain, it would wreak havoc in an adjacent domain. However, the government's entreaties about the importance of economic principles and not messing with them fell on deaf ears. The Shah was becoming convinced that he should dispense with the sermonizing economic counsel of his specialists and ministers, whom he believed may have been good accountants and bookkeepers but did not possess the necessary policy vision.

---

14 A soft budget constraint refers to situation when the unit for which a budget is established is incapable of keeping to its fixed budget, systematically surpassing it.
15 *Ettela'at*, 20 Khordad 1344.

On 17 June 1965, exactly a week after Hoveyda lectured the Shah about economic principles, His Majesty unburdened his thoughts on the matter. He expressed his candid opinion in a chat with Meyer, the American Ambassador, and Major General George Ekhardt, Chief of ARMISH/MAAG in Iran. The Shah "expressed his personal cynicism re economists, noting Iran has had sad experiences with experts who claim to know all answers and who disagree among themselves".

The Shah was satisfied with Iran's economic situation and that it had "now recovered from [the] handiwork [of] these economists". The Ambassador reported that the Shah was also "particularly pleased by what he considers [to be the] overwhelmingly favorable impact of his recent attack [on the] high-cost [of] living thru [through] setting prices for certain basic commodities".[16]

The Shah continued to voice his disapproval of Iranian economists. In his 2 March 1966 report, Meyer, the American Ambassador, commented "In recent conversations, [the] Shah has lashed out against foreign and domestic critics and pessimists who have been proved wrong by events. Privately, he has zeroed in on 'Harvard economists' (to which one may safely add Iranian economists trained in [the] US who are skeptical about growing Iranian commitments) and served blunt notice that [the] determination of what is best for Iran will henceforth be made by Iranians alone."[17]

In his annual 1966 report, the British Ambassador noted that "Despite warnings from his economic advisers of the serious foreign exchange difficulties likely to arise in 1968 and 1969, the Shah refused to cut back either on his rearmament or development programmes."[18] The Shah had concluded that his insight into the workings of the Iranian economy was greater than those of his Western-trained economists.

The disagreement between the Shah and his economists was not limited to differences in economic theory, analysis, and understanding but also revolved around the Shah's impromptu and irreversible decisions. One day (7 June 1965), he would call for maximum savings and threaten those who overlooked this axiom with severe consequences. Three months later (20 September 1965), the Shah would demand the immediate completion of a half-finished building earmarked for a teacher's training college in Hesarak (Karaj). Asfia had informed the Shah that the

16 FRUS, 1964–1968, vol. XXII, Iran, Document 90.
17 FRUS, 1964–1968, vol. XXII, Iran, Document 121.
18 FCO 17 351, EP 1/4.

initial cost projections of this unit would be exorbitantly high and asked to drop some of its lavish expenditures. The Shah's response was that, "For once, at least, a good building needs to be constructed." The Shah had then explained how important it was to train a group of leaders in a boarding school environment.[19] Asfia and some of the ministers not yet fully metamorphosed into functionaries must have walked out of that High Economic Council meeting wondering how strict savings and carefree profligacy could both be national priorities in the eyes of the Shah, either punishable or rewardable, depending on the Shah's mood.

YEARS OF ECONOMIC PROSPERITY, ALL THE SAME

By growth standards, 1966, 1967, and 1968 were excellent economic years. The rate of GDP growth continued to be an impressive 11.5%, 11.3%, and 14.4%, respectively, while income per capita increased from $267 to $281 and $320. Consumer prices or inflation registered –0.4% in 1966, followed by 1.6 in 1967 and 0.7% in 1968.[20]

Praise for Iran's economic performance between January 1966 and January 1969 was unanimous. In its National Intelligence Estimate of 10 January 1969, the CIA referred to Iran's more than 10% annual growth rate without inflation or any "serious balance of payments problems" or "a major increase in debt" during the past three years. It acknowledged that business confidence had been restored, and private sector investment increased rapidly, as did income per capita. The report characterized Iran's economic performance as "remarkable".[21]

Iran's economic boom was evident, and American, British, German, and Japanese firms were competing to gain a larger share of the Iranian market. On 13 June 1968, Walt Rostow, the theoretician and teacher of "Stages of Growth Theory", placed Iran on "that point on the development ladder where the 'take off' is just about finished".[22]

---

19 Nikpay (gerdavarandeh), *Surat jalesat-e showray-e 'aliye eqtesad dar pishgah Shahanshah Aryamehr, az Shahrivar 1343 ta 1345*. Surat jaleseh-e, 29 Shahrivar 1344, p. 154.
20 World Bank national accounts data, and OECD National Accounts data files.
21 FRUS, 1969–1976, vol. E–4, Documents on Iran and Iraq, 1969–1972. Document 1.
22 FRUS, 1964–1968, vol. XXII, Iran, Document 298.

The 1967–1968 Budget

On 19 February 1967, Hoveyda presented to the Majles the budget for the year 21 March 1967 to 20 March 1968. He reportedly spent 220 hours in various meetings over it. Once again, Iran had come a long way from months fraught with anxiety over reducing the deficit, late presentation to the Majles, and stressing over getting some budgetary help from the Americans. The 21.7 billion tomans ($2.9 billion) budget was presented a month before the 21 March deadline, and Hoveyda nonchalantly claimed that it had no deficit.

The two main objectives of the budget, with priority given to industrialization and maintaining high growth rates, followed by strengthening the country's military capabilities, remained the same as that of the 1965–1966 budget. The new budget ranked economic stability, maintaining the foreign trade balance, securing people's welfare, and high employment rates as its third to sixth priorities. Hoveyda hammered home Iran's self-reliance and independent national will, which went hand in hand with giving priority to Iran's defense capabilities. This budget allocated 80% of oil revenues to the Plan Organization for developmental projects.

Hoveyda's report to the Majles on Iran's economic performance in terms of high growth rates and almost zero inflation was upbeat, except for the country's balance of payments problems and the drain on Iran's foreign exchange reserves. He announced that expenditures on industrial projects would almost double and that of fuel and electricity would increase by more than double.

The novelty of this budget was threefold. First, its projected revenues included a provision entitled "the defense bond". This 300 million toman ($40 million) item was a traditional "war bond" but issued during peacetime. Hoveyda explained that by purchasing this bond, "people could voluntarily assist the government in maintaining the country's security." The Prime Minister did not speculate on what would happen to the budget deficit if people did not buy "the defense bond" voluntarily.

The other peculiarity of this budget was that cars and musical records were identified as luxury goods, and a consumption tax was imposed on them without specifying whether they were sales taxes, value-added taxes, or tariffs. In addition to those two sources of revenue, the government budgeted for the receipt of 15 million tomans ($2 million) from a consumption tax on home-assembled cars. Finally, there was a provision in the budget allowing the government to extend a loan of up to $13.8 million to Morocco to finance a dam.[23]

The Third Five-Year Plan in Hindsight

The Third Five-Year Plan (September 1962–March 1968) had to accommodate the unanticipated costs of implementing land reform and creating the literacy, health, and development corps. The budgetary support needed for the White Revolution "had not been included in the Third Plan". This factor, along with the growing oil revenues, caused several revisions to the Plan.[24]

Nevertheless, this Plan was much more successful than expected as it produced an average annual growth rate of 8.8% and surpassed its target of 6%. While during the first year and a half of the Plan, the economy was still in recession, total private actual investment ended up 75% higher than forecast, and actual total public expenditures ended up 45% higher than the original Plan. During the Third Plan, the industrial and mining sectors registered a 14% growth rate, while the agricultural sector grew by 3%. Foreign investment in Iranian industries jumped from 118 million tomans ($15.7 million) in early 1963 to 1.7 billion tomans ($234.8 million) in early 1966. By the end of the Third Five-Year Plan, Iran had a 40,000-kilometer road network compared to 25,000 in 1961. What made the Third Plan special was that substantial growth was attained with hardly any increase in the cost of living.[25]

The real engine of growth and the source of the Third Plan's unexpected success, however, remained government investment, fueled by rising oil revenues and its spillover into the private sector. Underutilized capacity during the recession period at the end of the Second Plan may have played a role in the planners' low-growth projects. During the Third Plan,

23 *Ettela'at*, 30 Bahman, 1 Esfand 1345. *Tehran Economist*, 12 Farvardin 1346.

24 H. Razavi and F. Vakil, *The Political Environment of Economic Planning in Iran, 1971–1983*, p. 26.

25 FRUS, 1969–1976, vol. E–4, Documents on Iran and Iraq, 1969–1972. Document 1. FCO 51 298. RR 6/7. *Tehran Economist*, 8 Bahman 1345. H. Razavi and F. Vakil, *The Political Environment of Economic Planning in Iran, 1971–1983*, p. 27, 29. Mehran, *Hadafha va Siyasathay-e Bank-e Markaziy-e Iran*, p. 65. Information in this paragraph is based on the above sources.

however, the actual average growth in annual oil revenues was around 14.8% compared to the approximately 10% projected.[26]

The rise in oil revenues was primarily due to external political factors in the region, and then the Shah's sound decisions to maximize Iran's benefits due to those exogenous circumstances. The economic fortunes of the Third Plan led the Shah to think of those results as the outcome of the soundness of his own economic decision-making capabilities, underplaying or ignoring the serendipitous conditions that had provided the circumstances for him to make those decisions.

The success of the Third Plan played a vital role in the Shah's further disregard for the counsel and the opinion of his economists. In 1961, the Shah had insisted on a minimum annual growth rate of 6% and even pushed for an 8% growth rate for the Third Plan. Both domestic and Western economists thought that even 6% was optimistic. At the end of the Third Plan, the Shah had been proven right, and the economists were wrong.

It subsequently became difficult to convince the Shah that it was to Iran's economic good fortune that the Syrians closed the Iraqi pipeline, and the 1967 oil embargo enabled Iran to raise its revenues. And, yes, he made the right economic decision for Iran's welfare not to join the Arab oil boycott. But these random, unpredictable, and exogenous events or positive economic shocks, were just exceptional episodes. Their recurrence could not be relied upon, and therefore they could not be factored in when drafting long-term economic plans.

The Third Plan, however, was less successful in achieving some of its main objectives. It did surpass its first objective of an average annual 6% growth rate. However, the Third Plan was less successful in obtaining its second and third official objectives: job creation and equitable distribution of income. The absence of specific quantitative benchmarks posed a serious problem for measuring the success of these two objectives. The literature on the outcomes of these two objectives remains largely mute. Razavi and Vakil observed that "matters of social justice never received proper attention". In its 1969 report on the Fourth Plan in Iran, the International Bank for Reconstruction and Development remarked that during the Third

26 FRUS, 1969–1976, vol. E-4, Documents on Iran and Iraq, 1969–1972. Document 165.

Plan, progress had "been slow" in terms of both job creation and a more equitable distribution of income.[27]

The same International Bank for Reconstruction and Development report observed that the average rate of per capita income increase during the Third Plan was "5% in real terms". This growth was "accompanied by an expansion of the middle class in the cities and a consolidation of income of the upper classes in Iranian society".[28] The rural-urban income gap widened during the Third Plan. The Plan Organization estimated that "the ratio of urban to rural income rose from 4.6:1 to 5.7:1 between 1959 and 1969.[29] This gap acted as a push factor encouraging greater rural-urban migration.

During the Third Plan, employment in the labor force fell short of Iran's growth in the labor force, while in the urban areas the migration rate outstripped the job creation rate. Iran's average annual population growth rate of 2.9% during the Third Plan, plus the average annual rate of rural-urban migration of some 7% over the 1960–1970 period, was becoming problematic in terms of generating employment in the urban area.[30]

During this period, the highly capital-intensive investments in modern manufacturing helped output, sales, and profits once the high initial machinery costs were met, but did not generate employment. Imported manufacturing machines were suited to export countries' relatively capital-abundant factor endowments. "The main labor absorptive industries in Iran, i.e., textiles and food processing, provided less than 10% of total employment."[31]

27 H. Razavi and F. Vakil, *The Political Environment of Economic Planning in Iran, 1971–1983*, p. 29. International Bank for Reconstruction and Development, *International Development Association. The Fourth Development Plan and the Economic Perspectives of Iran*. Vol. 1, February 25 1969; https://documents1.worldbank.org/curated/en/306061468050960546/pdf/multiopage.pdf (retrieved 14/8/2024).
28 International Bank for Reconstruction and Development International Development Association. *The Fourth Development Plan and the Economic Perspectives of Iran*. Vol. 1, February 25 1969, https://documents1.worldbank.org/curated/en/306061468050960546/pdf/multiopage.pdf (retrieved 14/8/2024).
29 FCO 51 298. RR 6/7.
30 Macrotrends, Iran Immigration Statistics, 1960–2024, https://www.macrotrends.net/global-metrics/countries/IRN/iran/immigration-statistics (retrieved 2024/8/16).
31 International Bank for Reconstruction and Development International Development Association. *The Fourth Development Plan and the Economic Perspectives of Iran*. Vol. 1, February 25 1969, https://documents1.worldbank.org/curated/en/306061468050960546/pdf/multiopage.pdf (retrieved 14/8/2024).

During the 15 January 1968 meeting of the High Economic Council, the Shah clarified his position on the question of appropriate technology for Iran and explicitly ruled on how to resolve the potential unemployment problem in the country. At this meeting, 'Ataollah Khosravani, the Minister of Labor, made a request to the Shah that labor-intensive projects should not be eliminated when priorities were being established for roadbuilding and other industrial activities. He argued that Tehran's new electricity-generating plant employed 69 workers. In comparison, a small electricity workshop in the past employed some 200 workers.[32] Khosravani advocated using labor-intensive technologies along with capital-intensive ones to avoid the increasing unemployment problem.

The Shah responded, "In those days, the country was underdeveloped, and now we need to see what the capital cities of advanced countries are saying instead of making decisions on our own. We cannot sacrifice the progress of the country for such matters." He argued that it did not make sense to "found inefficient and uncompetitive industries, just so that more people would be employed". The Shah's solution was that "if necessary, gather the unemployed in work camps, provide them with food and clothing and have them do some work." He added, "employ the same measures adopted in western European economies and the United States where they pay the unemployed but do not ruin their economies."[33] For the Shah, employing labor-intensive technology, which was an influential factor in making South Korea the economic giant that it became, was a sign of underdevelopment.

In terms of sectoral objectives of the Third Plan, the planned 4.1% increase in agriculture fell short of its target and reached only 3%. Finally, according to Razavi and Vakil, getting into the habit of making "arbitrary modification", as was the case in the Third Plan, "would become the nemesis of the regime during the Fifth Plan period".[34] The Third Plan began

32 G. Nikpay (gerdavarandeh), *Surat jalesat-e showray-e 'aliye eqtesad dar pishgah Shahanshah Aryamehr, az Shahrivar 1345 ta Shahrivar 1347*. Surat jaleseh-e, 25 Day 1346, p. 150.

33 G. Nikpay (gerdavarandeh), *Surat jalesat-e showray-e 'aliye eqtesad dar pishgah Shahanshah Aryamehr, az Shahrivar 1345 ta Shahrivar 1347*. Surat jaleseh-e, 25 Day 1346, p. 150. By August 1974, the Shah ordered his economists that "to the extent possible machines should replace workers." *Ettela'at*, 13 Mordad 1353.

34 H. Razavi and F. Vakil, *The Political Environment of Economic Planning in Iran, 1971–1983*, p. 30.

amid a deep recession, yet handed the development baton to the Fourth Plan amid an unprecedented boom.

Preparing the Fourth Five-Year Plan

The draft of the Fourth Plan was built upon the results of the Third Plan. During the Third Plan, Iran had transitioned to launching heavy industries. This period (1960–1968) could be loosely considered Iran's industrialization take-off. The private sector moved from producing household consumer goods, from soft drinks and biscuits to cooking oils and detergents, to more sophisticated household appliances, and finally, investment in motor vehicle production/assembly and processing, molding, and casting metal products. For its part, the government laid the foundations of the steel, machinery manufacturing, petrochemical, and aluminum industries.

Hoveyda and his team of ministers, planners, bankers, and economists gathered at Hotel Chalus on 13 September 1967 to review the details of the Fourth Five-Year Plan (1968–1973) prepared by Majidi's office at the Plan and Budget Organization. After two days of reworking the Plan, Hoveyda's team of sixteen travelled 8 kilometers to Nowshahr where they presented the Shah with the document for his consideration and examination.

Discussions on the Plan at Nowshahr were reported to have been "open and candid", and a smiling group picture of a relaxed Shah in casual summer garb standing with Hoveyda's economic lieutenants was published in the press.[35] The press reported that during all meetings, the "Shah consistently presented his views on all matters, and they were so logical and methodical that they determined the outcome of the Plan".[36] Nearly five months after the Nowshahr summit, on 6 February 1968, Hoveyda presented the Fourth Five-Year Plan (March 1968–March 1972) to the Majles. This plan, a detailed text of 601 pages and dubbed "Iran's grand plan", included four main objectives.[37]

The first two objectives of the Fourth Plan were similar to those of the Third Plan. They called for an increase in the growth rate, an equitable income distribution, and employment generation. The Fourth Plan,

35 *Ettela'at*, 23, 25 Shahrivar 1346.
36 *Tehran Economist*, 1 Mehr 1346.
37 *Khandaniha*, 21 Bahman 1346.

however, emphasized the importance of industry, the use of modern production techniques, and increasing productivity to attain higher growth rates. It also emphasized expanding social services in health, education, housing, workers' insurance, and rural development to reduce income inequalities.

The two new objectives of the Fourth Plan included reducing the country's economic dependence on foreign countries regarding agricultural and consumer goods and industrial inputs and final goods. The last overall objective of the Fourth Plan included an overhaul of the country's administrative system to provide improved administrative and managerial services in government ministries as well as bolstering and strengthening Iran's military capabilities.[38]

The Plan aimed at an average annual 9.4% GDP growth rate, which meant an increase of the per capita income from around $222 in 1968 to $310 by the end of the Fourth Five-Year Plan. The agricultural sector was to grow by 5% and the industrial sector by 15%. The Plan aimed to create 1 million new jobs over the five years. It was optimistically projected that by the end of the Fourth Plan, almost enough jobs (7,898,000) would be available for those actively seeking employment (7,959,000).

The Plan intended to add 14,500 hospital beds, 500 rural clinics, 275,000 housing units, 1,550 kilometers of railway, and 3,000,000 tons to the country's port capacities. The Plan made education compulsory and free for the first eight grades and aimed to increase school-goers by 1.5 million students. The government was to provide Abadan, Rasht, Esfahan, Esfahan, Shiraz, Tabriz, Mashhad, Kermanshah, and Gorgan with television coverage by the newly created state-owned National Iranian Television.[39] Finally, the Fourth Plan projected an 18.4% annual rate of increase in oil revenues, and based on those projections, it estimated $2.2 billion in external capital requirements.[40]

38 *Ettela'at*, 17 Bahman 1346. H. Razavi and F. Vakil, *The Political Environment of Economic Planning in Iran, 1971–1983*, p. 31. The information in the previous two paragraphs is based on the above sources.

39 *Ettela'at*, 17 Bahman 1346. *Khandaniha*, 21 Bahman 1346. The information in the previous two paragraphs is based on the above sources.

40 FCO 51 298. RR 6/7. International Bank for Reconstruction and Development International Development Association. *The Fourth Development Plan and the Economic Perspectives of Iran*. Vol. 1, February 25 1969, https://documents1.worldbank.org/curated/en/306061468050960546/pdf/multiopage.pdf (retrieved 14/8/2024). *Ettela'at*, 7 Shahrivar 1346.

The Extra-Economics of the Fourth Plan

The economic presentation of the Fourth Five-Year Plan by Hoveyda to the Majles on 6 February 1968 was overshadowed by two emerging ideological fixtures of post-coronation (26 October 1967) Pahlavism. First, Hoveyda referred to "some friends, especially foreign ones", who chided Iran for its "ambitious developmental plans". He argued that they were correct in their views, "but we too are quite right in what we have decided for ourselves". Reflecting the ideas of the Shah, whom he referred to as "patron" in French or "boss" in private, Hoveyda went on a passive-aggressive tirade against all those who dared to suggest that aspects of the Fourth Plan were unrealistic.[41]

Following the Shah's new "independent" posture, the Prime Minister put on a jingoistic nationalistic face. He announced that "we know best" how to run our economy and that the time has come to disregard foreigners. Hoveyda said, "Foreigners cannot open the doors that have been closed to us" and concluded, "We have to return to ourselves and our own spiritual and material sources and find in it the necessary forces to build our own future." As for foreigners, Hoveyda made the questionable claim that "we no longer rely on them, and if we have given some of them responsibilities in our country, they are here to serve us, and we are the decision-makers in Iran."[42]

Hoveyda, the Westernized modernist, was calling for a "return to ourselves", the details of which he knew not of, nor did he specify. As Ali Shari'ati would later say, "Which ourselves?" This ambiguous rhetoric of glorifying Iran's ancient past, which was partly responsible for its underdevelopment, was to become one of the pillars of Pahlavism. This contradictory mix of promoting an imaginary magnificent past as the key to joining the ranks of the most developed countries would be in full display during the October 1971 celebrations of 2,500 years of the Persian Empire.

Second, on the day that Hoveyda presented the Fourth Plan, a few members of the parliament had taken the floor before him. Asadollah Soleymani claimed that since a "just leader wears the crown" and constantly thinks about the progress and development of the country, Iran benefited from a high degree of God's protection like never before. Another

41 *Ettela'at*, 17 Bahman 1346.
42 *Ettela'at*, 17 Bahman 1346.

parliamentarian, Hoseyn Mo'ayeri, stated that "no country and people are graced with God's blessing as ours". He added that "due to Shahanshah Aryamehr's godsent being (*barekat-e vojud*) and because of his holy revolution, the new generation is benefitting from the good fortune of security, freedom, welfare, and justice."

Once Hoveyda finished presenting the broad contours of the Fourth Plan, he too began praising and eulogizing the Shah as the sole wise captain of the ship of state, one who single-handedly "guided the country through the darkest of tempests". Fawning over the Shah and flattering him on all occasions had become another common feature of Pahlavism. The powerful and rich engaged in this practice to maintain their positions, as did those who aspired to office and wealth. Such exaggerated exaltation by all around him only further swelled His Majesty's ballooning ego. In April 1969, the Shah would tell the elite gathered at the High Economic Council that "I think that I have never once erred in my assessment of this country's needs, capacities and potentials."[43]

43 Nikpay (gerdavarandeh), *Surat jalesat-e showray-e' aliye eqtesad dar pishgah Shahanshah Aryamehr, az Shahrivar 1347 ta Mordad 1348*. Surat jaleseh-e, 22 Ordibehesht 1348, p. 56.

20

Heavy Industries: The Soviet Dream-Makers Lead and the US Follows

In the 1950s and especially the 1960s, industrialization was deemed to be the key to less developed countries' economic development. It was also regarded as the sole vehicle for reducing reliance on the export of raw materials, diversification, and ending economic dependency on the import of industrial goods with higher value added. The pursuit of industrialization, through import protection, allowed home infant industries to flourish. This strategy implied specializing in their comparative disadvantage, namely the production of goods that could be obtained cheaper through imports. An import substitution industrialization (ISI) economic and trade policy meant substituting higher-cost home-manufactured and industrial goods for cheaper imports until that time when such home-produced goods could benefit from economies of scale, attain higher levels of productivity, and eventually lower costs equal to or cheaper than imports.

ISI was essentially the economic revolt of colonized, economically backward, and dependent Third World countries against the dominant comparative advantage trade theory. Pursuing the canon of the hegemonic neo-classical comparative advantage trade theory condemned less developed countries to remain non-industrial primary goods producers.

For ISI to work and industrialization to take root and perhaps produce internationally competitive goods, less developed countries needed to invest in industries. However, they also needed to possess a sizable domestic market with an increasing income, which would fuel demand for the newly manufactured goods. Industrialization needed an expanding domestic market and a growing middle class, which Iran's impressive growth rates between 1965 and 1968, thanks to the increasing revenues of its raw material, oil, provided. By 1966, however, industrialization had also become Iran's official economic policy and was mentioned as such in the Fourth Plan. The state, backed by its oil resources, was strongly invested in the industrialization drive.

The process of industrialization in Iran did not follow the step-by-step pattern found in early industrialized countries. If industrialization in advanced countries began with the production of producer goods, namely tools, machines, and factories, to first produce consumer goods such as textiles, food, beverages, and detergents and then produce durable consumer goods such as home appliances and cars, the Iranian process would be different.

Yet Iran's industrialization process resembled the pattern depicted by Albert Hirschman, who wrote, "ISI starts predominantly with the manufacture of finished consumer goods that were previously imported and then moves on, more or less rapidly and successfully, to the 'higher stages' of manufacture, that is, to intermediate goods and machinery, through backward linkage effects."[1] By backward linkage effects, Hirschman was referring to the pressure borne by an industry such as automobiles on another such as steel to produce its necessary inputs.

Almost all Iranian manufacturers followed that pattern and began their careers by importing products and then moved into production of the same products and brands with imported machinery. Two notable exceptions were Khalil Arjomand, the French-educated founder of Arj Industries, and Mostafa 'Alinasab, the founder of *Sanaye' Naftsuz* (Oil Burning Industries), whose formal education ended at a primary school certificate.[2] Arjomand and 'Alinasab were veritable innovators and entrepreneurs, developing and applying adapted home-bred technologies.

So, instead of beginning with producer goods, most importantly steel, and through forward linkages creating consumer durables, industrialization in Iran worked backward. The signing of contracts for building Iran's steel, chemical, and capital goods industries, and not their production,

1 A. O. Hirschman, "The Political Economy of Import-Substituting Industrialization in Latin America," *The Quarterly Journal of Economics*, Vol. 92, no. 1 (February 1968), pp. 1–32.

2 F. Shirinkam and I. Farjamniya, *Sargozasht-e panjah koneshgar-e eqtesadi-ye Iran*, Tehran: Farhang-e Saba, 1398, pp. 447–458 (on 'Alinasab) and pp. 167–174.

began in 1966, whereas the sporadic production of light and certain durable consumer goods had begun in 1952, and these were mass-produced between 1959 and 1963.

Iranian manufacturing remained an exercise in importing and imitating Western production processes. Machines and equipment embodying Western technology and using capital-intensive production methods implied using relatively less labor, Iran's abundant and relatively cheaper factor endowment. This kind of industrialization played an essential role in the country's inability to create enough jobs. Also, as Hirschman would say, this type of industrialization was "far less learning-intensive than had been the case for industrialization in Europe, North America, and Japan".[3]

The year 1966 marked the government's launch of three substantial heavy industries, preparing the ground for Iran's smooth Rostovian economic take-off. A new capitalist class was emerging in 1966–1967, establishing new and more sophisticated industrial ventures, which flourished under the state's patronage. By October 1969, Hoveyda referred to Rostow's theory of take-off and, using his charm, added that "under the judicious leadership of the Shah, spaceship Iran has now left the space of underdeveloped countries ... and it is now time to join the ranks of the developed countries as soon as possible."[4]

An essential feature of the government's industrialization drive was the creation of poles of growth. Iranian industries clustered around core industries, with linked ventures spreading away from them. These industries spun around themselves the necessary infrastructures and, most importantly, the housing and urban development required for the industrial units' workers, technicians, engineers, managers, and staff.

From the mid-1960s, Iran was dotted with industrial poles of growth outside Tehran, such as the steel mill in Esfahan, the Machinery Manufacturing Plant and Aluminum Plant in Arak, the Tractor and Machinery Manufacturing Plant in Tabriz, the petrochemical plants in the South (Bandar-e Shahpur, Abadan, and Khark), and the Pipe and Rolling Mill as well as the Navard Iran Company, both in Ahvaz.

3 A.O. Hirschman, "The Political Economy of Import-Substituting Industrialization in Latin America," pp. 1–32.

4 *Tehran Economist*, 26 Mehr 1348.

THE STEEL MILL DREAM

Since 1956, the Shah had been persistently looking for ways to get Western powers help Iran build a steel mill. An Iranian steel mill, the symbol of Iran's industrialization, had also been Reza Shah's dream. Negotiations, with ebbs and flows, were conducted with the Germans, the Americans and the British, but none yielded results.

Western governments were dubious about Iran's financial ability to fund such a project and the ability to repay loans on schedule. Most importantly, economists and decision-makers in the West were sold on the doctrine of comparative advantage, the pillar of neo-classical international trade. This dogmatic position was also repeated in developing countries like South Korea and Turkey in the early 1960s. Western administrations believed Iran should produce and export its comparative advantage, relatively cheap oil, and import its comparative disadvantage or relatively more expensive steel. For the Shah and Iranians, the steel mill symbolized national grandeur, dignity, and an economic necessity.

In April 1961, the Soviets signaled to Iran through their Ambassador, Nikolai Pegov, that they were ready "to help establish a steel plant in Iran" along with "every possible economic and technical aid without any preconditions whatsoever".[5] On 22 April 1961, the Shah held a press conference and without mentioning the Soviet proposal, confirmed that Sharif-Emami, the prime minister, was scheduled to pay a visit to Moscow.[6] Later when Amini replaced Sharif-Emami, he met with Pegov on 15 May 1961 and shut the door on the steel mill discussions by telling reporters that Iran had not received "any proposals of aid from the Soviet Union".[7]

It was not until 3 June 1961 that the news of the Soviet Union's offer to provide Iran with a steel mill became public. This critical information was relayed through the German news agency and not through Iranian authorities.[8] On 25 June, Ahmad Aramesh claimed that the Soviets had proposed the construction of a steel mill and that, had Sharif-Emami's government not fallen, the contract would have been signed during his official visit to the Soviet Union. Aramesh believed that Iran's "Western

5 FO 371/157624, EP 1102/13.
6 *Ettela'at*, 3, 4 Ordibehesht 1340.
7 *Ettela'at*, 26 Ordibehesht 1340.
8 *Ettela'at*, 13 Khordad 1340.

friends", implying the US, were opposed to the Soviets building a steel mill in Iran and, in fact, had sabotaged the deal.[9]

On the evening of 21 August 1961, Amini appeared on television and gave an hour-long interview on the economic situation. According to Sir Geoffrey Harrison, the British Ambassador to Iran, one of the highlights of Amini's comments was that "the building of a giant show-piece as a steel plant was out of the question at present."[10] Aware of the Shah's attachment to a steel mill, the Iranian press echoed a milder version of the Prime Minister's comments. One newspaper reported Amini as saying that the "steel mill issue was a complicated one" and that "We should not rush into this matter, set aside our ambitiousness and see if this project is really cost-effective and economically sound."[11] Another publication quoted Amini as saying, "Certain countries were ambitious and ruined their economies."[12]

Irrespective of how Amini's position on the steel mill issue was spun, it was clear that the Prime Minister was questioning, if not rejecting it. Amini and Ebtehaj's opposition to an Iranian steel mill was born from their firm belief in the validity of comparative advantage as an uncontestable pillar of international trade. With the departure of Amini and during the premiership of ʻAlam, the Shah embarked on a new foreign policy course. Intent on demonstrating his posture of independence in relation to CENTO and the US, the Shah adopted a calculated non-aligned economic position regarding the Soviet Union. This was an economic rapprochement that would eventually lead to a political one.

In July 1963, Alexey Sergeyev, the Soviet Vice-Minister of Finance, was in Tehran to sign an economic and technical cooperation agreement with Iran, for the construction of a dam on the Aras River, flowing between Iran and the Soviet Union. On 29 July 1963, he repeated the Soviet Union's interest in constructing a steel mill for Iran. The following day, Sergeyev met with ʻAlikhani, Iran's Minister of Economy to discuss among other things, the building of a steel mill.[13]

Some eight months later, in March 1964, Hasan-Ali Mansur, the new Prime Minister who fully supported the Shah on the need for a steel mill, made its realization one of his priorities. The responsibility of pursuing

9 *Ettelaʻat*, 6 Tir 1340.
10 FO 371/157629, EP 1111/34.
11 *Ettelaʻat*, 31 Mordad 1340.
12 *Tehran Economist*, 25 Shahrivar 1340.
13 *Ettelaʻat*, 8, 9 Mordad 1342. The previous two paragraphs are based on this source.

the steel mill project was entrusted to 'Alikhani's Ministry of Economy. 'Alikhani, in turn, appointed Amir-Ali Sheybani as general director of Iran's Steel Mill Company, a decision he ended up regretting.

On 9 April 1964, the press reported that Alfried Krupp, the German owner and director of Krupp Industries and the great-grandson of Alfred Krupp, was to come to Iran on 11 April. Krupp was to stay for twelve days, meeting with the Shah, the Prime Minister, the Minister of Economy, and several other state dignitaries. The purpose of his trip was to discuss the sale of industrial projects and the establishment of a steel industry in Iran.[14]

This was not the first time Krupp had shown interest in establishing a steel mill in Iran. Since 1939, there had been talks with Krupp, but negotiations had always fallen through. This time, too, rather mysteriously, Krupp and his team failed to show up, leaving the Iranians at the altar with no official explanation.

According to 'Alikhani, at the time, experts of IRSID, a French private research and consulting organization specializing in steel, had prepared a report for Iran's Steel Mill Company, identifying Esfahan as the ideal location for a steel mill with the capacity of approximately 500,000 tons a year. Esfahan was ideal since it had access to the three main inputs necessary for operating a steel mill. Zayandeh Rud, which ran through Esfahan, provided water, while the coal mines in Kerman and the iron ore fields in Bafq (Yazd) were nearby.

With the IRSID report on hand, the Iranian government had invited Krupp, with whom they had long been in contact, to come and finalize the steel deal. The Iranian Embassy in Bonn confirmed the arrival of the Krupp group. 'Alikhani informed the Shah of their arrival, and all was prepared for fruitful negotiations. On the day of their arrival, without any explanation, the Krupp group simply informed the Iranian authorities that they were not coming.[15] Mohammad Yeganeh, who was 'Alikhani's Deputy Minister for Industrial and Trade Development, maintained that it was upon US recommendation that Krupp desisted from becoming involved with Iran's steel mill project.[16]

---

14 *Ettela'at*, 20, 22 Farvardin 1343.

15 Ali-Naghi Alikhani, Iranian Oral History Collection, Harvard University, Transcript 12, Sequences, 218–219. The two previous paragraphs are based on this source.

16 Mohammad Yeganeh, Iranian Oral History Collection, Harvard University, Transcript 6, Sequence, 106.

On 31 August 1965, or some sixteen months after Krupp's sudden decision not to come to Iran, the Shah voiced his grievance to Armin Meyer, the US Ambassador to Iran. The Shah complained about how "Americans sabotaged [a] British-German steel mill project seven years ago" but made no mention of the Americans' supposed intervention in April 1964. Had the Shah believed that the Americans were responsible for Krupp's abrupt desistance, he would have probably mentioned it. In his same conversation with Meyer, a disappointed Shah even remembered how President Eisenhower had spoken to him "sneeringly of countries insisting on having 'damn steel mills'".[17] The West had turned down financing the Iranian steel mill because it was not "economically feasible".[18]

Upset at the turn of events in April 1964, the Shah went back to the drawing board and reconsidered the Soviet offer to help build a steel mill in Iran, which had been on the table since 1961. On 21 June 1965, or some fourteen months after Krupp snubbed Iran, the Shah, accompanied by the Queen, went on a thirteen-day historic official visit to the Soviet Union, his long-held ideological bogeyman. The Shah met with the leaders of the Soviet Union, visited Soviet industrial projects, dams, and electricity plants. In his speeches in the Soviet Union and after his return to Tehran, the Shah spoke fondly of his trip and expressed his admiration for the USSR's development and industrial achievements since his previous visit in 1956.[19]

On his return from Moscow (3 July 1965), the Soviet Ambassador to Iran, Grigory Zaitsev, revealed the essence of the Shah's discussions with the Soviet leaders. He announced that a team of ten Soviet experts would come to Iran in the next three weeks to study Iranian natural gas reserves and its export to the Soviet Union through a pipeline. In return for the export of gas, the Soviet Union would provide Iran with petrochemical and textile plants and a steel mill.[20] Some 90% of Iran's daily production of natural gas in 1965, which was about 32 million cubic meters, was burnt and wasted.[21]

On 4 July 1965, the Shah went to the High Economic Council and reported on the major themes of his gas-for-steel mill agreement with the

17 FRUS, 1964–1968, vol. XXII, Iran, Document 96.
18 Central Intelligence Agency, "The Character of Soviet and Eastern European Economic Involvement in Iran," July 1971, https://www.cia.gov/readingroom/docs/CIA-RDP85T00875R001700010077-5.pdf (retrieved 21/6/2024).
19 *Ettela'at*, 31 Khordad 1344; 1–12 Tir 1344.
20 *Ettela'at*, 13 Tir 1344.
21 *Ettela'at*, 19 Azar 1343; 1 Tir 1344.

Soviets. He called on 'Alikhani to quickly form a committee to negotiate the details with the arriving Soviet mission.[22] On 6 July 1965, Prime Minister Hoveyda confirmed the gist of Zaitsev's interview and reported that Iran was seriously exploring the purchase of a steel mill from the Soviet Union.[23]

On 3 September 1965, members of the Soviet mission arrived in Tehran. They met with the nine-man Iranian team headed by 'Alikhani and composed of Safi Asfia, Mohammad Yeganeh, Reza Niyazmand, Amir-Ali Sheybani, four others representing the NIOC, the Foreign Ministry, and two more from the Plan Organization.[24] German and French experts assisted the Iranian team on technical and engineering matters.

A month after the arrival of the Soviet technical and economic mission, the agreement for the construction of a steel mill by the Soviet Union in return for Iran's natural gas was signed on 5 October 1965. More specific issues, such as the pricing of the natural gas, the cost of the steel mill, the machine plant, the laying of the gas pipeline, and the conditions for the sale of Iranian natural gas, were to be quickly finalized before the deal was sent to the Iranian parliament for ratification.[25] Iranians enthusiastically welcomed the news of the steel mill agreement.

Two days after the signature of the agreement, 'Alikhani explained its colossal and momentous economic implications for the country. The steel mill project was to generate multiple and significant interconnected and associated ventures. The transportation of coal from Kerman and iron ore from Yazd to the steel mill location required constructing a railway line connecting Kashan, Kerman, and Yazd to Esfahan. The estimated cost of this approximately 1,300-kilometer rail project was between 360 to 370 million tomans ($48 to $49 million). The capacity of handling cargo, loading, and unloading at the railway station constructed next to the steel mill was projected to be twice the size of Iran's busiest port at Khorramshahr.

The pipeline, which stretched from Iran's southern oil fields to the north, exporting gas to the Soviet Union, also passed through Esfahan,

---

22 Nikpay (gerdavarandeh), *Surat jalesat-e showray-e 'aliye eqtesad dar pishgah Shahanshah Aryamehr, az Shahrivar 1343 ta 1345*, Surat jaleseh-e, 13 Tir 1344, pp. 104–105.

23 *Ettela'at*, 15 Tir 1344.

24 *Ettela'at*, 13, 14 Shahrivar 1334. Contrast the actual events with Mohammad Yeganeh's memory of the events in Mohammad Yeganeh, Iranian Oral History Collection, Harvard University, Transcript 6, Sequences 107–111.

25 *Ettela'at*, 14 Mehr 1344.

Qom, and Tehran, providing gas for the Esfahan steel mill. A contract was concluded with an Italian firm to construct a 75-thousand-kilowatt electrical plant. This 8.44 million toman ($1.12 million) plant provided electricity for the city of Esfahan, the industrial units situated around it, and the steel mill. The construction of the Shah Abbas Kabir Dam on Zayandeh Rud, costing some 300 to 350 million tomans ($40 to $46 million), was also to provide electricity and water for the steel mill.

The Esfahan steel mill, with an initial capacity of 600,000 tons per year, was to be completed in three years. Iranian authorities argued that the Soviet deal would save Iran 1.51 billion tomans ($200 million) per year, which it spent on the import of iron, metal pieces, and machines. The contract was also said to generate some 6,000 jobs in the steel and associated industrial, mineral, and services sectors. 'Alikhani was hopeful that the cost of producing Iranian iron and steel would be less than its CIF (cost, insurance, and freight) imported price, but he acknowledged that if that was not to be the case, Iran would indirectly subsidize its infant industries by charging home metal industries the CIF price for some years.[26]

In his 6 October 1965 speech to the members of Iran's legislative chambers, the Majles and the Senate, the Shah lauded the steel mill agreement and promised that Iran's petrochemical and aluminum industries would also be launched shortly.[27] In November 1965, the Shah told the American Ambassador to Iran that he believed that the steel mill had "become [a] dream of all Iranians, [a] dramatic symbol of Iran's movement into [the] modern world".[28]

Once the Iranian government ratified the final terms and details of the steel mill contract and its related projects, 'Alikhani left for Moscow on 27 December 1965. He headed a large mission, including Asfia, Yeganeh, and Sheybani, among others, to finalize specifics. After sixteen days of negotiations, the final deal on the steel mill, the gas pipeline, and the machinery manufacturing plant was signed in Moscow on 13 January 1966.

The Soviet Union agreed to extend 260 million rubles, or the equivalent of $286 million of credit, to Iran for twelve years. This sum was spent on

26 *Ettela'at*, 15 Mehr 1344; 1, 25 Day 1344. The information in the previous four paragraphs is based on these sources.

27 *Ettela'at*, 14 Mehr 1344.

28 FRUS, 1964–1968, vol. XXII, Iran, Document 108.

constructing the steel mill plant, part of the gas pipeline, and the machine plant. The Soviet Union pledged to provide Iran with all the necessary factories, machinery, and tools to construct the steel mill and the machinery and tools to extract the iron ore and coal needed for the operation. It also accepted full responsibility for providing the technical know-how and manpower training to construct and operate the steel mill. Iran, in turn, was responsible for extracting and providing lime and water, electricity, and transportation facilities.

A pivotal aspect of the Iran–Soviet deal was the export of Iranian gas. Iran agreed to transport gas through the 1,300-kilometer pipeline from South Iran's oil and gas fields to the town of Astara on the Soviet border for fifteen years, renewable for a further ten years. The initial volume of gas exported was about 6 billion cubic meters per year and would increase to 10 billion within five years. The gas price at Astara agreed between the two parties was $6.60 per 1,000 cubic meters, subject to adjustment given the variations in world prices. The contract also stipulated that 5 billion cubic meters of gas per year would be allocated to Iran's domestic use.

The gas pipeline project completed in October 1970 was divided into two parts. The stretch from the Southern oil fields to Saveh was Iran's responsibility, whereas the segment from Saveh to Astara was that of the Soviets. The pipes and telecommunication system to operationalize the transfer of gas was Iran's responsibility. The monies received by Iran from the sale of gas were earmarked for the purchase of machines, industrial complexes, and technical services from the Soviet Union, as well as repayment of the loans obtained from that country.

The total cost of the gas pipeline was estimated at $410–420 million by 'Alikhani and $700 million by US and British sources. Once the pipeline construction was underway, Iran obtained credit from Western countries to finance the project. The UK and France each contributed $72 million and $70 million, respectively, followed by Japan ($33 million), the US ($14 million), and the Netherlands ($1 million).

In a senate hearing, Senator Ali Vakili mentioned that the total cost of the steel mill and the machine factory was $700 million. Some $70–100 million of the costs were to be paid through the credits provided by the Soviets. With all its adjacent, complementary, and associated investments and ventures, the steel mill project was said to create some 20,000 jobs. The Majles ratified the steel mill contract and all its associated projects on

13 February 1966. The Senate followed suit on 23 February 1966.[29] Already by September 1966, some 1,200 workers were working under Soviet and Iranian supervision in the coal mines of Zarand, Kerman, which supplied the steel mill's coal input.[30]

On 13 March 1968, the Shah and the Queen flew by helicopter from Esfahan airport to the steel mill in Lanjan, some 45 kilometers southwest of Esfahan, where a large entourage of ministers and political, economic, and military dignitaries awaited them. At 10 a.m., they broke ground for Iran's steel mill. The Queen threw a few gold coins into the massive foundation of the blast furnace on which cement was subsequently poured, and the Shah placed a golden plate on the edge of where the blast furnace was to be built.

In their welcoming reports, both 'Alikhani, the Minister of Economy, and Amir-Ali Sheybani, general director of Iran's Steel Mill Company, acknowledged that Iran's steel mill was the brainchild of the Shah's visionary leadership and that the Shah had consented that the plant be called the Aryamehr Steel Mill. The Shah's speech on this occasion was unrelated to the steel mill. Instead, he took the opportunity to repeat his old self-glorifying notions that after the White Revolution, the royal "we" had put an end to "underdevelopment and reaction, inequality among people, and exploitation of man by man".[31]

The Shah was convinced that his White Revolution had resolved the contradiction between labor and capital, and had once and for all, laid to rest the notion of exploitation through profit sharing in Iranian industries. In so many words, the Shah viewed himself as the anti-communist political leader who had achieved what Marx had promised without communism.

In a speech at the Majles on 2 March 1966, the Shah claimed that "if by chance (*ahyanan*) an environment of hate and division existed between workers and employers in the past, and workers felt exploited ... now [after the White Revolution] that environment had dissipated." The Shah believed that "the profit-sharing law in factories has resulted in an environment of friendship (*ons*) and humaneness (*ensani*) and the disappearance

29 *Ettela'at,* 23, 27 Day 1344; 16 Bahman 1344; 4 Esfand 1344; 16 Khordad 1345. Central Intelligence Agency, "The Character of Soviet and Eastern European Economic Involvement in Iran," July 1971, https://www.cia.gov/readingroom/docs/CIA-RDP85T00875R001700010077-5.pdf (retrieved 21/6/2024). FCO 51 298. RR 6/7. The information in the previous six paragraphs is based on these sources.

30 *Ettela'at,* 24 Shahrivar 1345.

31 *Ettela'at,* 23 Esfand 1346.

of that feeling of exploitation. Now, the worker feels like a participant and shareholder in the factory's profits."[32]

In June 1968, a new economic contract was drawn up between Iran and the Soviet Union, increasing the production capacity of the Esfahan steel mill from 600,000 tons per year to 1.2 million tons.[33] The steel mill's blast furnace was completed in 1970. The USSR received its first delivery of Iranian natural gas in the same year. While in 1964, there were about 150 Soviet technicians in Iran, mainly working on the joint Soviet–Iran Aras Dam project, by 1967, this number had increased to 900, and by 1970, there were about 1,600 Soviet technicians in Iran, about two-thirds of them working on the steel mill.[34] The steel mill began production in the summer of 1972 and was officially inaugurated in March 1973.

An essential component of the Soviet deal in terms of Iran's heavy industry aspirations was the Arak industrial machinery and equipment manufacturing plant. The Arak Machinery Manufacturing plant, was officially inaugurated by the Shah on 19 September 1972, producing 8,000 tons of industrial equipment, annually. It planned to reach an annual capacity of 30,000 tons in some four years. It produced fifty-six different types of heavy machinery, including cranes, boilers, water tanks, accumulators, bridges, electricity pylons, spare parts for sugar and cement factories, and finally, agricultural tools and implements.

The total cost of this plant was $110 million, of which $23 million was to be covered by Soviet credit. The plant employed 1,270 workers, technicians, and engineers at its inception. A vocational center was constructed adjacent to the plant where 309 workers were trained in twenty different specialties since 1970, and another group of 505 new trainees were instructed by Soviet and Iranian engineers and technicians to run the plant.[35]

32 *Ettela'at*, 11 Esfand 1344.

33 *Ettela'at*, 2 Tir 1347.

34 Central Intelligence Agency, "The Character of Soviet and Eastern European Economic Involvement in Iran," July 1971, https://www.cia.gov/readingroom/docs/CIA-RDP85T00875R001700010077-5.pdf (retrieved 21/6/2024).

35 *Ettela'at*, 28, 29 Shahrivar 1351.

THE TABRIZ MACHINERY MANUFACTURING PLANT

On 29 January 1966, about a week after signing the Soviet–Iranian steel mill-for-gas contract in Moscow, Iran concluded an important industrial deal with Czechoslovakia in Tehran. Czechoslovakia extended $15 million of credit to Iran over ten years at an interest rate of 2.5%. With this sum, Iran would purchase a Czech foundry plant that produced machinery, lathes, diesel engines, pumps, and electric motors. The capacity of this plant, located in Tabriz, was planned to be 5,000 tons per year. Associated factories using the output of the Tabriz Machinery Manufacturing factory were established around this complex to produce various precision tools.

The Czech Tabriz Machinery Manufacturing factory was to be ready for the production of machineries before the Soviet Arak Machinery Manufacturing plant and the steel mill, and therefore it had to import its inputs until the time that the steel mill was ready for production.[36] Four months later, in May 1966, Czechoslovakia and Iran signed a second contract to establish a vocational and management center. Czech engineers and specialists were to train some 700 to 1,000 technicians, mechanics, and skilled workers, as well as the managerial personnel, necessary for operating the Machinery Manufacturing factory during its first year.[37]

Less than three months after signing the contract for the vocational center, Hoveyda went to Tabriz and broke ground for it. This school's first task was to provide three years of advanced technical training for the 200 high school graduates recruited. The school would also prepare semi-skilled and skilled workers for various tasks at the factory. These workers with six to nine classes of education would receive anywhere from three months to two and a half years of training. The center was to train some 2,000 workers and technicians for the Machinery Manufacturing factory, which was to begin production in 1969.[38]

On 11 September 1971, the Shah and the deputy prime minister of Czechoslovakia inaugurated the Tabriz Machinery Manufacturing (*Machin Sazi-ye Tabriz)* plant. The factory had a capacity of 10,000 tons per year and employed 1,294 workers, according to Ansari, the Minister of Economy, and 1,350 workers, according to the workers' representative. Its final cost was 560 million tomans (some $74.7 million), and plans to expand

36 *Ettela'at*, 28 Day, 6, 9, 10 Bahman 1344; 10, 23 Khordad 1345.

37 *Ettela'at*, 10 Khordad 1346.

38 *Ettela'at*, 1, 4 Shahrivar 1346.

the existing plant at the estimated additional cost of 500 million tomans were already underway.[39]

PETROCHEMICALS

The Shiraz Fertilizer plant, inaugurated in October 1963, was the first step to developing a petrochemical industry. Iran had all the necessary natural endowments for such an industry, with numerous forward linkages. In an interview on 24 February 1964, Asfia, the director general of the Plan Organization, spoke of the petrochemical industry as a "mother industry" comparable to the steel industry. He pointed out that a considerable market existed for its outputs, which formed the basic ingredients of the soap, tire, plastic, and textile industries.[40]

On 29 November 1964, the five-man board of directors of the National Petrochemical Industries Company (*Sherkat Meli-ye Sanaye' Petrochimi*), or NPIC, was announced. Manuchehr Eqbal, the chairman of the board of the National Iranian Oil Company, headed the board, while Baqer Mostowfi was appointed director general of the National Petrochemical Industries Company.[41] The Shah was impatient to find prospective industrial partners. At the High Economic Council meeting of 7 June 1965, he pressed his Minister of Economy to get the ball moving as quickly as possible on this bill.[42]

On 11 July 1965, the Iranian Majles ratified the Law on the Development of Petrochemical Industries. This Law enabled the National Petrochemical Industries to enter agreements with technically and financially eligible Iranian and foreign concerns to produce, transport, sell, and distribute petrochemical goods derived from natural gas and other carbohydrates. The law stipulated that Iran's share in partnerships with foreign entities could not be less than 50%.[43]

---

39 *Ettela'at*, 20, 21 Shahrivar 1351.

40 *Ettela'at*, 6 Esfand 1342. *Tehran Economist*, 10 Esfand 1342.

41 *Ettela'at*, 7 Azar 1343.

42 Nikpay (gerdavarandeh), *Surat jalesat-e showray-e 'aliye eqtesad dar pishgah Shahanshah Aryamehr, az Shahrivar 1343 ta 1345*, Surat jaleseh-e, 17 Khordad 1344, p. 91.

43 Majles showray-e melli, Majmu'ehe Qavanin-e dowreh-e Qanungozariy-e bizsto yekkom, 20 Tir 1344; *Ettela'at*, 20 Tir 1344.

On 24 October 1965, Manuchehr Eqbal and Baqer Mostowfi signed the draft of an important contract with the managing director of the Allied Chemical Corporation. At the time, Allied Chemical was the largest chemical company in the United States, specializing in petrochemicals, nylons, and plastics. The finalized contract was signed two months later.

This first petrochemical contract was a 50-50 partnership with an initial $100 million investment for constructing an ammonia and a sulfur factory, followed by producing methanol, melamine, formaldehyde, and polyethylene. The new petrochemical complex was built in Bandar-e Shahpur, in the south of Iran. The new installation initially produced 1,000 tons of ammonia per day, which would then be used to produce fertilizers. A new pipeline from Masjed Soleyman would bring gas to the petrochemical complex and produce 1,000 tons of sulfur and 300 to 400 tons of sulfuric acid daily.[44]

The petrochemical contracts with US partners snowballed, as did the steel, machinery, and tractor manufacturing contracts with the Soviet bloc. On 14 February 1966, Eqbal and Mostowfi signed two other substantial contracts with two American giants. The first was with the world-renowned American tire company, B. F. Goodrich, which had been present in Iran since 1958 and had dealings and partnerships with the Pahlavi Foundation. The second was with John. D. Rockefeller's Indiana Standard, the second-largest American oil company at the beginning of the 1950s.

Iran's partnership with B. F. Goodrich involved constructing a petrochemical plant that produced 20,000 tons per year of polyvinyl chloride (PVC) plastic goods, 24,000 tons per year of caustic soda, and 10,000 tons per annum of detergents. The cost of the new petrochemical plant, close to the Abadan refinery, was $28 million. Iran obtained a $13.1 million loan from the US Export–Import Bank. B. F. Goodrich owned 26% of the joint company, while Iran held 74% of the shares.

Iran signed a second contract with AMOCO, the American Oil Company, an Indiana Standard chemical company. This 50-50 partnership was to build a $52 million petrochemical plant on Khark Island. This plant was to produce 500 tons of sulfur and 450 tons of liquid gas daily. Whereas the products of the Abadan petrochemical plant, in partnership

44 *Ettela'at*, 3, 4 Aban 1344.

with B. F. Goodrich, were primarily for the domestic market, the output of the Khark plant was for export.[45]

After three years and some eight months, the Shah inaugurated the Abadan petrochemical project on 5 November 1969. The output of the Abadan plant, which was to provide for the domestic market, now fell short of the country's demand, and projects were already underway to expand its capacity. An affiliate of the Japanese Mitsubishi Company constructed the Khark petrochemical plant. The Shah inaugurated it on 6 November 1969.[46]

THE ARAK ALUMINUM PLANT

After his return from the May 1965 tour of Brazil, Argentina, and Canada, with a one-day stopover in New York, the Shah was keen to see Iran's aluminum industry launched. At the High Economic Council meeting of 7 June 1965, 'Alikhani informed the Shah that negotiations were underway with the US Reynolds Metal Company, and the Shah hurried to say that if such negotiations did not come to a quick conclusion, 'Alikhani should approach the Indian government.[47]

On 8 June 1966, a three-way contract was signed in Tehran between Iran, Reynolds Metal Company, and Pakistan to form a joint aluminum company. Eighteen months later (4 December 1967), the Iran Aluminum Corporation (IRALCO), with a capital of $46 million, was registered. Iran's aluminum plant, with a capacity of 50,000 tons per year, was to be built in Arak, right next to the Soviet-built Arak Machinery Manufacturing plant.

Some 20,000 tons of this output were earmarked for the Iranian and Pakistani markets, and the remaining 30,000 tons were to be exported. Iran held 70% of the shares, Reynolds Metal Company owned 25%, and Pakistan the remaining 5%.[48] Iran signed a contract with Australia to import more than 100,000 tons of alumina per year for the plant's input. The Arak aluminum plant, with a capacity of 45,000 tons per year and 705 laborers, technicians, and office staff, was inaugurated by the Shah on

45 *Ettela'at*, 25, 26 Bahman 1344. *Talash*, Mordad, Bahman 1345; Farvardin 1346.
46 *Ettela'at*, 14, 15 Aban 1348.
47 Nikpay (gerdavarandeh), *Surat jalesat-e showray-e 'aliye eqtesad dar pishgah Shahanshah Aryamehr, az Shahrivar 1343 ta 1345*, pp. 92–93.
48 *Ettela'at*, 17 Mordad 1345, 13 Azar 1346.

19 September 1972. The plant was able to increase output to 70,000 tons per annum in five years and finally reach 90,000 tons. The final cost of the plant was $50 million, with Germany covering $29 million with a loan.[49]

TABRIZ TRACTOR COMPANY AND AHVAZ PIPE ROLLING MILL

The year 1966 saw Iran warming up to the Soviet Bloc Comecon (Council for Mutual Economic Assistance) countries. The Shah traveled to Romania in May 1966 and visited the flagship Universal Tractor Company at Brașov on 30 May 1966. After industrial contracts with the Soviet Union and Czechoslovakia, on 8 August 1966, Iran signed an important commercial and industrial letter of understanding with Romania in Tehran. The commercial aspect of this agreement stipulated that for the next five years, Romania would export 3,000 tractors and 2,000 plows per year to Iran. The first batch of 500 tractors was expected to arrive in September 1966.

The Romanian government also constructed a tractor factory in Tabriz to assemble and produce universal tractors. Iranian sources suggested that both ventures were financed by selling oil to Romania. The contract was finalized between the representatives of the two countries in Tehran on 27 September 1967 in the presence of Gholamhoseyn Fuladiyoun, the director general of the Iran Tractor Company. The first phase of the factory was said to cost $120 million. The Iranian Tractor Manufacturing Company (*Sherkat-e traktor sazi-ye Iran*) was registered in Tabriz on 16 May 1968. On 11 September 1972, the Shah visited the Tabriz tractor factory, which employed 550 workers. The factory assembled 5,000 tractors per year.[50]

On 3 December 1967, the Shah inaugurated the pipe rolling mill at Ahvaz, which consisted of two factories. This complex, which belonged to the National Iranian Oil Company, was designed by and contracted to Los Angeles-based Torrance Machinery and Engineering. The plant's construction was subcontracted to Iranian firms, and Cyrus Arjomand's

49 FCO 51 298. RR 6/7. *Ettela'at*, 28, 29 Shahrivar 1351.

50 *Ettela'at*, 17, 19 Mordad 1345; 5 Mehr 1346; 21 Shahrivar 1351. Central Intelligence Agency, "The Character of Soviet and Eastern European Economic Involvement in Iran", July 1971, https://www.cia.gov/readingroom/docs/CIA-RDP85T00875R001700010077-5.pdf (retrieved 21/6/2024). All information in the previous two paragraphs is based on this source.

factory constructed the huge metal frames. The plants were ready for operation in a record nine months.

The two plants processed flat strips of steel into pipes of varying diameters. The flat steel strips were imported from France, Germany, Japan, and England and transported by rail from Bandar Shahpur to the complex. The necessary 4-kilometer rail extension connecting the complex to the Bandar Shahpur–Ahvaz railway was also a part of this project. The bigger plant specialized in pipes that were 18 to 48 inches in diameter, while the smaller plant produced 6-to-16-inch pipes. The output of this plant was to provide all the pipes necessary for the gas pipeline exporting Iranian gas from Aghajari to Astara and its extensions inside Iran.[51]

ARYAMEHR UNIVERSITY: TRAINING CADRES FOR INDUSTRIALIZATION

On 2 November 1965, the Shah issued a decree announcing the founding of the "Aryamehr Industrial University" to begin operation in September 1966. In his edict, the Shah stated that "advances in economic development and industrialization of the country necessitated the preparation of a labor force commensurate with the needs of Iran's future industrial requirements".[52] The Shah announced that he would personally take on the custodianship (*toliyat*) of this new learning establishment and appointed Mohammad-Ali Mojtahedi as his vice-custodian and director of the university.

Mojtahedi had masterfully directed Alborz, Tehran's prestigious and most highly competitive high school, and then Tehran's Polytechnic University. He was a most capable educator and administrator, highly respected and loved by his students, some of whom were members of Hoveyda's government. Mojtahedi was known for his fairness, frankness, honesty, and discipline. The Shah had chosen the ideal person for the job and gave him a free hand in creating and running Aryamehr University.

Aryamehr Industrial University was intended as a private, tuition-based establishment of higher education. It was to initially begin with departments of mechanical engineering, electrical engineering, sciences, iron smelting, and chemical engineering. The duration of study for the degrees

51 *Ettela'at*, 12, 13, 14, 19 Azar 1346.
52 *Ettela'at*, 11 Aban 1344.

offered was four to five years. The students who ranked first in the entrance exam of each department were exempt from paying tuition.

This new technical institution, named after the Shah's new title, bestowed upon him by the two legislative houses on 15 September 1965, was tasked to produce the skilled manpower necessary for operating, managing, and directing Iran's new heavy industries. The Shah also expected it to be a technological research center comparable to the most advanced institutions in the world. The Shah wanted an institution comparable to the Massachusetts Institute of Technology (MIT) and decreed that the best Iranian students graduating from top universities should be employed to teach at this new university.

Ironically, the news of the Shah's decree ordering (*moqarar farmudim*) the creation of Aryamehr University came on the very same day that some of the best Iranian graduates from top engineering and technical Western universities were being sentenced to death and long prison terms, up to life, by a military tribunal on trumped-up charges of plotting to assassinate the Shah.[53]

The Shah followed the developments at Aryamehr University closely and received regular fortnightly reports from Mojtahedi.[54] The entrance exams for six different technical degrees, including industrial management, were held on 25 and 26 June 1966. With the Shah's carte blanche and the sincere help of his old Alborz students and friends, Mojtahedi finished the construction of Aryamehr University in six months and opened its doors to 480 students.[55]

On 7 October 1966, accompanied by Queen Farah, the Shah visited the facilities at Aryamehr University and inspected the classes, laboratories, workshops, and canteen. Less than a month later, the Shah donned the academic gown and regalia and officially inaugurated Aryamehr Industrial University. The Shah and the Queen later joined the students at their dining room, sat among them, and ate their *morgh polo* (rice and chicken) and soup.[56]

---

53 For an account of the attempt on the Shah's life see: Ali Rahnema, *The Rise of Modern Despotism*, London: Oneworld, 2021, pp. 441–445.

54 Mohammad-Ali Modjtahedi, Iranian Oral History Collection, Harvard University, Transcript 5, Sequence 69.

55 Mohammad-Ali Modjtahedi, Iranian Oral History Collection, Transcript 6, Sequence 80, *Ettela'at*, 5 Ordibehesht 1345.

56 *Ettela'at*, 16 Mehr 1345, 11, 12 Aban 1345.

21

Iran's New Industrial Titans

During 'Alikhani's six-and-a-half-year tenure (1963–1969), Iran pursued a steady industrial policy, emphasizing manufacturing. Aside from direct government investment in heavy industries, such as steel, petrochemicals, machinery manufacturing, and aluminum, the government intervened in the private sector to encourage the development and growth of light and heavy industries. It also imposed controls to modernize and transform production processes, structures, and organizations with an eye to increasing productivity. 'Alikhani announced that "contrary to the past, we will not focus only on consumer goods, but to the extent of our capabilities, we will try and produce machinery and tools at home."[1] For both the Shah and 'Alikhani, home production of intermediary and final goods became a symbol of Iran's growing sense of economic independence, maturity, and nationalism.

As Iranian industrialists were moving beyond the production of simple light industries, such as textiles, beverages, sugar, biscuits, detergents, and cooking oil, into more advanced ones, such as home electronics, home appliances, and motor vehicles, 'Alikhani, pursued a policy of cajoling and even compelling Iranian industrialists to produce as many of their components as possible at home.

PUSHING FOR "MADE IN IRAN"

An integral part of Iran's industrial policy became the home production of not only components of light industrial goods but also the machines and

1 *Ettela'at*, 4 Esfand 1343.

tools used in their production. 'Alikhani encouraged the development of machine-tool industries in Iran and argued that they would not only generate employment but gradually free Iran from spending foreign exchange on the import of such goods.[2] The promotion of industries producing lathes, power saws, presses and drilling, milling and grinding machines, or basic machine tools, became a national priority.

The emphasis on increasing the home-produced components and parts of assembled manufactured goods picked up speed as importers of radio and television sets switched to varying degrees of assembly at home and called their goods "made in Iran". Habibollah Sabet's Iran Radio and Television Company was the first to move from importing RCA (US) and Hitachi (Japanese) radio and television sets to producing them at home.

In 1961, the Iran Radio Elektrik Company began producing/assembling eight models of "made in Iran" Philips radios, including transistor radios. Haj Mohammad-Taqi Barkhordar's Pars Elektrik Company, registered in February 1960, had the franchise for Toshiba (Japanese) and Schaub Lorenz (German) radios and televisions and was their importer.[3] By 1964 and 1965, he too was producing/assembling Pars Toshiba radio sets and Schaub Lorenz television sets. Other Iranian products included the Arj company's Arj Grandin transistor radio, which also appeared in 1964, and Shahab radios. Whereas in 1962, the number of "made in Iran" radio and television sets stood respectively at 8,580 and 600 units, in 1966, output jumped to 180,958 and 20,130, respectively.[4]

In December 1964, the Ministry of Economy issued a new set of directives regulating the establishment of companies and factories producing or assembling radio and television sets in Iran. This was a prelude to what would be applied to all manufacturing units. The new directive stipulated that within four years the lion's share of components and parts of radio and television sets had to be produced at home. As soon as home production of each component was attained, the import of such components would be prohibited to support home infant industries.

'Alikhani was becoming impatient with the small value added at home. He wished to minimize assembling and pushed for totally integrated home production. It no longer sufficed, for example, that frames of radios

2 *Ettela'at*, 4 Esfand 1343.
3 *Tehran Economist*, 13 Farvardin 1339.
4 Ali-Asghar Sa'edi, Fereydoun Shirinkam, *Zendegi va karnameh-e haj Mohammad-Taqi Barkhordar*, Tehran: Gam-e No, 1396, p. 192.

and televisions were produced at home, while all other technologically advanced components were imported as detached goods, free from import duties. He believed the time had come for Iranian producers to shift into a more advanced form of assembling.

To prevent the mushrooming of inefficient companies, the directive imposed strict conditions on the industrialists applying for permits to produce and assemble radios and televisions. The directive threatened producers with closure if they failed to abide by the detailed year-by-year agenda of producing components at home. Industrialists were obliged to begin production six months after they had been issued their licenses. In case of a delay, their licenses were revoked. The schedule set by the Ministry of Economy was precise. For example, by March 1966, the third of the four-year deadlines, assemblers were obliged to produce home electric transformers and oscillator coils.[5]

A month and a half after the government's directives, the press reported that eleven new plants had obtained licenses to begin construction of radios and had committed themselves to the four-year deadline to increase home-made components. These new plants were in provinces such as Esfahan, Tabriz, Rezaiyeh, Yazd, Abadan, Hamedan, and Babol. Pushing industrialists to build their factories out of Tehran, thus creating provincial poles of growth, was another main objective of the Ministry of Industry. The new provincial radio factories were to produce some one 100,000 radios per year.[6]

On 5 January 1965, 'Alikhani pushed ahead with his drive to increase home-produced components. In a new directive for industrialists seeking to set up truck-building assembly plants, the Ministry of Economy outlined in detail the qualifications of those who could enter this business and the specifics of the truck pieces they needed to produce at home. To qualify for a production license, manufacturers had to produce the following components at home: chassis, bumpers, the driver's compartments, radiators, hoods, windshield wipers, engines, and seats.[7] This was indeed a tall order and more of a wish than an attainable goal.

Iran's new industrial policy of pressing for higher levels of home-produced components of assembled goods was reiterated by Sharif-Emami, the chairman of the board of the Industrial and Mining Development Bank

5 *Tehran Economist*, 14 Azar 1343.

6 *Ettela'at*, 21 Day 1343. *Tehran Economist*, 1 Aban 1344.

7 *Ettela'at*, 15 Day 1343.

of Iran. On 17 June 1965, he noted that the import regulations of Hoveyda's government were compelling importers and assemblers of durable goods, such as buses, trucks, cars, refrigerators, bicycles, and air conditioners, to produce their component pieces at home.[8] In September 1965, 'Alikhani informed the Shah that by 1968, his ministry planned to have all components of trucks assembled in Iran to be home produced, except the engines.[9]

'Alikhani had the difficult task of juggling between various challenging objectives. He wished to support home industries and ensure that rudimentary assembly would become more advanced, rely less on imports, and more on home-spun technologically intensive production methods. Yet he also had to ensure that the quality of components and, eventually, final goods produced at home were on par with the standards of previously imported ones. Finally, for the import substitution industrialization strategy to work, the price of home-produced intermediary and final goods had to become competitive as compared to imported goods.[10]

The government's new industrial policy prepared the ground for the rise of a new industrial capitalist class that would take the initiative and risk to launch into uncharted industrial projects. From the early 1960s, Iran's roster of successful capitalists changed, and fresh faces appeared on the industrial horizon.

THE REZAI BROTHERS: MINES AND METAL WORKS

Ali Rezai was a typical representative of Iran's upcoming industrial magnates that suddenly appeared on the Iranian business scene in the 1960s. By the time Ali Rezai was elected to the thirty-person board of directors of the ninth Tehran Chamber of Commerce on 2 March 1967, he was a well-known and affluent businessman. The Tehran Chamber of Commerce was a highly exclusive, prestigious bastion, the hall of fame for the most successful and influential Iranian businessmen. Rezai, who obtained the fifth highest vote, now joined prominent old-timers of the Tehran Chamber of Commerce, such as Kazem Kuros, Habib Elqaniyan, Akbar

8 *Ettela'at*, 1 Tir 1344.

9 Nikpay (gerdavarandeh) *Surat jalesat-e showray-e 'aliye eqtesad dar pishgah Shahanshah Aryamehr, az Shahrivar 1343 ta 1345*. Surat jaleseh-e 29 Shahrivar 1344, p. 152.

10 *Ettela'at*, 28 Bahman 1343.

Lajevardiyan, Ja'far Akhavan, and Mohammad Bonakdar, who obtained fewer votes than him.[11]

The rise to economic and political power of the provincial Rezai brothers represented a fundamental shift in Iran's traditional elite "One Thousand Families". The four Rezai brothers, Ali, Mahmud, Abbas, and Qasem, worked together to build an impressive mining and metalwork empire. Two among them, Ali and Mahmud obtained greater fame. Their father, Mirza Mohammad Reza, better known as Salduz, was a prominent merchant and landowner who lived in Sabzevar (Khorasan) and subsequently came to Tehran. He made his wealth and reputation in Sabzevar, where he was said to have had a noticeable capital of over 300,000 tomans in the 1920s. He died when the children were young. Ali, the eldest, followed his father's path and became a merchant. He also developed an interest in mining.[12]

Members of the first post-coup parliament, the Eighteenth Majles, which opened on 18 March 1954, had been handpicked by Zahedi and the Shah and owed their appointment to their opposition to Mosaddeq before and during the coup. Mahmud Rezai was elected to the Eighteenth Majles from Sabzevar.[13]

Mahmud Rezai's election was a sign of his family's close political allegiance to the Shah, General Zahedi, or both. The Shah's political trust in the Rezai family was again displayed during elections to the Nineteenth Majles. Whereas numerous prominent members of the Eighteenth parliament were prevented from being elected or selected, the Rezai family sent another brother, Qasem, to the Nineteenth Majles, again as Sabzevar's representative.

With Prime Minister Zahedi out of office, members of the Nineteenth Majles were carefully handpicked by the New Prime Minister 'Ala and the court. Qasem, who was in the US studying during the elections and was elected/selected in absentia, nonchalantly sent word that he would return to take his seat once his academic term was over in August. Consequently, he missed the convention ceremony of the Majles on 31 May 1956.[14]

---

11 *Tehran Economist*, 13 Esfand 1345.

12 B. Aqeli, *Sharh-e hal-e rejal-e siyasi va nezami-ye mo'aser Iran*, Vol. 2, Tehran: Nashr-e Goftar, 1380, p. 728.

13 *Khandaniha*, 6, 13, 17 Bahman 1332.

14 *Sepid o Siyah*, 30 Ordibehesht 1335.

Mahmud and Mines

By 1959, the Rezai brothers operated their Esfandaqeh Company from an office in Tehran in front of Alborz High School. Esfandaqeh was the name of the location where they bought their chromite mines, in the south of Kerman Province. Mahmud Rezai oversaw the company's mining activities. They first expanded their chromite mining activities in Sabzevar and Beshagard and subsequently entered magnesite mining. By 1964, the Rezais created the Faryab Mining Company and became the leading mining family in the country.[15]

In early 1965, Mahmud Rezai bought the exploitation license of an obsolete mine in Sarcheshmeh, Kerman. This mine was Iran's biggest open-pit copper deposit and said to be second only to Chile's. From March 1966, the Rezai brothers registered one mining corporation after another, beginning with the Kashan Mines Corporation, followed by the Kerman Mines Corporation, and then the Anahita Mining Corporation.[16]

At the High Economic Council of 17 April 1967, while addressing 'Alikhani, the Shah encouraged the private sector to invest in activities "such as copper production".[17] Nearly seven months later, once again during the High Economic Council meeting of 13 November 1967, the Shah referred to the newly discovered copper mines, and pressed the Ministry of Water and Electricity to provide cheap electricity to Mahmud Rezai's chromite ventures rapidly.[18] Confident of the Shah's support for the Sarcheshmeh project, on 30 November 1967, Mahmud Rezai signed a contract with the British mining company, Selection Trust, to develop the Sarcheshmeh copper mines. The Rezai's Kerman Mines Corporation held 70% of the shares, while Selection Trust owned the remaining 30%. By the end of 1968, explorations proved that Sarcheshmeh had an estimated

15 Khorshid Mashreq, Sal-e sheshom, shomareh 22, Pai'z 1398, https://www.gsinet.ir/Contents.aspx?Module=Pages&PId=2256 (retrieved 9/9/2024).

16 *Tehran Economist*, 21 Esfand 1344; 17 Ordibehesht 1345. A. Baghini, *The State, Entrepreneur, and Labour in the Establishment of the Iranian Copper Mining Industry: The Sarcheshmeh Copper Mine 1966-1979*, Doctoral Thesis, Leiden, p. 110.

17 Nikpay (gerdavarandeh), *Surat jalesat-e showray-e 'aliye eqtesad dar pishgah Shahanshah Aryamehr, az Shahrivar 1345 ta Shahrivar 1347*. Surat jaleseh-e, 28 Farvardin 1346, p. 67.

18 Nikpay (gerdavarandeh), *Surat jalesat-e showray-e'aliye eqtesad dar pishgah Shahanshah Aryamehr, az Shahrivar 1345 ta Shahrivar 1347*. Surat jaleseh-e, 22 Aban 1346, p. 119.

reserve of 80,000 tons of copper, and by the end of 1969, this figure was revised upwards to 400,000 tons.[19]

On 6 January 1971, the press reported that according to Hushang Ansari, the Minister of Economy, the government would invest in developing Sarcheshmeh copper mines by partnering with European firms. Ansari said, "In the near future, Iran would be able to earn $160 million annually from the export of copper". The press reported that the new contracts would be between the Iranian government and foreign firms without the participation of Iran's private sector. Even though it seemed Rezai was being pushed aside, there were reports in the press that the government would enter a partnership with The Kerman Mines Corporation and foreign firms. Qasem Rezai gave an interview confirming this position.[20]

The unfolding events demonstrated how the government moved quickly to take over the Sarcheshmeh mine. First, on 23 January 1971, Ansari announced that the government had bought 50% of the Kerman Mines Corporation's shares, making it a 25.5% shareholder in the Rezai–Selection Trust joint company. The Minister of Economy insisted the government had obtained these shares with the Rezais' consent.

Then, on 7 April 1971, Ansari went on television and announced that the reserves of the Sarcheshmeh mines were estimated to be 800,000 tons, and the capital necessary for developing them was some $363 million, which neither the Kerman Mines Corporation nor Selection Trust could muster. He reported that, since only the government could financially shoulder such a cost, it had bought out Selection Trust, and the Rezais would only obtain a 10% share.[21]

Exactly a month before Ansari appeared on television, on 7 March 1971, Iran signed a "Memorandum of Principles" for developing the Sarcheshmeh copper mines with the representatives of Anaconda, the American copper giant active in Chile. This important news was kept secret from the public and had not made it to the press.[22] The Shah must have felt that the Sarcheshmeh mines were too lucrative to be left to the Rezais.

19 A. Baghini, *The State, Entrepreneur, and Labour in the Establishment of the Iranian Copper Mining Industry*, pp. 119–120. *Ettela'at*, 16 Day 1349.

20 *Ettela'at*, 16 Day 1349. *Tehran Economist*, 19 Day 1349.

21 *Ettela'at*, 18 Farvardin 1350. *Tehran Economist*, 21 Farvardin 1350.

22 Iran–US Claims Tribunal, Anaconda Iran v. Iran, 13 IRAN-U.S. C.T.R. 1986, at 199 et seq., p. 203, https://www.trans-lex.org/231800/_/iran-us-claims-tribunal-anaconda-iran-ltd-v-iran-13-iran-us-ctr-1986-at-199-et-seq/#toc_5 (retrieved 12/9/2024).

Finally, on 15 December 1971, Ansari made an important but curious announcement about the future of the Sarcheshmeh mines. He said the Shah had ordered the government to shoulder the cost of developing the Sarcheshmeh mines alone and without any foreign partnership. He claimed the project would be "one hundred percent Iranian" without any participation from the private sector or foreign firms.

Ansari added that the government would pay the Kerman Mines Corporation all compensations for the costs they had incurred, plus a just profit and bonus for having discovered the mines.[23] This was, in fact, the official announcement that Mahmud Rezai's Sarcheshmeh mines were being nationalized by the Shah's edict. Two days later, the Shah announced that "big industries and mines belong to society because their privatization would result in the exploitation of man by man".[24] On 26 September 1972, Iran signed a definitive agreement with Anaconda to conduct an extensive feasibility study, provide a detailed training program for personnel, and provide assistance "for the design, construction, placement into commercial operation and maintenance of" an opencast mine.[25]

Ali and Steel

While Mahmud Rezai was embarking on his copper mine venture, on 25 May 1965, the press reported on a happening in the Iranian economy forged by his brother, Ali. Iran was about to enter the ranks of heavy industry-producing countries. Navard Iran Company was going to "build iron", as Iranians liked to call it, or process, mold, and cast fresh iron metal bars, known as iron billet, into shape. On 14 April 1965, Ali Rezai, the owner of Navard, signed a contract with representatives of the German DEMAG steelworks company to build a light section rolling mill with a capacity of 65,000 tons of iron products per year.

This factory produced four kinds of iron products: angled, flat, T-bar, and rolled, essentially used in construction. The estimated fixed cost of construction, equipment, and machinery was 60 million tomans ($8 million). Navard Iran was a joint stock company. Its shares were divided between DEMAG (9%), the Philipp Brothers (31%), the Rezai brothers

23 *Ettela'at*, 24 Azar 1350.
24 *Ettela'at*, 27 Azar 1350.
25 Iran–US Claims Tribunal, Anaconda Iran v. Iran, 13 IRAN-U.S. C.T.R. 1986, at 199 et seq., pp. 203–204.

(40%), the Industrial and Mining Development Bank of Iran (15%), and the remaining shares were held by Iranian investors. DEMAG was the German giant specializing in heavy equipment production, and the British-based Phillipp Brothers was the largest metals merchant entity in the 1960s.

The plant was built on a seventy-two-hectare plot close to Ahvaz and used gas, coal, and gasoline as energy sources. A pipeline connected the factory to the oil and gas wells to the east. It used 6,000 kilowatts of electricity provided by the Dez Dam, an old Ebtehaj project that had begun operating in 1963. The essential input of the factory, raw iron or billet (ingots), was imported, heated in special furnaces in Iran, and then molded into desired shapes and sizes.

Rezai predicted that with the coming of Iran's own steel mill, the necessary iron billets would also be produced at home. Until that time, according to Rezai, given the $35 difference between the international price of raw and processed iron, Navard could save Iran considerable amounts of foreign exchange. The new iron plant was expected to employ some 5,000 laborers, office staff, engineers, and technicians and would begin production in January or February 1967. According to Rezai, this project had the full support and cooperation of 'Alikhani, Yusef Khoshkish, the governor of Bank Melli, and Abolqasem Kheradjou, the governor of the Industrial and Mining Development Bank of Iran.[26]

In January 1967, before the first factory began production, Rezai signed a contract with DEMAG and the Swiss Brown Boveri Company for a second light-section rolling mill with a capacity of 85,000 tons per year. This factory was also to be built in Ahvaz, close to the first plant. The investment for the two units was estimated at some 130 million tomans ($17.3 million), of which 40 million tomans ($5.3 million) came from Rezai and other smaller shareholders. The Industrial and Mining Development Bank of Iran, as well as the Bank Melli, continued to play an important role in financing this new project.[27]

On 3 December 1967, the Shah inaugurated Rezai's first Navard Iran factory, which was now renamed Shahriyar Navard Company. More than 300 government dignitaries, officials, and businessmen attended the factory site, 9 kilometers from Ahvaz. Germans constructed the factory, while

26 *Ettela'at*, 4 Khordad 1344. All information in the previous four paragraphs is based on this source.

27 *Ettela'at*, 21 Day 1345. *Tehran Times*, 24 Day 1345.

its metal frames were subcontracted to Cyrus Arjomand of Arj Industries and Alidad Farmanfarmayan of Nir Pars Company.

Ali Rezai reported to the Shah that work was already underway on his second light section rolling mill, for which he had already signed a contract. He announced that 80% of its machinery and equipment had been installed, and the plant would be finished by August 1968. The Shah pressed Rezai, saying that given the growing need for light metal products, plans should be made for a third factory. Rezai, in turn, informed the Shah that he was negotiating with DEMAG for a third factory with a capacity of 100,000 tons per year.[28]

Rezai's second factory, Shahin, and his third factory, Shahrokh, were built right next to the original Shahriyar plant in Ahvaz. The new factories benefited from credits extended by the Industrial and Mining Development Bank, Rezai's Iranian partner in these ventures. The total investment in the three factories was approximately 200 million tomans (around $27 million).

When the Shah came to Ahvaz to inaugurate the Shahin iron factory on 5 November 1969, Ali Rezai went out of his way to ingratiate himself with the Monarch while demonstrating his generosity and nationalism. First, as an act of gratitude for his support of the Navard projects, Rezai gifted 'Alikhani, who had been replaced by Hushang Ansari and was subsequently appointed the Rector of Tehran University, with one million tomans (about $133,000) to spend on Tehran University. He referred to it as a contribution towards one of the Shah's White Revolution principles, namely the advancement of education and science.

He then ordered the distribution of 200,000 tomans among the factory's workers and staff as a down payment towards the Shah's profit-sharing scheme. Finally, Rezai announced that he had allocated 500,000 tomans to create a housing cooperative for his workers.[29] All three cash contributions were to causes very close to the Shah's heart.

In December 1969, Navard began issuing shares on the Tehran Stock Exchange, which had begun operation in 1967. The price of each share was 900 tomans, and Navard's capital was quoted as 80.1 million tomans. By January 1971, Ali Rezai's Navard factories, with a capital of 160,200,000 tomans (some $21.3 million), became a leading private sector enterprise

28 *Ettela'at,* 16 Azar 1346. *Tehran Economist,* 9 Ordibehesht 1346.
29 *Ettela'at,* 15 Aban 1348.

in the country, second only to Khayami's Iran National with 200 million tomans in January 1970.[30]

During an exclusive international auction gala attended by the Queen and some 1,000 Iranian and foreign dignitaries for the benefit of an American charity organization, Small White Beds, and the Farah Pahlavi Charity Foundation, held on 28 October 1971 in Persepolis, Shiraz, Ali Rezai made a splash. In the bid for a diamond-studded golden box donated by the Queen to the charity auction, Rezai made the highest bid and obtained the box for the sum of 2.2 million French Francs.[31]

The fate of the Rezai brothers, Ali and Mahmud, both exceptional entrepreneurs and a tad ostentatious, was a compelling tale of capitalism under the Shah. On the morning of 18 December 1971, at Jondishapur University, the Shah announced the nationalization of the Sarcheshmeh mines, managed and principally owned by Mahmud Rezai. He told the students that large industries and mines had to be nationalized to prevent "the exploitation of man by man". In the afternoon of the same day, the Shah spent three hours visiting Ali Rezai's Shahdad and Shahrokh Metal Industries complex. He praised the "exceptional" industrial activities of Ali Rezai, and Rezai, in turn, thanked the "absolutely secure conditions" created by the Shah to allow the progress of his activities.

On the one hand, the Shah encouraged and allowed one family member to flourish while he took away what was contractually his from another member of the same family. The Iranian capitalist system, in the absence of its primordial prerequisite, an independent legal system assuring the security and sanctity of contract, was deformed, rigged, and arbitrary. The Shah's whim defined and directed it. Ali Rezai knew of the precarity of his enterprise and wealth and, therefore, hypocritically praised the secure business conditions that the Shah had created. This was the story of oriental despotism.[32]

---

30 *Tehran Economist*, 13 Day 1348; 27 Day 1348; 19 Day 1349.

31 *Ettela'at*, 8 Aban 1350. *Tehran Economist*, 15 Aban 1350.

32 *Ettela'at*, 27 Azar 1350. *Tehran Economist*, 4 Day 1350. The Rezais claimed that they were coerced into selling their lucrative mines. Eventually the Rezais and Selection Trust received full payment for all costs encumbered. In addition, Rezai's copper company received the rial equivalent of £2.5 million plus 4 million tomans (40 million rials). See A. Baghini, *The State, Entrepreneur, and Labour in the Establishment of the Iranian Copper Mining Industry*, pp. 125–6, 131–132.

KHAYAMI'S IRAN NATIONAL AND THE LEGENDARY PAYKAN

In 1935, Ali-Akbar Khayami's household in Mashhad was considered middle class. His two-story house had three bedrooms and a kitchen but no bathroom, with the toilet outside the main building. Ali-Akbar had a caravanserai that he had converted into a garage once motor vehicles, especially trucks and taxis, appeared in the city. He subsequently partnered with a friend, purchased twenty trucks, rented them out, or used them as taxis to carry passengers. Yet Mashhad remained a city of *doroshkehs* (carriages). Ali-Akbar's wife, Maryam, the daughter of Mohammad-Ebrahim Malek-o-Tojjar, had given birth twenty times, but only ten of them, three boys and seven girls, survived. Ahmad was born in 1924, and Mahmud in 1930.

In the years after Iran was occupied by the Allies in 1941, and while Ahmad was still at school, he began trading in sugar and sugarloaf. In his last year of high school, when he realized that his math teacher's monthly salary was 300 tomans while he was making 300 tomans a day trading, he quit school and went into commerce. It was in 1950 that Ahmad and his brother Mahmud, who had amassed some 2,000 to 3,000 tomans, rented their father's garage and soon obtained the distribution rights of Habibollah Sabet's Studebaker cars in Mashhad. In 1951 and 1952, even though Ahmad got caught up in Iran's political scene and took sides with Mosaddeq and Kashani, his business flourished, allowing him and his brother to buy their father's garage.

In the aftermath of the August 1953 coup, Ahmad Khayami obtained the distribution rights of Mercedes Benz in Mashhad. The prominent and established Sudavar family's Merrikh Company had the franchise of Mercedes Benz in Iran. The sale of Mercedes Benz in Mashhad proved to be most lucrative, and Ahmad soon moved to Tehran, where he became the distributor of Mercedes. Mahmud, however, remained in Mashhad, managing their garage and the sale of Mercedes. Ahmad recalled that Merrikh Company was the key to their good fortune.

Between 1957 and 1958, the Khayamis signed a contract to buy Mercedes-Benz bus chassis from the Sudavars. They subsequently outsourced the production of the body and began assembling buses and selling them to the private sector.[33] On 4 October 1962, the Khayami brothers

33 A. Khayami, ed. M. Khayami, *Paykan sarnevesht-e ma*, Tehran, Nashr-e Ney, 1403, pp. 17, 21–23, 33–34, 51, 53, 59, 61, 63, 71. Information in the previous four paragraphs is based on this source.

obtained a license to produce/assemble buses and mini-buses in Iran and registered the Iran National Company with a capital of 10 million tomans.[34]

Two years before the Khayamis' initiative, on 19 November 1960, the Sudavars had registered *Sherkat-e Otomobil Sazi-ye Khavar* (Khavar Automobile Company) to assemble Mercedes-Benz trucks and buses.[35] It must have been around 1961 that Ahmad Khayami broke ties with the Sudavars, his long-term business associates and almost mentors. Faced with the Sudavars' refusal to further sell him the Mercedes bus chassis to assemble in Iran, he went to Germany and independently signed a contract with Mercedes-Benz that obliged the Sudavars to sell him chassis and parts for buses and mini-buses to be assembled in Iran.[36]

On 4 August 1963, 'Alam, the prime minister, visited the Iran National motor vehicle factory, which was under construction. Iran National planned to become self-sufficient in buses, mini-buses, and agricultural trailers. Iran National's first products were city buses produced in cooperation with Daimler Benz and agricultural trailers produced in cooperation with the German Blumhardt Company.

The factory was located 18 kilometers from Tehran on the road to Karaj. The 18,000-square-meter construction was built on a 100,000-square-meter piece of land bought from Habibollah Elqaniyan. The construction, machinery, equipment, and raw materials cost the Khayami brothers some 30 million tomans (some $4 million). Daimler Benz provided Iran National with blueprints, factory plans, and technical assistance, including dispatching engineers and technicians to set up and run the bus-producing/assembling plant.

Huge imported lathe machines from Germany were installed to shape the steel sheets producing various bus parts. The quality of Iran National buses was to be identical to Daimler Benz's. During 'Alam's tour of the factory, Khayami acknowledged the prominent role of the Ministry of Economy in assisting this venture and overoptimistically, reported that within a year, 80% of the bus parts would be produced in Iran.[37] Six months after 'Alam's visit to Iran National, on 18 March 1964, the Shah, accompanied by the Queen, officially inaugurated Khayami's motor vehicle-producing plant. The first bus produced by Iran National was gifted to the

34 *Angah*, no. 3, Summer 2017, p. 98. Khayami, *Paykan sarnevesht-e ma*, p. 80.

35 *Tehran Economist*, 28 Aban 1339.

36 Mehdi Khayami, *Paykan sarnevesht-e ma*, p. 87.

37 *Ettela'at*, 15 Mordad 1342. Information in the previous three paragraphs is based on this source.

Farah Pahlavi Charity Foundation, and the ownership title was issued in the Queen's name.

Ali-Naqi 'Alikhani, the Minister of Economy, praised Khayami's efforts, and the speed at which his factory had begun production. He reported to the Shah that Khayami's home production of buses, mini-buses and trailers would save at least 38 million tomans of foreign exchange annually. Iran National was importing aluminum and steel to forge body parts rather than importing the body parts. It imported aluminum to produce suspension, wheels, and brake components. As such, the product was not yet "made in Iran" but was "largely made in Iran". According to the press, the Shah and the Queen were delighted with Khayami's factory and informed him of their satisfaction and patronage (*tafaqod o enayat*).[38]

'Alikhani was interested in industries that could produce a high percentage of their intermediate inputs at home rather than importing manufactured detached parts and simply putting them together. For him, like the Shah, high value added at home meant not only industrialization but was also a sign of Iran's economic grandeur and national pride.

Behind the scenes, Khayami's Iran National enjoyed the stern support of a most powerful advocate, the Shah. In the High Economic Council of 4 July 1965, the Shah singled out Iran National and said, "I have received reports that Iran National is doing an exceptional job." He displayed his discontent at government organizations not buying Iran National buses and ordered the National Iranian Oil Company to do so immediately. He also ordered the army to buy home-made buses.[39]

According to Ahmad Khayami, the Iranian Air Force bought some 100 of his buses for cash. Other government organizations, such as Tehran's Bus Service Company, henceforth bought their buses from Iran National. Khayami, however, maintains that at the time, most of the customers for his deluxe buses were private bus companies, such as Mihan Tour, TBT, and Guity Navard, which were providing bus services between major Iranian cities and had also started bus services to neighboring and even European capitals.[40]

---

38 *Ettela'at*, 8 Farvardin 1343. Information in the previous two paragraphs is based on this source.

39 Nikpay (gerdavarandeh), *Surat jalesat-e showray-e 'aliye eqtesad dar pishgah Shahanshah Aryamehr, az Shahrivar 1343 ta 1345*. Surat jaleseh-e, 13 Tir 1344, p. 109.

40 Khayami, *Paykan sarnevesht-e ma*, pp. 104–105, 109.

From Buses to Cars

Even though the idea of one day producing an Iranian car had long dwelled in Ahmad Khayami's mind, he recalled that it was the Shah's challenge that "we cannot produce cars in this country, so we must seriously pursue the establishment of a few car assembly plants", that rekindled the old quest in him.[41] Khayami wanted to prove to the Shah that within two years, he could manufacture an Iranian car suitable for Iranian roads with "at least 35 to 40 percent of its parts made in Iran", and that in ten to twelve years 90% of his car parts would be made in Iran.[42]

The ambitious entrepreneur responded to the Shah's challenge with a counter-challenge. He told the Monarch that if permitted to produce cars, he would expect no exemptions from paying the full sum of import duties on the car pieces. This interaction must have occurred on 18 March 1964, when the Shah and the Queen officially inaugurated Khayami's bus-producing plant. The day after Khayami's discussion with the Shah, he received a letter from 'Alikhani allowing him to produce cars.[43]

Having obtained the permit to produce cars, Khayami went on the road to meet potential foreign car partners and buy CKDs or completely knocked down spare parts and pieces to be assembled at home. The first firm on his list was Mercedes Benz, and the fifth and last was the relatively unknown British Rootes. One of the main problems that emerged in Khayami's negotiations, besides the high price of the CKD kits, was that he planned to produce 5,000 cars during his first year of activity. Foreign car producers, except for Rootes, regarded anything less than 15,000 to 20,000 as unprofitable.

At the time, Rootes planned to produce a version of the Hillman Hunter called Arrow. Once Khayami decided on Rootes, he proposed some modifications to the outward appearance of the Arrow, making it

---

41 Khayami, *Paykan sarnevesht-e ma*, pp. 111–113. Ahmad Khayami refers to mid-Fall 1965 (avaset pa'iz 1344) as the date of this challenge by the Shah and therefore the time when he actively began pursuing the idea of producing a car. He is mistaken in his date as the contract with Rootes was signed on 2 February 1965, and in August 1965 the government had already allocated 7,000 cars per year to Iran National and talk of Paykan as the name for Iran National's Iranian car was already circulating in the press by November 1965. See *Tehran Economist*, 30 Mordad 1344; 6 Shahrivar 1344; 6 Azar 1344.

42 Khayami, *Paykan sarnevesht-e ma*, p. 112.

43 Khayami, *Paykan sarnevesht-e ma*, p. 113.

look more like a Mercedes, which was accepted and applied. To finance his business and conclude the deal, Khayami obtained credit guarantees from British and German insurance firms.[44]

On 2 February 1965, the Coventry-based Rootes Group announced the signing of an agreement with the Iran National Company "for the production of passenger cars in Tehran". The contract was signed in London between Ahmad and Mahmud Khayami and Brian Rootes, managing director of Rootes.[45] Khayami benefited from some of the infrastructure, facilities, and equipment he used to produce his buses and mini-buses. However, the machinery for producing his cars was entirely imported from England, and some twenty British engineers and technicians were instrumental in installing them and operating the factory

In August 1965, the financial journal *Tehran Economist* reported that the Ministry of Economy finally decided how to divide the Iranian car assembly/producing market between various applicants. Iranians were given a glimpse of the future "made in Iran" cars. Khayami's Iran National was to produce 7,000 cars annually, Akhavan's Rambler was given a quota of 5,000 cars, and Antoine Ayseh's Iranian version of Citroën's Dyane was also given a share of 5,000 cars per year. By 4 January 1966, the government officially limited issuing car construction/assembly permits to these three types of cars and announced that it would not allow for any more.[46]

At a September 1965 meeting of the High Economic Council, the Shah inquired about the project of a single forging press for all car assemblers in Iran. 'Alikhani informed the Shah that Iran National had a 1,700-ton forging press running, which other car manufacturing/assembling companies could use. The Shah heeded the Minister of Economy to pursue this project quickly and have all other manufacturers use Iran National's press to save money.[47]

By this time, it was evident that Iran National had become the pet project of the Shah and 'Alikhani. When high dignitaries, such as the Austrian President Franz Jonas, visited the country, they would visit the Iran National factory, which was showcased as one of Iran's star industrial

44 Khayami, *Paykan sarnevesht-e ma*, pp. 115–124. Information in the previous two paragraphs is based on this source.

45 *Coventry Evening Telegraph*, 2 February 1965.

46 *Tehran Economist*, 30 Mordad 1344; 6 Shahrivar 1344. *Ettela'at*, 14 Day 1344.

47 Nikpay (gerdavarandeh), *Surat jalesat-e showray-e 'aliye eqtesad dar pishgah Shahanshah Aryamehr, az Shahrivar 1343 ta 1345*. Surat jaleseh-e, 29 Shahrivar 1344, p. 153.

complexes. During the grand exhibition of Iran's industrial products that began on 29 October 1965 and ended on 8 December 1965, the Shah visited the Iran National stand and praised Khayami. At the end of the exhibition, Iran National was awarded two medals, a gold for its industrial products and a silver for the design of its stand. Iran National was now considered Iran's leading industry, even before it launched into producing cars.[48]

In February 1967, word of mouth had it that Khayami's car factory was up and running, and its cars were even being test-driven on various roads. On 9 May 1967, a sizable first-page advertisement in the press informed Iranians of the "Paykan automobile", the "biggest industrial marvel of Iran's White Revolution". Paykan was the Persian translation of the Arrow, which was a plain, robust, cheap, mid-size family car in England. Four days after the launch of the Paykan advert, on 13 May 1967, the Shah and the Queen, accompanied by some 100 dignitaries, including Hoveyda, 'Alikhani, 'Alam, and Sharif-Emami, inaugurated the Iran National factory and witnessed the first Paykan roll out. Discreetly present was William Geoffrey Rootes, the chairman of Rootes Motors.[49]

Paykan was advertised as a national car, a special Iranian design with an Iranian name, and the product of Iranian labor and ingenuity. The British Arrow was expropriated and shown off as a genuine Iranian product. Ali-Asghar Amirani's *Khandaniha* stressed that Paykan was not the product of an assembly process but that of a genuine automobile industry and that other than its engine and the differential system, all its other parts were manufactured in Iran.[50] The *Tehran Economist* called Paykan a symbol of Iranian nationalism. Yet it suggested that only 25% to 40% of Paykan car pieces were home-produced and that this percentage would increase over time.[51] 'Alam believed that at its inception, 40% of Paykan car pieces were produced in Iran.[52]

A CIA intelligence memorandum dated February 1972 claimed that "Imports of machinery, component parts, and raw materials have increased in line with Iran's rapid industrial growth, much of which has taken the form of simple processing and assembly-type operations. The import

48 *Ettela'at*, 11 Mehr 1344; 27 Azar 1344.
49 *Ettela'at*, 24 Ordibehesht 1346. *Tehran Economist*, 30 Ordibehesht 1346.
50 *Khandaniha*, 26 Ordibehesht 1346.
51 *Tehran Economist*, 23 Ordibehesht 1346
52 A. 'Alam, *Yaddashtha-ye 'Alam*, ed. A.N. 'Alikhani, Vol. 7, Bethesda: IBEX Publishers, 2014, p. 46.

content of final products is more than 80% for such industries as motor vehicles, tires, pharmaceuticals, and synthetic fibers, and it is also fairly high in some other industries".[53]

Iran National began by producing ten cars daily and evolved into producing three different models: standard, luxury, and the sporty (GT) *Javanan* (the youth) brands. The original price of Paykan's standard model was 18,900 tomans ($2,520). Paykan quickly rose to the status of Iran's national car and became the proud symbol of the country's industrialization and modernization drive.

The Shah bought one of Khayami's first box-shaped Paykans. Hoveyda would often be seen behind the wheel of his Paykan; his ministers became Paykan owners, and the up-and-coming Iranian middle class, young and old, also became regular customers. Some eighteen months after the production of the first Paykan, or by October 1968, Paykan "accounted for 50 percent of all new car sales in Iran".[54] The mottos of "a Paykan for every Iranian" and "looking forward to the day when every Iranian would have a Paykan" placed Paykan and its producers at the center of Iran's economic modernization. In his annual review of 1968, the British Ambassador to Iran, Dennis Wright, noted with some pride and joy that, "The Iran National's equivalent of the Hillman Hunter car sold like hot cakes and seemed likely to outstrip Rootes' ability to keep apace with the demand for their knock-down chassis".[55]

On 22 June 1968, Paykan celebrated its first birthday and announced that it had sold 10,000 cars, well surpassing the initial output estimations.[56] Iran National threw a huge bash at the Vanak Hotel in Tehran. The event was so important that it was also televised. On that special night, Iran National gifted Iranians with a cultural and musical product that long outlived Paykan. Anushiravan Rowhani, the famous Iranian composer, produced a Persian happy birthday song for Paykan. The lyrics were a collective effort and intentionally did not make reference to the car. Rowhani considered it his "best" composition.[57] This piece of music, *tavalodat mobarak*, (happy birthday), was henceforth chanted as a standard birthday song by Iranians.

53 FRUS, 1969–1976, vol. E–4, Documents on Iran and Iraq, 1969–1972. Document 165.
54 *The Scotsman*, 3 October 1968.
55 FCO 17 849. NEP1/5.
56 *Ettela'at*, 1 Tir 1347.
57 Khayami, *Paykan sarnevesht-e ma*, p. 152. *Angah*, no. 3, Summer 2017, pp. 73, 75.

It outlasted the Shahanshahi national anthem, and it will likely outlast the Islamic Republic's national anthem.

In five years, the price of Paykan's standard model only increased by 1,100 tomans (some $146). The 1972 price of Paykan's basic model, now renamed *Paykan-e Kar* (the working man's Paykan) was 20,000 tomans (some $2,666), the deluxe model was 23,000 tomans, and the sports model was 27,500 tomans.[58] By July 1975, the Iran National factory was operating double-shifts of forty-eight hours and was producing 300 Paykans per day as compared to 10 in 1967, and still there was talk of a black market for Paykans.[59]

Iran National developed distribution agencies in all major cities of the country, and Paykan service stations equipped with spare parts made this car indispensable for the emerging Iranian middle class and those living outside the major cities. Soon, Tehran was studded with orange-colored Paykan taxis that replaced almost all other brands.

Paykan effectively replaced Volkswagen, DKW, and Fiat in Iran. But most importantly, Iranian taxi drivers who used to buy solid Mercedes-Benz Pontons switched to Paykans. They could get better terms and never had to worry about spare parts. The old importers of popular cars in Iran, such as Sabet (VW), Ali Kashanchi (Fiat), Hoseyn Vahabzadeh (DKW), and even Sudavar (Mercedes), were overshadowed by the success of Khayami's Paykan.

The Khayamis were self-made men. They built their fortune on hard work, risk, reliability, honesty, frugality, and a sense of public service. They possessed the work ethic, drive, and ambition that had made the old industrial titans of Western capitalism succeed. Ahmad Khayami was no Henry Ford, as he was neither an engineer nor an innovator. However, he was a successful imitator, and his Paykan was an ersatz and close duplication of Western technology. The changing of guards of Iran's business titans from 1953 to 1968 was well reflected in an accidental encounter in mid-air between Habibollah Sabet and Ahmad Khayami.

Ahmad Khayami recalled that on his way back to Tehran from England after signing his contract with Rootes, which must have been in early February 1965, he traveled in the same plane as Habibollah Sabet. Sabet, who was in the first-class cabin, walked through the aisle to the

58 *Tehran Economist*, 14 Esfand 1350.

59 *Ettela'at*, 22 Tir 1353.

economy class, where Khayami was seated. He told Khayami that he had heard about his intention to build cars in Iran and told him that his plan "was 100 percent impossible". Khayami responded that he thought building cars in Iran was possible and would do his utmost to realize it and serve his country.

Khayami thanked Sabet for giving him his first dealership in Khorasan in the 1950s and insisted that even if he lost his thriving bus and minibus manufacturing business, he could always go back to his garage business in Mashhad. Khayami added that even though he was earning 100,000 tomans a day, his standard of living had almost stayed the same since he had his humble garage. Khayami was giving Sabet a lesson in frugality.

Sabet assured Khayami that he would lose all his fortune in the pursuit of this quest and then warned him, "Whatever you do, you will not be able to take away Volkswagen's share of the market because this car is so popular in Iran that no other car can ever compete with it". Times had changed, and the old had to give way to the new. Paykan did replace Volkswagen, and Khayami proved Sabet wrong.[60]

The success stories of the Khayamis and Rezais were publicized as a direct outcome of the White Revolution, which was argued to have created the conditions for the realization of the new Iranian Dream.[61] Modern Iran, as the Shah often emphasized, not only provided opportunities for the industrious, paved the way for the upward social mobility of the hard-working and dexterous, but most importantly rewarded them handsomely. The Khayamis and Rezais showcased the Shah's claim that success in the new Iran resulted from initiative, diligence, and loyalty to the philosophy of the White Revolution and no longer from lineage and land ownership. The new self-made industrial titans were distinguished from Iran's old and successful names because their empires came on the heels of the White Revolution.

Paykan vs. Arya: 'Alikhani and Khayami vs. Sharif-Emami and Akhavan

With success came rivalries. Business ascendency in Iran ultimately required political connections. 'Alikhani was Iran's successful Minister of

60 M. Khayami, *Paykan sarnevesht-e ma*, pp. 52–53, 125. The previous two paragraphs are based on this source.
61 *Ettela'at*, 24 Ordibehesht 1346.

Economy during the country's economic transformation between 1963 and 1969. He did have the Shah's ears and confidence. Sharif-Emami, in his different capacities, cast a heavy shadow over Iran's political and economic scene, especially since he became Eqbal's Minister of Industries and Mines in April 1957. Once he became the Deputy Custodian of the Pahlavi Foundation in 1962, he had direct access to the Shah. Rivalry and clash of characters, as well as vying for attention from and proximity to the Shah, was most common among the Shah's men. Political men with economic power had their own patronage system in relation to the business community.

As much as 'Alikhani appreciated Khayami's Iran National and supported it, he had little respect for Jafar Akhavan's Willys Jeep and Ali Kashanchi's Fiat assembly plants. His economic argument against them was that they were sham assembly (*montage*) enterprises. But there was also a political lining to 'Alikhani's argument. He believed that Akhavan was in collusion with Jafar Sharif-Emami, the Minister of Industry between 1957 and 1960, and benefited from his patronage. 'Alikhani even accused Sharif-Emami of being in Akhavan's pay.[62]

When Akhavan, who already held the franchise to import American Motors' Ramblers, applied for a permit to assemble them in Iran, 'Alikhani's Ministry of Economy opposed the idea. It took some two years of behind-the-scenes political arms wrestling before Akhavan was finally issued a license.[63] On 19 October 1965, the press reported that Jafar Akhavan had finalized his contract with American Motors at the Paris Car Show to assemble/produce Ramblers in Iran.[64]

Sometime around the summer of 1965, Ahmad Khayami, who was busy importing heavy machinery for his Paykan factory and installing them, found himself short of cash. He applied for an 18 million toman credit from the Industrial and Mining Development Bank of Iran and provided the Bank with all the necessary documents. Khayami's loan application was rejected, and instead, the credit earmarked for car production was awarded to Akhavan's car project. Ahmad Khayami believed that favoritism was involved and that Sharif-Emami, who chaired the board of the Industrial and Mining Development Bank of Iran, had intervened on behalf of his

62 Ali-Naghi Alikhani, Iranian Oral History Collection, Harvard University, Transcript 4, Sequence 77.

63 *Tehran Economist*, 19 Tir 1344.

64 *Ettela'at*, 27 Mehr 1344.

"friend" Ja'far Akhavan. Khayami was convinced that the rejection of his credit was due to Sharif-Emami's animosity towards him.[65]

Friction between 'Alikhani and Akhavan continued. In August 1966, Akhavan began producing and selling Ramblers for 22,000 tomans (approximately $2,930). Shortly after the first assembled Ramblers were sold, the Ministry of Economy forced the factory to stop sales. It prevented the already sold cars from being registered and matriculated. The sale and registration of Ramblers resumed in September 1966.[66] Irrespective of the jealousies between Paykan and Rambler, very soon Akhavan realized that his two brands of Ramblers, renamed Arya and Shahin, were no match for Paykans.

---

65 Khayami, *Paykan sarnevesht-e ma*, pp. 126–128.
66 *Tehran Economist*, 26 Shahrivar, 2 Mehr 1345.

Conclusion

This study has tried to present the events, facts, and transformations of Iran's economic history between 1953 and 1968 based on the sources available. Readers can form their own opinions and pass their own verdicts. The conclusion reached by this study, however, is that the responsibility for the successes and failures of Iran's modernization project from 1953 to 1968 falls, in the first place, on the shoulders of the Shah. The entire Iranian ruling class was also a partner in the successes and failures. Those executive, legislative, and judiciary members and decision-makers of Iran's economic, financial, and banking organizations who knew that the Shah was making wrong and harmful economic decisions but did not resign from their posts were equally responsible for the failures.

Yet, economic successes would have been fewer without the technical and professional competence and the hard work and energy of some of those same ministers, planners, and bankers who stayed on until they were replaced. If only the Shah had allowed some of the country's brilliant minds to take the initiative, follow it through, and take full responsibility for it without intervening and making them submit to his whims. The Shah wasted the talent and potential of the country's educated, competent, and honest technocrats by failing to use their advice wisely and turning them into functionaries and bureaucrats. He also failed his country by turning a blind eye to the dishonest and the corrupt, instead of rooting them out. Giving His Majesty the benefit of the doubt, he could not be acquitted of a grave conflict of interest when it came to the activities of the Pahlavi Foundation.

Iran's business community, factory owners, managers, and skilled workers, the masons of Iran's economic modernization, were, by and large, independent entrepreneurs. They took risks and launched enterprises in areas of their expertise for private profit. Some benefited from state financial support and even the Shah's patronage and personal money through the Pahlavi Foundation. However, their share in the economic failures was minimal in the final analysis. They were playing according to the rules of the capitalist system in place.

Nevertheless, the Iranian private sector was not immune to the Shah's arbitrary and harmful interferences. The Shah had three economic nightmares: drought, inflation, and the inability to increase the military budget. After the oil boom of 1973, the Shah's fantastical economic ambitions against the counsel of his economic experts caused excessive government expenditures which in turn resulted in the 1974 demand shock, an inflationary period, and various major economic bottlenecks.

In the summer of 1975, the Shah ordered price controls to curb inflation which was around 18%. He would not listen to the simple economic logic that excessive government expenditures would cause inflation. The Shah believed that inflation was caused by profiteering and hoarding by producers and retailers and therefore called profiteering and price gouging "a variant of the exploitation of man by man", and ordered a crackdown.

The tides suddenly turned against the private sector, as thousands of industrialists, businessmen, wholesalers, petty shopkeepers, and bazaaris were arrested, jailed, banished, and heavily fined throughout the country. Some had their commercial licenses revoked, others had their heads shaved and their shops and business offices sealed. In Tehran alone, within a month of the Shah's edict, 16,000 profiteers were arrested and appeared in court. One thousand businesses and shops were padlocked, and the culprits paid 30 million tomans ($4 million) in fines.[1] Exactly ten years before, the Shah had ordered a much softer version of his war on profiteering, and Hoveyda, his newly appointed prime minister, had tried to carry it out. At that time, he had been successful due to exogenous factors, but not this time. On both occasions, the Shah and his vizier failed to obtain long-term results.

The fear of crossing the Shah or dissenting from his views, which threatened one's political or business position, bred two practices inimical to Iran's healthy economic development. First, to ward off the Shah's displeasure, prominent public and private sector figures chose to submit to his authority even on the most rudimentary technical and economic issues. Second, to endear themselves to the despot, they engaged in sickening sycophancy, only serving to make him feel higher, mightier, and more entitled to refuse sound advice. The worldwide curse of seeking personal ambition, power, and wealth at whatever cost may become economically

1 *Ettela'at*, 14, 26, 27, 29 Mordad 1354.

productive in democratic capitalist countries, but is a feeder of bad economic decisions for despots.

The Shah acted as though he owned the country. His key bankers and planners remarked that the Shah would make his economic decisions independently in areas such as military expenditures and foreign purchases of military hardware, oil, gas, petrochemicals, nuclear, steel, electricity, and water. He would then pass down his decisions to the prime minister, ministers, planners, and bankers to become incorporated into the budget and financed.[2]

When the Shah suddenly decided on an idea, such as land reform or a new project like the steel mill, nuclear power plants, building a military base at Chah-Bahar, or electrification of railways, the planners and economists, with no previous knowledge of his majesty's new plans or any proper cost-benefit analysis for them, had to "make room" for such expenditure items in the budget and the Five-Year Plans. The Shah's erratic behavior made planning and budgeting a mission impossible.

This study finds that surprisingly, from 1953 to 1968, the United States encouraged the Shah to allocate his resources more to developmental programs and less to military expenditures. The US contribution to Iran's economic development and modernization in this period is positive. Economic policies promoted and actions taken by various administrations were intended to push the country out of its underdevelopment and improve its welfare. It was with the presidency of Richard Nixon and the subsequent Nixon Doctrine that the US became an accomplice in Iran's economic failures.

One of the findings of this study is that Shah's gradual neglect of sound economic advice, which picked up speed and intensity around 1965, was sealed by 1968 when the gates of honest economic debate and discussion were firmly shut. The best that his economic and planning advisors could wish for was a minimal compromise on his part. So, the economic decision-making system became entirely the function of one man's will, without any accountability, until the 1979 revolution. From this point, absolute decision-making became the function of Khomeyni's will without the talented economic grey matter at the Shah's disposal.

---

2 Mehran, *Hadafha va Siyasathay-e Bank-e Markaziy-e Iran*, p. 121. Abdolmadjid Madjidi, Iranian Oral History Collection, Harvard University, Transcript 6, Sequence 132–133).

After 1968, fueled by ever-increasing oil revenues, the economy moved hurriedly and strictly according to the Shah's directives. In preparations for the Fifth Plan, a group of experts at the Plan and Budget Organization, led by Gholamreza Moqadam and Bahman Abadiyan, drafted a preliminary technical report on the state of Iran's economic, financial, and social prospects. Based on solid facts and reliable figures, the report was critical of prevalent policies, gave a bleak picture of what awaited the country, and went as far as arguing that unless the trends, inequalities, and the disequilibria of the past were amended and altered, Iran would experience "a socio-political explosion". The report was highly critical of the Third and Fourth Plan's negligence towards social issues, such as education, health, and rural welfare.[3]

Hoveyda judged that the report could not be presented to the Shah. He decided that it had to be attenuated and modified before he could present it at the High Economic Council. Faced with Moqadam's resistance and insistence, Hoveyda finally agreed to have Moqadam report to the Shah. For a long time, despite its name, the High Economic Council was not a space for discussion but one where only the Shah gave his orders. Once Moqadam finished reading a few pages of the report and got to the critical parts, the Shah became infuriated. He lashed out to Moqadam, "Who told you to write such things ... again, these economists are sitting and writing nonsense about the country, ignoring all the achievements and spreading disillusionment and pessimism ... You need not become involved in such matters because we know what we are doing ... I am vigilantly pursuing all these matters; you do your own work and do not concern yourself with such matters."[4]

Moqadam persisted and tried to explain to the Shah that the country's main economic problem was not a paucity of funds or a financial one that borrowing overseas or increasing oil revenues could solve. He pointed out that the fundamental economic problems were the country's national priorities (hinting at too much spending on the military), macro disequilibria, excessive unproductive government expenditures, infrastructural bottlenecks, and a shortage of skilled manpower. Moqadam spoke of

3 Gholam-Reza Moghadam, Iranian Oral History Collection, Harvard University, Transcript 4, Sequence 61.

4 Gholam-Reza Moghadam, Iranian Oral History Collection, Harvard University, Transcript 4, Sequence 63. Mohammad Yeganeh, Iranian Oral History Collection, Harvard University, Transcript 15, Sequence 290.

economic resource scarcities, and the Shah retorted that all problems could be solved by having enough money to make purchases.

The discussion between the two ended with the Shah saying, "I do not believe in these absurd notions and theories, and you economists do not know what you are talking about ... We know exactly what we are doing, and the country has a bright future before it." The Shah then stormed out of the room.[5]

On 6 November 1972, a vital economic conference was held in the Shah's presence at Takht-e Jamshid (Shiraz). Some 150 of the country's most prominent economists, planners, administrators, and bankers gathered to discuss and analyze the Fifth Five-Year Development Plan, which was to start on 21 March 1973. The Shah's top economic experts presented detailed reports on various aspects of the Fifth Plan. The Shah then stated his ideas, enumerated his objectives, and informed all present, "Now it is up to you to adjust your reports according to what I have just said." He added, "If you have not considered the points I have just made, get used to the new conditions." The Iranian press was not authorized to cover the detailed economic reports and discussions at the conference.[6]

Another fateful gathering, the Ramsar conference of 1 August 1974, was convened in the presence of the Shah to revise and reassess the Fifth Plan in view of the sudden increase in oil revenues after the first oil shock. The groundwork for this conference was laid at the Gajereh gathering, where Hoveyda, the prime minister, and his economic and financial specialists prepared specialized reports for presentation to the Shah.

At the opening of the Ramsar summit, Hoveyda reported to the Shah. After nine years of serving as prime minister, Hoveyda knew how to soften what may be construed as a blow to the Shah's exaggerated and extravagant economic dreams, which he took as reality. Hoveyda also remembered the Shah's rage at Moqadam's report at the High Economic Council and His Majesty's irritation at reports that were unpleasing to his ears.

Hoveyda said, "It is evident that the bottlenecks broached in the reports to His Majesty do not worry or scare us in any way. Our country has now become accustomed to the problem-solving will of Shahanshah, who, through revolutionary means, renders many impossibilities possible ...

---

5 Gholam-Reza Moghadam, Iranian Oral History Collection, Harvard University, Transcript 4, Sequence 63–65.
6 *Ettela'at*, 16 Aban 1351.

There exist no unsolvable problems which would restrain our country from attaining such spectacular development on the world scale."[7]

The wise vizier acted like he was at an Ilkhan, Safavid, or Qajar court. Hoveyda was giving the Shah the bad news of state affairs, but he was also assuring him that it need not dampen his mood, as he was the superior mind and master of the country who would finally find a solution. The Shah would hear the bad news but would not process it. Hoveyda's layers of soothing words would cover up his hints at looming problems, only making the Shah more adamant in pursuing his wishful dreams.

At Ramsar, Abdolmajid Majidi, director general of the Plan and Budget Organization, cautioned more than once that it was not to the benefit of the country for the government to spend $98.5 billion, the projected revenue from the sale of oil and gas during the Fifth Plan. He argued that the skilled manpower, energy, electricity, transportation, road, and port bottlenecks were major impediments to spending all of this sum on development projects at home.[8]

Given the projected substantial increase in oil and gas revenues, Majidi's team presented three government expenditure options for consideration and debate. The first option included all the ministries' upward-revised budgets. It meant spending some 90% (6,000 billion rials) of the new revenues (6,653 billion rials) at home. The second or minimalist option suggested spending slightly more than 50% (3,500 billion rials) of the new earnings at home. The third, or the in-between alternative, proposed spending 4,200 billion rials or some 63% of the increased revenues at home. The final figure agreed upon at Ramsar was 4,634 billion rials ($61.7 billion), which was almost double the 2,400 billion rials ($32 billion) of expenditure established for the Fifth Plan some sixteen months before.[9]

The Iranian press did not report on the discussions, arguments, or counterarguments at Ramsar. Instead, as it had become the established norm, it focused on the Shah's optimistic comments about Iran's bright future, the coming of the "Great Civilization", and how Hoveyda and Majidi had lauded the economic leadership of the Shah. Two well-placed economists at the upper echelons of the Plan and Budget Organization

7 *Ettela'at*, 10 Mordad 1353.

8 *Ettela'at*, 10 Mordad 1353.

9 Abdolmadjid Madjidi, Iranian Oral History Collection, Harvard University, Transcript 7, Sequence 153–154. *Ettela'at*, 10, 13 Mordad 1353. *Tehran Economist*, 19 Mordad 1353.

believed that nowhere was "the failure of the system more evident than in the acquiescence at Ramsar of the top echelons of the bureaucracy to the shah's programs".[10]

Years later, Hasan-Ali Mehran, who became the governor of Iran's Central Bank in October 1975, recalled that the Plan Organization presented three alternative expenditure packages with different economic trajectories and consequences for the country at the conference. The Plan Organization specialists were adamant that one option, which had adverse economic consequences, should not be adopted. According to Mehran, the one option the Plan Organization had advised against was finally adopted. Mehran believed the choice was not based on technical issues but was the Shah's political decision to move the country ahead as quickly as possible.[11]

Hossein Razavi and Firouz Vakil, bureau director and undersecretary at the Plan Organization, argued during this period that a month after the adoption of the revised Fifth Plan at Ramsar, "the plan was laid on the shelf, in favor of a spending spree, a frantic search of how to spend what was there".[12] The cautions and recommendations of the Shah's economic advisers, ministers and planners about the economic challenges, and bottlenecks that his hastiness and spurious directives presented went unheeded.

On 22 January 1976, Majidi privately met Asadollah 'Alam, the Minister of Court, and gave him a grim report of Iran's economic situation. Majidi mentioned the government's purchase of 4,000 trucks without drivers to operate them or sufficient roads to run them on. Majidi added that as the head of the Plan and Budget Organization, he would not know about extravagant purchases until after they were made. 'Alam was extremely alarmed and disconcerted. He confided in his diary, "The situation is such that it should logically (*qa'edatan*) lead to a revolution."[13]

The Shah was convinced that he knew better than anyone, and no one dared tell him otherwise. Therefore, he paved the path for doing and undoing the economic modernization that the country had witnessed since 1953. This study, therefore, ends before the post-1973 oil boom and bust period and the economic events leading to the revolution. As

10 H. Razavi, F. Vakil, p. 77.
11 *Tejarat*, 2 Khordad 1394.
12 H. Razavi, F. Vakil, p. 80.
13 Alam, vol. 5, pp. 404, 407.

for post-1979, Khomeyni did not believe in modernization but instead believed in the Islamization of Iran. Both the Shah and Khomeyni failed miserably to realize their respective grand designs. Iranians can neither be forced towards the "Great Civilization" nor through the doors of Paradise.

Select Bibliography

ARCHIVAL DOCUMENTS

British Foreign and Commonwealth Office (FCO)
Foreign Relations of the United States (FRUS)
Iran Oral History Collection, Harvard University
Mozakerat-e Majles-e Sena
Mozakerat-e Majles-e Showray-e Melli
Oral History of Iran Collection of the Foundation for Iranian Studies
Rockefeller Archive Center Research Reports
World Bank Oral Histories

WORKS IN PERSIAN

'Alam, A., *Yaddashtha-ye Alam*, ed. A.N. 'Alikhani, 7 volumes (Bethesda: Iranbooks/Ibex, 1992–2014).

Aqeli, B., *Sharh-e hal-e rejal-e siyasi va nezami-ye mo'aser Iran*, vol. 2 (Tehran: Nashr-e Goftar, 1380).

Be ravayat-e asnad-e savak, *Amir-Abbas Hoveyda*, vols. 1 and 2 (Tehran: Markaz-e barrasi-e asnad-e tarikhi-e vezerat-e ettela'at, 1382 and 1383).

Be ravayat-e asnad-e savak, *Rashidiyanha*, vol. 2 (Tehran: Markaz-e barrasi-e asnad-e tarikhi-e vezerat-e ettela'at, 1389).

Ebtehaj, A., ed. A-R. Aruzi, *Khaterate Abolhasan Ebtehaj*, vols. 1 and 2 (Los Angeles: Ketab Corporation, 2010).

Fardust, H., *Zohur va soqute saltanate Pahlavi* (Tehran: Entesharat-e Ettela'at, 1369).

Khayami, A., ed. M. Khayami, *Paykan sarnevesht-e ma* (Tehran: Nashr-e Ney, 1403).

Mehran, H.-A., *Hadafha va Siyasathay-e Bank-e Markaziy-e Iran, az 1339 ta 1357* (Tehran: Nashr-e Ney, 1394).

Nikpay, G., (gerdavarandeh), *Surat jalesate shoraye 'aliye eqtesad dar pishgah Shahanshah Aryamehr, az Shahrivar 1343 ta 1345* (Tehran: Chapkhaneh vezarat-e farhang va honar, n.d.).

Nikpay, G., (gerdavarandeh), *Surat jalesate shoraye 'aliye eqtesad dar pishgah Shahanshah Aryamehr, az Shahrivar 1345 ta Shahrivar 1347* (Tehran: Chapkhaneh vezarat-e farhang va honar, n.d.).

Nikpay, G., (gerdavarandeh), *Surat jalesate shoraye 'aliye eqtesad dar pishgah Shahanshah Aryamehr, az Shahrivar 1347 ta Mordad 1348* (Tehran: Chapkhaneh vezarat-e farhang va honar, n.d.).

Pahlavi, M.-R., *Mamuriyat baray-e vatanam* (Tehran: Chap-e artesh, n.d.).

Sabet, H., *Sargozasht Habib Sabet* (Los Angeles: Mazda Publishers, 1993).

Sa'idi, A.-A., *Zendegi va Karnemeh-e Ali Khosrowshahi* (Tehran: Nashr-e Ney, 1398).

Sa'idi, A.-A. and Shirinkam, F., *Zendegi va karnameh-e haj Mohammad-Taqi Barkhordar* (Tehran: Gam-e No, 1396).

Sa'idi, A.-A. and Shirinkam, F., *Mohammad-Rahim Mottaqi-Iravani* (Tehran: Gam-e No, 1398).

Sa'idi, A.-A. and Shirinkam, F., *Moqeiyat tojar va saheban-e sanaye' dar Iran-e asr Pahlavi, Khanedan Lajevardi va Lajevardiyan* (Tehran: Gam-e No, 1398).

Shirinkam, F. and Farjāmniya, I., *Sargozasht-e panjah koneshgar-e eqtesadi-ye Iran* (Tehran: Farhang-e Saba, 1398).

WORKS IN ENGLISH

Amuzegar, J., *Technical Assistance in Theory and Practice: The Case of Iran* (New York: Praeger, 1966).

Amuzegar, J., *The Dynamics of the Iranian Revolution: The Pahlavis' Triumph and Tragedy* (Albany: State University of New York Press, 1991).

Ansari, A., *The Shah's Iran: Rise and Fall* (London: I.B. Tauris, 2017).

Baker, R. L., *Business Leadership in a Changing World: A Report on the International Conference at San Francisco, September 11–15, 1961* (New York: McGraw Hill, 1962).

Baldwin, G. B., *Planning and Development in Iran* (Baltimore: Johns Hopkins Press, 1967).

Bharier, J., *Economic Development in Iran 1900–1970* (London: Oxford University Press, 1971).

Bostock, F. & Jones, G., *Planning and Power in Iran: Ebtehaj and Economic Development Under the Shah* (London: Frank Cass, 1989).

Elghanayan, S., *Titan of Tehran: From Jewish Ghetto to Corporate Colossus to Firing Squad – My Grandfather's Life* (New York: Associated Press, 2021).

Garlitz, R., *A Mission for Development, Utah Universities and the Point Four Program in Iran* (Colorado: University Press of Colorado, 2018).

Grathwol, R. P. and Moorhus, D. M., *Bricks, Sand, and Marble: U.S. Army Corps of Engineers, Construction in the Mediterranean and Middle East, 1947–1991* (Washington: Center of Military History and Corps of Engineers, 2009).

Ladjevardi, H., *Labor Unions and Autocracy in Iran* (Syracuse: Syracuse University Press, 1985).

Milani, A., *The Shah* (New York: Palgrave Macmillan, 2011).

Neuse, S. M., *David E. Lilienthal: The Journey of an American Liberal* (Lexington: Plunkett Lake Press, 2018).

Pahlavi, A., *Faces in a Mirror* (New Jersey: Prentice-Hall, 1980).

Pahlavi, M.-R., *Mission for My Country* (London: Hutchinson, 1961).

Rahnema, A., *The Rise of Modern Despotism in Iran: The Shah, the Opposition, and the US, 1953–1968* (London: Oneworld Academic, 2021).

Razavi, H., and Vakil, F., *The Political Environment of Economic Planning in Iran, 1971–1983: From Monarchy to Islamic Republic* (London: Routledge, 2019).

Warne, W., *Mission for Peace: Point 4 in Iran* (Indianapolis: Bobbs-Merrill, 1956).

Index